# Sundanese Print Culture and Modernity
in Nineteenth-century West Java

*Nanzan University Monograph Series*

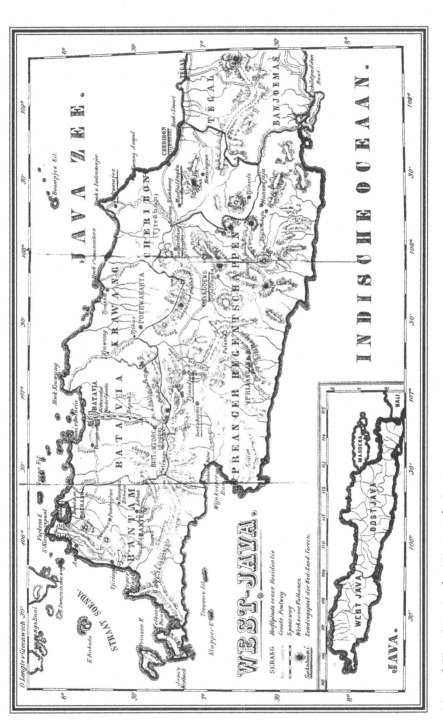

*Map of West Java in the Nineteenth Century*

Source: S. Coolsma, *West-Java. Het land, de Bewoners en de Arbeid der Nederlandsche Zendingsvereeniging.* Rotterdam: J.H. Dunk, 1881.

# Sundanese Print Culture and Modernity
## in Nineteenth-century West Java

*Mikihiro Moriyama*

NUS PRESS
SINGAPORE

© Mikihiro Moriyama

*Published by*:

NUS Press
National University of Singapore
AS3-01-02, 3 Arts Link
Singapore 117569
Fax: (65) 6774-0652
E-mail: nusbooks@nus.edu.sg
Website: http://nuspress.nus.edu.sg

Reprint 2018
Reprint 2019

ISBN 978-981-4722-99-5 (Paper)

All rights reserved. This book, or parts thereof, may not be reproduced in any form or by any means, electronic or mechanical, including photocopying, recording or any information storage and retrieval system now known or to be invented, without written permission from the Publisher.

*The first edition was published by Singapore University Press in 2005.*

Typeset by: Scientifik Graphics
Printed by: Markono Print Media Pte Ltd

*To Yuri*

# Contents

| | |
|---|---|
| List of Tables | ix |
| List of Figures | x |
| List of Illustrations | xi |
| Note on the Spelling | xii |
| Acknowledgements | xiii |
| Introduction | 1 |

1. Inventing a Language and Literature ..... 8
   *Language and Literature in the Sundanese-speaking Area*
   *Scholarship, Colonialism and the Canonization of Wawacan*

2. The Institutional Context ..... 55
   *Schools in the Sundanese-speaking Area*
   *Printing and Publishing Network*
   *A Mismatch: Print and Wawacan*

3. The Birth of the Author: Moehamad Moesa ..... 100
   *Moesa, the Man*
   *Moesa, the Author*

4. Reading Modernity in *Wawacan Panji Wulung* ..... 143
   *The Reception of Wawacan Panji Wulung*
   *Reading Wawacan Panji Wulung*

5. The Change in the Configuration ..... 184
   *The Changing Configuration of Sundanese Writing*
   *The Rise of a Kind of New Writing*

Appendix 1: List of Sundanese Printed Books Before 1908  206
    (1) By Year of Publication
    (2) By Author's Name

Appendix 2: *Wawacan Panji Wulung*  239
    (1) The Construction of Verse Form and Stanza in *Wawacan Panji Wulung*
    (2) Summary of *Wawacan Panji Wulung*

*Notes*  247

*Bibliography*  267

*Index*  282

# List of Tables

1. Number of elementary schools and students (from 1853 to 1872) — 60

2. Number of schools per million inhabitants (from 1857 to 1872) — 60

3. Number of schools per million inhabitants in 1904 — 63

4. Number of students at the various types of schools in the Priangan Regencies — 65

5. Textbooks used at elementary schools in Bandung in 1863 — 72

6. Total number of schoolbooks in Java by 1865 — 75

7. List of European/Eurasian printing/publishing houses for Sundanese books (from 1850 to 1908) — 89

8. Most frequently reprinted titles (from 1850 to 1908) — 96

9. Titles that were in the Landsdrukkerij's catalogue for more than 50 years — 98

10. Publications by Moehamad Moesa — 125

11. Sundanese Translations of European Stories in the Nineteenth Century — 192

# List of Figures

1. Number of schools (from 1853 to 1908)     62

2. Number of enrolment of students (from 1853 to 1908)     64

3. Printed books in Sundanese, by printing house
   (from 1850 to 1908)     83

4. Printed books, by printing houses (from 1850 to 1908)     84

5. Scripts used in Sundanese publications (from 1850 to 1908)     91

6. Number of reading books and printed *wawacan*
   (from 1850 to 1908)     95

# List of Illustrations

| | | |
|---|---|---|
| Plate 1. | Moehamad Moesa's tombstone | 102 |
| Plate 2. | Moehamad Moesa | 102 |
| Plate 3. | Mesjid Agung Garut | 103 |
| Plate 4. | Alun-alun Garut | 103 |
| Plate 5. | *Ali Moehtar*, published in 1864 | 135 |
| Plate 6. | Manuscripts of *Wawacan Panji Wulung* | 145 |
| Plate 7. | *Wawacan Panji Wulung*, published in 1871 | 159 |
| Plate 8. | Kartawinata and Lasminingrat | 191 |
| Plate 9. | The title page of *Carita Robinson Crusoë*, published in 1879 | 195 |

# Note on the Spelling

The original spelling is maintained as closely as possible. When words in Javanese or Arabic scripts are transliterated, present-day Indonesian orthography is used. All foreign words, including institutional names, are in italics.

# Acknowledgements

The idea of researching the genesis of modern Sundanese writing came to me during my first stay in Leiden in 1988. I decided to write this dissertation in Leiden following an unforgettable meeting with Professor Henk Maier, and he steadily encouraged and stimulated me throughout the process. Another unforgettable meeting with the late Dr. J. Noorduyn cannot be overlooked. He was willing to become the first contact person and gave me series of Sundanese classes. My interest in the language and literature of the Sundanese took root in 1980 when I was an undergraduate student at Osaka University of Foreign Studies, and I am indebted to two people I met there. Bapa Ajip Rosidi impressed me with his vast knowledge and his Sundanese "nationalism". The idea of a modern Sundanese readership formed in my mind as a result of lectures and personal conversations with Professor Hiroshi Matsuo during my studies in Osaka. The late Professor Kenji Tsuchiya at Kyoto University also had a great influence on the direction of my studies after I met him in 1981. In a hotel in Leiden five months before he passed away in 1995 he said to me, "Completing your dissertation on Sundanese language and literature is *ikita akashi* (the evidence of your life)."

Studying in Leiden was my dream from the time I started Indonesian studies in 1979, and a scholarship from the Netherlands Ministry of Education and Science allowed me to fulfil this dream. After returning to Japan in 1989, the Daiwa Bank Asia and Oceania Foundation (later renamed the Resona Foundation for Asia and Oceania) supported my further studies from 1990 to 1993. During this period I revisited Leiden and West Java to consult with my supervisors, as well as collect materials available in Leiden, Bandung and Jakarta. Beginning in 1992, I became an overseas research fellow for the Japan Society for the Promotion of Science for two years. The Department of Southeast Asian and Oceanian Languages and Cultures (TCZOAO) hosted me as a guest researcher and part-time lecturer in Sundanese. My final year in Leiden was spent as a Ph.D. student at the CNWS Research School (School of Asian, African, and Amerindian Studies) of Leiden University.

This study of Sundanese language and literature is a token of *mulang tarima* (returning thanks). I am grateful to be able with this study to make a contribution to the Sundanese people, especially my teachers, host families, and friends. I received a great deal of assistance from numerous people in Indonesia, especially in the Sundanese-speaking area. They are too many to mention, although I would like to thank in particular Professor Edi S. Ekadjati, who was my supervisor at the University of Padjadjaran in 1982 and continued to advise me as my research continued. Dr Iskandarwassid is my Sundanese teacher. With patience and sympathy, he taught me Sundanese grammar and how to read Sundanese literary works. Drs Nano S., the best known composer of Sundanese traditional music, and his wife Ibu Dheniarsyah, taught me much about Sundanese culture and always hosted me at their house. I always felt at home among them.

The library of the Royal Netherlands Institute of Southeast Asian and Caribbean Studies (KITLV) is a treasure-house for Indonesian studies and provided me with a comfortable space to write, especially in the summer when I revisited. The bibliographical part of this study owes much to its collection. In short, institutes in Leiden provided me with a stimulating research climate that I had never before encountered. Most of my stays in Leiden since 2000 were supported by a grant from Nanzan University in Nagoya (Pache Research Subsidy I-A and I-A-2) and this publication was made possible through subsidy from the Nanzan Academic Society. I am grateful to all the institutions that enabled me to carry out my studies.

I cannot forget the hospitality of three host families in Indonesia. The late Bapa Soekada Soemawidjaja and his wife Ibu Itje regarded me as one of their own children and offered me every possible assistance. During my field research, two families allowed me to stay at their house for a half year: Bapa Rd. Adang S. Kosdara and his family in Wanayasa, Purwakarta, and Bapa Yus Yusman and his family in Cikalong Kulon, Cianjur, hosted me as if I were family.

The Netherlands, especially Leiden with its academic atmosphere, has always been a source of inspiration and stimulus. Kind friends there have supported me. First I wish to thank Tom van den Berge and Jan van der Putten for all their help. Tom and Jan were always ready to share my joys and sorrows. I am sure I could not have completed my research without their sincere friendship. Will Derks, Hans van Miert, Ben Arps, Wim van Zanten, Els Bogaerts, Liesbeth Dolk, Palguna, Suryadi and Edwin Jurriëns are special colleagues, and I am indebted to them for stimulating discussions on a daily basis. Rogier Busser and Kuniko Forrer shared my distresses and joys in Japanese conversations. In Amsterdam, Michiel Verberne warmly received me at his place with good cheer when I really needed it.

Of course, there are those who supported me in Japan. Professor Tadataka Igarashi and Professor Noriaki Oshikawa were always there for me. Special thanks are also due to Benjamin G. Zimmer and Ruth Rose for reading the draft and correcting my English, and also for making a number of helpful comments.

Last but not least, I wish to express my gratitude to my family. My father-in-law, Professor Yoshihiko Kobayashi and his wife, Mrs. Yoriko Kobayashi, have always understood and supported me. I am indebted to *chichi to haha* (my parents) for their love. My wife, Yuri Moriyama, and our three children, Ruri, Saya and Kiminori, have always supported me with devotion and love.

# Introduction

This book suggests an alternative approach to studying the history of culture in Indonesia based on the evolution of writing in the Sundanese language, the predominant language used in the western part of Java and presently the mother tongue of about 32 million people.[1] The period of study is the nineteenth century, when Indonesia was a Dutch colony.

Early in that century, a small group of Dutch scholars and colonial officials reshaped Sundanese language and literature based on established Western concepts of print literature and culture. Driven by growing demand on the part of indigenous officials, a result of the growing intensity of Dutch involvement, the colonial administration established a number of schools for the indigenous population and introduced printing into the existing indigenous writing systems. These interventions had a great impact on Sundanese-speaking communities, and particularly on the aristocracy. The imposition of European standards of literary aesthetics shaped a colonial modernity that rejected traditional knowledge in favour of rational and empirical paradigms, promoted moralistic and other forms of useful knowledge, and instilled a sense of deference and loyalty towards colonial authority.

The period under study ends in 1908 with the establishment of the *Commissie voor de Inlandsche School- en Volkslectuur* (Committee for Indigenous Schoolbooks and Popular Reading Books), a government-subsidized institution that was to provide the growing number of literate people in the Indies with "good" and "appropriate" reading materials. This new institutional setting created a different context for Sundanese writing and led to the rise of a new genre: the novel.

Two key terms are discussed in this book: *wawacan* (a narrative poetry) and print literacy. The discourse around *wawacan* shows how the existing Sundanese writing tradition changed during the period of modernity, closely related to the introduction of schools, administration, machines and other innovations. Towards the end of the nineteenth century, the position of *wawacan* as a predominant genre was challenged by translations of European stories. Concurrently, the authority of traditional poetry (*dangding*) was challenged by prose (*omongan*), eventually taking the shape of novels. Print literacy implies various aspects of culture, and makes a contrast with manuscript tradition and orally- and chirographically-based literacies by bringing printing technologies and printed materials into focus along with reading activities. This study of Sundanese printed materials will trace how the configuration of Sundanese writing changed its form after the middle of the nineteenth century. At the same time, it suggests how manuscripts (including those related to Islamic topics) and oral presentations were gradually given a new place in the configuration in the process of transformation.

## Historical Background of Sundanese Language and Culture

After the fall of the kingdom of Sunda in the sixteenth century, the Sundanese did not have a single powerful cultural and spiritual centre that exerted a strong and lasting influence over the whole of the Sundanese region. Instead, *kabupaten* (seats of local chiefs) functioned as administrative and cultural centres in the western part of the island of Java. The absence of a single powerful cultural centre does not mean that the "production" of culture stopped with the fall of the Sundanese kingdom. Rather, it resulted in an accumulation and diffusion of knowledge that was different from that of other cultural communities in the archipelago. For instance, the Sundanese had maintained a rich oral tradition, such as the repertoire of *pantun*, an octosyllabic verse form which was (and still is) usually chanted by bards, and a tradition of writing in *lontar* manuscripts, dating from time immemorial. Javanese influence was overwhelmingly felt by the Sundanese after the Javanese king of Mataram conquered its neighbour in the seventeenth century. This influence extended not only to the arts but also to administration, lifestyle, and language: for almost two hundred years, Sundanese literature was developed according to Javanese aesthetics. One of the most remarkable examples is the adaptation of *macapat* poetry, a verse form that is called *dangding* in the Sundanese-speaking areas.[2]

For the colonial government in Batavia in the nineteenth century, the Priangan Regencies were particularly important for economic reasons, especially for coffee production.[3] Local officials were needed to act as intermediaries to enable the administration to work. To this end, formal education was introduced, primarily for the local aristocracy. As a result, the changing configuration of indigenous writing and literacy in West Java took place earlier than in other regions of the East Indies.

Since the arrival of Dutch merchants in the early seventeenth century, only a handful of European scholars and officials had studied the local peoples and cultures, including their languages and literatures. In the early nineteenth century, the Europeans "discovered" that Sundanese was a distinct language, and concurrently assumed that there must be a distinct Sundanese culture.

Towards the late nineteenth century, the Dutch colonial administration, in close cooperation with Dutch scholarship, divided the archipelago into distinct cultural units — Sundanese, Javanese, Madurese, Malay, etc. — each with its own language. In the process, the local population began to gain consciousness of linguistic and cultural differences in terms of the administrative borders that the Dutch constructed. Sundanese speakers, for example, became more aware of the differences between their own culture and that of the neighbouring Javanese. Once the colonial masters had pointed out the differentia among the ethnic groups, local elites tried to recognize their own language and culture as different.

Dutch colonial policy in the field of culture was somewhat paradoxical: the introduction of colonial tools to modernize the Indies led to the emergence of new literary genres — schoolbooks, newspapers, stories-in-translation. At the same time, efforts were made to understand and "freeze" the existing indigenous traditions in order to make use of them. This is what happened among the Sundanese language communities too; in the process, the existing Sundanese writing tradition changed. One of the most interesting examples of how a traditional genre changed is the *wawacan*, a type of narrative poetry.

*Wawacan*, in general terms, is a long narrative poem intended to entertain an audience. It was always chanted, often loudly. It is composed in a verse form called *dangding*. Tradition has it that aristocrats and Islamic teachers in the Sundanese-speaking area borrowed it from the Javanese literary tradition when West Java was part of the Javanese kingdom of Mataram. *Wawacan* was admired in Sundanese aristocratic circles, and pervaded the elite community. The Dutch saw *wawacan* as the most original and valuable kind of Sundanese writing and thought it the best way to convey modern information and enlighten the people. There were other visions of how local culture could serve colonial ends, however. The missionary S. Coolsma, for one, argued that prose should be developed among the people, even though he was aware of the Sundanese preference for poetry. Coolsma believed that *dangding* was too traditional to embody the novelties of modernity, and hoped that prose would lead to "a new spirit" (*een nieuwe geest*), paving the way to new and strong forms of writing (Coolsma 1881: 145). As it turned out, *wawacan* eventually lost its predominant position in Sundanese literary life.

## Print Literacy

Print literacy changed traditional objects and practices. Colonial officials collected manuscripts, giving them monetary value as well as a new aura. Print literacy also became the vehicle for new kinds of cultural objects, hybrids of tradition and modernity. As for language, print arrested linguistic drift and flexibility, standardizing the orally- and chirographically-based literacies.

Walter J. Ong's famous dictum, "Writing restructures consciousness", summarizes his theory of the effects of orality, chirographic literacy, and print literacy. Human consciousness is transformed when orality is replaced by literacy. The same can be said when print takes the place of handwriting: it reinforces and transforms the effects of writing on thought and expression (Ong 1982: 117).

It can be argued that the introduction of printing techniques causes greater changes in a language community than the introduction of writing. Print produces new kinds of reading materials, especially books. Smaller and more portable than manuscripts, they prepare the way for individual reading, and eventually for silent reading. In a manuscript culture, reading is usually a social activity, with one person reading to others in a group. Such reading makes for a different relationship between the reader and the authorial voice in the text, and calls for different styles of writing (Ong 1982: 122–32). This holds true for the formation of "modern" Sundanese writing; around the turn of the twentieth century, *omongan* (prose) was introduced as a new style of writing and silent reading grew in importance.

With the publication of the first Sundanese book *Kitab Pangadjaran Basa Soenda* (The Sundanese Language Textbook) in 1850, Sundanese writing entered a new era. Publishing was initially undertaken by Dutch individuals, such as K.F. Holle (1829–96), who took a serious and sincere interest in the locals but had very pronounced ideas of how "his friends" should be helped — but such ideas might not necessarily have been the best ones. Holle and his Sundanese friend Moehamad Moesa had a great influence on Sundanese education and schoolbooks. Their influence, however, was to disappear after the turn of the century.

Printing was done by the government printing house (Landsdrukkerij) in Batavia, close to the Sundanese heartland. The newly published books were more accessible than the manuscripts with which the population of West Java had been familiar long before the first printed book appeared, and thus a considerably wider audience was reached. This had consequences that the colonial masters could not have envisaged. As William Makepeace Thackeray observed in the 1860s, gunpowder and printing modernized the world. Indeed, printed books modernized Sundanese writing and thinking.

The publications of the Landsdrukkerij offered reading in a new visual form, with a new script and new forms of writing. The concept of writing and reading began to change. If only because the relationship between the reader and the authorial voice in the text changed, new styles of writing developed in which the Dutch took the lead through schoolbooks and translations or adaptations of European books. Schools and textbooks created a new type of reader and writer: they formed a new audience alongside the semi-illiterate one that was closely linked to the oral traditions that would remain predominant in West Java for a long time to come. Dutch educational policy stimulated the growth of a modern readership in the Sundanese communities, which gradually developed towards a single community. Increasing numbers of Sundanese children started to read and write in Sundanese. The new type of education produced a different sort of colonial subject, created by way of printed books in Roman script; that is to say, it produced modern literacy. However, the effects went beyond what the Dutch had envisaged.

The emergence of print literacy and everything that came with it — schoolbooks, newspapers, translated stories — shook the world of the Sundanese. They had to redefine their concept of verbal arts, for instance, and their notion of a "book", having to get used to the literariness of writing. They also had to get used to the Malay language, which was to play an important role in these changes. Carried along by the colonial administration and Islamic modernism, Malay made its presence increasingly felt. Even more than Sundanese itself, it was to become the vehicle of "new" knowledge (cf. Putten 1997: 719).

The literary works of the second half of the nineteenth century indicate that Sundanese writers tried to adopt a new way of giving meaning to the world around them. A key figure was the above-mentioned Moehamad Moesa (1822–86), a Sundanese aristocrat who, this study will suggest, lived in between tradition and modernity. He published 14 books covering a variety of topics. Moesa's writing assumed great importance in Sundanese literary life, and he gained recognition among Sundanese literates as well as Dutch colonial officials. His books were used in government-subsidized schools and were widely read, offering a new way to understand the modern world. Hence, they occupied an important position in the newly developing Sundanese writing. Moesa was an author in the European sense, producing a new type of writing that was unique in terms of circulation, form, and content, and reorganizing the Sundanese cultural tradition by combining elements of Western print culture, rationality, and colonial authority with indigenous knowledge. His most successful work, *Wawacan Panji Wulung*, serves as an illustration of how a new discursive configuration emerged in the Sundanese-language community. Published in 1871, it was read and admired widely until well into the twentieth century. Moesa's text is only one example from a corpus of *wawacan* which suggests a burgeoning of modernity.

Print literacy also created a new form of writing in Sundanese, starting with translations of European stories that engendered *omongan*, a term that was coined in the 1870s by the official Sundanese translator Kartawinata (1846–1906), Moehamad Moesa's son. Literally, *omongan* means "spoken word or everyday speech". Kartawinata introduced it as a new literary form that was to be propagated through translations: Dutch stories were translated or adapted in *omongan* and taught in schools alongside the major traditional written genre, *wawacan*. *Omongan* can be seen as the root of the Sundanese novel (the first one written by a Sundanese appeared in 1914), which emerged in the early twentieth century. At the time, colonial society was undergoing great changes as a result of the nationalist movement and the so-called Ethical Policy. Gradually, the novel began to push aside *wawacan* and other genres and became a prominent form of writing.

## Structure

This book consists of five chapters.[4] Chapter 1 is divided in two sections. The first gives an outline of how Sundanese language and writing were "discovered" and how Europeans (tea planters, Christian missionaries, and government officials) reached a certain consensus about the Sundanese as a distinct ethnic group with its own culture and language.

The second section provides an account of the debates among the Sundanese and Europeans about Sundanese literature and its genres, especially *wawacan*. The Europeans tried to find "literature" in the local Sundanese communities by mapping out a part of what they saw as Sundanese culture on the basis of their own particular literary concepts.

Chapter 2 gives a historical outline of the establishment of schools and printing, the material basis for the changes that were taking place in literary and cultural life. The schools and schoolbooks were the main tools in the implementation of colonial language policy. Government-subsidized schools played a leading role in the spread of print literacy, which brought about a gradual change in Sundanese writing. The second section of this chapter focuses on the effects of the introduction of printing into the Sundanese-speaking communities. First, a survey is given of the printed books published in Sundanese in the period 1850–1908, based on data collected in major libraries in Indonesia and the Netherlands. An analysis is then made on the basis of several variables: scripts (Javanese, Roman, Arabic), publishers (the government printing house Landsdrukkerij, European, indigenous), and forms of writing (*dangding*, prose).

Chapter 3 illustrates the developments described in Chapters 1 and 2 by focusing on the most prominent and productive author of the period under consideration, Moehamad Moesa, a Sundanese aristocrat and a *hoofdpanghulu* (head of Islamic leaders) in Limbangan, southeast of Bandung. Moesa was a key figure in West Java and his books were used in schools, becoming the core of the new writing which developed in close contact with the new types of schools and printing.

Chapter 4 offers a reading of *Wawacan Panji Wulung*, a representative work of Moehamad Moesa and a text written in the traditional form, which contains some of the novelties associated with modernity: rationality, realism, and reflexivity. The chapter begins by tracing the reception of the poem: Why was it so widely read for such a long time? Why did it lose its popularity in the long run? The chapter offers a reading of the dialectic between tradition and modernity in *Wawacan Panji Wulung*.

Chapter 5 concludes this study with a discussion of the formation of Sundanese printed writing in the second half of the nineteenth century as seen from the perspective of *omongan*, the newly emerging form of Sundanese writing. Parallel to the demise of *wawacan*, *omongan* gradually obtained a leading role in the literary tradition that was nurtured by print literacy — it was to lead to the Sundanese "novel".

# Chapter 1

# Inventing a Language and Literature

## 1. Language and Literature in the Sundanese-speaking Area

*Discovering the language*

An ethnicity (in Sundanese, *kabangsaan*; in Dutch, *een volk*) is defined by a language: this idea had come to be generally accepted in the Dutch East Indies in the early twentieth century. The prominent Sundanese scholar, Memed Sastrahadiprawira, expressed it in the 1920s as follows:

> The language forms a norm: the most evident and the most comprehensive symbols (notions) to distinguish one ethnic group from another. If the characteristics of a language disappear, the distinguishing features of an ethnicity will fade away as well. If an ethnicity no longer exists, the language of the ethnic group will also disappear in due course of time.
>
> Basa teh anoe djadi loeloegoe, pangtetelana djeung pangdjembarna tina sagala tanda-tanda noe ngabedakeun bangsa pada bangsa. Lamoen sipatna roepa-roepa basa tea leungit, bedana bakat-bakatna kabangsaan oge moesna. Lamoen ras kabangsaanana soewoeng, basana eta bangsa tea oge lila-lila leungit (Sastrahadiprawira 1929a: 99).[1]

There is a third element involved: culture. Here too, Dutch assumptions exerted a great influence on the thinking of a growing group of Sundanese intellectuals that a language is a representation, a reflection of a culture, and a culture defines as well as supports an ethnicity. This concept goes back to Romantic notions about the predominance of language.[2] An ethnic group is identified by a distinct language, and this language is the carrier of a culture. Lively and heated debates about the relationships between the three did not really take place in the Netherlands or the East Indies. The idea of a close connection between language, culture, identity, and ethnicity had become a self-evident one, so it seems, and was to play a prominent role in cultural policies in the colony.

People in the Sundanese-speaking areas of Java were made aware that they had a distinct Sundanese culture and identity, and this awareness could only be strengthened by the administrative boundaries that the colonial government imposed on the island of Java. However, before the Europeans came to their lands, the Sundanese people as subjects of the Sunda kingdom[3] had been implicitly aware that they were different from the Javanese, subjects of the Majapahit kingdom. The tale of Pasunda Bubat is a good example: Citraresmi (or Dyah Pitaloka) was the princess of Sunda, the glorious Sundanese kingdom in days of yore, and the western part of Java was more or less united under the kingdom of Sunda from the seventh to the sixteenth century (Ekadjati 1984: 81–7). At the instigation of his prime minister Gajah Mada, Hayam Wuruk, the powerful ruler of Majapahit, asked the princess to marry him. The court of Sunda at Pakuan Pajajaran accepted His Majesty's proposal, and sent the princess to Bubat in East Java. There she discovered that she had come not as a future wife but as a tribute, and she chose to kill herself rather than suffer humiliation. Then a war broke out between the Sundanese royal forces and Javanese forces in 1357 (Ekadjati 1995a: 6–7). Most Sundanese were familiar with this tale, and they remembered the incident with anger and rage.[4] The story suggests an anti-Javanese sentiment and, more importantly, an awareness of being different from the Javanese. The same awareness can be found in several manuscripts, such as the sixteenth-century *Sanghyang Siksakandang Karesian*, in which the writer tells his audience that one must speak Javanese when one goes to (the Javanese-speaking part of) Java, but that it is not appropriate to do so upon returning to Sunda (Danasasmita *et al*. 1987: 87, 111).

The arrival of the Dutch made the Sundanese even more conscious of their own language, and gave them an awareness that neighbouring languages carried cultures, identities, values and ideas that were not authentic to the people of West Java. The colonial administrators and scholars thus drove them to objectivize themselves in opposition to the "Javanese" and the "Malay".

The process of restriction and differentiation is aptly summarized in the words of Michael Bakhtin:

> [...] it is possible to objectivise one's own particular language, its internal form, the peculiarities of its world view, its specific linguistic

habitus, only in the light of another language belonging to someone else, which is almost as much "one's own" as one's "native language" [...] Where languages and cultures interanimate each other, language becomes something entirely different, its very nature changes (Bakhtin 1981: 62–5).

For Bakhtin, there is a decisive moment in the life of a language community when it encounters a powerful language other than its own. Suddenly, everything changes under the pressure of this newly-found "polyglossia" — the simultaneous presence of two or more (national) languages interacting within a single cultural system. The Sundanese awoke from their vague self-identification. The Dutch were to create a state of polyglossia that stimulated Sundanese intellectuals to think about their "own" language, and thus their "own" culture and identity, their "own" ethnicity.

In fact, the people in West Java had known a distinct language long before the Europeans arrived, using a script that was different from both the Javanese and Arabic ones. Inscriptions and texts (Ekadjati 1988) such as *Bujangga Manik* and *Carita Parahiyangan* (Noorduyn 1962) are evidence of what is now called Old Sundanese. The language had been used with its own script before Javanese Mataram influence spread over the region around the seventeenth century, but had largely been put aside as Javanese began to exert its influence in Sundanese-speaking areas well into the eighteenth century (Darsa 1994: 25).

Sundanese is mentioned as the *Zondase taal* (language of Sunda) by Herbert de Jager (1636–94), a Dutch scholar from Leiden (Haan 1911: vol. 2, 134). De Jager claimed that the language was used in the western part of Java. At that time, the term "Javanese" was already known by the Europeans, and from the seventeenth until the beginning of the nineteenth century they considered the language used in the Batavian hinterland and beyond, in the mountains, to be a Javanese dialect. The Dutch called it *bergjavaans* ("mountain" Javanese), suggesting that it was a mere variant of Javanese (Berge 1993: 13–7; Haan 1911: vol. 2, 256). The mountain peasants used a variant of Sundanese that was different from the language spoken by the ruling and administrative class. The language used by the local aristocrats, mostly living in and around the *kabupaten* (literally, the seats of indigenous chiefs, or *bupati*, which function as the centres of local government), was a more refined Sundanese heavily influenced by Javanese. The aristocrats considered Javanese to be "higher" and more "refined" than their own language

(Haan 1912: vol. 4, 513). When visiting the courts of Central Java to pay their respects, they were fascinated by Javanese etiquette and especially the language, which included various levels of speech that reflected social status. A sort of cultural involution started in the second half of the eighteenth century, centred at four royal houses in Yogyakarta and Surakarta.[5] Many aspects of culture, such as language, literature, batik, music and dance, became more refined and increasingly elaborate, and Sundanese aristocrats attempted to introduce speech levels into Sundanese. As a result, their speech became heavily interspersed with Javanese elements. European travellers, merchants and administrators mostly dealt with these aristocrats, and it is little wonder that they thought they were hearing a variant of Javanese.

To add to the confusion, the local aristocrats occasionally used a kind of Javanese among themselves, at least until the middle of the nineteenth century, because it was considered more prestigious than Sundanese, and they could show off their considerable knowledge (Berge 1993: 17). In particular, they wrote official letters in Javanese rather than in Sundanese, but spoke Sundanese among themselves in daily life.

As for writing, John Crawfurd observed: "The few who have any education aim at a little instruction in Arabic and Javanese, and even business is generally conducted in the latter" (Crawfurd 1820: vol. 2, 68). Arabic script, not the language (which Crawfurd mentions), was used to write Sundanese, mostly for non-administrative purposes. Meanwhile, Javanese had been the official language and script in the Sundanese-speaking areas for a long time. Sundanese was regarded as informal and vernacular, to the extent that it could be regarded as a humiliation if an aristocrat received a letter in Sundanese (Berge 1993: 16–7). Taco Roorda (1801–74), then a professor of Oriental Languages and Literatures and Theoretical Philosophy at Amsterdam, gives a remarkable comment in the preface of de Wilde's dictionary about the relation between Sundanese and Javanese at that time.[6]

> The regents in the Sunda region prefer to make use of Javanese in their correspondence with each other: even the address of a letter written in Sundanese to a regent should be in Javanese. We see from this that Sundanese is considered a vernacular by the upper class and is by no means placed on the same level as Javanese.
>
> De regenten in de Soendalanden maken in hunne brieven aan elkander bij voorkeur gebruik van het Javaansch; ook het opschrift van eenen

in het Soendasch geschreven brief aan eenen regent behoort in het Javaansch te zijn. Men ziet daaruit, dat door de voornameren het Soendasch meer als volkstaal beschouwd, en geenzins met het Javaansch op gelijken rang gesteld wordt (Roorda in Wilde 1841: x–xi).

This fact led K.F. Holle, a tea planter in Priangan Regencies and the most influential Dutchman in the Sunda region, to assume that Javanese had been the authoritative language in the Sundanese area since the rule of the Javanese Mataram dynasty (Holle 1890: 128–30). However, he thought their Javanese was not as refined as that used in the courts of Java: Sundanese themselves called it "Jaware", a blend of "Jawa saware" (half Javanese).

Besides Javanese, Malay also had its own significant position in Sundanese society. It had been a *lingua franca* for a long time in the archipelago, used between the Dutch officials and Sundanese aristocrats for administration purposes and daily conversation. Malay had an independent position in the Sundanese communities. The language map was thus a confusing one: Javanese, Malay, and a "refined" variant of Sundanese were used in the administrative and trade centres in the upland plains, while "mountain" Javanese or a plain variant of Sundanese was spoken in the highland areas.[7]

A first tentative effort to resolve the confusion was made by Josua van Iperen, a Dutch clergyman who in 1780 published a simple comparative translation of the four languages: *Nederduitſche Taal; Sundaſe of Berg-taal; Gemeene Javaanſe taal; Javaanſe Hoog Dalamſetaal* (Iperen 1780b: 289). Noteworthy here is that Sundanese was conceived of as a *taal* (language) among other *talen* (languages) — but it was to take another 60 years before Sundanese was fully recognized as a distinct language, and the Sundanese a people (*volk*) in their own right.

The British interregnum in Java from 1811 to 1816 gave strong impetus to the study of local history and culture. Thomas Stamford Raffles, the British Lieutenant Governor of Java, published *The History of Java* in 1817, and above-mentioned Crawfurd, who was the Resident of Yogyakarta (1811–6), published *History of the Indian Archipelago* in 1820. These two books were to have a great impact on subsequent Dutch scholarship, and both Raffles and Crawfurd recognized Sundanese as a distinct entity, albeit using different terminology. Raffles (1817: 357) wrote:

> The native population of *Java, Madura,* and *Bali,* islands most intimately connected with each other in every respect, use exactly the same

written characters, and it appears that one generic language prevails throughout these islands. Of this generic language, however, there are four dialects, differing so materially from each other as to be generally considered separate languages. It is, however, rather by admixture of other languages than by mere difference of dialect that they are distinguished. These dialects or languages are the *Sunda*, spoken by the inhabitants of the mountainous districts of Java west of *Tegal;* the *Jawa* or Javan, which is the general language of Java east of Cheribon, and throughout the districts lying on the northern coast of the island; the *Madura* and the *Bali,* being the dialects or languages belonging to those islands respectively.

Is "the *Sunda*" a language or a dialect? In "A Comparative Vocabulary of the Malayu, Javan, Madurese, Bali, and Lampung Languages", which was added to his monumental book as an appendix, Raffles reveals his uncertainty about how to distinguish between the two. Sundanese is not given an independent place in the word lists, but it is included in the "Javan" column instead. It is clear that the Lieutenant Governor of Java considered Sundanese to be a variant of Javanese.

Crawfurd had a more distinctive idea of Sundanese: he classed it among "Minor languages of the Archipelago", which, in his words, are the "many written languages of tribes less powerful and cultivated than the great nations of Java". Under the major languages of the archipelago, he included Javanese, Malay, Bugis, and Macassarese. Crawfurd was primarily interested in languages that had a written tradition; only those which had manuscripts were really worth studying. European academic tradition's insistence on writing was still paramount in this period.

Although their terminology may have been confused and confusing, both British scholar-administrators clearly appreciated the Sundanese language as a distinct entity, and that in itself represents a break in European scholarship about Java.

That the British saw Sundanese as a distinct entity is also clear from their efforts to estimate the number of those who spoke it. Raffles guessed that the number "does not exceed one-tenth of the population of the whole island; the remaining nine-tenths speak Javan" (Raffles 1817: 358). Recent population research in Indonesia suggests that this figure was underestimated (Boomgaard 1991: 105). According to the statistical research of P. Boomgaard and A.J. Gooszen, the population of the Sundanese-speaking regencies (Banten, Buitenzorg, Krawang, Priangan, Cirebon) in 1815 was 566,294.[8] (It is surprising that Dutch colonial officials kept detailed records of indigenous populations.) The population of Java was 4,322,031, and about one-seventh of the island's population seems to have spoken Sundanese. This proportion of Sundanese to Javanese speakers had not changed much by 1930 (one-fifth), when a credible census of ethnic groups was made. Raffles underestimated the number of Sundanese speakers because of the confusion of the language map (Raffles 1817: 356–60). He may have counted only the speakers of "mountain" Javanese, which was spoken in the highland areas, leaving out the speakers of refined Sundanese, or *Jaware*, spoken in the upland plains. Raffles' estimate is repeated by Crawfurd's account (1820: vol. 2, 66):

> The *Sunda* is the language of the mountaineers of the western part of Java, of perhaps one-third of the area of the island, but, in round numbers, probably of not more than one-tenth of its inhabitants.

Andries de Wilde, a Dutch coffee planter in Sukabumi, published an ethnographic study of the Priangan Regencies in 1829. He considered *de Soendasche taal* (the Sundanese language) as an independent language, as the following paragraph makes clear:

> The language that is spoken in these Regencies is Sundanese; this differs from Javanese and Malay. However there are many words which have crept in or been adopted from the latter languages. The script of the priests is Arabic; most of the local chiefs know it too; if not, people generally use the Javanese script.
>
> De taal, welke in deze Regentschappen gesproken wordt, is de Soendasche; dezelve verschilt van het Javaansch en Maleijsch, echter zijn er van beide laatste talen vele woorden bijingeslopen of aangenomen. Het schrift der priesters is Arabisch; de meeste Hoofden kennen het ook; anders wordt het Javaansch karakter, over het algemeen, gebruikt (Wilde 1829: 108).

For the revised edition of 1830,[9] de Wilde collected many Sundanese words about agriculture, customs, and Islam. The vocabulary indicates that he studied Sundanese by himself.[10] However, he seems hesitant about using the term *Soendasche* (Sundanese) for the words he collected. Above all, the book gives us an impression of the writer's confusion about the people he dealt with in West Java; in 230 pages the word *Soendasche* is used only three times: *de Soendasche taal* (the Sundanese language), *de algemeene Soendasche naam* (the general Sundanese name), and *Soendasche volkeren* (Sundanese peoples). In particular, the plural *Soendasche volkeren* is intriguing: somehow de Wilde must have assumed that many kinds of cultural entities living in the Priangan Regencies could be summarized one way or another under the term *Soendasche*. However, he does not use the term *Soendasch* but *Javaans* to refer to the local population: *Javaan/Javanen* (Javanese) is used no less than 35 times, the adjective *Javaansche* eight times, and *Berg-Javaan/Berg-Javanen* ("mountain" Javanese) four times. In other words, these people were somehow *Javaans* (Javanese) and *Soendasch* (Sundanese) at once. What was the most appropriate name for them? Did de Wilde perhaps just repeat what the locals told him? His confusion is not really surprising: about 1830, the existence of a distinct ethnicity in West Java had not yet been acknowledged, and de Wilde must have been simply bewildered by the languages he heard during his long stay in the area. How to order a linguistic (and cultural) continuum? How to draw a map over the area so that its heterogeneity could be curbed and organized, and the local people could be made aware that they were Sundanese while others were Javanese? These issues were colonial concerns.

In 1841, the Sundanese language was formally recognized with the publication of the first Sundanese dictionary: the *Nederduitsch-Maleisch en Soendasch Woordenboek* (Dutch-Malay and Sundanese Dictionary), published in Amsterdam by Roorda, who was considered to be the most authoritative scholar of Oriental languages. The vocabularies in the dictionary had been collected by de Wilde. The existence of Sundanese was now sanctioned by an authority in academia far away from the speech community. In the preface, Roorda makes a significant remark about Sundanese:

> This [dictionary] is useful in the first place, especially in order to become more closely acquainted with a language of which our knowledge is little and imperfect at this till now; the language is spoken in the western part of the Java island, which is called *Sunda* or *Sundalanden* by the natives, differing from the eastern part of the island; the language differs considerably from that properly called Javanese as well as from Malay, the language of the foreigners in the Dutch East Indies Archipelago.

> Het dient in de eerste plaats, en vooral, om ons nader bekend te maken met eene taal, waarvan ons tot hiertoe slechts weinig, en ook dat nog gebrekkig, bekend was; de taal namelijk, die door de inboorlingen gesproken wordt in dat westelijk gedeelte van het eiland Java, hetwelk,

in onderscheiding van het oostelijk gedeelte des eilands, *Soenda*, of de *Soendalanden*, genoemd wordt; eene taal, die van het eigenlijk gezegd Javaansch zoowel als van het Maleisch, de taal der vreemdelingen in den Indischen Archipel, zeer aanmerkelijk verschilt (Roorda in Wilde 1841: v).

In the early nineteenth century, Johann Gottfried Herder's (1744–1803) *Abhandlung über den Ursprung der Sprache* (On the Origin of Language), published in 1772, had great significance for Romanticism in the West. Jostein Gaarder gives a wonderful summary on this point:

> Herder showed that each historical epoch had its own intrinsic value and each nation its own character or "soul" … The National Romantics were mainly interested in the history of "the people", the languages of "the people", and culture of "the people" in general. And "the people" were seen as an organism unfolding its innate potentiality — exactly like nature and history (Gaarder 1995: 270).

Romanticism influenced Dutch scholars, too. They were searching for "the people" and the language of "the people" in their colony. Roorda defined Sundanese as an independent language, not a dialect of Javanese. He believed in the relationship between a people (*een volk*) and its language (*zijn taal*): "the language is the living natural product of the spirit of a people; the spirit of every people manifests itself in the language in its own manner" (Noordegraaf 1985: 352). He established the linguistic distance between Sundanese and both Javanese and Malay. Sundanese became a language, no longer a dialect, in the eyes of Europeans.

Roorda also insisted on the importance of Sundanese, based on scientific principles. He said:

> From this it becomes clear that Sundanese is considered a vernacular by the aristocrats which is not at all viewed as being on the same level as Javanese. This does not mean, however, that knowledge of Sundanese is of no less importance, not only for communication with the inhabitants of the Sundanese area, who do not understand Javanese, but also in purely linguistic terms. Sundanese, like Javanese, is a distinct, peculiar branch of language, and because of it, of equal importance considered from a linguistic point of view.
>
> Men ziet daaruit, dat door de voornameren het Soendasch meer als volkstaal beschouwd, en geenzins met het Javaansch op gelijken rang

gesteld wordt. Daarom is de kennis van het Soendasch echter niet van minder belang, niet alleen voor het verkeer met de bewoners der Soendalanden, die het Javaansch niet verstaan, maar ook uit een taalkundig oogpunt beschouwd. Het Soendasch is, zoowel als het Javaansch, een eigene, bijzondere taaltak, en daarom uit een taalkundig oogpunt beschouwd van hetzelfde belang (Roorda in Wilde 1841: xi).

His metaphor of a "branch" shows that his idea of language is rooted in the thinking of Herder and the theory of evolution.

The next step in the emergence of Sundanese language and culture was its differentiation from other *volken* (ethnicities). In 1842, Wolter Robert van Hoëvell, a clergyman in Batavia from 1836 to 1849 and co-founder of the *Tijdschrift voor Nederlandsch-Indië* (Journal for the Dutch Indies), presented the results of his research. In his article "*Onderzoek naar de oorzaken van het onderscheid in voorkomen, kleeding, zeden en gewoonten, taal en karakter tusschen de Soendanezen en eigenlijke Javanen*" (Research into the reasons for the differences between the Sundanese and the Javanese proper in terms of appearance, dress, customs and traditions, language and character), he discusses in ethnographic terms the distinction in physical features between the *Djalma Soenda* (Sundanese people) and the *Wong Jawa* (Javanese people). This article amounted to an acknowledgement, not only of Sundanese as a linguistic unity but also of the people living in western Java as a distinct ethnic group, the *Soendanezen* (Hoëvell 1842: 139–45). It is of interest that language and ethnicity were discussed together, another echo of Herder's work.

The most important event in the development of the study of Sundanese was soon to occur. Pieter Mijer, the secretary of the Bataviaasch Genootschap van Kunsten en Wetenschappen, announced on 9 October 1843 that a prize consisting of 1,000 guilders and a gold medal (or another 300 guilders) would be awarded for a Sundanese dictionary. After pointing out the incompleteness of de Wilde's Dutch-Sundanese dictionary, he announced the following requirements for the new dictionary:

A Dutch-Sundanese dictionary, as comprehensive as possible, in which Sundanese words appear in both Javanese and Roman characters; explaining which words are the *kromo* language and which words are the *ngoko* language, and in which part of the Sundanese areas every word is used; and clarifying the meanings of words with examples from daily life.

> Een, zoo veel mogelijk, volledig Nederduitsch-Soendasch Woordenboek, waarin de Soendasche woorden met Javaansche en Latijnsche karakters moeten geschreven zijn; waarbij tevens moet worden opgegeven, welke woorden tot de kromo- en welke tot de ngoko-taal behooren, en in welk gedeelte der Soendalanden ieder woord in gebruik is; en waarin de beteekenis der woorden, met voorbeelden van spreekwijzen uit het dagelijksche leven, moet worden opgehelderd (Mijer 1843: x).

What was the reason for this prize? First, the colonial government had become aware of the necessity to study indigenous languages for the sake of administration. As Dutch involvement deepened, more direct contact with the indigenous people increased. However, knowledge of Sundanese was scarce in Dutch scholarship, especially in comparison with Javanese. The idea of the prize was supported by the increasing interest of scholarship in a "newly-found" distinctive language. Dutch officials required a more practical and comprehensive dictionary because they considered de Wilde's compilation inadequate.

The government also drew attention to the need for textbooks and grammars. It insisted that the study of Sundanese by Europeans was as useful in practical terms as the study of Javanese: in the interior of Java, Malay was incomprehensible to both the Javanese and Sundanese (Mijer 1843: v–vi). The most significant effect of the announcement of the prize was the shared recognition of Sundanese as a distinct language in Java, which proved to be a stimulus for the study of Sundanese among the Europeans.

The first foreign-language dictionary for the Sundanese language came out in 1862, titled *A Dictionary of the Sunda Language of Java*. Its compiler, Jonathan Rigg, was an English tea-planter who lived south of Buitenzorg (the current Bogor). He had compiled it in 1854, thirteen years after the publication of de Wilde's dictionary. Rigg's dictionary marked an epoch in the history of the Sundanese language. The British had succeeded in West Java, unlike the Dutch, and it is not difficult to imagine the frustration felt by the latter in this respect. Although the Dutch had long been concerned with the East Indies and had studied them, it was the British (Raffles, Crawfurd, and Rigg) who had made the most important scholarly contributions, especially with regard to the Sundanese language. Dutch scholars bitterly criticized Rigg's dictionary. Daniel Koorders, for example, began his review of the book as follows:

> It has pained me that the compiler was not a Dutchman; that, just as the first man to give us a general view of the fundamental rules of our

colonial policy was a foreigner, so, too, the first person to give us the practical means for the knowledge of the language of the people of western Java was a foreigner. It did surprise me that in a dictionary that is supposed to have been written mainly for Dutch people the spelling of the Sundanese words is accorded to the English pronunciation.

Wel deed het me leed, dat geen Hollander de samensteller was; dat, gelijk een vreemdeling de eerste geweest is, door wien ons een algemeen overzicht werd gegeven van de grondregelen onzer koloniale politiek, het wederom een vreemdeling was, die ons het eerste bruikbare hulpmiddel voor de kennis der volkstaal van Westelijk Java kwam brengen. Wel verbaasde het me, in een woordenboek, dat geacht moet worden hoofdzakelijk voor Hollanders geschreven te zijn, bij de spelling der Soendaneesche woorden de Engelsche uitspraak der letters gevolgd te zien (Koorders 1863: 1).

Koorders had doctorates in both theology and law and was sent to the Indies in 1862 as a high-ranking official. He was ordered to study Sundanese and to establish a Teachers' Training School. Koorders concluded his review as follows:

In light of the importance of the study of Sundanese, which could be taken down a completely wrong path by Rigg's book, I feel obliged to make a disapproving judgment [...].

In het belang van de Soendaneesche taalstudie, die door het boek van Rigg in een geheel-verkeerd spoor zou gebracht worden, achtte ik me verplicht, mijn afkeurend oordeel uittespreken [...] (Koorders 1863: 21).

It is interesting that Rigg does not attempt any lengthy explanation of the language in the preface of his dictionary. Presumably, he thought no explanation was necessary to justify its status as an independent indigenous language in the island of Java, suggesting that the existence of Sundanese had already become common knowledge in the Dutch East Indies. Some seventy years after the first vocabulary list was compiled by Van Iperen (Iperen 1780b), Sundanese was recognized as a language in European scholarship.

The following years were marked by the activities of missionaries and scholars, who tried to define what Sundanese was, and attempted to establish orthodox/authoritative knowledge of the language. This period lasted until the 1880s, when the divergence of opinion among the missionaries and scholars was largely solved, and the discussion settled: many dictionaries were compiled, grammar books published, and spelling rules established. One of the most important discussions centred around which variety of Sundanese was "pure". Interestingly, they assumed that every language has a pure form. In the course of their publishing efforts, the Dutchmen tried to seek a "pure" Sundanese.

## "Pure" Sundanese

Descriptive and normative studies of a language are generally carried out first, chiefly by scholars outside the speech community and are therefore written in other languages (Ferguson 1959: 325–40). Hence, studies of Sundanese were undertaken by outside scholars, especially Dutch scholars and missionaries. In the 1860s, the idea of Sundanese as a different language from Javanese became commonly accepted among the Europeans. However, their knowledge of the "newly-found" native language was minimal and they began studying it in the island of Java itself. Protestant missionaries came to West Java to disseminate their religion and study Sundanese mainly as part of their attempts to translate the Bible. Meanwhile, scholars who were sent by the government compiled dictionaries and wrote grammar books. Both the missionaries and scholars were almost obsessed by the belief that every language had a pure form.

The idea of a pure language also influenced Sundanese intellectuals of the time. One of the most influential Sundanese aristocrats and writers, Moehamad Moesa (1823–86), thus attempted to purify his own language. Moesa was the chief Muslim leader in Limbangan (present-day Garut) and an intimate friend of K.F. Holle. He wrote in a poem in 1867:

| | |
|---|---|
| Reja make doewa basa,[11] | Many people use two languages, |
| nja eta salah-sahidji, | namely one of these |
| Malajoe atawa Djawa, | Malay or Javanese. |
| nja bener hade teh têing, | This is actually exceedingly good and |
| kaäsoep djalma radjin, | one is counted among diligent people, |
| ngarti Djawa djêng Malajoe, | understanding Javanese and Malay. |
| tatapi oelah tinggal, | But do not forget |
| basa asal nini-aki, | the native language of the ancestors. |
| mangka natrat basa asal toetoeroenan. | May the native language be passed on. |

| | |
|---|---|
| Kawoela soekoer ka Allah, | I thank Allah |
| Goesti anoe sipat rahim, | The Lord who is merciful |
| sareh kersa noe kawasa, | It is the Almighty's wish |
| Soenda dihoedangkên deui, | that Sundanese was revived, |
| oepama anoe gering, | like one who was ill and |
| ajeuna eukêr mamajoe, | now he is recovering, |
| ngan tatjan tjagêr pisan, | but he has not fully recovered yet. |
| manawa sakêdêng dêi, | Likely in a little while, |
| moega-moega sing toeloej djagdjag waringkas. | Hopefully he will be completely well again. |
| | |
| Anoe matak basa Soenda, | The reason why the Sundanese language can |
| diseboetkên hoedang gering, | be said to be in the process of recovering, |
| tapi tatjan djagdjag pisan, | but not yet completely well, |
| boektina tatjan walagri, | the evidence that it is not yet healthy, |
| basana tatjan bêrsih, | is that the language is not yet pure, |
| tjampoer Djawa djêng Malajoe, | mixed with Javanese and Malay, |
| soemawon basa Arab, | even with Arabic. |
| eta noe reja teh têing, | That is too many, |
| malah aja noe enggeus lêngit djinisna. | There are even some which have lost its original form. |

(Moesa 1867: 5)

Moesa often thanked either the Dutch or the colonial government in his writing because they raised the position of Sundanese to the same level of Javanese, but did feel that Sundanese as an ancestral language was still in a weak position. Moesa was afraid of losing the purity of Sundanese because of influences from other languages.

One point needs to be clarified about the different notions of pure language held by Moesa and the Dutch. Pure Sundanese, for Moesa, was language that was not mixed with Javanese and Malay, while for the Dutch it meant a purer dialectal form of Sundanese. The missionaries and scholars were trying to settle on a "pure" form to standardize the language, so their question was which regional form of Sundanese was the most proper. In the end, they determined that the Sundanese spoken in Bandung represented the "purest" form.

We often hear that the Sundanese people themselves claim the Sundanese dialect in Cianjur to be the most mellifluous in terms of pronunciation. By contrast, the Sundanese dialect outside the Priangan Regencies is considered to be less refined in terms of pronunciation and lexicon. In the first half of the nineteenth century, Cianjur prospered and had a relatively larger population than other towns. In fact, it had been the administrative centre of West Java up to 1864. The colonial government had made Cianjur the capital of the Priangan Regencies mainly for economic reasons, as it occupies an important geographical position connecting the interior of West Java to Batavia. Agricultural produce such as coffee, which was collected from the plantations, was brought through the city. However, proportional to the shift in the importance of the market economy, Bandung was gradually becoming more important than Cianjur for the colonial government. In 1865, the capital of the Priangan Regencies was moved to Bandung as a result of the changing of the transportation route for plantation produce (Ohashi 1994: 87–114). In fact, Bandung had functioned as the centre of the eastern part of the Sundanese region for a long time before this administrative move. The event led to accelerated centralization in many aspects.

The population in Bandung began to increase rapidly as it became the centre of Sundanese culture and government (Antlöv 1995: 16–27; Kunto 1984). However, Cianjur maintained its reputation in the cultural field. R.A. Koesmaningrat, the Regent in Cianjur from 1834 to 1863, was highly respected in the field of Sundanese culture. He was very fond of music and promoted it. This is reflected in the name of a musical genre, *tembang Sunda Cianjuran*, still used today (Zanten 1989: 21–3). The language in Cianjur maintained its respected status as *lemes* (soft, refined) Sundanese. In contrast, at the beginning of the nineteenth century Raffles had declared that "in *Bogor* and *Chai-anjur*, the *Sunda* is pronounced in a more drawling manner than in *Cheribon*,[12] where it is probably most correctly spoken" (Raffles 1817: 358). His remarks are understandable as Raffles considered Sundanese to be a "mountain" dialect of Javanese. Unlike the British, the Dutch scholar Roorda defined the Sundanese-speaking area in exact terms in his introduction to de Wilde's dictionary:

> Sundanese is spoken in completely pure form throughout the whole of the Priangan Regencies, as well as in Banten and Cirebon, except in the coastal area of Banten, in the direction of the Sunda strait, and in the Cirebon area, in the north close to Tegal. In these areas, as is common in boundary areas, a mixed accent is spoken.

> Geheel zuiver wordt het Soendasch gesproken in de geheele uitgestrektheid der Preanger Regentschappen, alsmede in Bantam en Cheribon, uitgezonderd alleen in het Bantamsche de strandbewoners naar den kant van straat Soenda, en in het Cheribonsche die, welke naar het noorden en digt aan het Tegalsche wonen, daar in beide deze steken, gelijk veelal in grensgewesten, een gemengde tongval gesproken wordt (Roorda in Wilde 1841: v).

Roorda did not specify which dialect was the purest. In the following three decades, various research on the "pure" form was undertaken by missionaries such as S. Coolsma, A. Geerdink, C. Albers, D.J. van der Linden, G.J. Grashuis, and W.H. Engelmann, and by scholars such as D. Koorders, H.J. Oosting, and J.R.P.F. Gonggrijp.[13] The colonial government declared in 1872 that Sundanese was spoken in its "purest" form in Bandung. Bandung Sundanese, together with the Javanese spoken in Surakarta, the Batak in Mandheling, and the Malay spoken in Melaka and the island of Riau, became the designated languages of education in Dutch indigenous schools.[14] Is it not the case that these "pure forms" were ideological creations, based on the belief that a variant of the language in a specific place is "pure" and can be clearly distinguished from its other dialects in terms of particular linguistic aspects? It is especially difficult to tell the differences between them when the language is written, because the distinction of a "pure" variety is based mainly on its oral aspect. "Pure" Sundanese was chosen and began to be taught in schools. This official statement was an epoch-making event in the development of the language, representing a truly colonial situation: a dialect had been chosen to be the standard by the colonial authority.

With regard to the standard languages, the colonial authorities issued another statement in 1912. The contents of the declaration were the same: the Bandung dialect was to be recognized as the standard for Sundanese.

> In making the rule [of spelling], we principally follow the pronunciation of the words as they are most commonly pronounced in the standardised

languages (chief dialect of Sundanese: Bandung, Malay: Riau, Javanese: Surakarta).

Netepkeun palanggeran teh babakoena pisan noeroetkeun kana ngoenikeunana ketjap noe pangloembrahna dioenikeun dina basa anoe djadi loeloegoe (hoofddialect Soenda: Bandoeng, Malajoe: Riau, Djawa: Soerakarta) (Commissie voor de Volkslectuur 1912).

Language is dynamic and changing by its own nature. However, in a sense "correct" Sundanese was "invented" by the Dutch. After "pure" Sundanese was found, the specific form of the language was codified as unitary, as a result of the influence of scholars, lexicographers, grammarians, and missionaries. They compiled dictionaries of "correct" Sundanese words and systematized the language in grammar books. Ironically, the language of these grammar books and dictionaries has come to be considered as the "correct" one by the Sundanese themselves until the present day.

The government declaration quoted above was published in a booklet on spelling in Roman script. It shows that, in the case of Sundanese, this process extended to the level of script and orthography. A system of spelling and transliteration is evidence of the "invention" of the language. The Dutch created an alphabet for Sundanese according to their own concepts in place of the existing script.

## Sundanese in Aksara Walanda (Roman script)

Before the Dutch introduced Roman script to the Sundanese-language area in the nineteenth century, it was written in Arabic script (called *huruf pegon*) and in one based on the Javanese script. The Arabic script had been introduced by Muslim scholars in the fifteenth century and was used in and around Islamic institutions. The Javanese script had been introduced in the seventeenth century when Mataram made its influence felt in the western part of Java, and the *menak* (local aristocrats) followed the Javanese examples in admiration for the courts of Central Java. The Arabic script was used for almost every kind of writing, whereas the Javanese script was used only for official reports submitted to the Javanese Mataram dynasty and later to the Dutch government, as well as for the *menak*'s correspondence.

The administrators who re-established Dutch authority over West Java after the British interregnum worked with the *menak* and were hardly aware of the fact that local intellectuals also made use of the

Arabic script. When they began to establish schools, it was self-evident for them that, next to the Roman script, only the Javanese script was worth considering.

The admirable catalogue of Sundanese manuscripts compiled by Ekadjati (1988) serves to show how Sundanese used the three scripts in their writings.[15] Ekadjati lists 488 manuscripts that are kept in domestic public collections, 789 in collections abroad (mostly in the library of Leiden University), and 554 that are still in private hands in West Java. The great majority of manuscripts in domestic collections are written in the Arabic script, whereas in Leiden the number of manuscripts in Javanese script is nearly the same as that in Arabic script. Sundanese manuscripts in the Roman script are also not uncommon in domestic or overseas collections; they suggest that manuscript culture continued to flourish beside print culture even after the Roman script was introduced. Printed books in the Roman script were probably copied by hand, creating a new tradition. This suggests how ingrained the handwriting practice was in the community. Finally, private collections have hardly any manuscripts in Javanese script.

Why are there so many Sundanese manuscripts in the Javanese script in Leiden and so few in Indonesia? The answer is simple: the Javanese-script manuscripts were collected by the Dutch based on their ideas about Sundanese.[16] The main Dutch collector was Snouck Hurgronje, who purchased 400 Sundanese manuscripts for the Leiden collection. The others are Hazeu (52), Rinkes (36), Koorders (35), Roorda (8), the Netherlands Bible Society (NBG: Nederlands Bijbelgenootschap) (117), and several minor collectors. On the basis of Ekadjati's findings we can conclude that the collection in Leiden does not give a balanced picture of nineteenth-century writing practices in West Java: Arabic script was predominant among the Sundanese communities, and the domestic collections are a more faithful reflection of the actual state of things. It is important to note that about 80 per cent of the collection in the Jakarta National Library was compiled by the Dutchmen K.F. Holle and C.M. Pleyte.[17] Holle, a government advisor on indigenous affairs and one of the main collectors of manuscripts, undoubtedly knew that most of the Sundanese could read and write Arabic better than the Javanese script, but suggested to the colonial government that the Javanese and Roman scripts should be used for educational purposes in the Sundanese region. He insisted that Islamic elements should be avoided in government-sponsored education (Holle 1867: 450–2), and the government in Batavia followed his advice: Islam was seen as dangerous.

Illustrative of the complex situation of scripts used are the remarks of Ahmad Djajadiningrat, a well-known aristocrat, in his autobiography.[18] Before Ahmad left home to attend a Dutch-language school for aristocrats' children in Batavia, his father had sent him to a private school at Pandeglang in the Banten Regency, where he received private lessons in writing and reading *huruf Belanda* (Dutch script). Like most Sundanese children, he had learned to read and recite the Koran near his house, and had been taught the Javanese script at home, as suited a young aristocrat. However, he managed to learn the new script: "Within a few weeks I was able to read rather well and write neatly [in Roman script] with a pencil" (*Na eenige weken kon ik vrij behoorlijk lezen en vrij netjes met potlood schrijven*) (Djajadiningrat 1936: 24).

For most Sundanese literates, the Arabic script, *pegon*, was more familiar than the Javanese script because of the traditional education in Islamic schools, called *langgar* and *pasantren*. No wonder that a Dutch administrator in the Banten Regency questioned the wisdom of the government's educational policy: "Nobody here can read the books in Javanese script. If we were sent printed books in Arabic script, they would be read" (Steenbrink 1985: 10). In the peripheral regions such as Banten, Karawang, Cirebon and Buitenzorg, a special provision was made in the curriculum: the Roman and Arabic scripts and the Malay and Javanese languages were taught as Arabic script was predominant, and the two languages were used next to Sundanese, and sometimes even preferred (VIO 1867: 13). On the insistence of Holle, however, Arabic script was gradually expunged from the education system in the whole of the Sundanese region,[19] and the Roman script was promoted by the government as time went on.

Looking back at some fifty years of education, the *Palanggeran noeliskeun basa Soenda koe aksara Walanda* (Handbook of writing Sundanese in Dutch script), written by Dutch and Sundanese language and education specialists, could safely argue that neither the Javanese nor Arabic script was suitable for the Sundanese as the Javanese script contained sounds that were not used in Sundanese, and the Arabic script needed new letters and vowel marks on each syllable (Commissie 1912: 8–12). An additional reason for relying on the Dutch or Roman script was the fact that it was cheaper to print. Moreover, "Sundanese in Dutch script is easy for other ethnic groups and foreigners who want to read Sundanese; thus, the Sundanese will be as respected as other ethnic groups when the books are well produced" (ibid.: 11–2).

The Roman script thus became the dominant and, later, the sole script for printed Sundanese. The Arabic script was maintained in the manuscript tradition, whereas the traditional Javanese script for Sundanese was discontinued and replaced by Roman script. The Roman alphabet, educationalists and missionaries argued, was based more directly on sound than the other scripts, reducing sound directly to spatial equivalents, and in smaller, more analytic, more manageable units than the syllable-based writing of Javanese and Arabic.

Initially, Dutch residents of West Java transliterated without much reflection, rendering Sundanese words in Roman script according to their aural perception. In 1862, Holle proposed a standardized orthography in his *Kitab Cacarakan Sunda* (Sundanese Spelling Book) (Holle 1862: 1–2). In the process of transliteration, the discussions focused on the long *pepet*, which in the ears of the Dutch was most characteristic of the Sundanese language and thus became the touchstone. Koorders, however, criticized Holle's spelling method in his bitter review of Rigg's dictionary (Koorders 1863: 3, 9), and so did W.H. Engelmann, translator of the Netherlands Bible Society in his correspondence with that same institution (Engelmann 1867). Soon enough, Holle recognized the inadequacy of his own method, and accepted Engelmann's suggestions — *e* for short *pepet* and *eu* for long *pepet*.

The colonial government decided to adopt Holle's transliteration of Sundanese, partly based on that of Engelmann (Holle 1871: 94);[20] it was generally accepted, albeit not wholeheartedly. Two years later, S. Coolsma, a missionary of the Netherlands Missionary Union (NZV: Nederlandsche Zendingsvereeniging), published a grammar of the Sundanese language. In his preface, he confessed to have used the transliteration that the government prescribed, but with great reluctance. This not only confirmed the strained relations between Holle and the missionaries, but also Holle's influence on the colonial government.

> What gave me great pleasure was the positive advice concerning my handbook that was submitted to the government of the Dutch East Indies by Mr. K.F. Holle, Honorary Advisor on Native Affairs, which yielded a government grant for the cost of the publication, for which I am most grateful. That support has obliged me, as far as this booklet is concerned, to use my transliteration of Sundanese in accordance with the system adopted by the government.
>
> Hoogst aangenaam was voor mij het gunstig advies, door den Heer K.F. Holle, Adviseur honorair voor Inlandsche Zaken, over mijne handleiding uitgebracht aan de Ned. Ind. Regeering, hetwelk tengevolge

had tegemoetkoming van de zijde der Regeering in de kosten der uitgave, — door mij bij dezen dankbaar erkend. Die ondersteuning legde mij de verplichting op mijne transcriptie van 't Soendaneesch, voor zooveel dit boekske aangaat, in overeenstemming te brengen met het systeem door de Regering aangenomen (Coolsma 1873: [i]).

The first edition of Coolsma's Sundanese-Dutch dictionary in 1884 seems to have set the norm,[21] and the now formalized spelling was to be used in the Sundanese books of the government publisher (the Landsdrukkerij[22]), which had been printing Sundanese books since 1853.

Finally, some 30 years later, in 1912 the Committee for Indigenous Schoolbooks and Popular Reading Books published *Palanggeran noeliskeun basa Soenda koe aksara Walanda* (Handbook of writing Sundanese in Dutch script) for their Sundanese publications. It was written by the agricultural expert H.C.H. de Bie, a teacher at the Willem III Gymnasium, the Sundanese ethnologist C.M. Pleyte, and four Sundanese intellectuals who played an important role in Sundanese literature, namely M. Moehamad Rais, M. Partadiredja, D. Ardiwinata, and M. Amongpradja. This showed that the Sundanese elite itself was also willing to accept the formal spelling. A government decree concerning indigenous languages, issued in 1918, made the spelling official.

> In recent years, it has seemed desirable for the spelling of the indigenous languages which are written in Roman script to be fixed accurately, especially for the benefit of education.
>
> In de laatste jaren bleek het gewenscht om — inzonderheid ten behoeve van het onderwijs — de spelling van de Inlandsche talen, welke met Latijnsche karakters worden geschreven, nauwkeurig vast te stellen ([Commissie voor de Volkslectuur] [1918]: 1).

The handbook, translated into Malay, Javanese, and Sundanese,[23] is an interesting example of how the indigenous languages were interpreted in terms of the language of the colonial masters:

> In choosing the scripts and signs, the Dutch equivalents are looked at first. When a certain sound does not exist in the latter language, the equivalent sign for the Dutch sound which comes closest to the vernacular is used. For example, the so-called long *pepet* in Sundanese, which is not encountered in Dutch, is represented by *eu*, since the sound represented by this sign indicates approximately that of Sundanese.

> Bij de keus van letters en teekens is in de eerste plaats rekening gehouden met de waarde, welke deze in het Nederlandsch hebben. Indien een bepaalde klank niet in de laatstgenoemde taal voorkomt, is gebruik gemaakt van het teeken voor de Nederlandsche klank, welke de Inlandsche zoo dicht mogelijk nabijkomt. Voorbeeld De z.g. lange pepet in het Soendaasch, welke in het Nederlandsch niet wordt aangetroffen, is weergegeven door *eu*, daar de door dit teeken voorgestelde klank die van het Soendaasch bij benadering aangeeft ([Commissie voor de Volkslectuur] [1918]: 2).

Sundanese orthography was developed for those who knew Dutch, with the assumption that Dutch was superior to the indigenous languages and should be used as the universal standard.

In sum, the transliteration of Sundanese from Javanese script into Roman script was discussed and "invented" by the Dutch between the 1860s and the 1880s. The orthography was made based on the logic of the Dutch language: to educate the "uncivilised" Sundanese, Roman script was better than the existing scripts — that is, Javanese and Arabic — as well as cheaper to print. First, the Dutch made a distinction between Sundanese and Javanese. Then they attempted to find a "pure" Sundanese and created an orthography for the language. "Pure" Sundanese and its orthography was taught to the Sundanese people through Dutch schools and schoolbooks. The Dutch-made orthography was convenient for the Dutch administrators who were in charge of the Sundanese-speaking area and assumed that the local people would follow their example.

The same holds for the missionaries who, by compiling dictionaries and prescriptive grammar books, made an important contribution to scholarship. They translated the Bible and gospels into Sundanese, mostly using Roman script.[24] However, they were less successful than the administrators. Their failure to spread Christianity in the Sundanese-speaking area can partly be explained by the influence of Holle on the government to formulate a policy against the propagation of Christianity in West Java so as not to encourage a reaction by "fanatic" Muslims, but also partly by the missionaries' lack of understanding of Sundanese culture.

The Sundanese did not reject the newly "invented" orthography. Apparently, they did not insist on using their existing script but readily received the new script as a symbol of modernity, with hardly any resistance to the language policy of the Dutch. Dutch education served the colonialists' own interests and they were not afraid of losing the

Javanese and Arabic scripts. However, the number of literates in the community was quite small and the new Roman-script literates, the product of a Dutch education, constituted an even smaller group. The new form of Sundanese was, of course, more than the script and orthography presenting the "right" Sundanese, as formulated in grammar books and "pure" words compiled in dictionaries. The Sundanese that was arranged by the Dutch during the second half of the nineteenth century came to be considered the "right" Sundanese by the people themselves. Nowadays, the Sundanese consider the language recorded at the time in grammar books and dictionaries to be *asli* (original) Sundanese. In fact, a new kind of Sundanese language was formulated — one that reflected the colonial ideology.

## Discovering the "literature" without writing

The Europeans in the Indies operated on the assumption that each ethnic group had a distinct language and culture. Some ethnic groups were advanced while others were backward, and some cultures were more developed than others. One criterion to measure the level of development of a culture was the presence or absence of "literature".

Influenced by Romantic ideas of the nineteenth century, European scholars had hoped to find a particular kind of literature in Sundanese culture, even though they had only a vague idea of what it should be like. "Literature" was something lofty, gathered in canonical works, and, of course, it had to be written. Working with these vague notions — no scholar had ever tried to formulate a definition — they failed to find what they were looking for, or were disappointed by what they found. In the process of defining the Sundanese language, they concluded that Sundanese writing lacked artistic dimensions, and that the Sundanese did not have a literature. This allegedly showed that the local population of West Java was not well developed.

As discussed in the previous section, the Europeans began to take the indigenous cultures, including their languages, more seriously after the beginning of the nineteenth century. The British played an important role in setting the tone. Crawfurd maintained that "there are no books in the Sunda language, for the Sunda has no national literature" (Crawfurd 1820: vol. 2, 68). He recognized Sundanese as a distinct language, but could find no writing using it. One wonders what knowledge Crawfurd based his blunt statement on. Jonathan Rigg, who compiled the first Sundanese-English dictionary, did not find a Sundanese literature either:

"The Sunda people possess no literature to which reference can be made, and it is consequently a purely oral language spoken by a little better than two millions of people" (Rigg 1862: xiii). It is obvious that Crawfurd and Rigg considered literature to consist of something written, as the word's etymology would indicate, and that the idea that artful language could be used in oral forms was beyond them. Rigg showed his ignorance even more explicitly in that he assumed that all the texts the Sundanese wrote in Javanese script were in the Javanese language.

Roorda, professor of East Indies languages, could also not find anything he could call literature. The work of de Wilde convinced him that Sundanese was a distinct language in West Java, but following de Wilde,[25] he did not think it very likely that Sundanese speakers had a literature:

> Mr. de Wilde was never informed about an indigenous Sundanese literature during his many years stay in the Preanger Regencies, so that it is not probable that any such thing exists.
>
> Van eene eigene Soendasche literatuur heeft de Heer de Wilde, gedurende zijn veeljarig verblijf in de Preanger Regentschappen nimmer iets vernomen, zoodat het niet waarschijnlijk is, dat er zulk eene bestaat (Roorda in Wilde 1841: xi).

By denying the possibility of the Sundanese having a literature, Roorda put them on a lower level of civilization than the Javanese who, he claimed, had a lofty literary tradition, witnessed by the manuscripts that he could study in Holland.

H. Neubronner van der Tuuk, Roorda's contemporary, had a completely different notion of literature, however. An expert in several indigenous languages, he asserted that Sundanese was an independent language and had *menak* words (words of aristocrats, upper-class vocabulary) and *kuring* words (words of the common people), a distinction he considered equivalent to the Javanese *kromo-ngoko* speech levels. At Buitenzorg during a period of recuperation from a serious illness, van der Tuuk obtained Sundanese manuscripts, including religious books, narrative poems and letters, and criticized de Wilde as follows:

> That absolutely no Sundanese literature exists, as de Wilde mentions, is completely incorrect, and I believe that we will still have little to say about it as long as the civilised (who are, as a rule, the most pious) Muslims are unwilling to show us infidels what sort of literature they possess, for fear of having to hand it over or seeing it contaminated.

> Dat er volstrekt geen Sundanesche litteratuur zou bestaan, zoo als De
> Wilde vermeldt, is geheel onjuist, en ik geloof, dat hierover nog weinig
> stelligs te zeggen valt, zoo lang de beschaafde (en dit zijn in den regel
> de meest godsdienstige) Mahommedanen ongenegen zijn aan ons
> ongeloovigen te laten zien, wat zij van letterkunde bezitten, uit vreeze,
> dat te moeten afstaan of verontreinigd te zien (Tuuk 1851: 341).

This was written ten years after de Wilde's dictionary was published. Van der Tuuk seemed to work on the assumption that where there is a language, there is a literature, even though for him the term "literature" primarily referred to everything written rather than to artful language. "Literature" is a confusing term, and it should not be surprising that even the most important Dutch linguist of the nineteenth century hesitated to give a clear definition of it.

Van der Tuuk's doubt about de Wilde's position, based on the reluctance of the Sundanese to show the Dutch their writings for religious reasons, is probably justified. Many Sundanese-language manuscripts were written in the Arabic script, as we have seen from Ekadjati's catalogue, and people often thought those manuscripts to be sacred or holy objects (*pusaka*), just as a dagger (*keris*) can be. Van der Tuuk also reported that the Sundanese had Javanese-language manuscripts that were written in the Arabic script. Whatever the language, a text written in the Arabic script had to be protected from contamination. In the mid-nineteenth century, the use of script and language in manuscripts in the Sundanese-speaking area was a confusing one: both Sundanese and Javanese were written in Javanese as well as the Arabic script. The indigenous Sundanese script had been lost nearly a hundred years before.

Holle's work represented a turning point.[26] He went to the Indies in 1843 and started to study local language and culture from the time he was appointed a government clerk in 1846. He came to love Sundanese culture, and when he retired from government service and went to work at a tea plantation in Cikajang (in the present-day Garut district) in 1858, he became deeply involved in its study and decided to devote himself to the "enlightenment" of the Sundanese. In Holle's view, the Sundanese used their language as an oral medium and Javanese as the written medium. He believed that the script used in the manuscripts on palm leaf had been lost. He wished to revive Sundanese as a language to define Sundanese culture:

> The writing system in manuscripts is at present completely unknown
> to the descendants, and only for some years now have they been

written in Sundanese, instead of faulty Javanese. Yes, I still remember the response of a regent when I told him that the *panghulu* of Garut had composed a Sundanese poem, *wawacan*: "That is impossible: Sundanese is not a language!".

Het schrift der MSS. zelfs is thans ten eenenmale aan het nageslacht onbekend, en eerst sedert een jaar of wat wordt er, instede van in gebrekkig Javaansch, in het Soendaasch geschreven. — Ja, ik herinner mij nog het antwoord van een regent, toen ik hem verhaalde, dat de Panghoeloe van Garoet een Soendaasch gedicht (*wawatjan*) had gemaakt: "dat is onmogelijk: het Soendaasch is geen taal (*boekan bahasa*)!" (Holle 1867: 451).

However, Holle did not try to revive the old Sundanese script, but tried to revive the language as a written medium. He suggested to literate Sundanese aristocrats that they should write their stories in Sundanese. His friend, Moehamad Moesa, was one of the most prolific among those who took up his suggestion. Holle then selected some texts and edited them for schoolbooks, which were published by the government printing house Landsdrukkerij. In the 1860s, no less than 23 such books were published by the government under Holle's supervision.

Whether there existed Sundanese literature was not a point of discussion for Holle; the matter at hand was which writing should be selected as suitable to publish for use in schools. There was no talk of "verbal art" in Sundanese either. The purpose of publishing texts in Sundanese was not to edit manuscript materials that were considered to be valuable from a scholarly point of view, as Engelmann and others had attempted,[27] but to publish schoolbooks. The main goal of the Dutch authorities was to lead the locals and raise their "level of civilisation". The research on the Sundanese language and literature was therefore done for more practical reasons.[28] The results were to be used for the implementation of colonial policy.

In 1863, the government commissioned D. Koorders to evaluate the schoolbooks in use at the time. Koorders, the scholar, immediately came into conflict with the autodidact Holle, the pragmatist. Koorders' evaluation of Holle's works was mostly negative. He deemed them inadequate for the purpose of teaching Sundanese to the Sundanese, for a number of reasons: most of the texts were written in verse (*dangding*) and were unsuitable for teaching a pure or correct form of the language (Koorders in Meinsma 1869: 260-4). Koorders assumed that the indigenous peoples of the Indies did not have a "literature" equivalent to that in Dutch. The criterion for his evaluation of Sundanese printed books was whether the contents were sufficiently didactic and whether the language usage was correct. No attempts were made to evaluate the texts in literary terms, and Romantic notions of verbal art were not considered at all. As a colonial official, Koorders felt that the Dutch were obliged to teach the Sundanese the proper Sundanese language. In other words, the Dutch thought that they knew Sundanese better than the Sundanese people themselves (cf. Maier 1988).

## No "literature"?

After having published a number of schoolbooks in Sundanese, Dutch scholars began to wonder about the artistic merits of the language. They searched in vain for "literature" and concluded that Sundanese writing was worthless from the "literary" point of view.

In the early nineteenth century, *letterkunde* was the common term used to refer to literature in the Netherlands, although the concept of literature itself was not clear. *Litteratuur* was a new word borrowed from French (*littérature*), with the newly established meaning of "literature". However, as Michel Foucault has observed, the concept of literature was itself relatively new to European civilization in the nineteenth century (Foucault 1985). At that time, the Dutch felt that the French were superior with respect to language and culture, and accepted the French term *littérature* without establishing a clear definition for it; they presumed that there was something self-evident about it and lost sight of its ideological nature (Bork *et al.* 1986). In Dutch, *letterkunde* and *litteratuur* became interchangeable terms, and nobody knew exactly what either meant. The Dutch scholars thus tried to adapt their notion of literature to indigenous writing without having a clear definition of the term.

As we have seen, van der Tuuk was the first scholar to address the issue. He claimed that there was writing in Sundanese but adopted a vague notion of literature to Sundanese writing. The result was to be expected: no "literature" could be found. Grashuis, initially sent to West Java as a Bible translator by the Netherlands Missionary Union and in 1877 appointed a lecturer of Sundanese language at Leiden University, was to continue the discussion. He did find *litteratuur* in the sense of *geschriften* (writings), but failed to find any artfulness in them; thus, he also found no "literature". In his introduction to an anthology of Sundanese writings, *Soendanesche Bloemlezing* (1881), he wrote:

"[Sundanese writings] lack every artistic merit" (*zij missen alle kunstwaarde*), and continued as follows:

> Though they are important from a linguistic point of view, they cannot claim to be named artistic products of literature. The poetry is simple rhyming, and the prose remains very down to earth.
>
> Van belang, uit een taalkundig oogpunt beschouwd, hebben zij geene aanspraak op den naam van litterarische kunstvoorbrengselen. De poëzie is gerijmel, en het proza blijft laag bij den grond (Grashuis 1881: xi).

Grashuis' position on Sundanese writing remained consistent after his first anthology was published in 1874. He saw Sundanese poetry as a mere imitation of Javanese poetry, lacking any original artistic value, and showing a deep influence of Islam (Grashuis 1874: iv). Besides poetry, the Sundanese had very few prose writings, and those that existed merely served as didactic aids. Art and science had never flourished in the Sundanese-speaking area of Java, Grashuis argued, and the reasons were simple: since the fall of Sunda, the Sundanese lacked a kingdom and palaces that could function as cultural centres, as well as rulers who could patronize the arts.[29] He was always comparing Javanese language and literature with those of the Sundanese, and constantly finding the latter inferior.[30]

Although Grashuis was of the opinion that the Sundanese had no "literary products of art" (*litterarische kunstvoorbrengselen*), he compiled three anthologies of Sundanese writing from the corpus of texts available to him.[31] He did so for the sake of knowledge of indigenous languages in the Indies, and not because of its artistic merit. In the introduction to the first anthology (1874: xiii), he announced that the Sundanese language was no less worthy an object of study than Javanese as a distinct language. This was meant to be a textbook for anyone who wanted to learn the language of West Java, in particular those who were trained in Delft and later in Leiden to be colonial officials. Grashuis' anthologies emphasized the pragmatic selection of "pure" Sundanese, relatively free from the influence of other languages, such as Javanese, Malay, and Dutch. Textbooks had to provide examples of proper language usage rather than of a refined dialect, that is to say, Sundanese in Bandung. This idea is consonant with Moesa's idea of "healthy Sundanese". He chose texts that were stylistically "original", although the criteria he used to determine originality are not clear.

Grashuis aimed for variety. He chose letters, fables, and Islamic tales from manuscript sources, *pantun* stories from oral sources, and stories from printed books, including a translation into Sundanese of Defoe's *Robinson Crusoë*. He even presented some fragments of *wawacan*, the well-known narrative poetry among the Sundanese, but they were few and only for purposes of comparison with other writings. Poetry, artful and artistic, was not really suitable for learning a language. Moreover, "there is a deep gap between our poetry and Sundanese poetry" (*welke eene diep klove er gaapt tusschen onze poëzie en die der Soendanezen*), for one is art and the other is not (Grashuis 1891: v–vi). Other Dutch scholars did not disagree with that opinion, apart from Coolsma who was outside the academic circles.

Grashuis' opinions of Sundanese writing came to be commonly accepted. They were taken up, for instance, in the *Encyclopedie van Nederlandsch Oost-Indië* (Encyclopaedia of the Dutch East Indies) which, published in four volumes in 1905 and reprinted in eight volumes from 1917 to 1937, summed up the views and knowledge of the Dutch scholars and officials involved with the East Indies. The *Encyclopedie* was taken as the authoritative reference work on the Indies, to be quoted again and again. Under the entry "*Soendaneesch*", the *Encyclopedie* had this to say:

> It is no wonder then that in the past the Sundanese has been unable to produce what is properly called *literature*. Imitating the newer Javanese poetry, they gradually started to produce *pieces of poetry* or, more accurately, *pieces of rhyme*. These lack any truly artistic value and are noteworthy only as evidence of the influence of Islam on the inhabitants of the Sundanese part of Java for more than four centuries.
>
> Geen wonder dus dat de Soendanees voorheen geene eigenlijk gezegde *literatuur* heeft kunnen voortbrengen. Wel is hij er echter allengs toe gekomen om, in navolging van de nieuwere Javaansche poëzie, in zijn eigen taal *dichtstukken* of liever gezegd *rijm werken* op te stellen. Deze missen echter alle kunstwaarde en strekken alleen ten bewijze van den invloed, nu reeds bijna vier eeuwen lang, door den Islam op den bewoner van het Soendaneesche deel van Java uitgeoefend (*Encyclopedie* 1921: vol.4, 20).

This entry from the 1905 edition was repeated word for word in the 1921 edition, an indication that the official opinion on Sundanese literature had not changed as a result of the poor knowledge of Sundanese writing as well as a lack of Dutch experts. It was Memed

Sastrahadiprawira, the most respected and well-known Sundanese intellectual of the time, who refuted this view. In an article in *Djawa*, the journal of the Java Institute, entitled *"Over de waardeering der Soendaneesche litteratuur"* (On the evaluation of Sundanese literature) he wrote:

> 1st. Grashuis' judgment, [—], that the Sundanese have no literature in the proper sense of the term is inconsistent with reality; 2nd. The opinion that existing pieces of poetry are totally lacking in artistic value shows that the critics do not have sufficient knowledge and are, therefore, unable to appreciate beauty, the more so because they are using idiosyncratic criteria. Errors in an Encyclopaedia have a persistent life, but we *keep* on hoping for a judgment, if possible an appreciation, that is based on a deep *knowledge* and an affectionate *understanding*.

> 1e. het oordeel van Grashuis, [—],als zouden de Soendaneezen geen eigenlijk gezegde literatuur hebben, niet overeenstemt met de werklijkheid; 2e. dat de meening, als zouden de bestaande dichtwerken alle kunstwaarde missen, van onvoldoende kennis van den beoordeelaar getuigt, waardoor het hem niet mogelijk was het schoone te genieten, mede vanwege den eigenaardigen maatstaf, welken hij aanlegde. In een Encyclopaedie vervatte dwalingen hebben een taai leven, doch wij *blijven* hopen op een oordeel, zoo mogelijk op een waardeering, gegrond op diepgaande *kennis* en liefdevol *verstaan* (Sastrahadiprawira 1929b: 21).

It is noteworthy that Sastrahadiprawira wrote the article in Dutch, not in Sundanese or Malay, as if his words of protest should be read by Dutch scholars, the true power-holders in the East Indies. On the other hand, by engaging in a debate with Dutch scholars he removed himself from the Sundanese tradition and alienated himself from his fellow Sundanese; in his arguments he used the terms of Indology which had been formed by Dutch scholars.[32]

Sastrahadiprawira deplored the fact that the negative evaluation of Sundanese literature had not changed since the first publication of the *Encyclopedie*, and pointed out that that the evaluation had originated with Grashuis' 1874 anthology. He also remarked that some 150 Sundanese books had been published by 1921, the date of the revised edition of the *Encyclopedie*, and demonstrated the richness of Sundanese *litteratuur* by listing the names of authors like Moehamad Moesa, Moehamad Soeëb, and Aria Bratadiwidjaja.

Sastrahadiprawira criticized the author of the *Encyclopedie* article for his inadequate judgements and unsatisfactory knowledge. Of course, what was to be included exactly in the *litteratuur* category is not evident. Sastrahadiprawira discussed Sundanese "literature" only in the context of the Dutch notion of *litteratuur*. He did not explain the literariness of Sundanese writing on its own terms.

This vague notion of Sundanese literature came to be taken over by Sastrahadiprawira's successors, who also failed to think or write about their own writings in terms different from those of the Dutch. They only transformed *litteratuur* into *sastra*[33], without clearly defining the category.

## 2. Scholarship, Colonialism and the Canonization of *Wawacan*

After the "discovery" of Sundanese writing, a particular form of it known as *dangding* became the focus of Dutch scholars' attention. Believing this form to be borrowed from Javanese literary tradition, they called it *tembang* and did not look for the Sundanese term for it. Despite their low regard of Sundanese writing, they continued their studies, using European notions in their description of Sundanese literature (cf. Sweeney 1991: 26–7).

In terms of form, Sundanese poetry can be roughly divided into two categories: *dangding* and *kawih*. The first is a generic term designating poetry in 17 verse forms, known as *pupuh*. Each *pupuh* has its own name, such as *dangdanggula*, *kinanti*, *asmarandana*, *sinom*, and so forth, with its own rules of composition, melody, and number of lines. Etymologically, the word *dangding* derives from the sound of the voice when the text is sung: "dang-ding-dung, dang-ding-dung". The song has a free-rhythm, called *tembang* or *mamaos*.

Formally speaking, *kawih* is simpler than *dangding*. Each line has eight syllables, the last syllable of the lines rhyme, and the total number of lines varies.[34] *Kawih* is a rhythmic song and is sometimes accompanied by *kacapi*, a Sundanese zither.[35] A good example of *kawih* performance is the recitation of *pantun*, where a bard chants a story the whole night long.[36] *Kawih* is chanted and sung in measures of four stresses, employing a different melody from *dangding*. It is considered to be "the simpler, less refined form of vocal music" and can be called a kind of folk song (Zanten 1989: 15–6).

*Dangding* was usually written while *kawih* was not. In the nineteenth century, *dangding* was mainly for the *menak* (aristocrats), and *kawih* was for the *cacah* (commoners). *Kawih* seemed to be unimportant in the eyes of Dutch scholars, especially because the idea of oral literature did not exist in their conception of "literature"; there are hardly any descriptions of it. The paradox lies in the fact that the Dutch looked for original verbal art, such as *kawih*, in the Sundanese-speaking communities, whereas *dangding* was a verse form imported from the Javanese literary tradition.

## The Dutch view of Dangding

By the middle of the nineteenth century, the Dutch had concluded that *dangding* was the most dominant and favourite form of writing among the Sundanese-speaking communities. Hence they considered it the most effective means for the education of Sundanese children; *dangding* was called *tembang* by the Dutch until the beginning of the twentieth century. The inspector of native education, J.A. van der Chijs, wrote that only *dangding* would be effective in the education of the Sundanese (Chijs 1867a: 6–11). His idea originated with the "Sundanese specialist" K.F. Holle, who had written an important report on native education, especially on the creation of Sundanese schoolbooks (Berge 1993: 19–20). According to van der Chijs, the following should be included in the teaching of Sundanese:

> Sundanese legends as readers, a reader about local customs and good manners, [and] Sundanese poetry *(tembang)*. Learning the various melodies, in which the poetry has to be read or preferably sung, is not superfluous and certainly interesting for the Sundanese; knowledge of it is considered a sign of civilization and good education.

> Soendasche overleveringen als leesboeken, een leesboek omtrent den adat en goede manieren; Soendasche gedichten (tembang). Het leeren van de verschillende zangwijzen, waarop de gedichten moeten worden gelezen of liever gezongen, is niet overbodig en voor den Soendanees zeer aanlokkelijk; wordende de kennis daarvan als een blijk van beschaving of goede opvoeding aangemerkt (AVSS 1861: 214).

On the basis of Holle's suggestions, the government began printing Sundanese schoolbooks in the 1860s, most of them in *dangding*. An evaluation of the printed books was conducted by Dutch scholars/administrators soon afterwards. Van der Chijs and others approved them as suitable materials for education, but not everyone did. For instance, in his 1863 report to the Secretary-General of the Dutch East Indies government in Batavia, Koorders considered *dangding* inappropriate for schoolbooks. He gave three reasons:

> Firstly, they [*tembang* verses] spoil the purity of the language.[...] Secondly, *tembang* violates the external form of words and the rules of sentence structure in every possible way.[...] Thirdly, the nature of *tembang* is unsuitable to give a strong impetus to development and civilisation [...].
>
> Vooreerst: ze bederven in den grond de zuiverheid der taal.[...] In de tweede plaats: de tembangs doen zelfs den uitwendigen vorm der woorden en de regelen van zinbouw op alle mogelijke wijzen geweld aan.[...] In de derde en laatste plaats: de tembang is uit zijn aard ongeschikt om aan ontwikkeling en beschaving een krachtigen stoot te geven[...] (Koorders in Meinsma 1869: 261–4).

It is noteworthy that Koorders mentions the purity of the Sundanese language, as if he knew what Sundanese was while the Sundanese themselves did not. It is a good illustration of the arrogance of the colonizers. As for *dangding*, Koorders had noticed the prominent position of *dangding* like most of the Dutch, but he had difficulties judging it as poem because of his conception of literature. The following statement demonstrates his confusion:

> It is inaccurate to translate the word [*tembang*] as *poem*. They have nothing in common with our poems. Perhaps they could be called *songs*. However, only because of the lack of a proper Dutch word, we say that *tembangs* are *sung*, not *read*. Only the English word *chanting*, as far as I know, conveys a correct and complete understanding of the word.
>
> Het is onnauwkeurig, dat woord door *gedicht* te vertalen. Ze hebben met onze gedichten niet-het-minste gemeen. Veeleer zou men ze dan noch met den naam van *zangstukken* kunnen bestempelen. Maar het is enkel bij gebrek aan een eigen Hollandsch woord, dat we plegen te zeggen: de tembangs worden *gezongen*, niet *gelezen*. Alleen het Engelsche *chanting* geeft, voor zoover mij bekend is, het begrip juist en volkomen weer (Koorders in Meinsma 1869: 260–1).

Koorders would not translate *dangding* simply as "poem", because Sundanese verse lay beyond the concept of poetry (*gedicht*) that was held among the Dutch. Sundanese poetry was always chanted or sung loudly. This view was consonant with the belief of Dutch scholars and administrators that the Sundanese did not have a "literature". Hence, Koorders called *dangding* "songs".

The manner in which *dangding* was read is also important here, as Koorders noted. Somehow, van der Chijs was aware of the intriguing reading habits of the local people:

> The indigenous man has two ways of reading: the first is our way, be it with the difference that he rarely understands the purport of recitation; the second is reading while singing (*nembang, matja*). He only uses the first when the second is impossible, because for him the latter is by far the most favoured and actually the true way.

> De inlander heeft twee manieren van lezen; vooreerst onze manier, met dit onderscheid, dat hij van voordragt zelden begrip heeft; in de tweede plaats het zingende lezen (nembang, matja). De eerstbedoelde manier past hij alleen toe dan, wanneer de tweede onmogelijk is. Want deze laatste is voor hem verre weg de meest geliefde en eigenlijk de ware manier (Chijs 1867b: 7).

From van der Chijs' remarks, it can be concluded that in the second half of the nineteenth century, "reading" still implied "reciting" for the Dutch scholars; for him, the difference between "us" and the locals was not silent reading versus recitation, but reading aloud versus singing to a melody. The first way of reading was thus reading aloud, while the second was singing. He saw singing as the true way of reading for the Sundanese, but that opinion may have been the result of yet another confusion on the part of the Dutch. They clearly did not understand the difference between *nembang* and *matja*; *nembang* (the nasalized form of *tembang*) referring to reading *dangding*, and *matja* (from *batja*) to reading in general.[37] Equally interesting in van der Chijs' remarks is his assumption that the indigenous people barely understood what they were reading unless they sang it. This cannot but be akin to the recitation of the Koran: children allegedly learned to recite the Koran without understanding the meaning. Van der Chijs called this "mechanical reading" (Chijs 1867b: 12).

The Dutch colonial government could not promote its language policy without taking *dangding* into account. Somehow, the topic was made important enough to become an issue in parliamentary discussions in the motherland in 1867, where Koorders, the representative for Haarlem, protested that the schoolbooks in *dangding* were "bungled and were no more than waste-paper" and that publication with government budgets should be suspended immediately (Berge 1993: 22–3). Koorders' biting critique sounded like a personal attack on K.F. Holle, but did not have the result he must have hoped for: the government did not take immediate action to stop the publication and distribution of these schoolbooks. However, in the 1870s the publication of Sundanese *dangding* books showed a clear decline for different reasons, which will be considered in Chapter 2.

In the 1870s, Grashuis began an extensive study of Sundanese "literature". Grashuis acknowledged the significance of *dangding* and attempted to understand it, but failed to find it "poetic".

> It is poetry in form, yet so little of a poetic nature did I find among the thousands of Sundanese lines of poetry I had (unfortunately!) to struggle my way through, that I did not come across a single grain of poetry, even a poetic simile. Nothing but words with a certain measure, very often words and idioms, spoilt because of that very rhythm, made longer or shorter, whenever necessary.
>
> Poëzie namelijk wat den vorm aangaat, maar zoo weinig poëtisch, dat ik onder al de duizenden Soendanesche dichtregels, welke ik helaas! heb moeten doorworstelen, geen grein ware poëzie heb aangetroffen, geen enkele dichterlijke vergelijking. Niets anders dan woorden in maat, zeer dikwijls woorden en uitdrukkingen, om die maat verknoeid, verlengd of verkort, al naar het noodig was (Grashuis 1874: i).

What Grashuis expected to find in Sundanese poems abounded in European poetry: elegance, emotion, lyric. In the introduction to his first book on Sundanese language and literature, *Soendaneesch Leesboek* (Sundanese Reader), published in 1874, he said that Sundanese verse lacked every poetic quality. Such remarks remind us of Koorders and his colleagues, and of the *Encyclopedie van Nederlandsch-Indië*. It seems that Dutch scholars would hardly ever come to develop some kind of literary appreciation for Sundanese writing. Perhaps more noteworthy is that this expert on Sundanese language and literature expressed his preference of prose over poetry:

> Furthermore, those writings reveal that the Sundanese, if left completely to themselves, can write prose which is not without errors but is tolerable. That prose favourably distinguishes itself from the language and style of *wawatjan* (poetry) by its purity and regularity. The

Sundanese prose writer usually says in his simple manner what he thinks, and stays away from the artificial style of poems which often no longer express any substantial thought, but only place concepts next to one another.

Verder blijkt uit die geschriften dat Soendanezen, geheel aan zich zelven overgelaten, wel geen onberispelijk, maar toch dragelijk proza kunnen schrijven. Dat proza onderscheidt zich gunstig van de taal en den stijl der wawatjan (gedicht) door zuiverheid en regelmaat. De Soendanesche prozaïst zegt gewoonlijk op eenvoudige wijze, wat hij denkt, en blijft ver van den gekunstelden stijl der dichtstukken, die somtijds geene wezenlijke gedachte meer uitdrukken, maar slechts begrippen nevens elkander plaatsen (Grashuis 1874: xi).

"No substantial thought", "tolerable" and "artificial"—Dutch arrogance in a nutshell once again. His preference for prose was not in line with the official government policy that tried to promote *dangding* as the most adequate means of enlightening the indigenous population.

In retrospect, perhaps it is not so surprising that Dutch scholars in the second half of the nineteenth century had a limited knowledge of Sundanese writing. They were too focused on written sources, they often did not stay "in the field" for long periods of time, their local informants were not always reliable, and some of them had never even set foot in the Indies. Roorda comes to mind, as well as P.J. Veth, who published a widely acclaimed four-volume book, *Java*, between 1875 and 1884. When Veth solicited comments on the book from K.F. Holle in West Java, Holle answered as follows:

What you say about Sundanese literature is not quite correct, and incomplete. *Tembang* and *pantun* are worlds apart. The *pantun* (properly the Sundanese wayang) is very old (I have a *lontar* that is undoubtedly 400 years old). Mainly prose, with now and then some songs. The melody is peculiar. And then there are *sindirs* or *pangbalikans*, and lastly *dongengs*.

*Tembangs* are new. *Panata istri*[38] was written by the *panghulu* of Garut when he was still assistant *panghulu*.

I definitely disagree that the writings of the *panghulu* of Garut, especially the latter, belong to *santri* literature. This is a misrepresentation, which was brought into the world by the intolerance of missionaries. See, for example, *Panji Wulung*, *Wulang Krama*, *Wulang Tani*, *Ali Mohtar*, *Elmu nyawah*, *Dongeng pieunteungeun*, and so forth. Even *Abdurahman jeung Abdurahim*!

> Wat u zegt omtrent de Soend. litteratuur is niet heel juist en onvolledig. Tembang en pantoen verschillen hemelsbreed. De pantoen (eig. de Soend wajang) is heel oud (ik heb er een op lontar, stellig 400 jaar oud). Hoofdzakelijk proza, met gezang nu en dan afgewisseld. De wijs is een eigenaardige. Verder de sindirs of pangbalikans eindelijk dongengs. Tembangs zijn nieuw. Panata istri is door den pangh. v. Garoet gemaakt, toen hij nog hulppang. was. Ik kom er bepaald tegen op dat de geschriften v.d. panghoeloe v. Garoet, vooral de latere, tot santri-litteratuur behooren. Dit is een scheve voorstelling, door de onverdraagzaamheid der zendelingen in de wereld gebragt. Zie b.v. Pandji Woeloeng, Woelang Krama, Woelang Tani, Ali Mochtar, Elmoe njawah, Dongeng pieunteungeun, etc. Abdoerahman dj. Abd. zelfs![39]

Veth, who based his work on the knowledge that had been collected by Dutch scholars in the Indies, such as Grashuis, was quite misinformed about Sundanese writing (Veth 1875: vol. 1, 443–5). However, Holle himself explained *pantun* inaccurately in terms of verbal composition. *Pantun* was neither Sundanese *wayang*, a distinct genre of story-telling among the Sundanese-speaking communities, as it was in Java, nor prose: it was octosyllabic poetry.

Holle criticized missionaries like Grashuis for their ignorance, sometimes rightly so. However, some missionaries had a good knowledge of Sundanese language and writing, and particular mention should be made of Sierk Coolsma, who was sent to the Sundanese-speaking area in 1865 by the Netherlands Missionary Union. Coolsma's knowledge is best illustrated by his scathing commentary on 30 books, consisting of about 2,000 pages, published by the government: "the language is often artificial, not natural, and mixed with other writings, and the contents are of little value, with a few exceptions" (Coolsma 1881: 143 note). His advice was that the government should stop publishing these schoolbooks.

Coolsma had a sharper insight and a deeper knowledge of Sundanese language and writing than any other missionaries (or any other officials for that matter), but even his thorough knowledge was not a guarantee for success as a missionary: very few Sundanese were ever convinced of the superiority of Christianity. Be that as it may, his writings can only help us to acquire a better understanding of Sundanese writings.[40]

> People tend to complain that little or no poetry can be found in *tembang*. I think that is wrong. *Tembang* is not poetry, and it should not be treated as such. Nevertheless, in some of the best *tembangs*, in the *Abdul Muluk*, the *Rangganis* and the *Panji Wulung*, poetic elevation

and depiction can certainly be found. And *tembang* is a writing in verse form; it is composed to be sung, not to be read. It consists of one or more stanzas. If the writing is longer, then some variation is made in these stanzas. I know of seventeen kinds of verse forms.

> Men heeft zich wel eens beklaagd dat er in de tembangs weinig of geen poëzie wordt gevonden. Mijns inziens ten onrechte. De tembang toch is geen poëzie, en moet ook daarvoor niet worden gehouden. Niettemin zal in sommige der beste tembangs, o.a. in de Abdoel Moeloek, de Rangganis en de Pandji Woeloeng, dichterlijke verheffing en schildering niet te vergeefs worden gezocht. En tembang is een geschrift in dichtmaat, alzoo opgesteld, niet om te worden gelezen, maar om te worden gezongen. Zij bestaat uit een of meer zangen. Heeft het geschrift eenige uitgebreidheid, dan tracht men in deze zangen zooveel men kan afwisseling te brengen. Zeventien zangwijzen zijn mij bekend (Coolsma 1881: 144).

According to Coolsma, *dangding* is not poetry but "a writing in verse form", and he showed more appreciation for it than any of his colleagues, acknowledging that some *dangding* were elegant. His was a voice in the desert, however, as nobody seemed to take him seriously. This may have been due to his status as a missionary, which gave him a peripheral position in the European community and made it impossible to develop warm friendships with the local Sundanese aristocrats, who often refused to receive him (End 1991: 176). Moreover, missionary activities were restricted by the government in order to avoid possible Muslim opposition.

Coolsma did not have an optimistic view of Sundanese writing: "The situation of literature is unfavourable, and the people's perception of it is even more unfavourable".

> What suits the taste of the people is verse sung in the evenings or at night by someone who can read. And thus knowledge reaches many people who are always willing to listen. Prose, however, is rarely read and much will have to change before pen and press obtain some power among the Sundanese. At first a new spirit must emerge and they should abandon their indifference. They should learn and develop an interest in themselves and in their surroundings.

> Wat in dichtmaat is valt wel in den smaak, wordt 's avonds of 's nachts door iemand die lezen kan gezongen, en komt zoo ter kennis van velen, daar er altijd gevonden worden die zoo iets gaarne hooren. Proza echter wordt weinig gelezen, en veel zal er nog moeten veranderen eer

> pen en pers een macht worden onder de Soendaneezen. Eerst zal er
> in hen een nieuwe geest moeten komen, zullen ze hunne onverschilligheid
> laten varen en in zich zelven en wat buiten hen is belang leeren stellen
> (Coolsma 1881: 145).

Coolsma hoped that prose would develop among the people for a reason different from that of Grashuis: "a new spirit" had to emerge. He was aware of the fact that the Sundanese had a strong preference for *dangding*, and was familiar with their "reading" habits. He wanted to spread the gospel, and decided that prose was the most appropriate for this. The state of mind of the people had to be changed. Even though he knew *dangding* was the most effective way to convey knowledge to the people, Coolsma did not translate the Bible into *dangding*. He and other missionaries translated its books into prose, hoping that a new spirit would emerge through the new writing. *Dangding* was thought to be too traditional to convey new ideas. Moreover, it would be difficult to translate the New and Old Testaments into *dangding*.[41]

Contrary to this view was the fact that Coolsma admired *Injil anu kasuratkeun ku Mattheus* (The Gospel of St. Matthew) which was translated into *dangding*, and printed in 1854.[42] He regarded it as the greatest "Sundanese book" produced in such unfavourable conditions (Coolsma 1881: 146). Coolsma also noticed that the people read Arabic script instead of Javanese and Roman scripts even though the government had been trying to spread knowledge of the Roman script by way of schoolbooks. In the nineteenth century, being literate meant primarily being able to read Arabic script; only a small elite could read Javanese and Roman scripts. Hence, Coolsma published the *Book of St. John* and the *Acts of the Apostles* in Arabic script, although printing Arabic script was much more expensive than printing Roman script.

Coolsma made an important contribution to the study of the Sundanese language. Besides translations of the Bible, he also published an unrivalled Sundanese dictionary and a grammar book which the Sundanese still consider the most authoritative work on the language. However, as mentioned above, his views were not taken seriously until the 1930s, when K.A.H. Hidding appeared on the scene and analysed his predecessors' misunderstandings about *dangding*:

> Now before we turn to what is called literature in a proper sense, we
> should first have a closer look at *dangding*, the so-called verse forms.
> Because in this melodious language poetry plays a completely different
> role than that in present-day Western literature, this term easily causes

misunderstanding. When talking about poetry and art in general, it is better for people not to think purely in aesthetic terms in the first place, because the differentiation of the various domains of life did not take place to the same degree as it has in the West.

Voordat wij ons thans wenden tot wat in meer eigenlijken zin literatuur te noemen is, doen wij goed eerst de reeds enkele malen ter sprake gekomen *dangding*, de z.g. dichtmaten, nader te beschouwen. Want de poëzie speelt in deze melodieuze taal een geheel andere rol dan in de huidige Westersche literatuur en daarom wekt deze term zonder meer licht misverstand. Als er van poëzie en van kunst in het algemeen sprake is, doet men goed zich dit alles niet in de eerste plaats louter aesthetisch te denken, daar de differentiatie van de verschillende levensgebieden zich hier lang niet in die mate als in het Westen voltrokken heeft (Hidding 1935: 126).

Hidding's observations concurred with Coolsma's opinions about Sundanese poetry; they had sufficient authority to silence, at long last, not only Holle's but also Koorders' and Grashuis' ideas about Sundanese writing.

## The Sundanese view of Dangding

The Sundanese had considered *dangding* a highly artistic or artful form of composition since the time of intensified Javanese cultural influence. This fact had been noticed not only by the Dutch (as we have seen earlier), but also by the Sundanese themselves. Writing about the period when the Sundanese-speaking area was under the influence of the Javanese Mataram kingdom, one of the most prominent present-day Sundanese critics, Ajip Rosidi, recently formulated it as follows: "In general, what was considered beautiful, that is: writing which had literary merit, had to be written in *dangding*" (Rosidi 1995: 4).

In the second half of the nineteenth century, Moehamad Moesa, one of the most prolific Sundanese authors of schoolbooks, was regarded as the best writer in terms of his command of the Sundanese literary language (*Encyclopedie* 1921: vol. 3, 22–3). When he wrote and translated, he was conscious of the differences among the forms of writing. It is interesting that he offered his readers an apologetic explanation about the form of writing, because he did not employ *dangding,* in the preface to one of his frequently reprinted books, *Dongeng-dongeng Pieunteungeun* (Model Stories), published in 1867.

It suggests that *dangding* was the writing norm — in fact, even letters between aristocrats were usually composed in *dangding*, seen as an indication that the writer was a cultivated person and, at the same time, respected the addressee. In short, for the Sundanese people, to write meant to compose in *dangding*, and therefore Moesa had to explain why he composed the stories in *kalimah*, a term that Moesa seems to have invented to refer to prose.

Although Javanese was still the language of prestige in the Sundanese communities, Moesa's letters as well as those of his family members were composed in Sundanese, though partly Javanese, verse (Danoeredja 1929). The following is part of such a letter, written by Moesa's first wife, R.A. Perbata, between 1882 and 1885, and addressed to her daughter-in-law, the wife of the Regent of Lebak:

| | |
|---|---|
| Embok enggeus tampi serat, | I have received your letter |
| pandjang sarta nganggo dangding, | long and written in *dangding*. |
| pinareng noedjoe koempoelan, | Unexpectedly people gathered, |
| sadaja ais pangampih, | even including servants, |
| djedjel pinoeh di boemi, | the house was packed, |
| di poengkoer sareng di pajoen, | in the back and in the front. |
| ladjeng serat diboeka, | Then the letter was opened. |
| awit koe embok pribadi, | I started reading it by myself, |
| ladjeng bae ditembangkeun koe Ki Djaksa. | then it was sung by the Prosecutor. |

(Danoeredja 1929: 20)

Of course, this letter was composed in *dangding*; moreover, it shows that the people were used to listening to *dangding*. For the Sundanese, reciting *dangding* (*ditembangkeun*) was at once entertaining and educational, and this was true of letters too. Moesa was very much aware of the superior position of *dangding*, yet decided to write stories in prose, thus introducing a new form of writing.

As seen above, knowledge about Sundanese language and literature was primarily collected and then shaped by Dutch administrators, scholars, and planters — and this knowledge was often taken over by the Sundanese intellectuals who were educated in the government-subsidized schools. R.I. Adiwidjaja is a good example of a Sundanese intellectual who received a Dutch education in the full sense. He was a language teacher of Sundanese and Malay at the Teachers' Training School of Bandung and became one of the most prominent literary critics in the first half of the twentieth century (Nataprawira 1955). He played the role of a disseminator of knowledge on writing among his fellow Sundanese. An article in which he tried to explain the meaning of the Dutch word *gedicht* (poem) speaks volumes:

> I suppose that there are still many Sundanese who do not really know what is meant by *gedicht* (poetic language) as the Dutch call it. People usually assume that *gedicht* means only *tembang*. This assumption is not absolutely incorrect, because Sundanese poetry usually consists of *dangding*. [...] An utterance which contains the thought of poets and is made of fine structure, concise and carefully arranged, and with beautiful diction is called *gedicht* (poetic language).[43]

> Koe panginten, masih keneh seueur oerang Soenda, anoe hanteu atjan tarerangeun leres, naon ari noe koe oerang Walanda disebat *gedicht* (basa kaboedjanggan). Njangkana gedicht teh moeng woengkoel kana tembang bae. Eta panjangka kitoe teh, henteu lepat-lepat teuing, margi kawen Soenda gelarna babakoena dina dangding. [...] Omongan anoe ngandoeng pikiran boedjangga, kawoewoeh sae bangoenna, beres gekgekanana, rapat raprapanana mamanisna basa, tah eta noe disebatna *gedicht* (basa kaboedjanggan, basa kawen) teh (Adiwidjaja 1926: 6–7).

In attempting to define *gedicht*, Adiwidjaja also explained that Sundanese poetry was — or should be — more than *dangding* alone. The sentence suggested that *dangding* had remained at the centre of other poetic genres, but Adiwidjaja tried to combine the knowledge of the Dutch and the Sundanese, explaining the Sundanese view of poetry while embedding it in a Dutch conceptual framework. It seems that, for Adiwidjaja, *gedicht* meant all verbal art, and not only poetry, but that he thought of poetry as the centre of verbal art. In this sense, his attempt to unify the knowledge failed. Perhaps Sundanese intellectuals like Adiwidjaja were not always aware of the discrepancy between the Dutch and Sundanese views of poetry. However, Adiwidjaja was satisfied with the knowledge he learned at school, and so were most Sundanese intellectuals, it seems: the descriptions and definitions of Sundanese writing have been reproduced literally, or with only minor changes in wording. The same materials were used even after World War II. Sundanese intellectuals who had received a Dutch education still wrote schoolbooks or works of *kasusastran* (literature), sometimes without any trace of what constitutes verbal art, by their own definitions.[44] Thus, *dangding* remained the pinnacle of Sundanese verbal arts. Ajip Rosidi criticized such views:

> [...] the form of *dangding* held a significant role and became the common norm of Sundanese literature since the middle of the 19th century. *Dangding* was considered the sole and highest form of literature, and the view continued until the Japanese period and afterwards.

> [...] bentuk dangdinglah jang memegang peranan dan mendjadi norma kesusastran Sunda jang umum sedjak pertengahan abad ke-XIX. Dangding dianggap sebagai satu-satunja bentuk kesusastran jang tertinggi dan anggapan itu berlaku terus hingga djaman Djepang dan sesudahnja (Rosidi 1966: 55).

This does not mean that the Sundanese were not conscious that something was wrong with the colonial understanding of *dangding*. They were aware that it did not fit with their own perception of Sundanese writing. On this point too, Ajip Rosidi made an interesting remark, noting, on the one hand, the unique position of *dangding*, and on the other hand, pointing out that *dangding* was not the traditional form of writing. He criticized sharply the knowledge of the older generation as follows:

> And the original poetic form of Sundanese, which already had a high position in its culture, is *dangding* according to them [the older generation]. In their view, the highest form in the literary tradition is *wawacan*. It is *dangding* that properly suits the structure, feeling and spirit of the Sundanese. It is *dangding* that expresses the Sundanese tradition of our ancestors. It is *dangding* that represents the absolute norm of Sundanese literature. [...] As I said before, *dangding* is not the original form of Sundanese literature. *Dangding* has been also influenced by the outside, that is to say, it was imported from... Javanese literature, presumably since the time Sultan Agung reigned in the Mataram kingdom (in A.D. 1613–45). Thus it has been at most only three centuries in Sundanese literature. There is no doubt that *dangding* became a new and common form of poetry and was accepted in Sundanese society for the short period of the last hundred or hundred-and-fifty years only.

> Dan bentuk puisi Sunda jang asli, warisan leluhur Sunda jang katanja sudah tinggi kebudajaannja, menurut mereka adalah ... dangding! Dan bentuk sastra tertinggi warisan leluhurnja menurut mereka adalah ... wawatjan! Dangdinglah jang paling tepat dengan susunan bahasa,

perasaan dan alundjiwa orang Sunda. Dangdinglah jang mendjadi warisan karuhun Sunda. Dangdinglah bentuk puisi jang mutlak dalam kesusastran Sunda. [...] Tadi sudah saja katakan, bahwa dangding bukanlah bentuk kesusastran Sunda jang asli. Dangdingpun pengaruh dari luar, jaitu diimpor dari ... kesusastran Djawa, kira-kira dimulai pada djaman Sultan Agung bertahta di Mataram (1613–45 M.). Djadi usianja dalam kesusastran Sunda paling lama baru tiga abad sadja. Tidak mustahil dangding sebagai bentuk puisi baru umum dan diterima dalam masjarakat Sunda, dalam waktu satu atau satu setengah abad jang terahir sadja. (Rosidi 1966: 55).

Ajip Rosidi rejected the views that had been held and imposed in colonial times when the aristocracy collaborated with the Dutch. When *sajak-bebas* (free poetry) was introduced into Sundanese writing in the late 1940s, the older generation did not accept it as poetry because of its distorted (that is, Dutch-influenced) ideas about tradition:

> So it is clear that when Sundanese people reject free verse and criticise it as an inauthentic form of Sundanese literature while defending *dangding* and *wawacan* as their own cultural heritage and that of their ancestors, it shows only their lack of knowledge about their own history, art and literature.
>
> Djadi njatalah, bahwa orang Sunda jang menolak sadjak dan menuduhnja sebagai bukan bentuk kesusastran Sunda sambil mempertahankan dangding dan wawatjan sebagai warisan kebudajaan karuhunnja sendiri, hanja menundjukkan kekurangan pengetahuan mereka sadja tentang sedjarah, kesenian dan kesusastran Sunda sendiri (Rosidi 1966: 55).

Ajip claims that the authoritative position of *dangding* was the result of colonial scholarship. He criticized the intellectuals educated in the Dutch schools, but did not offer a new conception of Sundanese writing. At least it shows that he was conscious of the fact that the Sundanese elite or intellectuals had embedded Sundanese verbal art in the framework of European concepts. Thirty years later, Ajip Rosidi noted once again that the European way of defining Sundanese verbal art had left its mark on its writing:

> The word *puisi* (poetry) is not pure Sundanese. It is used to denote a corpus of language expressions that are different from everyday language, the so-called *basa lancaran* or *prosa* (prose). The division of language expressions into two, *puisi* and *prosa*, follows the Dutch

> (West), who divide literature into *poezie* and *proza*; [...] The division into two groups, *puisi* and *prosa*, has become common in each language and cultural context.
>
> Kecap *puisi* lain pituin Sunda. Digunakeun pikeun nyebut hiji golongan éksprési basa anu béda tina basa sapopoé nu disebut basa lancaran atawa *prosa*. Ngabagi éksprési basa kana dua golongan, puisi jeung prosa, téh nurutan urang Walanda (Barat) anu ngabagi sastrana kana *poezie* jeung *proza*; [...] Ngabagi dua basa kana puisi jeung prosa téh, ayeuna mah geus ilahar dina unggal basa jeung lingkungan budaya (Rosidi 1995: 3).

Apparently even Ajip, although very much aware of the Dutch-invented tradition of writing, has given up the effort to define Sundanese writing on its own terms. He too has accepted the dichotomy between prose and poetry, a dichotomy that had been taken as self-evident in the time of Grashuis and Moesa. The question of whether these European literary notions are relevant for describing and understanding Sundanese writing has remained unaddressed.

Most of the Sundanese intellectuals who had been educated at Dutch schools also accepted the dichotomy of prose and poetry. They thought that the division between prose and poetry played a meaningful role in understanding their verbal art, and was therefore not bothered by arbitrariness. Of course, there were a few exceptions. For instance, a writer who called himself *Goeroe* (Teacher) did not classify Sundanese writing into two kinds. Instead, he identified three categories of writing, as follows:

> If we follow the rule of the language, Sundanese literature can be divided into three parts: first the flowing language, second *tembang* (*wawacan*), and third a kind of *tembang* not so restricted by the rule of the number of syllables and the last sound, such as *sisindiran*, *kawih*, *doa nyawer*, and children's *kakawihan*.[45]
>
> Lamoen noeroetkeun atoeran basa, djadi kasoesastran Soenda beunang diatoer didjieun 3 bagian: kahidji basa diladjoer, kadoea tembang (wawatjan) djeung ka tiloe sabangsa tembang noe teu pati katalian koe atoeran reana engang atawa sora toengtoengna, saperti: sisindiran, kawih, doa njawer djeung kakawihan baroedak (Goeroe 1926: 14).

This quotation shows that alternative views were in existence within the Sundanese communities, perhaps only in an embryonic state and never developed. Meanwhile, thorough inventories of available and existent texts were never made. Apparently, the Sundanese did not feel the need to classify them, and it was only a century later that Ekadjati made a first inventory of the Sundanese manuscripts in today's Sundanese-speaking areas (Ekadjati 1988). In his laborious work, Ekadjati found that a variety of generic names were used for the total of 1,831 texts, including manuscripts in Sundanese, Javanese, Malay, Dutch, and Arabic. The inventory's primary organization is still in terms of *prosa* and *puisi* (prose and poetry), which does not tell us very much about the Sundanese perceptions of verbal art — but the titles of the manuscripts do tell us more, and they certainly could be used by future historians of Sundanese literature.[46] The Sundanese must have had some kind of implicit or unconscious poetics, and Ekadjati's list could be of great use to make sense of Sundanese writing in terms of form, content and function.

## The present state of Wawacan

Some words about the present state of *wawacan* are in order here. In the Sundanese-speaking communities, *wawacan* is rarely read now, let alone chanted. Only the older folks sometimes read them, but they hardly ever recite them for an audience. The exception is *beluk,* performed as part of a ritual by villagers when awaiting the birth of a child, celebrating the fortieth day after the birth (*opat puluh dinten*), and at the ceremony of cutting the baby's hair (*parasan*). In olden days, *beluk* was also sung when villagers watched the rice drying in the fields at night. Normally, a manuscript would be selected which fits the purpose of the gathering. In a singing circle, the chorus master would first recite the text, then a participant in the chorus (five to ten men) would sing the text one by one, following the chorus master in accordance with a metrical melody of the verse form. No musical instruments are used. When the text reaches a changing verse form, the chorus sings. *Beluk,* however, is gradually disappearing.[47]

Another exception is *tembang Sunda.*[48] It is still sung by people who love traditional music. The text used for *tembang* is limited to a small repertoire and consists of fragments of *wawacan* and *guguritan*. The singing is accompanied by two Sundanese zithers (*kacapi*) of different sizes, a bamboo flute (*suling*), and a fiddle (*rebab*).

According to Ajip Rosidi, *wawacan* declined in popularity when *sajak* (free verse) started to replace *dangding* in the 1960s (Rosidi 1995: 14). What does *wawacan* mean to the Sundanese people today? In the preface of a reprint of *Wawacan Panji Wulung*, Ajip Rosidi wrote that reading *wawacan* was useful for knowing the Sundanese literary tradition:

> *Wawacan* is a part of the wealth of Sundanese literature, and it must not disappear from the spiritual life of the Sundanese people. In fact, if someone composes *wawacan* today, he will be considered to be behind the times. However, the *wawacan* written in former times should be read so that the Sundanese will know the spiritual heritage of their ancestors.
>
> Wawacan minangka bagian tina kakayaan sastra Sunda, sawadina ulah nepi ka leungit tina kahirupan batin urang Sunda. Memang, lamun kiwari aya nu nganggit wawacan, baris dianggap tinggaleun karetaapi, tapi ari wawacan anu kungsi ditulis dina basa Sunda mah perelu dibaraca sangkan urang Sunda wanoh kana warisan rohani karuhunna (Rosidi in Musa 1990: 12).

This is obviously a stereotypical expression of admiration for a cultural heritage. *Wawacan* has become a relic of the golden age.

# Chapter 2
# The Institutional Context

## 1. Schools in the Sundanese-speaking Area

As Tony Bennett puts it, reading and writing "literature" is not a disinterested activity: "By 'Literature' here, I have in mind not the literary as a neutral totality of imaginative or fictional writing, but Literature as 'an ideologically constructed canon or corpus of texts operating in specific and determinate ways in and around the apparatus of education', in short, the canonised tradition" (Bennett 1992: 189). The canonized tradition can be seen in the formation of various literatures in the Dutch East Indies in the second half of the nineteenth century. Sundanese literature was one of them; it was promoted by the Dutch colonial masters in and around government-subsidized schools in West Java through the production of schoolbooks that introduced students to the concept of "literature" as well as alternative forms of writing, thereby making them aware of a standardized form of Sundanese. Formal education is an important force in creating and shaping the "literature" of a language community: schoolbooks and the discourse they evoke play a prominent role in its development (and in many cases, the emergence) as a distinct group of texts. The following attempts to contextualize the emergence of a group of texts designated as Sundanese literature within the new type of colonial education.

To begin with, some words on the concept of literacy. "Literacy", the capacity to write and read, had a wide meaning among the Sundanese-speaking communities. Initially, it referred to the ability to read and write Arabic and/or Javanese scripts. In and around the educational apparatus, a third form of literacy emerged: the ability to read and write texts in the Roman script, inspired by the textbooks that were produced under the supervision of the colonial government. Literacy in the Roman script produced a modern readership which developed in a complex interplay with the Javanese and Arabic manuscript traditions as sustained by traditional forms of education. At the same time, literacy in the Roman script was to create new forms of belonging.

## The schools

In the early nineteenth century, the education of the indigenous population of the East Indies came to be seen as a duty of the colonial government. In 1808, the then Governor-General Herman Willem Daendels (1762–1818) issued a decree that Regents had to establish schools for the indigenous children and appoint qualified teachers. However, it was not until 1818 that this decree was given legal recognition: the *Regerings Regelement* (Government Code of the Netherlands Indies) stated that the government had the duty to provide indigenous children with education facilities that were the same or similar to those for European children (Chijs 1864: 213–4). On paper it sounded beautiful, but then paper is patient.

Governor-General van der Capellen (1816–26) made the first effort to establish schools for indigenous children by setting up educational facilities in Pasuruan, Karawang, and Cianjur (Chijs 1864: 220–3). These schools were simple: a teacher taught reading and writing to a small group of children for a couple of hours a day. The government made a budget available for the schools and paid the teacher's salary. In the case of the school in Cianjur, the Regent of Cianjur and other aristocrats warmly supported it because it offered their own children an education that they expected would open many doors to the government. Twenty students, including two sons of the Regent, learned reading, writing, and simple arithmetic in Sundanese as well as Malay. The school was to be a model for other schools in the region. However, the new form of education failed to attract the attention of the locals who, unfamiliar with this novel institution, preferred to send their children to *pasantren* and *madrasa,* mainly to learn to recite the Koran and read religious texts (Snouck Hurgronje 1924: 155–81). Moreover, they were reluctant to send their children to a school with *kafir* (infidels) (Chijs 1864: 220–3). Perhaps the existing schools also did not operate very efficiently: their number did not increase for a long time.

A royal decree in September 1848 was needed to make the colonial education policy a reality:

> Our Governor-General of the Dutch East Indies is authorised to allocate to the budget of the East Indies the amount of Dfl. 25,000

per year, in order to establish schools for the Javanese, primarily intended to train indigenous officials.

Onze Gouverneur-Generaal van Nederlandsch-Indie wordt gemagtigd om op de Indische begrooting uittetrekken eene som van f 25,000 's jaars voor de oprigting van scholen onder de Javanen, voornamelijk bestemd tot opleiding van Inlandsche ambtenaren (AVSS 1853: 319–20).

Once the Governor-General was given a separate budget for schools (the term "Javanese" was meant to refer to the indigenous population of the island of Java as a whole), he took the matter seriously, the more so because there was a growing demand for local officials, concurrent with a deeper colonial involvement in local affairs. The money allocated was shared: Dfl. 12,300 was to be spent on a Teachers' Training School (*kweekschool*), and Dfl. 10,400 was used for the establishment of 20 provincial schools (*provinciale scholen*).[1]

In September 1851, the first Teachers' Training School, with a four-year programme was established in Surakarta. Its students were mostly of Javanese origin, and the language of instruction was Javanese. At the beginning, Madurese was used occasionally and Sundanese not at all (AVSS 1854: 129). However, some 10 years later, Sundanese began to be taught at the school to prepare Sundanese students for the opening of the Teachers' Training School of Bandung, which was established in 1866 as a result of the strong support of K.F. Holle. More schools of this type were subsequently established in other cities in the East Indies, such as Fort de Kock, Padang, Makassar, Ambon, and Yogyakarta.

Provincial schools, known as regency schools (*regentschaps-scholen*) and later renamed primary schools (*lagere scholen*), were established mainly on the islands of Java and Madura, which at the time were the centres of colonial activities. This type of school only offered an elementary education. It was designed for indigenous children, and although the students were relatively few, this was the form of education that was to play an important role in the emergence of a modern readership in the second half of the nineteenth century.

The first regency school was established in Pati, in the Jepara Regency of Central Java, in 1849. In the Sundanese-speaking area, the first regency school was opened in Cianjur in 1851.[2] Until the establishment of the Teachers' Training School in Bandung, this school in Cianjur initially also trained teachers for the primary schools. In other towns in the Priangan Regencies similar schools were opened. By the end of 1853, the school in Cianjur had 39 students, the school in Bandung 25, Sumedang 21, Sukapura 27, and Garut (Limbangan) 13 (AVSS 1854: 137).

In 1854, an important law concerning the education of the indigenous population was passed in Parliament, establishing that "The Governor-General has the responsibility of establishing schools for the benefit of the indigenous population" (Chijs 1867a: 250). The law came into effect in the Dutch East Indies the following year and gave some momentum to the establishment of three-year elementary schools. Every Regency now had the obligation to open an elementary school — and subsequently schools were opened in Cirebon, Ciamis, Kuningan, Majalengka, and Indramayu. By 1863, the total number of elementary schools in the Sundanese-speaking area had grown to 12. The number of students was still small, and it is obvious that the schools did not function the way the government had planned.

In the Priangan Regencies, the Resident at that time, C.P.C. Steinmetz, drew up regulations for indigenous education which consisted of eight articles (AVSS 1854: 132–6). They were remarkably explicit, beginning with the purpose of education, and followed by a survey of subjects taught, holidays and time schedule, the social position of the students' parents, budgets, teachers, examinations, and supervision. The regulations clearly showed the purpose of these local schools (training young Sundanese to become good administrators) as well as the leading principle (to separate local students from European children). For instance, Article 1 says:

> The establishment of these schools has the purpose of giving the children of the indigenous chiefs the opportunity of acquiring education and training, so that in the future they will be suited to occupy positions in the government administration as respectable indigenous chiefs. In other words, they may not have the tenor to make them accept European customs, clothes, etc., which are incompatible with their own.

> De oprigting dezer scholen heeft ten doel de kinderen der Inlandsche hoofden onderwijs te doen genieten en hen te bekwamen, om later geschikt te zijn betrekkingen in 's Lands dienst te vervullen als fatsoenlijke Inlandsche hoofden. Het mag dus niet de strekking hebben hen Europesche, met de hunne niet strookende gewoonten, kleeding, enz., te doen aannemen (AVSS 1854: 132).

In theory, the newly-established educational institutions were meant for children of the local elites, that is, the sons of those holding the titles of *regent* (regent), *papati* (vice-regent), *hoofdpanghulu* (chief Islamic leader), *koffij-gecommitteerde* (commissioned agent of coffee cultivation), and *districtshoofd* (district chief) — in other words, those occupying significant positions in economic and administrative life (AVSS 1854: 132). Only boys aged 10 to 18 were accepted; girls were not admitted (some girls had attended Dutch schools earlier). Chinese children were not explicitly mentioned in the regulations that Steinmetz had designed; as it turned out, some attended missionary schools or had private teachers at home (Tio [1963]: 17–9). Special permission from the Resident was necessary if an aspiring student did not meet the formal qualifications — and that happened more than once, as the number of commoners' children soon increased considerably.

Before long, practice subverted Steinmetz's regulations. The school in Cianjur, for instance, had 73 students of whom only 3 were the sons of the so-called indigenous chiefs, whereas 17 students were sons of lower officials and the others, sons of commoners. Age restrictions were also overruled. For instance, in 1858, of the 159 students who attended the five schools in the Priangan Regencies,[3] 22 boys were between 6 and 10 years old, 120 were between 10 and 20, and 17 students were older than 20. The annual General Education Report in the East Indies (*Algemeen Verslag van den Staat van het Schoolwezen in Nederlandsch-Indië*) contains very detailed and explicit information about the many problems and issues faced by the schools. For instance, at the school in Cianjur, the number of students was 23 in January 1858, and 13 in December (AVSS 1859: 11–4): parents had stopped their sons from going to school after several months because of religious reasons. This is just one illustration of the many hardships Steinmetz's regulations had to overcome — and never really did. They were easy to read, but hard to implement.

Most of all, the Reports tell us that the Dutch education system did not easily take root in West Java. Schools were opened and strict regulations were formulated, but the number of students remained small, and no efforts were made to integrate European and local children into a single educational system. Be that as it may, compared with other regions in Java and Madura, the colonial efforts to establish schools were rather successful in the Priangan Regencies. This was just the beginning, and relatively speaking, West Java has always had more educational institutions than other places.

**Table 1.** Number of elementary schools and students (from 1853 to 1872)

| Year | Schools (students) | | |
| --- | --- | --- | --- |
| | Priangan | West Java | Java and Madura |
| 1853 | 5 (125) | 7 (175) | 23 (827) |
| 1857 | 5 (149) | 8 (179) | 37 (1305) |
| 1862 | 5 (254) | 7 (305) | 46 (2099) |
| 1867 | 5 (237) | 12 (568) | 62 (3434) |
| 1872 | 9 (383) | 16 (859) | 83 (5512) |

Note: The figures in parentheses show the number of students.
Source: *Algemeen Verslag van den Staat van het Schoolwezen in Nederlandsch-Indie* (AVSS) (1853, 1854, 1859, 1880).

Table 1 shows the number of elementary schools and students in the Sundanese-speaking area, compared with Java and Madura as a whole.[4] The column "West Java" represents the Priangan Regencies plus its surrounding regencies, Karawang, Cirebon, and Banten, where some people spoke Sundanese and others Javanese.

In the two decades after 1851, when the elementary school at Cianjur was opened, the number of schools in the Priangan Regencies doubled and the number of students tripled. Moreover, the number of schools per million inhabitants established in the Priangan Regencies was much higher than elsewhere — almost twice, as Table 2 shows.[5] Obviously, the government paid much attention to West Java, and it did so for various reasons. The colonial centre of Batavia, in the periphery of West Java, needed locally trained officials. The Priangan Regencies were of great importance to economic expansion, and the government needed local officials to mediate between their own officials and the native Sundanese to keep the colonial machine moving.

**Table 2.** Number of schools per million inhabitants (from 1857 to 1872)

| Year | Priangan | West Java | Java and Madura |
| --- | --- | --- | --- |
| 1857 | 6.15 | 3.50 | 3.24 |
| 1862 | 5.92 | 2.80 | 3.49 |
| 1867 | 5.44 | 4.46 | 4.18 |
| 1872 | 8.06 | 5.10 | 4.84 |

In addition to the above-mentioned elementary schools, a different type of school was designed, the so-called district school. In 1863, there were four such schools in West Java, with a total of 43 students (VIO 1868: 79–81). However, this kind of school was bound to fail because it laid a heavy financial burden on the local population; the government provided the teachers and paid their salaries, but the rest of the operation was to be paid by the local communities.

There were few missionary schools in the Sundanese-speaking area compared with other regions of Java because missionary activities were restricted so as to avoid conflicts with the local Muslims. School education in the region, in other words, was mainly provided by the colonial government; missionaries did not make a substantial contribution, whereas the Islamic schools still played an important role in the communities.

As the schools gradually expanded, slowly implementing the official procedures, a special institution was deemed desirable to exercise supervision. In January 1867, the Department of Education was founded in Batavia, and in May 1871, the new department issued the Fundamental Education Decree (Brugmans 1938: 160–1) which brought about two significant changes in the colonial government's education policy. Firstly, the government would be responsible for everyone's education, not only the indigenous elite. Secondly, education was to be given in the local languages (*volkstalen*), and where this was not possible, the language of teaching should be Malay. After this decree was gazetted (Staatsblad No. 104), Sundanese was used more than ever before as the language of instruction; moreover, it was taught as a subject at elementary schools. This was the best method of language standardization, and an effective way to attract more students.

In the decree, the already existent hierarchy of languages became more visible, running largely parallel with the social hierarchy. Dutch was at the top, followed by Malay; at the bottom were the local languages, such as Sundanese. The Dutch, at the highest level of society, used Dutch, while some spoke a variant of Malay. Most of the local officials usually spoke their local language with the population, and used Malay with the Dutch officials. Given the fact that the colonial government wanted to have a group of local officials to rely on in day-to-day affairs — they were cheaper and more effective than the Europeans — while still excluding Dutch as a language for the indigenous population, it is not surprising that Malay was given the same importance as Sundanese.

These practical considerations of incorporating locals into the modern state-run administration were not straightforward, however: the colonial

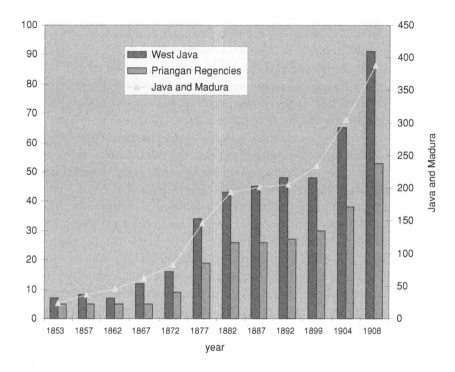

Figure 1. Number of schools (from 1853 to 1908)

authorities wanted to strengthen and give recognition to a Sundanese identity and culture, by "settling" it administratively in order to avoid a destabilization of the local communities. It was felt that the Sundanese should have their own distinct language, literature and culture. The use of Malay had also to be strengthened, but the same was true of "local traditions" — a confusing and contradictory endeavour indeed.

It was obvious that the education policy that was being formulated and implemented was closely connected to the colonial ideology. The natives should remain not-quite-natives, and education should be accessible to "everybody" — but in reality it was primarily intended to meet the growing need for local officials. Schooling produced a new type of colonial subject who became familiar with printed books in the Roman script, thus opening the door to modernity to a growing number of Sundanese youngsters, slowly but steadily.

Figure 1 shows the number of schools in three categories. The left column represents the number of schools in the Priangan Regencies and

Table 3. Number of schools per million inhabitants in 1904

|  | Priangan | Java and Madura |
|---|---|---|
| Schools | 38 | 305 |
| Population | 2,630,514 | 29,654,035 |
| Per million | 14.45 | 10.29 |

West Java, and the right column, the number of schools in Java and Madura. For instance, in 1908 there were 53 schools in the Priangan Regencies, about 90 schools in West Java, and 400 in Java and Madura.

This figure shows that the 1871 decree initiated a considerable increase in the number of schools, not only in the Priangan Regencies but also in the islands of Java and Madura as a whole, although this does not say anything about the quality and attendance: having a school in a community does not necessarily mean a good school. In the 1880s and 1890s, the number of schools remained the same. It can be speculated that the levelling off was due to the diversification of school types. The budget for indigenous education was shared with other types of schools, such as a Chiefs' School (*hoofdenschool*) and a Teachers' Training School (*kweekschool*). In the first decade of the twentieth century, the number sharply increased again, both in the Priangan Regencies and in Java and Madura as a whole.

The higher number of schools for the inhabitants in the Priangan Regencies did not change later into the twentieth century (see Table 3). It seems that the Priangan Regencies had a special position under colonial rule, and this may have been due to economic considerations, for the operation of plantations, as well as the enthusiasm of (a small group of) Sundanese for education in general.

Parallel with the increase in the number of schools, the enrolment of students also increased, as Figure 2 shows. The left column shows the number of students in the Priangan Regencies and West Java, and the right column, the figures for Java and Madura. In 1877, about 1,000 students were studying at schools in Priangan, and 2,000 students in West Java. About 13,000 students were enrolled in schools in Java and Madura.

Roughly speaking, the bar charts and the line graph show a parallel upward tendency. Two sharp rises can be seen, between 1872 and 1877 and between 1899 and 1904, corresponding to the increase in the number of schools shown in Table 1. The numbers should be read with

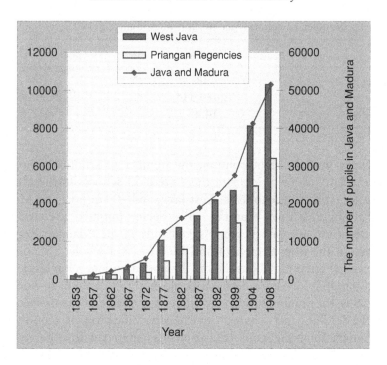

Figure 2. Number of enrolment of students (from 1853 to 1908)

care, however; given the total population in the East Indies, only a small percentage of local children went to government schools.

The data in Figure 2 does not include students at other types of institutions, such as missionary schools, those managed by individuals, those subsidized by the government (non-government schools), and Islamic schools. The non-government schools were operated mostly by local chiefs but some were by Dutch gentlemen. Some schools were subsidized by the government and some were not. The teaching was mostly based on the European style. In other words, the government did not fully operate its own schools in the beginning. Table 4 shows the number of students at the various types of schools in the Priangan Regencies.

The drastic increase in the number of students in non-government schools from 1868 to 1872 can be explained by the zeal of the local chiefs for the new type of education. They built schools with subsidies from the government and teachers were also usually sent by the government. The sharp decline from 1872 to 1892 can be explained by

Table 4. Number of students at the various types of schools in the Priangan Regencies

| Year | 1868 | 1872 | 1892 |
|---|---|---|---|
| Government schools | 258 | 383 | 2,470 |
| Non-government schools | 48 | 1,005 | 57 |
| Missionary schools | 63 | 53 | 43 |
| Islamic schools* | — | — | 23,068 |

Note: * No figures are available for 1868 and 1872.

their incorporation into the government schools. As mentioned earlier, there were relatively few missionary schools in the Priangan Regencies in order to avoid conflicts between Muslims and Christians. However, insofar as students in the non-government and missionary schools learned to read and write the Roman script in a kind of European system of education, the schools were significant in terms of supporting the rise of modern literacy.

A considerable number of children attended Islamic schools. For instance, in 1892, there were 23,068 students in the Priangan Regencies alone, almost ten times the number of students at government schools (AVIO 1894: 218–9). J.A. van der Chijs, the Inspector of Indigenous Education, was fully aware of this: "the indigenous people, following their centuries-old customs, prefer to send their children to a religious school" (VIO 1867: 38). However, it is conceivable that a number of children attended a government school in the morning and an Islamic school in the afternoon.

It should be noted that another kind of literacy was being nurtured in the Islamic educational institutions which followed methods of learning different from those at government schools. Even though, in a strict sense, these Islamic schools did not have a direct connection with Roman script literacy, it is important to realize that the Sundanese-speaking communities of West Java were a fertile soil for education.

Further specifications are needed for Table 4 as the official reports about indigenous education sometimes give three figures for the number of students. The first is the number of students registered, the second is the average attendance, and the third covers those who were present on 31 December. In the figures and tables presented here, the third number has been used. For instance, 23 children were registered at the school in Cianjur, but 10 left school in the course of the year (AVSS 1859: 11–4). The annual *verslag* (report) tended to show the positive achievements of the colonial administration. What is written in the reports does not always coincide with reality, and numbers can be deceptive.

In short, the basis of Dutch school education had been laid by the turn of the century; towards the end of colonial rule, the number of schools and students in the Sundanese-speaking area continued to grow. Given the total population, however, the rate of literacy in the communities of West Java remained low: a small group of people functioned as the motor of novelty, becoming the driving force of modernity.

## The education in practice

By the middle of the nineteenth century, teaching at the colonial government schools was done in a novel style, different from the methods that were followed at existing educational institutions, Islamic schools, and tutorials for aristocrats. One of the most important aspects of Dutch education was its pragmatism, as described by Johannes A. Wilkens (1813–88), a government educationalist for the Javanese language in Surakarta, in a report that was quoted in the first government report on school affairs in the Dutch Indies (*Algemeen Verslag van den Staat van het Schoolwezen in Nederlandsch-Indië*) in 1852. His opinion constituted part of official policy from the start:

> The purpose of education for the indigenous people must be exclusively *practical*. The goal is not to train the indigenous people to obtain a profound knowledge of their language. It is not more than teaching them reading and writing of their own language and Malay in a sufficient way for daily use, in particular for official duties, and further teaching them the arithmetic, geography and land surveying that is needed to perform official duties.
>
> De strekking van het onderwijs voor den inlander moet eene uitsluitend *praktische* zijn. Het doel is niet, den inlander op te leiden tot de grondigst-mogelijke kennis van zijne taal; het is niets anders dan hem zijne taal en het Maleisch te leeren lezen en schrijven op eene voor dagelijksch gebruik, vooral in "s lands dienst, voldoende wijze, en hem voorts zooveel van het rekenen, de aardrijkskunde en het landmeten te laten leeren, als ook vooral in "s lands dienst vereischt wordt (AVSS 1853: 367–8).

Two languages had to be taught, a local language and Malay. Knowledge of Dutch was not necessary for those who were going to be local officials in the colonial administration. Wilkens' suggestions were accepted, and hence two languages and three kinds of script were to be used in schools in the Priangan Regencies: Sundanese in Javanese/Roman script and Malay in both Arabic and Roman script. Initially, official reports observed that in the early years of the introduction of European education students had great difficulties in reading Sundanese in Roman script, and that Javanese and Arabic scripts were considerably easier for them to master (VIO 1865: 13). A decade later, practically seven subjects were taught at indigenous schools: reading Sundanese, reading Malay, writing Sundanese, writing Malay, and arithmetic, geography and land surveying in Malay.[6]

Some of the practical aspects of schooling at the elementary level in the Priangan Regencies can be deduced from government documents and reports on indigenous education. In the 1850s, school hours were set from 8.00 to 11.00 a.m. and from 1.00 to 4.00 p.m; Friday and Islamic feast days were holidays (AVSS 1854: 133). However, this schedule gradually changed, with schools beginning at 8 o'clock in the morning and ending at noon. Sundays became holidays and the Islamic fasting month was made into a long vacation. School buildings were usually constructed in the courtyard of the local Regent's residence to facilitate supervision.

In the beginning, teachers were not well prepared. Before the Teachers' Training School was established in Bandung, there was some kind of training in Surakarta[7] — but it took some time to improve the quality of education. It is indicative that in December 1864, of the 54 teachers at the regency schools in Java only 35 had received training at the Teachers' Training School in Surakarta (VIO 1867: 37–8). Most of the local teachers were from aristocratic families for whom the teaching profession was new. For example, in the 1860s both teachers at the school in Bandung were of aristocratic descent: Soeriadikoesoemah oversaw senior classes, and Tjakra Wiria oversaw junior classes.[8] Education offered an honourable status and stable career; individuals received a regular salary and respect from the local population.

The Sundanese people were used to reading aloud, as van der Chijs, the Inspector of Indigenous Education, noted: "The indigenous people do not know reading silently" (Chijs 1867b: 7). The Sundanese even preferred reading poetry aloud with a certain melody. As seen in the previous chapter, *dangding* was the most favoured form of poetry. In the curriculum and schoolbooks, this chanting of texts was therefore given due attention. Many schoolbooks were written in *dangding*, demonstrating a kind of paradox: the school was modern, and the reading materials were traditional. However, *dangding* was seen as a vehicle, a means to convey new forms of information, new kinds of thinking, rather than a goal in itself (Chijs 1867b: 10). Apparently, students recited the textbooks, individually and together, but the Dutch gradually tried to teach them to read silently. On the basis of their experience with Koranic recitation, the colonial masters assumed that chanting a text implied a lack of understanding. They believed that the lessons in silent reading would bear fruit; hence "modern readers" emerged, as will be seen in the last chapter.

For the practice of writing, a slate board and chalk were used as paper was still expensive in the second half of the nineteenth century. Along with the slate board, the *pisang-blad* (banana leaf) was used; students wrote letters on a banana leaf with a sharpened quill pen. Both forms of writing were cheap, and students could practice penmanship and composition at will in order to learn to write beautifully, according to van der Chijs.

At a later stage of the curriculum, *taalkunde* (the systematic learning of language) was taught. Knowledge of the Sundanese language gave students, among other things, an awareness of the importance of standardization. The lessons in *taalkunde* were closely related with the lessons in translation: Sundanese texts were translated into Malay and the vice versa. "Translation" was considered important to teach students the standardized language which would facilitate the performance of administrative and official duties; it was a practical lesson. The educational reports tell us more than once that translating from Sundanese (and Javanese) into Malay was more difficult for students than the other way round (VIO 1867: 30).

It is ironical that the Sundanese that was being taught was standardized by Dutch officials. Yet another irony is that the Sundanese (and Malay) that was being taught was primarily a written form of language; frozen in textbooks, it exerted a growing influence on spoken language, limiting the dynamics of Sundanese as a whole and establishing categories such as "good" and "bad", "standard" and "substandard" Sundanese. In retrospect, the local teachers unknowingly became the agents of colonial forms of knowledge — and of modernity.

## Schoolbooks

The Sundanese language that the Dutch authorities considered "correct" and "pure" was taught by way of schoolbooks, which proved to be effective in imposing the will of the colonial authorities on those who belonged to the local elites. In the preparation and composition, as well as the distribution and use of schoolbooks, Wilkens' proposals were taken as the starting point:

> Further the government wants to spread easily intelligible reading materials among the indigenous people, also of a *practical* and in particular *moralistic* character; these will inspire their thinking abilities and guide them in the right direction. It is less important whether those books are written in *pure* Javanese, Sundanese, Madurese or Malay, but it is of *highest* importance that they are written in the language which is understood by *most* of the people.
>
> Wijders verlangt het Gouvernement, zoo veel mogelijk ligt bevattelijke leesboeken onder den inlander te verspreiden, mede van *praktischen* en inzonderheid *zedelijken* aard, ten einde zijn denkvermogen op te wekken en ten goede te leiden. Het is eene zaak van minder belang, of die boeken geschreven zijn in het *zuiverste* Javaansch, Soendasche, Madureesch of Maleisch; maar het is eene zaak van het *hoogste* belang, dat zij geschreven zijn in de taal, welke door de *meesten* verstaan wordt (AVSS 1852: 368).

Initially, practical and moralistic aspects were given heavy emphasis, but soon enough the purity and correctness of the Sundanese language were given special attention too, as seen in the virulent discussions among Dutch officials in the 1860s and 1870s, mentioned in the previous chapter (cf. Putten 2000: 112–27).

The first schoolbook in Sundanese, *Kitab Pangadjaran Basa Soenda* (Sundanese Language Textbook), was designed and printed in Holland in 1849 or 1850. As many as 1,490 copies of this 24-page book were sent to the Dutch East Indies, together with Javanese and Malay schoolbooks.[9] Meanwhile, in the Indies, the involvement of K.F. Holle in the education of the Sundanese started with his reading book, *Tjarita koera-koera djeng monjet* (The story of the turtle and the ape),[10] co-authored with his brother Adriaan Walraven Holle. It was produced in 1851 by a private publisher, Lange en Co. in Batavia, and was to be the start of a series of books for the new generation of students in West Java.

> Concerning *Sundanese*, while releasing Mr. Wilkens from this part of the task entrusted to him, the offer of Mr. K.F. Holle and Mr. A.W. Holle has been accepted to prepare books in that language. Indigenous specialists in the Priangan Regencies have stated that the Sundanese fable which they published in *Batavia* shows (a certain) knowledge of the common language of the peasant class. In October 1852 they submitted a *Sundanese reader*. Capable and civilised indigenous people in Priangan were again consulted and they expressed the feeling that the book would provide the Sundanese with good reading materials.

> Wat het *Soendasch* betreft, met vrijkenning van den heer Wilkens voor dit gedeelte der hem opgedragen taak, is gebruik gemaakt van het aanbod der heeren K.F.Holle en A.W.Holle om zich met het vervaardigen van boeken in die taal te belasten. Eene door hen te *Batavia* in druk uitgegeven Soendasche fabel werd door deskundige inlanders in de *Preanger Regentschappen* verklaard blijken te dragen van kennis aan de gewone taal der landbouwende klasse. In Oktober 1852 boden zij een *Soendasch leesboek* aan. Kundige en beschaafde inlanders in de Preanger werden weder geraadpleegd, die het gevoelen uitten, dat het boek eene goede lektuur voor den Soendanees verschaffen zoude (AVSS 1853: 369).

No doubt, one of the "capable and civilised" indigenous men who were consulted was Holle's friend, Moehamad Moesa, who was close to the Dutch administrators. It is no wonder that the book was accepted.

Of the books used in the schools in West Java, only three were in Sundanese: the one shipped from Holland, a spelling guide, and an arithmetic book. The other books used in the 1850s were in Malay, such as *Kitab akan di batja anak-anak di skola Djawa* (Reader for children at schools in Java), *Kitab ilmoe boemi* (Book of geography), and *Soerat oekoem oendang oendang atas tanah Nederlandsch Indië* (Law book of the Dutch East Indies). This was a result of the government policy as designed by Wilkens, who had propagated the use of Malay with Roman script in the schools: Malay was important in the archipelago, it was "*de lingua franca in deze gewesten*" (the lingua franca in these regions) (AVSS 1853: 368).

In the *Javasche Courant* of 21 July 1855, the government announced that it would award a prize of 1,000 Dutch guilders to the person who wrote a reader in Javanese, and three years later a similar award was announced for a book in Malay. As for Sundanese schoolbooks, a different arrangement was made. In 1861, a sum of 1,200 Dutch guilders was granted to K.F. Holle for the preparation of Sundanese readers and schoolbooks (AVSS 1861: 208). In those days, 1,200 guilders was a considerable sum of money: it was the monthly salary of the Resident of the Priangan Regencies (Doel 1994: 55). Holle's good friend, Moehamad Moesa, a *hoofdpanghulu* (Islamic leader) in Limbangan, was invited to assist him.

> Also the *Hoofd-Panghulu* of Limbangan, Radhen Mohamad Moesa, was told that the government would be very happy indeed if he assisted Mr. Holle with the compilation of Sundanese readers, given his knowledge of language and poetry.

> Ouk aan den Hoofd-Panghoeloe van Limbangan, Radhen Mohamad Moesa werd te kennen gegeven, dat het der Regering aangenaam zal zijn, indien hij den heer *Holle* behulpzaam wil zijn met zijne taalkennis en dichtkunst bij het zamenstellen van *Soendasche* leesboeken (AVSS 1861: 208).

Holle was given a monopoly for Sundanese schoolbooks, and no doubt the government's commission was partly inspired by the report Holle had submitted shortly before, in which he had made a summary of the Sundanese schoolbooks that should be made available to the students in the newly established schools (AVSS 1861: 208-6). Holle had recommended no less than 16 textbooks, such as a Sundanese ABC and spelling book, a Sundanese conversation book, a traditional reader, in *tembang* form, a guide to letter-writing, an arithmetic book, a book on agriculture, a book on practical surveying and levelling, and so forth (AVSS 1861: 212-6).

Holle's report, it seems, became the main guideline for government policy in the nineteenth century. The books that were used in the elementary schools in Bandung in 1863 are clear evidence of the proposal (Table 5).

After the government decision of 1861, Holle set about his task, and achieved impressive results in a short period. The number of Sundanese books increased remarkably, replacing Malay schoolbooks. What is obvious in the list is that all of the books on reading and writing were in Sundanese in both Roman and Javanese scripts, whereas "common knowledge" and geography were taught with Malay books that were used elsewhere in Java, and Madura too. Malay was used by the Dutch as a vehicle for "new" knowledge, which concurred with the role of

**Table 5.** Textbooks used at elementary schools in Bandung in 1863

| Sundanese books |
| --- |

1. *Tjaritana Ibrahim* (The story of Ibrahim), Anonymous
2. *Ijeu wawatjan tjarita Ibrahim* (This *wawacan* is the story of Ibrahim), Anonymous
3. *Ijeu wawatjan tjarita Noeroelkamar* (This *wawacan* is the story of Nurulkamar), Anonymous
4. *Katrangan tina prakawis mijara laoek tjai* (Guide for raising freshwater fish), Mohamad Oemar
5. *Wawatjan Djaka miskin* (*Wawacan* of Djaka *miskin*), Wira Tanoe Baija
6. *Kitab tjonto-tjonto soerat pikeun moerangkalih anoe ngaskola* (The book of examples of letter-writing for school children), K.F. Holle
7. *Wawatjan woelang poetra* (*Wawacan* teaching lessons for children), Adi Widjaja
8. *Wawatjan woelang krama* (*Wawacan* teaching good manners), Moehamad Moesa
9. *Wawatjan woelang tani* (*Wawacan* teaching lessons for the farmer), Moehamad Moesa
10. *Wawatjan Radja Darma* (*Wawacan* of King Darma), Danoe Koesoema
11. *Wawatjan Radja Soedibja* (*Wawacan* of King Soedibja), Moehamad Moesa
12. *Kitab pikeun moerangkalih anoe mimiti adjar matja Soenda* (Book for children beginning to read Sundanese), Anonymous
13. *Kitab tjatjarakan Soenda* (Guidebook of Sundanese spelling), K.F. Holle
14. *Kitab ilmoe itoengan* (Book of arithmetic), Anonymous.

| Malay books |
| --- |

1. *Bagei bagei tjeritera* (A variety of stories), J.R.P.F. Gonggrijp
2. *Bahwa inilah kitab pemoela-an pengataoe-an dan ilmoe ilmoe, jang terkarang akan di batja oleh kanak kanak di sekola Djawa dan Malajoe adanja* (This is an introductory book of general knowledge, composed for school children, in Jawa and Malay), Anonymous
3. *Kitab akan mengadjar permoelaän dari ilmoe boemi* (An introduction to geography), J.A. Wilkens

Source: VIO 1865: 30.

Malay, which was associated with modernity in the entire archipelago. Noteworthy too is that most reading books were composed in *dangding*, in accordance with the government policy and the preference of the Sundanese people themselves, which was reflected in the answers to a questionnaire sent to the Regents in the Priangan Regencies concerning schoolbooks and reading books. Most of the Regents responded that the people liked to read *dangding* at home in the evenings and at gatherings, such as weddings, circumcision, and childbirth.[11] Moreover, most of the 13 available readers had been written by Moesa, Holle's close friend who had the authority to select the "appropriate" draft manuscripts and send them to the government publisher in Batavia to be printed. The authors of the other books came from Holle's circle in and around Limbangan Regency.

Moralistic themes were emphasized in the books. The point had already been made by Wilkens, but Holle stressed it again as he wrote in the above-mentioned report:

> *Moral stories and poems* of which the subject contains some virtue or vice, which stimulate good from the former and evil as a consequence of the latter. In particular dealing with chastity, parental and brotherly love, love for one's neighbour, loyalty, truthfulness, justice, devotion, modesty, humbleness, contentment, charity, expansivity, commiseration, hospitality, honesty, zest for work, tidiness, proper thrift, moderation and cleanness.
>
> Furthermore about hate, envy, vindictiveness, egoism, wrong ambition and discontent with status and rank, conceit, slander, love of mockery and impertinence, hypocrisy, lying, deceit, superabundance, waste and ostentation, voluptuousness, laziness and dirtiness.
>
> The nature of the main characters in the story (if it is a story) may represent these virtues and vices.
>
> *Zedekundige verhalen of gedichten* tot onderwerp hebbende de een of andere deugd of ondeugd, het goede van de eerste, de kwade gevolgen van de laatste ontwikkelende. Vooral handelende over kuischheid, ouder kinder- en broederliefde, liefde tot zijn naaste, trouw, waarheidsliefde, regtvaardigheid, eerbiedigheid, bescheidenheid, nederigheid, tevredenheid, barmhartigheid, mededeelzaamheid, medelijden, gastvrijheid, eerlijkheid, werklust, ordelijkheid, gepaste spaarzaamheid, matigheid en zindelijkheid.
>
> Wijders omtrent haat, afgunst, wraakzucht, zelfzucht, verkeerd geplaatste eergierigheid en ontevredenheid met stand of rang, verwaandheid, laster, spotlust en onbeschoftheid, schijnheiligheid, leugen, bedrog, overdaad, verspil- en praalzucht, wellust, luiheid en morsigheid.

Het karakter der hoofdpersonen van het verhaal (zoo het een verhaal is) kan deze deugden of ondeugden voorstellen (AVSS 1861: 213).

The Dutch considered the indigenous people rather uncivilized and immoral, and believed that they had to be educated and enlightened in the name of culture, and for the sake of control and management. For instance, a spelling book compiled by Holle, *Kitab Cacarakan Sunda* (Sundanese Spelling Book) reads as follows:

Story 12
A monkey broke into the house of a rich man, who was a stingy fellow who never helped the poor. When the stingy fellow was not at his house ...
Lesson of this story: if people want to be blessed, money should be properly managed.

Aja koenjoek hidji asoep kana imah anoe benghar, tapi koret katjida, tara bae mere ka noe mararat. — Anoe koret eker te aja di imah ... Tegesna ije dongeng: Djalma lamoen hajang salamat, doewitna koedoe hade metakenana (Holle 1862: 8).

The reader will undoubtedly be reminded here of Aesop's and other European fables (Fabius 1906). In the above list (Table 5) there are three books with the title *woelang* (teaching, lessons); they were collections of tales with a strongly didactic tenor in that each protagonist plainly represented right or wrong. Holle drafted curricula and schoolbooks for the Sundanese in a way that he himself thought appropriate. Through the spread of these schoolbooks, the ideas of the colonial government, especially of Holle in the case of the Priangan Regencies, were disseminated among the people. Colonial education and schoolbooks were preparing the ground for new forms of Sundanese writing.

The students were native children, some belonging to the elite, some to the lower classes. Holle thought that education should be given in Sundanese because, in his view, "original" Sundanese culture should be strengthened, and language was the most important medium for culture. His motto *"Taal is macht"* (Language is power) reflects his thoughts (Holle in Kartawinata 1891: [i]; Berge 1993: 29–30). Part of the lessons was in Sundanese and about the Sundanese, but another part was in Malay, which was considered indispensable for the colonial administration, the growing medium of communication among various *volken* (peoples), and for the acquisition of practical knowledge (Putten 1997:

Table 6. Total number of schoolbooks in Java by 1865

|  | Javanese 19 | Sundanese 20 | Malay 23 |
|---|---|---|---|
| Reading | 11 | 18 | 18 |
| Arithmetic | 4 | 1 | 2 |
| Geography | 1 | 0 | 2 |
| Land surveying | 2 | 0 | 1 |
| Language knowledge | 1 | 1 | 0 |

719). There was another reason for distributing and using schoolbooks in Malay: they could be used in all schools in the archipelago, and thus the costs of production could be kept low. Noteworthy too was that the higher the level of education, the more Malay and the less Sundanese books were used. For instance, at the Teachers' Training School in Bandung in 1866/7, half of the curriculum's reading and writing books were in Malay (Commissie [1941]).

Apart from the first reader that had been published in Holland, schoolbooks were printed in Batavia, mostly by the government printing house, Landsdrukkerij, in Weltevreden. Table 6 shows the variety of languages used in the schoolbooks (VIO 1867: 31–7).

By 1865, the total number of schoolbooks amounted to 62 titles and some 180,000 copies were made available for Java. Van der Chijs remarked that there was *veel kaf onder het koren* (much dead wood) among these schoolbooks. Compared to Javanese and Malay books, he claimed that Sundanese schoolbooks had better content — an implicit word of praise for Holle's endeavours. Javanese readers were mostly translations of European stories by prominent official translators, such as C.F. Winter, Palmer van den Broek, and Tjondro Negoro (VIO 1867: 4). According to van der Chijs's evaluation, the stories in the Malay readers were alien to the indigenous people as they contained many Christian elements; Gonggrijp's *Bagej-bagej hikajat dhoeloe kala* (Various tales of old times) was just one example. On the other hand, Sundanese readers were more appropriate, with a variety of stories suited to local tastes (VIO 1867: 32). The number of printed copies of these books was between 2,000 and 4,000 for the first impression (VIO 1866: 275–7), with the exception of Holle's books: 10,000 copies were printed for his *Modellen van verschillende brieven* (Models of various letters), and 20,000 copies for his *Soendaasch spelboekje* (Sundanese Spelling Book).[12]

The books were distributed to the Sundanese-speaking regencies of Banten, Batavia, Buitenzorg, Karawang, Priangan, and Cirebon.[13] For example, Moesa's *Wawatjan Woelang Krama* (*Wawacan* Teaching Courtesy), published in 1862 in the Javanese script, was distributed to each regency in the following quantities: Banten, 200 copies; Batavia, 259; Buitenzorg, 200; Karawang, 200; Priangan, 450; and Cirebon, 200. They were presumably used at elementary schools and at the Teachers' Training School in Bandung. Apparently, more and more printed schoolbooks found their way to the Sundanese communities, even though the number of students remained limited and the books were not widely read: distribution was poor and the students could not always afford them (Chijs 1867a: 4). Sometimes a student possessed only a spelling book; to learn to read, students often borrowed books from their well-to-do friends (Chijs 1867a: 12).

Some indications on the sales of such books can be found in the response of Regents to the above-mentioned 1864 questionnaire. The Regent of Bandung received 602 schoolbooks and readers of 10 different titles; 302 books were sold. The Regent of Sumedang received 190 books, of which 174 were sold. The Regent of Sukapura received 671 books of which 559 were sold.[14] However, sometimes schoolbooks lay idle in the storehouse in a Regent's residence. For example, the Regent of Ciamis bought 1,000 copies for 50 Dutch guilders in order to gain favour with the Governor-General, but most of them remained in the storehouse of the Regency (Berge 1993: 25).

Some authors of books were outside the "Holle clan": they were mostly Dutch schoolteachers.[15] After 1890, new reading and arithmetic schoolbooks began to replace the old ones — in other words, Holle's schoolbooks. A good example was the fate of Holle's spelling book, which was gradually replaced by a spelling book by C.J. van Haastert (who was to become the director of the Teachers' Training School in Bandung). Holle taught students Javanese script first and then the Roman script, whereas Haastert started with the Roman script on the very first page, working from the assumption that Javanese script was too difficult for Sundanese students and not very practical at that (Haastert 1894: III). Haastert's book was based on the idea that students should learn to read by way of complete words that consist of syllables, whereas Holle had worked from letters. In the last part of Haastert's book, a series of these words constituted sentences. For instance, Lesson 23 reads as follows:

23
sa-ko-la ka-ka-ra di-boe-ka a-jeu-na lo-ba
noe ka-da-ri-toe.
a-ri ka sa-ko-la koe-doe ma-wa boe-koe (Haastert 1894: 15)

as soon as school opens, many
go there
when (you) go to school, (you) must bring (your) book

Haastert's spelling book was used until the end of colonial rule. Other books, such as van Gelder's compilation of European stories in Sundanese, titled *Mangle,* was reprinted at least six times and used in many schools. However, it is important to realize that in the second half of the nineteenth century, Sundanese language policy was dominated by a small group of people with a distinct view of language, morality, and *volk*. Only after the establishment of the Committee for Indigenous Schoolbooks and Popular Reading Books in 1908 did their role begin to diminish. Nonetheless, they were the ones who introduced a new world to Sundanese readers, who were greatly influential albeit limited in numbers.

The soil of a new literacy was prepared in West Java, but one should not overlook the literacy in Arabic and Javanese scripts and those who continued to work with them. Islamic schools were numerous, and students there were learning to read and write Arabic in manuscript form. In private tutorials, young aristocrats were taught reading and writing in the Javanese script. Roughly speaking, the Arabic and Javanese reading stratum of the communities was synonymous with so-called chirographically-based literacy, while the Roman reading stratum was synonymous with print literacy.[16] Conflicts and tensions between these two strata were to remain an important element in the cultural life of West Java; the modernity and modernization which came with the printed materials in Roman script had counterparts whose authority should not be underestimated.

## 2. Printing and Publishing Network

The Sundanese community had a tradition of manuscript reading. This tradition did not vanish after the emergence of mechanically printed books, but changes did occur in the configuration of reading activities, so beautifully described by Walter Benjamin:

> [...] that which withers in the age of mechanical reproduction is the aura of the work of art. This is a symptomatic process whose significance points beyond the realm of art. One might generalise by saying: the technique of reproduction detaches the reproduced object from the domain of tradition. By making many reproductions it substitutes a plurality of copies for a unique existence. And in permitting the reproduction to meet the beholder or listener in his own particular situation, it reactivates the object reproduced (Benjamin 1970: 223).

Mechanical reproduction had newness: each book has the same shape in appearance and exactly the same type-letters on its pages instead of the wild variety of manuscripts. Uniformity through printing confirmed the tendencies towards strengthening the unity of the language community. Moreover, people began to share tastes in and knowledge of writing, and thus became a new community of sorts. New cultural practices of reading and writing emerged, creating fresh patterns of solidarity and belonging in which the authority of manuscripts began to be questioned — and hence manuscript culture began to wither.

People in West Java could obtain more reading materials than ever before, given the availability of money and a willingness to be connected with the colonial government. For some, book reading gradually became a daily activity (Lenggang Kantjana 1887: 1–2). The layout and presentation of books forced readers to reorganize their assumptions and concepts, and their contents guided them to a new interpretation of the world. Moehammad Moesa played the most significant role in this process; supported by Holle, he was the pioneer of the new style of writing.

In her fascinating book on the emergence of printing techniques in Europe, Elisabeth Eisenstein writes, "Typography arrested linguistic drift, enriched as well as standardised vernaculars, and paved the way for the more deliberate purification and codification of all major European languages" (Eisenstein 1983: 82). The same seems to apply to the indigenous languages in the Dutch East Indies in the middle of nineteenth century. In printed books, the Malay, Sundanese and Javanese languages were arrested in their linguistic drift, gradually becoming standardized. Printing preserved and codified vernaculars, and sometimes even created new ones. Having fortified language walls between one *volk* and another, Dutch colonial policy tended to homogenize what was within each of them. In short, by way of print, the Sundanese language strengthened its identity among other languages, and Sundanese speakers and readers with it.

It is not easy to describe this process of homogenization. Some material questions need to be asked first: How many books were printed? What kind of books were Sundanese books? Who were the authors? Which printing houses produced Sundanese books? The description will be concrete and statistical in nature. In the following section, the material basis regarding the new reading community in West Java will be described. The period covered comprises the years between 1850 and 1908 as the first printed materials reached West Java in about 1850, while in 1908 the Committee was established, which served to confirm the authority of the printed and standardized word.

## Sundanese books in print

One of the leading Dutch scholars on the indigenous languages of the Indies, J.R.P.F. Gonggrijp,[17] gave the following Malay summary of the colonial government's initiative in printing activities:

> In the old days, before people knew about printing techniques, all books were written by pen. At that time the price of books was very expensive and only few people mastered reading and writing. But nowadays His Excellency the Government publishes very cheap books so that all people, low and high, may read and receive the benefits of reading.
>
> Dhoeloe-kala, sabelomnja orang tahoe ilmoe menera itoe, maka segala kitab djoega tersoerat dengan kalam. Koetika itoe segala kitab terlalo mahal arganja dan adalah sedikit orang sadja jang mengarti membatja dan toelis. Tetapi pada sakarang ini Kangdjeng Goebernemen mengaloewarkan kitab jang moerah sakali sopaja segala orang ketjil, besar, boleh membatja, dan sopaja orang beroleh goena deri pada batjanja itoe (Gonggrijp 1866: 6).

Gonggrijp used the term *kitab* to refer to books in general, both in manuscript and in print. Holle, for example, gave his spelling book published in 1862 the title *Kitab Tjatjarakan Soenda* (Guidebook for Sundanese Spelling), and in doing so suggested a perpetuation of tradition: *kitab* was introduced to refer to printed books aimed at teaching and giving counsel.

Each manuscript was titled according to its contents, character, and form of writing. For instance, in Sundanese there are terms such as *carios* or *carita* (story, tale), *wawacan* (narrative poem), *dongeng* (story), *sajarah* (history), and *serat* (writing). This was reflected in the titles of the early printed books, such as *Tjaritana Ibrahim* (The story of Ibrahim) and *Wawatjan Radja Soedibja* (The *wawacan* of King Soedibja). The first usage of the term *boekoe*[18] in the title of a printed book in Sundanese was in 1881: *Boekoe Batjaan Salawe Toeladan Pikeun Moerid-moerid Pangkat Panghandapna* (Reader of Twenty-five Model Stories for Students in the Lower Class), compiled by W. van Gelder, the head-teacher of the Teachers' Training School in Bandung. Gradually, the word *boekoe* came to be used for every kind of printed book. The new notion of a book was imported into Sundanese culture together with the dissemination of printed books. On the other hand, the term *kitab* continued to be used for books that gave counsel, and in practice this often meant religious counsel.[19] *Kitab Indjil* was the term coined for the translation of the Bible, while books with an Islamic message were given the name *kitab kuning* (Bruinessen n.d.).[20] Thus, Gonggrijp's usage of the term *kitab* for all books did not last long.

It is also interesting to note in Gonggrijp's statement above the price of *kitab* in manuscript form. Before the arrival of the Europeans, manuscripts had never been commodities that could be bought and sold; they were considered sacred treasures, concrete proofs of knowledge. The European scholars were willing to pay for them, and not only did this change the function and status of the manuscripts already available, it also inspired local literates to produce more of them and to sell them to those who were willing to pay for them, thus starting lending libraries (Chambert-Loir 1991).

Gonggrijp expected "everyone" would read books once they became cheaper, but that was not the case: books were cheaper than manuscripts, but not really for everyone. The number of literates was also very small, and certainly not "everyone" read. Moreover, contrary to Gonggrijp's expectations, manuscripts continued to be produced and "consumed" in the Sundanese-speaking communities even after the introduction of printed books.

In other words, printing did not spell the end of the manuscript culture. On the other hand, it cannot be denied that the use of schoolbooks changed the existing concepts of writing and reading which, in West Java, had been associated with enjoyment and entertainment and not necessarily with what Gonggrijp called *goena* (use). However, it was this very concept that Moehamad Moesa used in his preface to one of the reading books, "reading is not only for enjoyment, but it must bear fruit for the reader" (Moesa 1867: 4).[21]

The last interesting point made by Gonggrijp is that he called the colonial government *Kangdjeng Goebernemen* (His Excellency the

Government). The term can be found in many of the printed books and reports in the second half of the nineteenth century. The Landsdrukkerij in Batavia called itself *Kantor Tjitak Kangdjeng Goepernemen di Batawi* (Printing Office of His Excellency the Government in Batavia) on the title pages of Sundanese books. The word *kangdjeng* was originally a honorific title reserved for high-ranking indigenous people, such as kings, sultans, and *bupati* (regents). The word had never been used for an institution — and here it seems like an effort to personify an anonymous office and place it in the colonial hierarchy. A Sundanese writer who had a Dutch education was to explain the use of *kangdjeng*:

> The word KANGDJENG has nearly the same meaning as ZIJNE EXELLENTIE (His Excellency), or *Hoogedel Geboren Heer* (Distinguished Gentleman) in Dutch. So we should not be careless with *kangdjeng* and should respect distinguished people to avoid receiving something unexpected. Those we can call *kangdjeng* are only the Governors-General, members of the Raad van Indie, Residents, Directors of a Department, Regents and other high-ranking people.
>
> Eta ketjap KANGDJENG, ninggang meueusan kana basa Walanda ZIJNE EXELLENTIE handap-handapna Hoog-edel Geboren Heer. Djadi anoe kitoe, atoeh oerang teh oelah hamboer teuing kana kangdjeng teh, oelah ditatamboeh ka anoe lain adjangna, bisi padjar njoengkoen. Anoe merenah diseboet kangdjeng di oerang ngan Toean Besar, Lid Raad van Indie, Residen, Direktoer Dipartement, Boepati-boepati sareng sapapadana (Sastrawinangoen 1925: 346).

The first book printed in Java was in Dutch, in the mid-seventeenth century.[22] Not until the mid-eighteenth century were books printed in the local languages, first in Malay, the language of communication in the archipelago, and then in Javanese, the main language of Java and central to Dutch activities. It was to be another hundred years before the first Sundanese books began to appear (AVSS 1853: 320–67). The number of printed books in Sundanese — mainly schoolbooks — remained relatively small, prompting the most productive Sundanese author in the second half of the nineteenth century, Moehamad Moesa, to lament:

| | |
|---|---|
| basa Soenda noe kalipoet, | Sundanese has been concealed. |
| tanda jen kalipoetan, | The sign that it is concealed is |
| boektina di Soenda sepi, | that Sunda is desolate, |
| hanteu aja boekoe woengkoel basa Soenda, | no book was written in Sundanese only. |

> Reja make doewa basa,  Many of them use two languages.
> nja eta salah-sahidji,  Namely one of these,
> Malajoe atawa Djawa.  Malay or Javanese.
> (Moesa 1867: 5)

One of the most important civil servants during that time, Levyssohn Norman, Secretary-General of the Dutch East Indies government from 1873 to 1877 and then a member of the Council of the Indies, observed the lack of Sundanese schoolbooks in a more casual manner:

> The government has fostered the Javanese language very well, but Sundanese has been ignored, for the reason that at that time there were no indigenous schools in Sundanese-speaking areas, but what was the use of such a school if there were no books which might be used?
>
> Goepernemen sangat memliharaken bahasa Djawa, tetapi bahasa Soenda tiada diperdoelikan, maka dari sebab itoe sahingga itoe koetika belom ada sekola negri di dalem tanah Soenda, tetapi apakah bergoena demikian, djikaloe tiada ada kitab pangadjaran jang boleh di pake?
> (Levyssohn Norman 1888a: 19)

Sundanese was given less attention by the government than Javanese. Malay and Javanese were seen as more important languages and given higher priority until the end of the colonial era. The Sundanese lived "in a valley between two high mountains, Javanese and Malay", Moesa chanted — and he was not the only one who feared that his language would vanish in the course of time (Moesa 1867: 5).

## Inventory of Sundanese books

This section will take stock of the books printed in the Sudanese language,[23] beginning with the first book, *Kitab Pangadjaran Basa Soenda* (Sundanese Language Textbook), printed in 1849 or 1850 in Holland, and ending with the establishment of the *Commissie voor de Inlandsche School- en Volkslectuur,* later called Balai Poestaka, in 1908. As long as a publication was in Sundanese it was included in the list (see Appendix 1).[24] No newspapers and magazines in Sundanese were published during this period of "modernization".[25]

After the turn of the century, Sundanese writing experienced a remarkable change in its contents and form, concurrent with social and

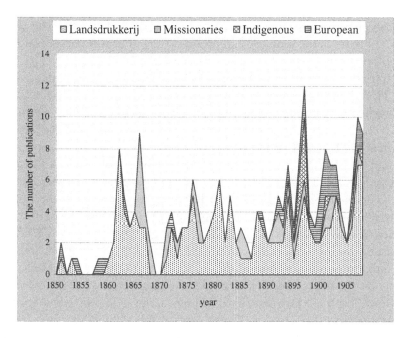

Figure 3. Printed books in Sundanese, by printing house (from 1850 to 1908)

political movements in the colony. Publishing was institutionalized with the establishment of the Committee. After 1910 indigenous publishers and printing houses appeared like mushrooms after a heavy rain: Sundanese writing truly entered a new phase in the early twentieth century.

Between 1850 and 1908, there was reference to 222 books printed in Sundanese: they were printed by the government printing house Landsdrukkerij, the missionary presses, European/Eurasian private printing houses, and indigenous printing houses.[26] The number of books are shown chronologically in Figure 3.

In 1897, for instance, five books were published by Landsdrukkerij, one by missionaries, four by indigenous printing houses, and two by European/Eurasian printing houses. The figure shows three peaks in the number of publications: the first one was in 1866 (9 titles), the second in 1897 (12 titles), and the third in 1907 (11 titles).

In 1866, six books were published by the missionaries. They were spelling and arithmetic books for use at their own schools. The year 1897 was, so to speak, an Islamic year: 4 of the 12 books were publications by Sayyid 'Uthmân, whose activities will be discussed later. The third peak in Figure 3, the year 1907, represents the publication of several new schoolbooks that were to replace those of Holle.

Initially, the educational policy in West Java was largely steered by K.F. Holle but his influence, if not supervision, started to decline after 1890 when new writers, inspired by newly developed teaching methods, began to produce schoolbooks. Not surprisingly, most of these writers taught at the Teachers' Training School in Bandung. The above-mentioned C.J. van Haastert, for instance, compiled a spelling book, *Boekoe Edjahan Djeung Batjaän, Pikeun Moerid-moerid dina Pangkat Panghandapna di Sakola-Soenda* (Spelling Book with Reading, for Students in the Lower Class of Sundanese schools). Not only the writers, but also the publishing houses began to diversify. Apart from the government printing house Landsdrukkerij, (Indo-)European printers (such as A. Bisschop in Cirebon) and indigenous printers began operations. Their activities increased after 1890. On the other hand, some books were reprinted while others were re-issued, both in Javanese and Roman script with different covers, amounting to 60 books, or 27 per cent of the total. Thus, two-thirds of the 222 titles were original, while one-third were reprints or revised editions.

## Landsdrukkerij

Figure 4 shows the number of publications by the various printing houses: the Landsdrukkerij, missionary printing houses, indigenous printing houses, and (Indo-) European/Eurasian printing houses.

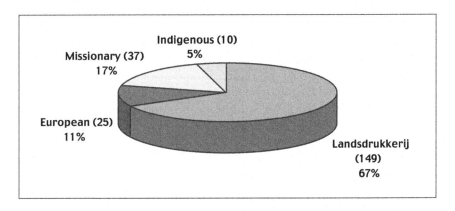

Figure 4. Printed books, by printing houses (from 1850 to 1908)

One hundred and forty-nine titles were printed by the Landsdrukkerij, which accounts for 67.6 per cent of all Sundanese books. These titles roughly consisted of three kinds of books: readers (114), spelling and arithmetic books (24), and official publications (8). Most of these publications were produced for use in schools established by the colonial authorities. D. Koorders once remarked that it was difficult to make "the odd difference between schoolbooks and popular readers" (Koorders in Meinsma 1869: 269). The third group of publications was clearly different from the other two, being primarily meant for local officials rather than for young students. Some official publications were translated into Sundanese after the 1870s; they consisted of regulations which directly concerned the local people, such as *Boekoe Wet hal pangadilan hoekoeman baris oerang priboemi di Indië-Nederland* (Book of the criminal law court for the indigenous people in the Dutch East Indies), published in 1889. The government had an official translator for Sundanese after 1880. He was none other than the son of Moehamad Moesa, Kartawinata. Two important law books and a book of prison regulations were made accessible to Sundanese readers.

The number of books illustrates that the government enterprise, Landsdrukkerij, played an extremely important role in the nineteenth-century book market in Java. It had been made a governmental institution in 1809 by Governor-General Herman Willem Daendels (1808–11). He combined the two existing printers in Batavia, the Stads-drukkerij, which had operated under the management of an Asian-born European family, and the Landsdrukkerij, known as Kasteel-drukkerij and owned by the Dutch East Indies Company (VOC) since 1750. The newly-reorganized Landsdrukkerij had an office in Molenvliet, several miles inland from the old Castle of Batavia.[27]

In 1871, the Landsdrukkerij had become a serious business: it had 8 power-driven printing machines (*snelpersen*) on site, 13 old manual printing machines, 2 folding machines, 2 rolling machines, and 1 steam machine with a six-horsepower engine (Departement van Gouvernementsbedrijven 1912: 15). It had an exclusive monopoly on the production of official publications, such as *De Javasche Courant, Het Staatsblad van Nederlandsch-Indië* (Official Gazette of the Dutch East Indies), *Het Bijblad op het Staatsblad* (The Supplemental News of the Official Gazette), *Den Regeeringsalmanak* (Governmental Almanac), and *De Naam- en Ranglijst der officieren van de Land- en Zeemacht in Nederlandsch-Indië* (Name and Ranking List of Officials of the Army and Navy). Apart from these Dutch-language publications, it also produced books in different languages and scripts: Arabic, Javanese, Lampungese, Mandhelingese, Makassarese, Balinese, Greek, Sanskrit and Chinese (Departement van Gouvernementsbedrijven 1912: 6). In the nineteenth century, the distribution of these books was not always easy. Some of the books lay dormant in storehouses for a long time because of the lack of a proper distribution network (Holle 1869: 137). Things only improved gradually, beginning with the new arrangements of 1863:[28]

> The sale of those Javanese, Malay and Sundanese books, available only by cash at the Landsdrukkerij in former days, increased only in the latter half of 1863, when the arrangement was made that they could be obtained from salt warehouse masters, coffee warehouse masters, and indigenous teachers.

> De verkoop dier Javaansche, Mal. en Soend. boekjes, die aanvankelijk slechts á contant ter Lands-drukkerij geschiedde, is eerst in de laatste helft van 1863 aanzienlijk geworden, toen zij over geheel Java bij alle zoutverkoop-pakhuismeesters, koffijpakhuismeesters en inlandsche onderwijzers verkrijgbaar zijn gesteld (Chijs 1867b: 4).

In 1876, the government set up a separate organization, the Government Depository of Schoolbooks in Weltevreden (*'s Lands Depot van Leermiddelen*), which started a mail-order service and produced catalogues of schoolbooks and readers that were sent all over the colony beginning in 1882. Everyone in the Dutch East Indies could now buy books, sending money by post, and the catalogue gave information on how to order in Dutch and Malay:

> All books and other printed materials in this catalogue will be sent by mail to you if they are not needed by the government itself. You pay for the books with cash or postal money order; there is no need to purchase stamps. Please send your letter with the postal money order to the following address: "The Administration of Government Depository in Weltevreden".

> Segala boekoe-boekoe dan barang lain soerat tjitakan jang terseboet di dalam Daftar ini, djika tiada akan di pakei sendiri bagi goebernemen itoelah akan di kirim dengan pos, dengan ta'oesah di bajar prankonja melainken perloe di bajar boekoe-boekoe itoe, baik dengan oewang, baik dengan soerat wisselpos. Adapon soeratnja membeli boekoe itoe apalagi soerat wissel itoe, alamatnja ja'ni: "kapada Administrateur goedang kitab Goebernemen di Weltevreden" (Landsdrukkerij 1891).

Once the Sundanese books were printed, they were partly kept in Weltevreden, ready to be sent by mail to whoever made a purchase through a mail order, and partly distributed to the urban centres of West Java to be sold. Until the early twentieth century, no printing machines were used in the Priangan Regencies; only then did private printing houses emerge in the larger cities in West Java. The production of books was to remain an urban activity. From the cities, modernity spread to the countryside.

## Other printing houses

The second largest group of publications was made up of books produced by missionaries, which numbered 37 altogether, or 17 per cent of the total number of publications. The books — mostly translations of the Bible and largely schoolbooks for missionary schools — were published by the Netherlands Bible Society (NBG) and the Dutch Missionary Society, and printed in the Netherlands. A.W. Sijthoff in Leiden, who specialized in Oriental languages (and their various scripts), printed three missionary books in the Arabic script. Books in the Roman script were produced by printing houses in Rotterdam, of which D. de Koning was the most important. Later, printing houses in the Indies, such as Rehoboth-Zending Press in Meester-Cornelis and Zending Press in Bogor, also printed missionary books.

The readership of the books that were published by the Protestant mission remained small, mainly because of the restrictive policy of the government, which was afraid of provoking the ire of the Muslims. The missionary contribution to the nurturing of print literacy, however, has been considerable: G.J. Grashuis and S. Coolsma devised a spelling system and wrote grammar books that played an important role in the process of standardizing the language (Berge 1993: 33–61). Indicative of the importance of the missionaries is the fact that Coolsma's grammar book, *Handleiding bij de beoefening der Soendaneesche taal* (Handbook for the study of the Sundanese language), was used in educational institutions in West Java (AVVIO 1880: 8). Ironically, the ultimate products of Coolsma and his colleagues — their translations of the Bible — were hardly known or used.

Indigenous printing houses accounted for 5 per cent of the total number of Sundanese publications, ten in all, and mostly Islamic books. Eight books, lithographed in the Arabic script, were the creations of Sayyid 'Uthmân (1822–1914), a scholar of Arabic descent, who wrote books on Islamic topics in both Malay and Arabic and printed them on a lithograph machine in his own house in Batavia.[29] Some of Sayyid 'Uthmân's books were translated into Sundanese by Raden Haji Azhari in Bandung.[30] Sayyid 'Uthmân played an important role in Muslim circles in the colony, not only because of his numerous publications. He was also the Honorary Advisor on Arab Affairs, an important informant of yet another Government Advisor, Christiaan Snouck Hurgronje, and later made a member of the *Orde van de Nederlandse Leeuw*.[31]

The other two books were printed by Ikhtiar in Bogor, and Toko Tjitak Afandi in Bandung, respectively. Toko Tjitak Afandi was established in 1903 in Bandung and was one of the earliest indigenous printing houses that produced Sundanese books. Printing houses such as Ikhtiar and Afandi seem to have published books quite at random, and were driven not only by ideological or religious fervour but also by financial considerations. Books were not just good for morality and knowledge, but also for making money: publishing became a business through the growing literacy in the Dutch East Indies society.

Apart from these books, mention should be made of *Wawatjan Gendit Birajoeng*, a lithograph that Snouck Hurgronje found in Banten, probably in 1896. This text, without an author's or publisher's name, suggests the existence of a network of printed materials that escaped the searching of the colonial government. The Sundanese books printed in Singapore in the first decade of the twentieth century (numbering at least three) equally suggest that printing activities and the circulation of the books were taking place beyond the colonial boundary.[32] In 1882, the number of Islamic schools in the Priangan Regencies was 935, with a total enrolment of 16,475 students;[33] thus, there existed a readership besides the so-called "Dutch-made" readership, and there must have been many more than the ten printed Islamic books in circulation.

The Chinese in West Java do not seem to have been actively involved in publishing Sundanese books in the nineteenth century. The famous Lie Kim Hok, who bought a printing machine in Buitenzorg from the missionary van der Linden in 1885, did not publish any Sundanese books. The Soekaboemische Sneldrukkerij, established in 1903 and owned by a Chinese in Sukabumi, published a Malay weekly newspaper after the turn of the century, but had no interest in publishing a Sundanese one.[34] Malay had a potentially larger modern readership in the Dutch East Indies and publishers looked forward to the growth of literacy in Malay and profit increases from their publications in the coming decades. A look at Eurasian authors and stories in Malay newspapers in Batavia supports this argument (Pramoedya 1980). The Eurasians and the Chinese, so important in the development of modern Malay writing, did not become writers of Sundanese.

The 25 books (17 per cent of all Sundanese books) published by private European/Eurasian printing houses were quite diverse, as the printing houses tried their hand at printing anything that could make money, unlike the subsidized Landsdrukkerij. Competition must have been tense as there were 86 printing houses in Java (Batavia, Semarang, Surabaya, Pasuruan and Surakarta) in 1870 and 18 in the Outer Islands.[35] The larger houses, most of them in Batavia, such as Albrecht & Co., G.C.T. van Dorp & Co. and Lange en Co. published mainly Dutch-language books and printed few indigenous language books.[36] In West Java, European/Eurasian printing houses appeared a little later. They include A. Bisschop in Cirebon in 1885, and G. Kolff & Co. in Bandung in 1897.

Table 7 shows the printing or publishing houses owned by Europeans/Eurasians which had printed Sundanese books before 1908.

Next to the Landsdrukkerij, the printer/publisher Lange & Co. in Batavia was the second largest company in terms of titles published in the Dutch East Indies in the second half of the nineteenth century. It

Table 7. List of European/Eurasian printing/publishing houses for Sundanese books (from 1850 to 1908)

In the Dutch East Indies:
- Lange & Co., Batavia: 3 books in Javanese script, 1 book in Roman script.
- G. Kolff & Co., Bandung: 1 book in Roman script.
- G.C.T. van Dorp & Co., Samarang: 8 books in Javanese, 4 books in Arabic script.
- Albrecht & Co., Batavia: 1 book in Roman script.
- Ogilvie & Co., Batavia: 1 book in Roman script.
- A. Bisschop, Cirebon: 6 books in Javanese script.
- De Vries & Fabricius: 1 book in Roman script.

In the Netherlands:
- E.H. Tassemijer, Rotterdam: 2 books in Roman script.
- D. De Koning, Rotterdam: 9 books in Roman script.
- S.E. van Nooten & Zoon, Schoonhoven: 1 book in Roman script.
- D. van Sijn & Zoon, Rotterdam: 11 books in Roman script.
- A.W. Sijthoff, Leiden: 3 books in Arabic script.

produced mainly Dutch books and some indigenous language books, numbering altogether 410 between 1845 and 1869. Lange's Sundanese books dealt with Islamic teaching or contained didactic Christian stories, traditional Sundanese stories, and adaptations of Dutch stories. G. Kolff & Co. in Bandung, G.C.T. van Dorp in Semarang, and Albrecht & Co. in Batavia were established around 1890, the first two being branches of their mother company in Batavia. They also published hundreds of books in many languages; apparently their trade was a profitable one, since they stayed in business for a long time.

A. Bisschop in Cirebon published the first Sundanese almanac in Javanese script in 1892. It consisted of a calendar, a list of the names of government officials, and some reading materials. The publication of this almanac was stopped in 1897, the very year another almanac in Javanese script was published, this time in Semarang by G.C.T. van Dorp, which continued until 1903, side by side with a similar almanac in the Arabic script after 1900, by the same publisher. It seems that Sundanese almanacs, no matter what the script, did not sell well, compared with almanacs in Malay, which appeared in a steady stream.

By the end of the nineteenth century, the Sundanese modern readership had not yet grown enough to make private publishing houses decide to try their luck with Sundanese publications alone — only the government-subsidized printing house Landsdrukkerij remained a steady factor.

## *Script*

Three scripts were used for Sundanese publications: Javanese,[37] Roman and Arabic (called *pegon* by the Sundanese). Figure 5 shows the proportion of scripts used in the Sundanese publications.

There were 94 books in Javanese script, and 95 in Roman script. The large number of texts in Javanese script (in the early years) can be explained as the result of K.F. Holle's idea that Javanese script was preferable for printing Sundanese books, given the kind of literacy of the potential readers. Arabic script was never suggested because of the fear of "Islamic fanaticism". In the early period, 11 dual-script books were published, with the right-hand page in Roman script, and the left-hand page in Javanese script on a two-page spread. This type of book gradually disappeared because of the high cost of printing (Moriyama 1995: 451–2). Perhaps Koorders' bitter criticism also played a role in its demise:

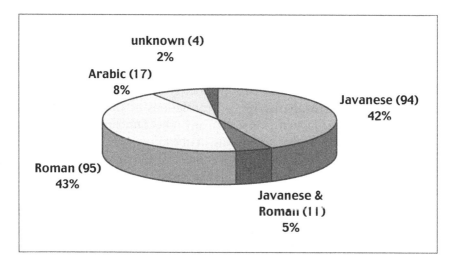

Figure 5. Scripts used in Sundanese publications (from 1850 to 1908)

[...], I do not favour the form of some popular Sundanese books for the reason that those books printed in a two-page spread with Javanese-Sundanese script and Roman script are useless and a waste of money ... Now the buyer has to pay twice for the same; the books are so expensive that it hampers their distribution, and the government cannot conclude from the sales whether there is already some kind of a reading public for books in our script.

[...], die ik tegen den vorm van sommige Soendaneesche volksboeken heb; de bedenking namelijk, dat het tegen-over-elkaar drukken van den tekst met Javaansch-Soendaneesche en Latijnsche karakters nuttelooze, ja schadelijke geldverspilling is .... Zoals de zaak nu geregeld is, moet de kooper tweemaal hetzelfde betalen; de boekjes zijn zooveel-duurder, hetgeen natuurlijk nadeelig teruchwerkt op hun verspreiding, en de regeering kan uit het debiet niet opmaken, of werkelijk voor boekjens in ons letterschrift reeds een lezend publiek van eenigen omvang aanwezig is (Koorders in Meinsma 1869: 268).

As time went by, fewer and fewer books (and fewer total pages) were printed in Javanese script, and more were printed in the Roman script. Apart from ideological reasons — the Roman script was associated with modernity — there were also economic ones: Javanese script needed double the space of the Roman script.[38] After 1902 the Landsdrukkerij no longer published Sundanese books in Javanese script, apart from some reprints.[39]

The missionaries developed their own ideas about the locally used scripts. The Dutch Missionary Society printed all their publications in Roman script. The Netherlands Bible Society in Amsterdam published three books in the Arabic script — translations of the Bible and the Gospel, by S. Coolsma, who, more than any other Dutchman, was aware of the fact that the Arabic script was better known than the Javanese script among the Sundanese (only members of the elite read Javanese script). However, even in this more familiar script, the efforts to proselytize were doomed to failure.

The government was not completely unaware of the Sundanese familiarity with the Arabic script, as seen in *Wawatjan Piwoelang Panoelak Panjakit Kolera* (Wawacan Teaching the Prevention of Cholera), which was published in the Arabic script in an apparent effort to reach as many readers as possible.[40] This so-called Arabic literacy did not decline but developed parallel with the growth of Roman literacy, and until the present day, the Arabic script is used and sometimes even printed in the Sundanese-speaking areas, especially in and around Islamic institutions. On the other hand, the Javanese script has completely vanished in these areas.

Two printing techniques were used for the production of Sundanese books: lithography and typography. Lithography is best seen as an extension or a variation of the traditional way of producing manuscripts. It is not clear how widely this technique was used, but almost all of the lithographs that have been preserved (seven) were produced on Sayyid 'Uthmân's machine in Arabic script. However, it is not known how many lithographs were used in institutions of Muslim education. Typographic techniques were used to print books in all three scripts, although those in the Arabic script seemed to be very few. Typographically produced texts were radically different from manuscripts, in form as well as in distribution. When people read a manuscript, they could see evidence of the human hand and perhaps even hear the human voice between the lines of the page. Typography, on the contrary, gave the touch of a machine, a wonderful and overwhelming feeling.

## K.F. Holle

Karel Frederik Holle began to contribute to Sundanese education after 1851, when he and his brother Adriaan Walraven Holle published a book of fables. Until the 1880s, he played an important role in the production of books in Sundanese written by Sundanese authors (Berge 1993: 17-8). Many of the early books bear the imprimatur "under the supervision of K.F. Holle" on their title pages. In 1868, he expressed his satisfaction with his endeavours in a letter to the Board of the Batavian Society:

> It is not that I want to claim that the published Sundanese books are perfect, but the books, written by Sundanese, offer a considerably greater guarantee for pureness and intelligibility than the ones written in that hodge-podge Malay.

> Ook niet, dat ik wil beweren, dat de in het Soendaasch uitgegeven boekjes perfect zijn, ofschoon zij, door soendanezen geschreven, een veel grooteren waarborg voor zuiverheid en verstaanbaarheid opleveren dan die in 't zoozeer geraadbraakte Maleisch geschreven.[41]

Under Holle's supervision, Sundanese books were produced by a small group of writers, most of whom lived near his residence in Garut, about 50 kilometres southeast of Bandung. They were Moehamad Moesa, the *hoofdpanghulu* (Islamic chief) in Limbangan; Adi Widjaja, the *patih* (vice-regent) of the Limbangan Regency in Priangan; and Bratadiwidjaja, the former *patih* of Galuh in Sukapura Regency, all of whom were high-ranking local officials and members of the aristocracy. Holle's monopoly on the production of Sundanese books continued at least throughout the 1880s; the last book he supervised was *Pagoeneman Soenda djeung Walanda* (Sundanese-Dutch conversation book, 1883), and the last book he edited was *Mitra noe Tani* (Friend of the Farmer, 1895). When he died in 1896, Kartawinata, a son of Moesa, wrote a memorial booklet which symbolized the end of an age ([Soerja Nata Legawa 1897]).[42]

## 3. A Mismatch: Print and *Wawacan*

> Among those who are literate, very few people have reached a level that they can read the Roman script, in addition to the Arabic and Javanese-Sundanese script.

> Onder degenen, die lezen kunnen, zijn maar zeer weinigen, die het zoover gebracht hebben dat ze, buiten het Arabiesche en Javaansch-Soendaneesche ook-noch het Latijnsche letterschrift lezen kunnen (Koorders in Meinsma 1869: 268).

Print literacy grew side by side with manuscript literacy, although both were still restricted to a small number of people in the Sundanese-speaking communities of West Java in the second half of the nineteenth century. Some works were read in manuscript form while others were read separately in print.[43] Readers did not stop consuming manuscripts as they had distinct cultural meanings, a distinct "aura" that could not be replaced by printed books. Still, those who had read manuscripts in the past were the same people who began to read printed books too. As the number of schools increased, so did the number of printed books, and the circle of those who acquired print literacy became wider. Thus, print literacy was to constitute the basis for a modern readership, in which innovations and alterations were introduced into the configuration of Sundanese writing.

No more than 200 titles were printed in the second half of the nineteenth century. It is hard to say if this was a large number or not, but in retrospect it is clear that these printed books, fostered in the schools, changed Sundanese writing and hence the cultural life of West Java. Local printing houses were established, new forms of writing — such as journals, newspapers, and translations of stories — were developed, and a group of people emerged who had progressive ideas. "Print" was not the only avenue towards modernization in Sundanese writing. Others included: the Islamic institutions, the development of Malay, colonial efforts to standardize the "Sundanese language", and the establishment of schools. "Modern Sundanese writing" was the knot that tied them together.

When printing was introduced into Sundanese writing in the middle of the nineteenth century, *wawacan*, a traditional genre of narrative poetry, was so popular among the Sundanese that Dutch scholars concluded that it was the "most traditional" and the "most prestigious" form of Sundanese writing, and the most favourable means for education. As a result, *wawacan* was given a prominent role in the educational materials that were produced by the colonial authorities. However, *wawacan* gradually lost its predominant position: its poetic form and its conventions of storytelling suited neither print publication nor the demands of modernity.

Thus, more prose came to be written and produced in print. The form of writing, of course, interacted with and altered reading habits. Gradually, it became less common for people to share stories in the traditional, more or less ritualized way, and intoning or reciting was no longer the sole manner of "reading a book", as was discussed in the

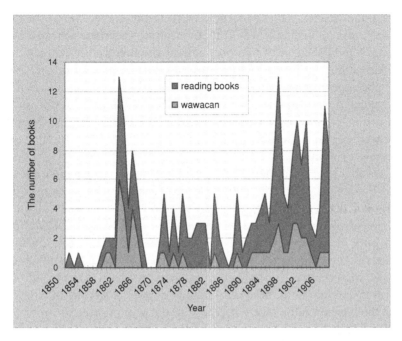

Figure 6. Number of reading books and printed *wawacan* (from 1850 to 1908)

previous chapter. Prose writing in print was read by individuals, silently. *Wawacan* and the printed book proved to be a mismatch.

Almost 70 per cent of all publications in Sundanese in the second half of the nineteenth century were produced by the Landsdrukkerij. Of the 87 reading books, 51 publications were *wawacan* texts, which represented almost 60 per cent of the total. Figure 6 shows chronologically the number of printed *wawacan* among the reading books during the period 1850–1906.

Many *wawacan* were published mainly during two periods: first in the 1860s, then around the turn of the century. In the earlier period most publications were *wawacan*, especially those produced by the Landsdrukkerij. This was due to the involvement of K.F. Holle, who believed that *dangding*, a "traditional form", was most effective in simultaneously strengthening the identity of the Sundanese and bringing enlightenment to the people.

The first *wawacan*, entitled *Ijeu Wawatjan Tjarita Ibrahim* (This Wawacan is the Story of Ibrahim), was published in 1859.[44] It was the first of a series of *wawacan*, 11 of which were written by Holle's friend,

Moehamad Moesa. Moesa's largest work in the genre, *Wawacan Panji Wulung*, was published in 1871; it could be seen as representative of all *wawacan* published in the second half of the nineteenth century.

Altogether, Holle and Moesa produced 17 *wawacan* in the 1860s which became important schoolbooks and readers for the students at the educational institutions in West Java. The second peak period in the publication of *wawacan* was in the late neneteenth century. Most of these were reprinted editions of those published in the 1860s. New titles were few in number.

Another way to understand the special position of *wawacan* is to study the frequency of their publication. Certain titles were reprinted (with or without revisions), often more than once.[45] In the catalogue of the Landsdrukkerij, the words *habis* (finished) in Malay and *uitverkocht* (sold out) in Dutch are found against some titles, but this does not necessarily mean that they were well purchased or were actively used in schools: sometimes piles of old editions were preserved in the storehouse. However, comparisons between catalogues over a period of 60 years show that certain books were indeed sold out within three or four years. Table 8 lists the most frequently reprinted titles.

All except *Mangle* were authored by Moesa. These books were intended for schools. However, *Wawacan Panji Wulung* was not only used in schools but also read widely by the Sundanese people. It is interesting to see that only this *wawacan* is on the list of the most frequently reprinted titles, while the other three books are works of prose.

Most of the reprinted books were in prose. *Carita Abdurahman jeung Abdurahim* (The Story of Abdurahman and Abdurahim) was almost always available, and collections of fables like *Dongeng-dongeng Pieunteungeun* (Model Stories) and *Mangle* (The Anthology of Model Stories) were also reprinted many times. The following fable is taken

Table 8. Most frequently reprinted titles (from 1850 to 1908)

- *Wawacan Panji Wulung* (first published in 1871), reprinted eight times
- *Mangle* (first published in 1890), reprinted eight times
- *Dongeng-dongeng Pieunteungeun* (first published in 1867), reprinted six times
- *Carita Abdurahman jeung Abdurahim* (first published in 1863), reprinted five times

from *Dongeng-dongeng Pieunteungeun,* one of the most successful books in prose. Such fables had moralistic teachings.

> 20. Garuda Bird and Turtle
> A turtle wanted to be able to fly and often asked the garuda to teach him. Every time the turtle asked the garuda, the bird scolded, "You keep talking about something which is not at all appropriate!" The turtle kept asking, the bird kept warning, and at last the turtle's wish was fulfilled because he really annoyed the bird's heart. The garuda grabbed the turtle with his two feet and carried him into the air. When they had come high up, the bird dropped the turtle, and the result was exactly what the garuda had said: the turtle fell down to the earth and was smashed to pieces.
> This story means: do not wish what you cannot do; it often comes from your arrogance and causes damage in the end.
>
> 20. Manoek Garoeda Djeung Koeja
> Aja koeja boga nijat bisa hiber, remen ngomong ka manoek garoeda, neda diwoeroekan. Oenggal ngomong ka manoek garoeda, tjarek garoeda: "Sok ngomong teu patut djeung teu pantes kana pipatoeteunana!" Bawaning keukeuh noe hajang, keukeuh noe njarek, toengtoengna nja dianteur karepna, tina ngaroedetkeun kana ati batoer. Toeloej koeja diranggem koe manoek garoeda sarta kebat dibawa hiber. Barang geus nepi ka loehoer, diragragkeun, kadjadjadianana njata saomong manoek garoeda, koeja ragrag kana taneuh, awakna remoek.
> Hartina ijeu dongeng: oelah sok nganijatan noe teu pikalakoneun, karep kitoe eta bidjilna ti ati takaboer, noe noengtoen kana karoeksakan (Moesa 1867:19).

Many of the Sundanese prose readers were translations of Dutch stories, sometimes via a Malay version. For instance, the title page of *Dongeng-dongeng nu araneh* (The wonder stories), published in 1866, says that "one half is composed [in Sundanese], the other half is translated from Malay into Sundanese". Holle and Moesa may not have foreseen that people would love these translations and adaptations in prose better than *wawacan*. Were their *wawacan* not "original" and in the poetic form the Sundanese loved most? It seems that those were the very two features that did not please the students of modernity. Printed *wawacan* were not overwhelmingly popular among the print-literate Sundanese, in spite of the promotion by Holle and the government.

Another way to understand printed *wawacan* is to look at those which had a long life-span. Some titles were listed in the catalogue of

**Table 9.** Titles that were in the Landsdrukkerij's catalogue for more than 50 years

- *Wawacan Dongeng-dongeng Tuladan* (Wawacan Telling Model Stories) published in 1863, reprinted three times;
- *Dongeng-dongeng Pieunteungeun* (Model Stories), published in 1867, reprinted six times;
- *Carita Abdurahman jeung Abdurahim* (The Story of Abdurahman and Abdurahim) published in 1863, reprinted five times;
- *Wawacan Carios Ali Muhtar* (Wawacan Telling the Story of Ali Muhtar), published in 1864, reprinted once;
- *Caritana Ibrahim* (The Story of Ibrahim), published in 1853, reprinted once;
- *Wawacan Katrangan Miara Lauk Cai* (Wawacan Explaining the Raising of Freshwater Fish), published in 1866, not reprinted.*

Note: * The catalogue says that this *wawacan* was printed again in the same year with a special binding, but the special edition cannot be found in the collection of any of the libraries.

Landsdrukkerij for a long period while others were not. For each edition, about 3,000 to 6,000 copies were printed and some were reprinted again and again. Thus, certain titles remained in the series of catalogues for more than 50 years, such as *Wawacan Panji Wulung*, which was reprinted eight times. Other titles remained in the catalogues because they were never sold out, like *Babad Tanah Pasundan* (The History of the Sundanese Lands, 1880), a Sundanese translation of a Dutch text by J.A. van der Chijs.[46] Table 9 shows other books that were in the catalogue for more than 50 years.

Some of these titles also appear in the list of the most frequently reprinted books (Table 8). Among the six titles, including the above-mentioned two books, were three *wawacan*. Two of them, *Wawacan Panji Wulung* and *Wawacan Dongeng-dongeng Tuladan*, were reprinted many times. *Wawacan Katrangan Miara Lauk Cai*, however, was never reprinted but remained in the catalogue for more than 50 years. This means that most *wawacan* did not sell well, even though many titles were published. On the other hand, most prose books were on the catalogue for 30–40 years and were reprinted several times. It was a paradoxical phenomenon: the Dutch promoted *wawacan* as the means to enlighten the Sundanese; but printed *wawacan*, with a few exceptions, did not really succeed. *Wawacan* and the printed book were increasingly incompatible, so it seems.

This does not mean that *wawacan* was not popular, however. Ekadjati's catalogue (1988) shows that in many places in West Java *wawacan* have been preserved in manuscript form. *Wawacan Amar Sakti*, or *Wawacan Ogin,* for instance, can be found in many places; apparently this work was often copied by hand.[47] New manuscripts were made even in the middle of the twentieth century (Ayatrohaedi 1991). *Wawacan* continued to circulate in the chirographic tradition, separate from printed *wawacan*.

Most of the Dutch considered *wawacan* to be the "purest" and "best" of the traditional genres of Sundanese "literature" and they tried to use it to bring information to the people. Sundanese writers were therefore asked or ordered by Holle to compose *wawacan* that could be published. Hence, *wawacan* became the prima donna, pushing other genres aside. But then, these printed *wawacan* were more informative and didactic in nature than the "traditional" *wawacan* which, preserved in manuscripts, were composed primarily for entertainment. For instance, *Wawacan Seca Nala* (Wawacan of Secanala), published in 1863, was intended to inform peasants and merchants about things and ideas that were considered useful by Holle and Moesa. The form of writing was familiar to the people, but this kind of *wawacan* contained a variety of unknown and unfamiliar elements which led to the slow demise of *wawacan*. New content in old form — a strange combination, characteristic of many educational endeavours in the Indies, and doomed to failure.

## Chapter 3

# The Birth of the Author: Moehamad Moesa

### 1. Moesa, the Man

In the backyard of the central mosque in Garut there is a cemetery where the high officials of the Limbangan Regency and their relatives have been laid to rest. Moehamad Moesa is buried in a plot together with his crippled son Djenal (or Zainal) Asikin (1852–1915), who succeeded his father as *hoofdpanghulu* of Limbangan. Their graves are in front of the oldest cemetery unit, in which the Regent XIII, Toemenggoeng Djajaningrat (Dalem Sepoeh, ?–1871); Regent XIV, Adipati Aria Wiratanoedatar (?–1915); and his wife Lasminingrat (1843?–1948), one of Moesa's daughters and a well-known writer herself, are buried. Going from the cemetery along a narrow path that is next to a ditch is the place where Moehamad Moesa's house stood in the nineteenth century.

The inscription on Moesa's tombstone has his name, R.H. Mhd. Moesa, and tells us that he was born in 1822 and died on 10 August 1886. From other sources we know that his father, Raden Rangga Soerjadikoesoemah, was a *patih*, the second highest position in the Limbangan Regency.

Moehamad Moesa played a key role in the emergence of a new form of Sundanese writing. Immersed in Islamic tradition, he was aware of the new age, and realized that he and his people were living in strange times. Moesa assisted his Dutch friend, Karel Frederik Holle, in producing books in Sundanese. He advised Holle in the latter's efforts to find tales that could be used for appropriate reading materials at the newly established schools. He himself also composed tales and books for these schools. They represent a kind of writing that was novel in Sundanese literary life, both in terms of appearance and content, as they were not hand-written manuscripts but printed books, and dealt not only with days of yore but also with contemporary situations. *Wawacan Panji Wulung* became his best-known work. It was to be greatly appreciated in decades to come by generations of Sundanese people. Only in the 1950s, when books and print had become self-evident manifestations of modernity and the colonial context had come to an end, was its authority radically questioned.

## Sundanese aristocrat and Islamic leader

Moehamad Moesa received his first formal education at an Islamic school (*pasantren*) in Purwakarta, north of Bandung. As a young boy, he also spent some time in Mecca, an unforgettable experience for any Muslim. Moesa believed that he was destined to be a cleric and when still a young man, he rejected the government's offer of a job to become a warehouse chief (Levyssohn Norman 1888b: 94). Instead, he became a *panghulu* (Islamic leader) and in 1864 was appointed *hoofdpanghulu* (chief *panghulu*) of the Limbangan Regency (Almanak en naamregister 1862: 83, 1863: 87), a position that he held until his death.

Limbangan had been a political centre, more or less in competition with Sukapura, Bandung, Parakan Muncang, and Sumedang ever since the days of the Javanese Sultan Agung of Mataram in the seventeenth century.[1] In the nineteenth century, it was generally seen as one of the most "advanced and prosperous" regencies in Java (Bezemer 1924: 32). Within the colonial administration, the position of *panghulu* was one of the highest possible for indigenous people, next to *regent* or *bupati* (local chief), *patih* (vice- regent), *jaksa* (prosecutor) and *wadana* (district chief). In the traditional community, the *panghulu* played an important role for the people. However, when *panghulu* were integrated into the Dutch administration, their religious and political role was diminished. The colonial government made use of the traditional role of *panghulu* to keep colonial order if they agreed to cooperate with the Dutch (Kobayashi 1991: Hisyam 2001). Moesa received an annual salary of 900 Dutch guilders, plus an additional 720 guilders in compensation for corvée labour service (Levyssohn Norman 1888b: 94). It was a good salary, as that of a *bupati*, the highest position in the same period, was 200 guilders, and that of a *patih* between 225 and 300 guilders.[2] The *hoofdpanghulu* of Limbangan was an authoritative and wealthy man.

During his lifetime, Moesa had six wives who gave him 17 children, and 66 grandchildren (Brata di Widjaja 1897: 28). His family acquired positions in almost all the Priangan Regencies, and even in Central Java.

**Plate 1.** Moehamad Moesa's tombstone
*Source: M. Moriyama.*

**Plate 2.** Moehamad Moesa
*Source: One of Moesa's descendants, Mr. A. Rachman Prawiranata, of Bandung.*

**Plate 3.** Mesjid Agung Garut
*Source:* M. *Moriyama.*

**Plate 4.** Alun-alun Garut
*Source:* M. *Moriyama.*

The correspondence between Moesa's family from 1882 to 1885 was collected and compiled in *Serat-sinerat djaman djoemenengna Raden Hadji Moehamad Moesa* (Correspondence at the time when Raden Hadji Moehamad Moesa was on duty).[3] This book offers some insights into the ways local chiefs and aristocrats in Java established and maintained their social network, not only by way of marriages but also through regular contacts with colleagues within the Dutch administration (Danoeredja 1929). Besides correspondence, visits were essential to maintain and expand these networks; for instance, in *Serat-sinerat* mention is made of a journey that Moesa (together with his wife and two other family members) made to visit his eldest son, then Regent of Lebak at Rangkasbitung, and also of his visits to Batavia, Serang, Bogor, Cipanas, Cianjur, Cimahi, and Cicalengka to meet relatives and friends, all members of the local elite. The *menak* (aristocrats) clearly formed a community of their own with shared interests in every sense of the word.

The relationships between aristocrats and the common people (*cacah*) were hierarchical, and were strengthened by the machinations of the colonial administration which appointed members of the aristocracy in high administrative and bureaucratic positions so as to preserve peace and order in the region. *Menak* and *cacah* lived in complementary worlds; contacts were formal and distant, based on power and intimidation rather than intimacy and sympathy. Not least because of his warm friendship with K.F. Holle, Moehamad Moesa enjoyed the confidence of a number of colonial officials, both in West Java and in Batavia, the glorious centre of the Dutch East Indies government. The fact that his name was well-known in the European community helped him to extend his network. It strengthened his status among the *menak*, and confirmed his authority among the *cacah*.

The following poem, a fragment of a memorial verse for K.F. Holle which the well-known poet Aria Brata di Widjaja, the *patih* of Mangunreja in the Priangan Regencies, composed ten years after Moesa's death, shows how well-respected Moesa was in his community (Danoeredja 1929: 79–82).

| | |
|---|---|
| Halijah padoeka toewan, | The great master, |
| K.F. Holle ti mimiti, | K.F. Holle, from the beginning |
| dongkap ka wekasannana, | until the very end of his life |
| beunangna ngagolang ilmi, | was able to use his knowledge |
| mitraning anoe tani, | for his friends, the peasants. |

| | |
|---|---|
| goejoeb djeung Raden Panghoeloe, | Together with the Panghulu's, |
| djoeragan Hadji Moesa, | Mr. Haji Moesa, |
| reja noe djadi pertawis, | Many were the signs |
| tawis dalit koentjara djeung kanjataän. | of their intimate friendship, that was the fact. |
| Beunangna saekapraja, | They carried out the same duties and |
| djadi sakoelit sadaging, | became one in body and soul. |
| djenat *Raden Hadji Moesa*, | The late Raden Hadji Moesa was |
| sajakti menak sinelir, | a prominent aristocrat and |
| kaselir koe noe singgih, | liked by his admirers. |
| sanadjan pangkat Panghoeloe, | Even though his status was Panghulu, |
| moebjarna kahoermatan, | his respectability was glorious. |
| kanggep sami djeung Boepati, | He was regarded as high as a regent, |
| pon toeroenan kasertaän koe boediman. | virtue runs in his family. |

(Brata di Widjaja 1897: 27)

Moesa was obviously as much a politician as he was a man of religion — at the time, Islamic leaders often played a political role in that they knew how to handle administrative affairs, such as the collection of taxes, appointments, and issues of education, and use these as a way to gain power and control. In West Java, the *panghulu* was just as involved as regents in the maintenance of law and order: it was an area where many people prided themselves in being pious Muslims, and the colonial authorities had to move very cautiously.

Moesa seemed to be more aware of the benefits and importance of the European way of education than most of his colleagues. European knowledge was beneficial for his family and his flock, in terms of well-being and welfare. Strangely enough, he himself never mastered Dutch, but saw to it that his children were given the proper Dutch education — an effective guarantee, he thought, for prestige and status for his family:

So much the *Panghulu* of *Garoet* could have contributed, had he understood our language! So often he complains that he has no access to our literature! One of his sons, a smart boy, is now at the Dutch school of the Regent of *Soemedang*.

Wat had de *Panghoeloe* van *Garoet* niet kunnen leveren, als hij slechts onze taal goed verstond! Hoe dikwerf zucht hij niet, dat hij geen toegang heeft tot onze litteratuur! Een zijner zonen, een vlugge jongen, is thans op de Hollandsche school van den Regent van *Soemedang*.[4]

For his relatives' benefit, Moesa established a European school (*bijzondere Europeesche school*) in Garut; and its two European teachers were paid by Sundanese chiefs.[5] It was one of the few schools for both European and local children and, equally rare, for boys as well as girls. The number of students reached almost 100. From 1876, the *bijzondere school* received a government subsidy of 100 guilders per month (Levyssohn Norman 1888a: 24). Moesa believed that education was equivalent to mastering script and languages — and that boys and girls should be separated once they reached puberty:

| | |
|---|---|
| Kakara ngangkat birahi, | When reaching puberty, |
| menggah istri-pamegetna, | girls and boys are |
| saena geus lepas bae, | better being separated. |
| ajeuna sedeng diadjar, | Now is the time to learn, |
| ngolah ilmoe oetama, | to obtain superb knowledge. |
| sanggeus iskolana tjoekoep, | When schooling has been sufficient, |
| ladjeng kana padamelan. | then they go to work. |
| | |
| Saniskara damel istri, | All kinds of female skills |
| oelah aja kapetolan, | must not be ignored: |
| ngeujeuk njoelam njoeat njongket, | embroidering and weaving, |
| kitoe deui olah-olah, | and also cooking. |
| panedja sim koering mah, | What I mean is that |
| lamoen iskolana tjoekoep, | when schooling has been sufficient, |
| aksara djeung basa-basa. | [they have mastered] script and languages. |

(Danoeredja 1929: 52)

The *hoofdpanghulu* of Limbangan recognized the significance of schooling for girls, but in the case of his own daughters he followed a newly developed custom among the *menak*: he sent his daughters to live with Dutch families so that they could learn the language and become familiar with European discipline and hygiene. Holle explained this custom in a letter to Governor-General, J. Loudon (1872–5), as follows:

> The second wife of the Regent, a daughter of the *hoofdpanghulu*, who stayed with the family of Levyssohn in Sumedang for a considerable time before her marriage, not only speaks Dutch and has assimilated many good things such as discipline and cleanliness but now also translates Dutch into Sundanese for the purpose of indigenous education. A daughter of the *panghulu* was taken care of by the wife of the Assistant Resident, a daughter of the *patih* by the wife of the controller, while another daughter of the *hoofdpanghulu* and a daughter of *patih* are taken care of by the family of Stam (a teacher). Moreover, a sister of the Regent, a daughter of the Regent of Sumedang and a daughter of a *wedana* attend the school, while they are trained in female fancywork by the Teacher's wife after school. The effect of good European companionship on the children is clearly visible, and no doubt they will have a favourable effect on their husbands and children once they are married. That will surely not damage our prestige.

> De 2e vrouw van den Regent een dochter van den Hoofdpanghoeloe, die voor haar huwelijk geruimen tijd bij de familie Levyssohn te Soemedang aan huis was spreekt niet alleen Hollandsch en heeft veel goeds zooals orde en zindelijkheid overgenomen, maar vertaalt thans uit het Nederlandsch in het Soendaasch ten behoeve van het inlandsch onderwijs. Een dochtertje van den panghoeloe is door de echtgenoote van den Assistent Resident aan huis genomen, een dochter van den patih bij de echtgenoote van den controleur, terwijl nog een dochter van den hoofdpanghoeloe en een van den patih bij de familie van Stam (de onderwijzer) aan huis zijn. Wijders bezoeken eene zuster van den Regent, een dochter van den Pangeran van Soemedang en eene dochter van een wedana de school terwijl zij na schooltijd bij de echtgenoot van den onderwijzer zich in vrouwelijke handwerken oefenen. Merkbaar is dan ook de invloed welke goede Europeesche omgang op die kinderen heeft en lijdt het geen twijfel of zij zullen later, getrouwd zijnde op hunne echtgenooten en kinderen een gunstigen invloed uitoefenen, die zeker niet ten nadeele van ons prestige zal zijn.[6]

Moesa's expectations came true: his sons were given high positions in the government administration, and his daughters married equally Europeanized *menak*. That was how, for instance, his eldest son, Soeria Nata Ningrat, became the Regent of Lebak in the Banten Regency. His second son Kartawinata became the *patih* of Sumedang. His sagacious daughter Lasminingrat was married to the Regent of Limbangan, and the others were to have official positions too. No wonder his family was praised in a poem by Brata di Widjaja:[7]

| | |
|---|---|
| Lain woengkoel salirana, | Not only he himself who has |
| nampi parmaning jang widi, | received the mercy of God |
| diraksa koe toewan Holla, | was taken care of by Mr. Holle, |
| poetrana pameget istri, | also his sons and daughters, |
| ti kawit moerangkalih, | from early childhood, |
| didjoeroeng disoewoek ilmoe, | were stimulated to increase their knowledge, |
| diadjar kaboedajan, | and learned culture. |
| sadaja poetra ngadjadi, | All children were successful. |
| djadi pinter taja hidji katjingtjalang. | All of them became clever without exception. |
| Asal djoemlah toedjoeh welas, | Seventeen was the number[8] |
| poetra pameget djeung istri, | of sons and daughters, |
| sadaja meunang angkatan, | all obtained positions. |
| diangkat *Boepati Patih*, | They were appointed as *Bupati* or *Patih*. |
| dalasan para istri, | As for the daughters, |
| tjoendoek loenggoeh Raden Ajoe, | they became the first wives of high officials |
| poetra mantoe ambtenaar, | and daughters-in-law of officials. |
| patitis baris pinoedji, | They are properly respected |
| kapoedjian midji ka menak Limbangan. | praised examples of the *Limbangan* nobility. |

(Brata di Widjaja 1897: 28)

In short, Moesa's life was a success story, except perhaps for one incident: the so-called Cianjur affair which must have been a black page for him and his relatives (Suminto 1985: 64–6). Around 1885, the government became increasingly worried about the activities of an Islamic brotherhood, *tarekat Naqshabandiyya*, of which not only commoners but also local high-ranking officials, such as the Regent of Cianjur, the *hoofdpanghulu* of Cianjur, the *hoofdpanghulu* of Sukabumi, and the *patih* of Sukabumi, were active members. Both Holle and Moesa described the brotherhood, which had its centre in Cianjur, as "fanatical" and therefore a threat to public peace and order, and Holle suggested in his letter to the Resident of Priangan, a man named Peltzer, that the *hoofdpanghulu* of Cianjur and the *hoofdpanghulu* of Sukabumi be dismissed. Sayyid 'Uthmân in Batavia published a pamphlet in which he criticized the brotherhood, using Islamic arguments. However, the Resident of the Priangan Regencies and the Assistant Resident of Sukabumi did not take the *tarekat Naqshabandiyya* very seriously, and refused to listen to Holle's manifold warnings as well as prohibited the circulation of Sayyid 'Uthmân's pamphlet.

At about the same time, Habib As-Sagaf, a man of Arab descent, who had been dismissed as the *penghulu* of Kampung Jawa in Banda Aceh, came into conflict with the *patih* of Sukabumi because he could not pay his debts. He sent a maliciously slanderous letter to L. Brunner of the *Java-Bode*, who then published a sensational article in his newspaper dated 28 September 1885 about the religious activities of the *patih* of Sukabumi and his deep involvement in *tarekat Naqshabandiyya*. A *Perang Sabil* (Holy War) seemed imminent, according to the article, and rumours that all Europeans would be murdered at the annual horse-races in Bandung began to circulate. It was only a single episode in a very hectic period of the history of the Priangan Regencies, which eventually ended in a strengthening of Dutch control and a growing fear of possible Islamic fanaticism.[9]

In retrospect, it is obvious that Moesa moved in murky waters: he wanted his youngest son, Djenal Asikin, the *naib* (a lower-ranking Islamic position) of Wanaraja, to become the *hoofdpanghulu* of Cianjur, and his eldest son, Soeria Nata Ningrat, to replace the Regent of Cianjur. The father was worried about the future of Djenal, crippled as a result of a fall from a horse, and he was unhappy because Soeria Nata Ningrat was the Regent of Lebak in the Banten Regency — in the eyes of the Priangan aristocrats a mere backwater. Nothing came of these plans and designs, however. When Moesa realized that he had made serious miscalculations, he wrote a letter to the then Governor-General, van Rees, with whom he was personally acquainted, and asked him to dismiss him as *hoofdpanghulu* and appoint Djenal Asikin in his place. His proposal was squarely rejected by Batavia. Moesa died one year later.

### Bosom friends: Moesa and K.F. Holle

Crucial for Moesa's prestige and authority was a Dutchman named Karel Frederik Holle (1829–96).[10] Holle came to know Moesa in 1857 when he moved to a tea plantation at Cikajang in the Limbangan Regency. They developed a friendship that lasted for nearly 30 years and had a great influence on each other, having had many conversations about agriculture and education in West Java, and Sundanese as well as European culture.

Moesa's second wife, Banonagara, was proud of the friendship between the two. She told her relatives more than once how close Holle was to her family — how, for instance, the Dutchman once came to Moesa's house to hear the latter's stories about her journey to Lebak, Batavia, and Bogor. This letter was addressed to her daughter-in-law in Lebak:

| | |
|---|---|
| Toean Hola meunang tiloe wengi, | For three nights Mr. Holle |
| di dajeuhna teu aja kersana, | had nothing to do in the city, |
| ngan hojong nanggap tjarios, | but to listen to the stories. |
| miloe tjalik di poengkoer, | He joined us in the back of the house, |
| sila bae dina alketip | sitting cross-legged on the carpet, |
| sasaoeran djeung Djoea | while chatting with Djoea.[11] |
| djeung embok nja kitoe, | And also to me. |
| henteu njana koe Nji Djoea, | Unexpectedly since her return from Lebak |
| sadatangna ti Lebak sedjen parangi, | Djoea looked different |
| djadi sonagar pisan. | She had become puffed up with pride. |

(Danoeredja 1929: 22)

Another witness, the above-mentioned Brata di Widjaja, wrote a memorial verse for Holle in 1897 in which he gave a picture of the warm friendship between Moesa and Holle:

## The Birth of the Author 111

| | |
|---|---|
| [...] | [...] |
| saharita di Garoet, | at that time in Garut was |
| Rahaden Hadji Moesa, | Raden Haji Moesa, |
| panghoeloe noe mashoer, | the famous *panghulu*, |
| djembar kaboedajannana, | he had wide knowledge of culture, |
| ngolah sara radjin bangkit mitra tani, | devoted and willing to encourage peasants, |
| berboedi pangabaran. | and was virtuous and modest. |
| | |
| Toewan Holle misaderek dalit, ka Raden Hadji Moehamad Moesa, | Mr. Holle was like an intimate brother of Raden Hadji Moehamad Moesa. |
| koemaraket roekoen sae, | were very close and on good terms. |
| kaseboet noeroeb tjoepoe, | They were called an ideal pair, |
| toenggal tjegah toenggil pamilih, | united in effort and consideration, |
| sareundeuk sakeupatan, | one in action and movement, |
| samaksoed sasoehoed, | one in intention and hope, |
| poehara saekapraja, | completely [devoted to] the same duties, |
| sasarengan ngolahkeun harti pangarti, | together obtaining meaning and understanding, |
| djarijah kasantosan. | of good deeds and power. |

(Brata di Widjaja 1897: 23)

Holle introduced his Sundanese friend to his Dutch friends. For instance, W.H. Engelmann, a translator working for the Netherlands Bible Society (NBG) and a good friend of Holle, wrote the following report to the Secretary of the High Officials of NBG in 1865:

> I have developed a warm relationship with the indigenous chiefs through his [Holle's] introduction, in particular with the *Hoofdpanghulu* who is considerably enlightened (for an indigenous person, that is) and not averse to European ideas, famous as a writer of various Sundanese schoolbooks published by the Government.
>
> Door zijn (Holle) introductie ben ik met de inlandsche hoofden aldaar op een zeer goeden voet, vooral met den Hoofd-panghoeloe, een (voor een inlander altijd) vrij verlicht en van Europeesche denkbeelden

niet afkeerig man, bekend als schrijver van verscheidene door het Gouvernement uitgegeven Soendaneesche leerboekjes (Veth 1869: 257–8).

For the Muslims, Europeans were *kafir* (infidels), dangerous and a nuisance (Chijs 1864: 220–3), but Moesa did not share such sentiments. Although a prominent Islamic leader, he had an open mind for "Europe". He tried to understand European thinking, although it is not clear what role opportunism rather than sincere curiosity played in this: he gained the trust of the Europeans and the colonial government, and leaning on their authority he managed to expand his networks and confirm hierarchy — and to accumulate considerable wealth. The warm relationship between Moesa and Holle was confirmed by the marriage of one of Moesa's younger sisters, possibly the above-mentioned Djoeariah, to Karel Holle (Berge 1998: 21). That strange mixture of opportunism, friendship, and curiosity drove both Moesa and Holle, who not only had a good time with his friend but also used him as an informant in Sundanese affairs and won his advice in political and administrative problems that the Dutch Indies government was facing.

When Holle was ill in 1879 and had to go to Buitenzorg (Bogor) for recuperation, Moesa sent him letters and prayed, so he wrote, for his friend's recovery. When there was no reply from Karel himself, Moesa sent a card in Malay to his brother, Herman Holle, at Kebon Sirih in Batavia (20 November 1879):

> I hope you will send word to me about your brother, Mr. K.F. Holle. How about his sickness? I am afraid that he has suffered a relapse again, because I have not received any letters for a long time and I have not received a reply to my three letters. Therefore I am very afraid that he has become ill again.
>
> Hareplah sabot soeka membri kabar pada saja, dari hal soedarah Toean K. F. Holle, bigimana dari sakitnya? Saja takoet komboeh lagi, sebab soeda lama saja tida dapat soerat, dan saja soeda 3 kali kirim soerat bloem dapat balasan; Dari itoe terlaloe mendjadi ketjil hati saja, takoet merasa lagi sakitnja.[12]

Holle recovered from his illness, and then it was Moesa's turn: he was diagnosed with diabetes, and after a long illness Moesa passed away in the arms of Karel Holle on 10 August 1886 (Levyssohn Norman 1888b: 95). His friend saw to it that the news of Moesa's death was delivered by printed cards in Dutch to his friends on the following day.[13]

Holle showed his deep grief and offered his condolences to the bereaved family. Some months later Kartawinata, one of Moesa's sons and *patih* of Sumedang, wrote a moving letter in eloquent Dutch to Herman Holle in the Hague. "Uw hooggeachte broeder" (your respected brother) refers to Karel Holle.

> Dear Sir:
>
> Also in the name of my family I express our hearty thanks for your well-meant words of condolence on the great and painful grief caused by the demise of our beloved father.
>
> He died of exhaustion, caused by his old disease (diabetes) and had a gentle and calm passing.
>
> I cannot tell you how sad we are about his departure, and how big the loss is for his children, but there is nothing for us to do but accept the wise decisions of the Almighty God. Your respected brother feels the loss as much as we do. A more profound, sincere friendship between two noble men would have been difficult to find, I believe. We consider your brother our second father, a substitute for his trusted friend.
>
> Your brother spent his time with Papa during his sickness to the very end, and he stayed with us some days more after the funeral to comfort and encourage us.
>
> Holle [?][14] is fine and will publish a life history of Papa one of these days.
>
> In the hope of hearing something from you soon, I close, offering our hearty and sincere greetings.

> Zeer Geachte Heer!
>
> Ook namens de familie betuig ik U onzen hartelijken dank voor Uwe welgemeende woorden van deelneming in ons smartelijk en groot verlies door het overlijden van onzen dierbaren vader.
>
> Hij is van uitputting van krachten ten gevolge van zijn oude kwaal (diabetes) gestorven en heeft een zacht en kalm sterfbed gehad.
>
> Ik kan U niet zeggen hoe diep wij zijn heengaan betreuren en hoe groot het verlies voor ons zijn kinderen is, doch er is voor ons niets te doen dan in de wijze besluiten van den Almachtigen God te berusten. Ook Uw hooggeachte broeder gevoelt het verlies even zwaar als wij. Inniger, oprechter vriendschap als die tusschen die twee edele mannen kon men geloof ik moeielijk vinden. Wij beschouwen Uw broeder dan ook als onze tweede vader, vervanger van zijn trouwe vriend.
>
> Uw broer heeft tijdens de ziekte tot het laaste oogenblik bij Papa doorgebracht en bleef na de begrafenis nog eenige dagen bij ons om ons te troosten en moed in te spreken.

Holle[?] maakt het thans uitstekend en zal eerstdaags een levensgeschiedenis van Papa laten uitgeven.

In de hoop iets naders van U te mogen vernemen, teeken ik na aanbieding onzer hartelijke groeten hoogachtend.[15]

## Relationship with the Dutch

Moesa's family was close, if not intimate with Dutch officialdom. For instance, Levyssohn Norman, the Secretary-General of the government and one of the most influential men in the Indies, reminisced on his first meeting with Moehamad Moesa in 1860 in an essay he published in the Dutch magazine, *Eigen Haard*, in 1888 (Levyssohn Norman 1888b: 93–6). Accompanied by Karel Frederik Holle, he tells his readers, he paid a visit to Moesa at his house, next to the mosque in Garut, and was impressed by Moesa's appearance and attitude; the *panghulu* was open-minded and frank, traits that a Dutch official did not expect to find in an indigenous aristocrat.[16]

> When we entered the residence I was greatly surprised because I saw a wealthy Sundanese who had a round and open face with a vigorous moustache, wearing a colourful turban and, apart from that, was dressed more or less as a European, comfortably sitting with his wife and children in cosiness around the tea table and reciting a folk tale; this was nothing of the ascetic appearance one would expect when meeting a Muslim cleric in Java.

> We traden de woning binnen en niet weinig was ik verrast toen ik, in tegenstelling van de ascetische verschijning, die men zich gewoonlijk denkt van een Mohammedaanschen priester op Java, een welgedanen Soendanees gewaar werd met een goedrond, open gelaat en forschen knevel, met een veelkleurigen tulband op en overigens min of meer op zijn Europeesch uitgedost, die met vrouw en kroost gezellig aan de theetafel was gezeten en met het voorlezen van het een of ander volksverhaal bezig was (Levyssohn Norman 1888b: 94).

For her part, Raden Ajoe Banonagara, Moesa's second wife, left a description of the visit she and her husband paid to Levyssohn Norman and his wife in Batavia:

| | |
|---|---|
| Aja anoe matak seuri, | What made us smile was |
| loetjoe pisan mariksana, | his funny way of asking |
| Kangdjeng Ideler Levishon, | His Excellency Esquire Levyssohn |

| | |
|---|---|
| ari njaoerna ka ama, | when he said to our father, |
| begimana sakarang,[17] | "How are you doing? |
| apa soedah djadi gemoek, | Has he gained weight, |
| Raden Toemenggoeng di Lebak. | the Raden Tumenggung in Lebak? |
| | |
| Dahoeloe koeroes sekali, | In the past, he was very thin. |
| sajah harep banjak makan, | I hope he eats a lot. |
| misti banjak makan telor, | He should eat lots of eggs |
| dan lagi minoem bir djoega, | and also drink beer, |
| soepaja djadi koeat, | so that he will become strong." |
| ladjeng koe ama diwangsoel, | Then my husband answered: |
| koeatnja tiada koerang. | "His strength has not diminished. |
| | |
| Tatapi koeroesnja masih, | But he is still thin. |
| tida maoe gemoek djoega, | He does not want to be fat." |
| goemoedjeng toean Levishon, | Mr. Levyssohn smiled. |
| ngalahir deui njonjana, | Then his wife spoke, |
| njang koeroes lebih koeat, | "Thin people are stronger |
| dari pada orang gemoek, | than fat people |
| asal boekan sakit sadjah. | as long as they are not ill." |

(Danoeredja 1929: 22–23)

This casual conversation shows their close and unusual relationship. In Betawi (Batavia), they met not only with Levyssohn Norman but also with other Dutch gentlemen and ladies. Many of them were newcomers, the effect of all sorts of far-reaching changes in colonial life after 1870 in which the growing number of women (the majority were wives and daughters of government employees and private entrepreneurs) played a prominent role (Doorn 1983: 19–20). Most of these new immigrants lived in the cities — Batavia, Semarang, Surabaya and, later, Medan — and formed a community and culture that tried to emphasize Dutchness. The Sundanese *menak* may have been greatly intrigued by this unfamiliar lifestyle.

Moesa and his wife were invited to receptions that impressed both (Danoeredja 1929: 23). Together with her and two relatives, Djoeariah and Adang, he paid a visit to J.H.B. Kuneman, who later became the Resident of Buitenzorg. Moesa's wife was to describe the meeting as follows:

| | |
|---|---|
| Ladjeng bae ama pamit, | Then our father took leave |
| poekoel satengah dalapan, | at seven thirty. |
| ama embok ladjeng bae, | Our father and I |
| ngandjang ka toean Kuneman, | paid a visit to Mr. Kuneman. |
| Nji Djoea hanteu tinggal, | Ms. Djoea also came along, |
| Adang oge hanteu kantoen, | and Adang joined us too. |
| barang gok tepoeng djeung toean. | At the time we met the gentleman. |
| | |
| Semoe langkoeng soeka ati, | His face showed his delight, |
| reh geus lawas hanteu tepang, | because we had not met for a long time. |
| soemawonna sareng embok, | Especially with me, |
| teu tepang geus lawas pisan, | he had not met for a long time. |
| tapi mangsa harita, | But at that time |
| njonjana keur rada ngangloeh, | his wife was rather ill and |
| teu jasa tjalik di loear. | she could not sit outside. |
| | |
| Kasawat borang koe angin, | I feared she would expose herself to the wind. |
| ladjeng embok sareng Djoea, | Then Djoea and I were |
| ditjandak bae ka djero, | brought inside the house. |
| barang gok oge patepang, | At that time we met each other, |
| langkoeng-langkoeng ngakoena, | she really respected us. |
| eling keur djaman kapoengkoer, | She remembered the time, |
| tepang di Tasikmalaja. | when we met in Tasikmalaya. |

(Danoeredja 1929: 24)

This poetic description suggests that Moesa and his family entertained quite informal relationships with the Dutch officials, and the description of his subsequent meetings with other authorities merely confirms this: the inspector of indigenous education and his wife received the Sundanese *panghulu* and his relatives at home, and while he was discussing educational issues with his Dutch superior, "an old friend" (*sobat lawas*), the women were chatting away in Dutch about household affairs (Danoeredja 1929: 25).

Of course, Moesa considered the meeting with His Excellency the Governor-General of the Dutch East Indies, Frederik s'Jacob himself, as the highlight of this journey. They met in s'Jacob's residence in Bogor, an indication that Moesa was considered an important figure by the government. s'Jacob arranged for Moesa's wife and Djoeariah to meet with his sister-in-law and daughter-in-law, and the next Sunday, at 9 o'clock in the morning, the two of them went to the Governor-General's residence without Moesa. Moesa's wife retold her meeting with the ladies, as follows:

| | |
|---|---|
| Di gedoeng teh embok langkoeng soeka ati, | Inside the building I was very pleased |
| ningal kalangenan, | to see the lovely things |
| sarwa aloes sarwa rasmi, | all beautiful and pleasant. |
| tambah aja hidji njonja. | And there was a lady, |
| | |
| Noe bareto basa madjoe teu kapanggih, | whom I had not met at the time of the audience, |
| tjarios iparna, | She told us she was the sister-in-law |
| Goepernoer Djenderal van Indi, | of the Governor-General of the Indies. |
| langkoeng sae panampina. | She received us very cordially. |
| | |
| Jasa basa Malajoe oelatna manis, | She could speak Malay, and had a sweet face. |
| rea mariksana, | She asked all sorts of things |
| hal Banten hal di Batawi, | about Banten and Batawi |
| ka embok sareng ka Djoea. | to Djoea and me. |
| | |
| Kitoe deui njonja s'Jacob anoe manis, | The friendly Mrs. s'Jacob did the same. |
| ka Djoea mariksa, | She asked Djoea |
| naon-naon noe kapanggih, | about things she had seen |

| | |
|---|---|
| Lebak Pangdegelang Serang. | in Lebak, Pangdegelang, and Serang. |
| | |
| Ka embok mah ngan imoet ngadjakan seuri, | To me she only smiled charmingly, |
| minangka ngakoena, | as she respected me. |
| djeung Djoea bae ngetjewis, | She chatted with Djoea only, |
| tjarita basa Walanda. | speaking in Dutch. |
| | |
| Henteu kesel tina boga lawan deui, | I was not bored for I had a person to talk to, |
| njonja ipar tea, | that was the sister-in-law. |
| djeung embok bae ngetjewis, | She chatted with me only. |
| njonja mantoe sareng Djoea. | The daughter-in-law was with Djoea. |
| | |
| Pirang-pirang soesoegoehna noe aramis, | There were plenty of sweets, |
| sagala inoeman, | all kinds of drinks. |
| koekoeehan warni-warni, | There were all kinds of cakes. |
| embok henteu petot heran. | I could not help being surprised, |
| | |
| Tina tjara oerang narima tatami, | compared to how we receive guests. |
| bet nganggo njoegoehan, | After entertaining us with refreshments, |
| ladjeng njandak ngider deui, | we were given a tour, |
| ngasoepan sagala kamar. | we entered all the rooms. |

(Danoeredja 1929: 27)

Still, there were some Dutchmen whom Moesa evaded at all costs: the missionaries. The letter that one of them, Christian Albers, who lived at Cianjur from 1863 to 1885 and worked for the Netherlands Missionary Union (NZV) (Coppel 1986: 18), wrote to his superiors in Rotterdam is telling:

> The hostility is bitter, even among the Muslims who are praised as being liberal or rather "enlightened". I asked the *Panghulu* of Garut,

Moehammad Moesa, to grant me a meeting during his stay in Cianjur. He declined to receive me in the polite indigenous manner, yet his house is open to the Chinese as well as Hollanders.

Die vijandschap is bitter, ook bij die Mohammedanen, die men als vrijzinnig of liever als "verlichte" uitkrijt. [...] De Panghoeloe van Garoet Mohammad Moesa vroeg ik om belet tijdens hij op Tjiandjoer was. Op de inlandsche beleefde manier, weigerde hij mij te ontvangen; terwijl zijn huis open is, zoowel voor Chinezen als Hollanders.[18]

Albers faced difficulties and hostility from the beginning, and did not succeed in making close contacts with the Sundanese in the Priangan Regencies. The Muslims were hostile and distrustful, and the Dutch authorities, inspired by Holle, were also not very positive with respect to the missionaries (End 1991: 102, 157). Holle too had a deep distrust of their activities, and no doubt shared these feelings with his good friend Moesa. For instance, in a letter to P.J. Veth, Holle wrote:

That Christian intolerance has brought much harm, especially Koorders: he saw to it that the *panghulu* (Moesa) did not dare to write anything, a reluctance I still have not been able to overcome completely.

Die christelijke onverdraagzaamheid deed een boel kwaad. Vooral Koorders, die oorzaak was, dat de panghoeloe er tegen op zag iets te schrijven, een weerzin die ik nog niet geheel heb kunnen overwinnen.[19]

The feelings of distrust and contempt were mutual.[20] Koorders called Moesa "a sly hoofdpanghulu" and was very bitter and sour about the writings of Holle's friend (Koorders in Meinsma 1869: 275–89). He was not the only European who thought that Moesa was a cunning opportunist who tried to curry favour with Dutch officials in every possible way for his personal benefit (Levyssohn Norman 1888b: 95).

The government made use of people like Moesa, an aristocrat with his own agenda, to collect information and intelligence about the local people and situations. More than once Moesa was sent on an inspection tour. Time and again, he was asked advice on matters of agriculture and religion,[21] and more than once he accompanied Dutch officials on their tours in Java. With Holle, he made journeys to Aceh (1871) and to Singapore (1873) to investigate how the Islamic community in Singapore supported the Muslims in Aceh (Levyssohn Norman 1888b: 95).

The *panghulu* of Limbangan could also be used to convey the will of the government to the indigenous population. The colonial administration needed figures like him. A good illustration of Moesa's good services is the way he was involved in the reorganization of the so-called *Preangerstelsel* (Preanger System). Until 1870, villagers were obliged to provide the government (and their local representatives) with land and labour so that commercial crops could be produced and sold for fixed prices. The Agrarian Laws of 1870 brought radical changes in the way land was owned and products were traded. The government gained more direct control over the peasants than before, and their local chiefs were made salaried government officials. In West Java, the implementation of these laws was supervised by Otto van Rees, who later became Governor-General (1884–8). Moesa came to know him personally and worked in close cooperation with him, persuading local chiefs and clerics to agree with them. Not least because of Moesa's activities, the government did not face any serious opposition from the local chiefs in the Priangan Regencies, even though their income and privileges were curtailed. Eventually the government awarded him a gold medal as a sign of gratitude for all the work he had done. It was not the only medal Moesa received: several times he was rewarded for his books and for his work as a civil servant.

Equally honourable was his honorary membership in the Batavian Society of Arts and Sciences.[22] It was another key for widening his social network and strengthening his status among the Europeans as well as the Sundanese.

In a letter to the wife of the Regent of Sumedang, Raden Ajoe Radjapamerat, Moesa tacitly showed his pride in being acquainted with the *toean-toean* (gentlemen) in Batavia:

| | |
|---|---|
| Djisim koering remen ngoeping, | I often hear that |
| toean-toean noe ngaroepat, | the gentlemen are gossiping about you, |
| tapi lain ngoepat awon, | but not saying bad things |
| ngan ngagoengkeun ka gamparan, | only honouring you |
| dina hal kadaharan, | for your dinners. |
| di Betawi enggeus mashoer, | In Betawi it is well known |
| di Soemedang ngeunah dahar. | that in Sumedang the food is tasteful. |
| | |
| Noe kakoeping koe sim koering, | I heard that |
| lain hidji doea toean, | not just from one or two gentlemen, |

| | |
|---|---|
| malah Kangdjeng Toean van Rees, | even His Excellency Mr. van Rees, |
| noe djadi Besar ajeuna, | who has become important nowadays. |
| kitoe oepatanana, | He speaks like this: |
| Raden Ajoe nomer satoe, | "Raden Ajoe is number one, |
| jang bisa oeroes sagala. | she can take care of everything." |

(Danoeredja 1929: 52)

As the last two lines in the above poem shows, conversations between the indigenous people and Dutch officials were usually in Malay. Moesa and his wife could speak and write Malay (Danoeredja 1929). Malay had become the major language of communication in the Dutch East Indies' civil service in the second half of the nineteenth century. As Moesa noted, a growing number of Malay words were entering the Sundanese vocabulary, both "Dutch-made" and everyday words, and this process intensified when government-subsidized schools were established and printed books began to be read. Malay was to play an increasingly important and significant role in the Sundanese community, as it was the language of modernity.

Moesa tried to write "clean" or "pure" (*bersih*) Sundanese, but in the preface of *Dongeng-dongeng Pieunteungeun*, published in 1867, he confessed that it was not easy. The following stanzas, already quoted in the first chapter, are worth reading again in this context:

| | |
|---|---|
| Anoe matak basa Soenda, | The reason the Sundanese language can |
| diseboetkên hoedang gering, | be said to be in the process of recovering, |
| tapi tatjan djagdjag pisan, | but not yet completely well. |
| boektina tatjan walagri, | The evidence that it is not yet healthy, |
| basana tatjan bêrsih, | is that the language is not yet pure, |
| tjampoer Djawa djêng Malajoe, | mixed with Javanese and Malay, |
| soemawon basa Arab, | even with Arabic. |
| eta noe reja teh têing, | That is too many, |
| malah aja noe enggês lêngit djinisna. | there are even some which have lost their original forms. |

| | |
|---|---|
| Koela lain pisan ngoepat, | I am not talking about others. |
| gês karasa koe pribadi, | I have felt this myself. |
| poegoeh koela oerang Soenda, | Certainly I am a Sundanese, |
| tatapi hese teh têing, | but it is very difficult |
| noelis soepaya bêrsih, | to write purely |
| masing basa Soenda woengkul, | using only Sundanese. |
| tatapi tatjan bisa, | But I am not yet able, |
| sangkilang diati-ati, | no matter how careful I am, |
| koedoe bae aja basa noe njampoeran. | there must be other languages mixed in it. |

(Moesa 1867:5)

In this quotation, Moesa mentions three languages (*basa*): Javanese (*Jawa*), Malay (*Malayu*), and Arabic (*Arab*). "Not yet completely healthy" summarizes in a natural metaphor his perception of the Sundanese language at the time, considered only as a spoken language by the majority of Europeans and Sundanese aristocrats. Sundanese was not a language for writing, least of all for use in official correspondence. Moesa was realistic enough to recognize the importance of Javanese and Arabic as well as Malay. Javanese was still a symbol of elite culture, a norm of literary writing, and a sign of education (Djajadiningrat 1936: 1–64). Moesa was born into a traditional and well-to-do aristocratic family and he wrote in Javanese (in both Javanese and Roman scripts) when performing his official duties for the Dutch administration as *hoofdpanghulu*. Brought up in an Islamic environment, having made the pilgrimage to Mecca, and working as a *(hoofd) panghulu*, he was familiar with Arabic writing too. Indeed, Moesa lived in the complexity of various languages and scripts but was conscious of the differences.

### Retrospect

Fifty years after the death of Moesa and forty years after the death of Holle, the Regent of Cianjur, Soeria Nata Atmadja, kept the memory of the close friendship of Moesa and Holle alive:

> With great gratitude and deep respect many Sundanese remember the days those two eminent figures, who were bosom friends, were the talk

of the town: Mr. K.F. Holle and R.H. Moehamad Moesa, *Hoofd-Panghulu* of Limbangan, now the Regency of Garut.

Met groote erkentelijkheid en diep ontzag denkt menige Soendanees aan den tijd, dat die twee eminente figuren, boezemvrienden van elkander, op ieders lippen waren, terug. Het waren de heer K.F. Holle en R.H. Moehamad Moesa, Hoofd-Penghoeloe van Limbangan (het tegenwoordige regentschap Garoet) (Soeria Nata Atmadja 193?: 13).

The friendship became a legendary one, but its aura turned fragile in the early twentieth century. Open criticism of Moesa began after 1945, when the Dutch lost its influence on Indonesian politics and society. He came to be seen as an opportunistic and ambitious man; the fact that he bowed so often to the Dutch was seen as a disgrace. Rumours spread that the colonial government had rewarded him for his devoted services in many ways: had not his seven descendants been made regents, including R.A.A. Musa Suriakartalegawa,[23] the last Regent of Garut (Salmoen 1955: 438)? Such stories are still known among the Sundanese today, especially in the Garut area.[24] The local people know that Moesa's family was the wealthiest in the region, and it is easy to link this to his cooperation with the Dutch. In short, many people hold negative opinions of him, although some speak in admiration of Moesa's and Holle's contributions to agriculture.

There is a well-known poem which ridicules the *wadana* (district chief) of the Suci district in Garut:

| | |
|---|---|
| Ajang-ajang agoeng - goeng, | Two men are walking shoulder to shoulder, |
| goeng goongna ramé - mé, | a big drum rings loudly, |
| menak ki Mas Tanoe - noe, | an aristocrat Mr. Tanu, |
| noe djadi Wadana - na, | he becomes Wadana, |
| naha mana kitoe - toe, | why does he do so? |
| toekang olo-olo - lo, | he is a flatterer, |
| loba anoe giroek - roek, | many people do not like him, |
| roeket ka koempeni - ni, | he is close to the colonial government, |
| nijat djadi pangkat - kat, | his intention is to become a high official, |
| katon kagorèngan - ngan, | his evil is exposed, |

ngantos Kangdjeng Dalem - lem,    he waits on the Regent,
lempa-lempi-lempong,    lempa-lempi-lempong
ngadoe pipi djeung noe ompong.    cheek to cheek, toothless.

(Poeradiredja 1919: 407)

At the First Congress for Language, Geography and Ethnography in Java in 1919, this satirical poem was introduced as one of the most well-known Sundanese poems by R. Poeradiredja, the chief editor for the Sundanese language in the office of *Volkslectuur*, and M. Soerijadiradja, a teacher of Sundanese and Malay in the *Opleidingsschool* (training school) at Serang. They argued that the poem was composed by the people to ridicule the excessive ambitions of Moesa. To the joy of many, it was sung at the Congress.[25]

Quite by accident, the author was told in an interview conducted in 1994 that this *kawih* had been a creation of Moesa himself.[26] He had been afraid that his sons would be defeated by a rival, the chief of Suci district, a man named Tanoe. Knowing that gossip and rumours could be a sharp weapon, he had seen to it that the song became known. Tanoe's capabilities were questioned, his cunning ridiculed, but little did Moesa know that his song would backfire on himself.

It was a surprise to hear Sundanese children singing the same *kawih* in the remote village of Cikalong Kulon close to Cianjur, where the author lived for four months in 1984. They were singing cheerfully and clapping hands in a circle while enjoying and shouting out the rhyming words. This *kawih* about a cunning *wadana* has been sung for more than a hundred years! Most people do not know the name Moesa any longer, but a handful of old Sundanese said that the song was about Moesa, "that friend of the Dutch", "a deceitful and cunning man".

## 2. Moesa, the Author

In the context of an oral, largely chirographic culture such as the Sundanese, the novelty of Moesa's writing was primarily that it was produced in print.[27] He was one of the first local writers whose creations were made into printed books, and in so many copies that they initially outnumbered not only all manuscripts but also all other printed books.

As seen earlier, with the help of Holle, Moesa's handwritten texts were brought from Limbangan to Batavia, where they were printed by the Landsdrukkerij, each book having between 2,000 and 4,000 copies for the first impression (VIO 1866: 275-7). *Ali Moehtar* (The Story of Ali Muhtar), for instance, had 3,030 copies printed and was sold for 0.08 Dutch guilders each.

Altogether, Moehamad Moesa published 14 books, most of which were reprinted several times (see the list of his publications in Table 10). For instance, *Tjarita Abdoerahman djêng Abdoerahim* was published in

Table 10. Publications by Moehamad Moesa

| | |
|---|---|
| 1862 | *Wawacan Raja Sudibya* (*Wawacan* of King Sudibya); Javanese script, *wawacan*. |
| 1862 | *Wawacan Wulang Krama* (*Wawacan* Teaching Courtesy); Javanese, *wawacan*. |
| 1923 | – in *Soendaneesche Volksalmanak*, Roman script. |
| 1862 | *Wawacan Dongeng-Dongeng* (*Wawacan* of Fables); Javanese, translated from a Malay adaptation of European fables. |
| 1862 | *Wulang-tani* (Lessons for Farmers); Javanese *wawacan*. |
| 1863 | *Carita Abdurahman jeung Abdurahim* (The Story of Abdurahman and Abdurahim) Roman/Javanese, prose, translated from Arabic? |
| 1881 | – in the anthology compiled by G.J. Grashuis, Roman script. |
| 1884 | – 2nd ed., Javanese. |
| 1885 | – Roman. |
| 1906 | – 3rd ed., Javanese. |
| 1908 | – 3rd ed., Roman. |
| 1911 | – 4th ed., Roman. |
| 1877 | – Javanese translation by Raden Angga Baja |
| 1925 | – Malay translation by Balai Poestaka |
| 1863 | *Wawacan Seca Nala* (*Wawacan* of Seca Nala); Roman/Javanese, *wawacan*, 3050 ex., f. 0.11. |
| 1864 | *Ali Muhtar* (The story of Ali Muhtar); Roman/Javanese, *wawacan*, 3030 ex., f. 0.08. |
| 1883 | – 2nd ed., Roman. |
| 1864 | *Elmu Nyawah* (A Guide for Wet Rice Cultivation); Roman/Javanese, *wawacan*, 4050 ex., f. 0.22. |
| 1865 | *Wawacan Wulang Murid* (*Wawacan* of Lessons for Students); Javanese, *wawacan*, 2050 ex., f. 0.06. |
| 1865 | – Roman. |

*(cont'd overleaf)*

**Table 10.** *Continued*

| | |
|---|---|
| 1865 | *Wawacan Wulang Guru* (*Wawacan* of Lessons for Teachers); Javanese, *wawacan*, 550 ex., f. 0.04. |
| 1865 | – Roman. |
| 1866 | *Dongeng-dongeng nu Araneh* (The Wonder Stories); Javanese, prose, 3050 ex., f. 0.16. |
| 1884 | new ed., Javanese. |
| 1890 | 2nd ed., Javanese. |
| 1867 | *Dongeng-dongeng Pieunteungeun* (Model Stories); Roman, prose, 3,050 ex., f. 0.28. |
| 1867 | – Javanese., 6,050 ex., f. 0.48. |
| 1888 | – new ed., Roman. |
| 1901 | – Roman. |
| 1904 | – Roman. |
| 1907 | – Roman. |
| 1912 | – Roman. |
| 1871 | *Wawacan Panji Wulung* (*Wawacan* of Panji Wulung); Javanese, *wawacan*. |
| 1876 | – Roman. |
| 1891 | – 2nd ed., Javanese. |
| 1901 | – new ed., Roman. |
| 1904 | – Roman. |
| 1908 | – 3rd ed., Javanese. |
| 1909 | – Roman. |
| 1913 | – reprint ed., Roman. |
| 1922 | – 4th ed., Javanese. |
| 1879 | – Javanese translation by Pangeran Adipati Ario Mangkoe Negoro IV, Javanese. |
| 1872 | *Wawacan Lampah Sebar* (*Wawacan* Guide for Seeding); Roman/Javanese *wawacan*. |
| 1872 | – *Lampah Sebar*, Roman/Javanese, prose. |
| 1874 | – *Katrangan Lampah Sebar* (Explanation of Seeding), Javanese, *wawacan*. |
| 1881 | Santri Gagal (A Santri Fell into Error); in the anthology compiled by G.J. Grashuis, Roman, prose. |
| 1881 | *Hibat* (The Gift) in the anthology compiled by G.J. Grashuis, Roman, prose. |

1863 for the first time, in a combination of Roman and Javanese scripts. In 1884, 1885, 1906, 1908, and 1911 it was published in Roman and Javanese script separately. A Javanese translation appeared in 1877 and a Malay one in 1925. Moesa wrote extensively over at least a ten-year period. His range of topics was diverse and can be divided into four categories: "belles-lettre" (4 titles plus 2 short stories); *wulang* (lessons or teachings) (4); books on agriculture (3); and fables (3).

Some of the titles are translations and adaptations, while some of them were written based on the knowledge provided by Holle (especially the books on agriculture, the *wulang* books, and fables). The so-called "belles-lettres" books are mostly original. Moesa's masterpiece is *Wawacan Panji Wulung*. Javanese and Roman scripts were used for the publications, but not the Arabic script.

There are many *wawacan* among his writings, 11 in total. Holle's ideas influenced the writing of his friend considerably: poetry was the symbol of Sundanese culture and the best media for enlightenment. The other three works are in prose, all translations. The two short stories were published in the anthology compiled by Grashuis: *Hibat* (The Gift), and *Santri Gagal* (A Santri Fell into Error).[28] Technically, every kind of writing can be composed in *dangding*, but Moesa believed that translations of foreign tales were more effective in prose. He himself explained, "it is not difficult to make *dangding*, but prose will be more effective. Prose will never be disturbed by songs, and stories can progress fast. Story is not perturbed by *dangding*, so it is pleasant to listen to and easy to understand" (Moesa 1867: 5). It is an interesting remark: apparently prose was thought to be more transparent than poetry. In this he seemed to follow Dutch ideas so that prose gradually gained the upper hand over poetry. This will be discussed later.

## *Recognition*

During the second half of the nineteenth century and in the early twentieth century, the Dutch regarded Moesa as the best Sundanese author, or at least the most prominent one. Grashuis, one of the nineteenth-century specialists on Sundanese language and literature, wrote of him in the introduction to his anthology of Sundanese writing in 1881:

> From the linguistic point of view they may be important, [but] these writings cannot claim to be works of literary art. The poetry is doggerel, and the prose remains at a low level. I will not say anything

more about the first. As for the second, I can merely state that the *Panghulu* of Garoet is the master, leaving his predecessors far behind. Though, in his verse style he may have his equals, in his prose he stands alone, like a wonderful forest tree in the middle of scrub. He is really the first Sundanese who has his own style; those who produced prose before him did not rise above the daily manner of speech, in narrative or argument. However, it is a pity that he has composed too many poems and does not restrict himself to writing prose, or at least focus on that.

> Van belang uit een taalkundig oogpunt beschouwd, hebben zij geene aanspraak op den naam van litterarische kunstvoortbrengselen. De poëzie is gerijmel, en het proza blijft laag bij den grond. Van de eerste spreek ik te dezer plaatse niet verder. Wat het laatste betreft, ik kan slechts getuigen dat de Panghoeloe van Garoet daarin een meester is, die al zijne voorgangers verre achter zich laat. In zijn dichtstijl moge hij worden geëvenaard, zijn proza staat geheel alleen, als een prachtige woudboom te midden van laag kreupelhout. Hij is wezenlijk de eerste Soendanees, die een eigen stijl heeft al de anderen, die voor hem proza hebben geleverd, verheffen zich niet boven den dagelijkschen spreektrant, hetzij in het verhaal, hetzij in het betoog. Alleen is het jammer, dat hij te veel verzen maakt, en zich niet uitsluitend of althans hoofdzakelijk toelegt op het schrijven van proza (Grashuis 1881: xi).

The Dutch did not appreciate Sundanese poetry, which they thought to be simple, boring, and repetitive — and poetry was what most Sundanese writers produced. Moehamad Moesa was the first contemporary who wrote prose that was more or less acceptable.

The recognition of Moesa as "the best Sundanese writer" gradually became a conventional phrase, and found its climax in the lemma "*Soendaneesch*" in the authoritative Encyclopaedia of the Dutch East Indies:

> Sundanese is very well suited to a simple and clear prose style, and a good writer, such as the late Radén Hadji Moehammad Moesa, who was the respectable *Panghulu* in Garoet, knows how to handle his mother tongue so that smoothness and ease of composition give evidence of the excellence of the language and of the large reservoir of words and expressions that it possesses.

> Het Soend. heeft veel geschiktheid voor eenvoudigen en duidelijken prozastijl, en een goed schrijver, zooals wijlen Radén Hadji Moehammad Moesa, de verdienstelijke Panghoeloe van Garoet, weet zijne moedertaal zoo te hanteren, dat de losheid en gemakkelijkheid der rede bewijs

levert van de voortreffelijkheid der taal en van den ruimen voorraad van woorden en uitdrukkingen, waarover zij te beschikken heeft (*Encyclopaedie* 1921: vol. 4, 22).

Equally important in the canonization of Moesa's work must have been the positive opinion that one of the most influential scholars of the Dutch East Indies, Snouck Hurgronje, had for the contribution of Karel Holle and Sundanese intellectuals like Moesa in the field of indigenous publishing. In contrast with his predecessors, Snouck Hurgronje appreciated both prose and poetry in Sundanese. [29]

> Kohlburgge, who can only speak scornfully of the Malay readers that have been published by the government, seems not to know that forty years ago Karel Holle inspired some intellectual Sundanese (the *Hoofdpanghulu* of Garut, Raden Haji Moesa, his son who later became *Patih* of Sukabumi, the *Patih* of Mangunreja Atmadibrata and so forth, all of them now deceased) to write civilising popular books, some in prose, some in indigenous poetry. He does not know either that these Sundanese books, written by Sundanese, found some acceptance even without the tactful, almost cunning, manner of introduction, which Kohlburgge wrongly believes necessary.
>
> Kohlburgge, die slechts smalend weet te spreken van Maleische leesboeken, die van Regeeringswege zijn uitgegeven, schijnt niet te weten, dat reeds veertig jaren geleden Karel Holle een aantal intelligente Soendaneezen, thans evenals hijzelf reeds overleden, (den Hoofdpanghoeloe van Garoet, Raden Hadji Moesa, diens zoon, den lateren Patih van Soekaboemi, den Patih van Mangoenredja Atmadibrata, enz.) tot het schrijven van zulke beschavende volksboekjes, deels in proza, deels in inlandsche dichtmaat, wist te inspireeren en dat die Soendaneesche, door Soendaneezen geschreven werkjes gereedelijk ingang vonden ook zonder de meer dan beleidvolle, bijkans listige wijze van introductie, die Kohlbrugge daarvoor geheel ten onrechte nodig acht (Snouck Hurgronje 1927:117).

This is not to say that all Dutch scholars praised Moesa. In Chapter 1, mention was made of Koorders, the Sundanese specialist sent by the government to West Java. Koorders did not think much of Holle's friend's activities: their main aim was to make money, he claimed. In a report to the Governor-General in Batavia in 1864, he bitterly criticized Moesa's *Wawacan Woelang Krama* (Wawacan Teaching Courtesy) (Koorders in Meinsma 1869: 285–8). Moesa was a "repetitious writer" and his books were almost completely useless:

I feel obliged to ask the government's attention for the *panghulu*'s tendency to be long-winded, because it is surely an expensive hobby for the state. I think that an honorarium of 100 guilders for sixteen pages in small octavo of Sundanese script is really a stunning sum of money, it exceeds by at least five times what men such as van Oosterzee or Opzoomer earn in our Fatherland. If we take the daily needs and income of a native into consideration, it is truly an astonishing sum of money.

Ik acht me verplicht, ook-daarom de aandacht der Regeering op die neiging van den pangoeloe tot omslachtigheid te vestigen, omdat het een, voor den Lande zeer kostbare liefhebberij is. Me dunkt, een honorarium van honderd gulden voor zestien bladzijden klein 8° Soendaneesch letterschrift een honorarium, minstens vijf malen overtreffende wat aan mannen als van Oosterzee en Opzoomer in ons Vaderland wordt toegekend, en als men de gewone behoeften en inkomsten van een inlander in aanmerking neemt, een waarlijk verbazingwekkende som zulk een honorarium is te hoog, om een dergelijke omslachtigheid te kunnen dulden (Koorders in Meinsma 1869: 286).

Moesa did indeed earn a considerable amount of money. For his 14 publications, totalling some 1,200 pages, he received at least 7,500 guilders from the government. In some cases, the money was easy: Roman script on the left page and Javanese script on the right page gives a double income for one and the same composition. With the composition of *Wawacan Lampah Sebar* (Wawacan Guide for Seeding, 1872), Moesa earned fivefold for a single piece of work: the text was published in *wawacan* and in prose, printed in the two scripts on facing pages, and then another version in Javanese script. No wonder Koorders expressed his annoyance about the misuse of government funds, and he may have touched some sensitive chords: the government wanted everything to be cheap.

Not only the honorarium but also the quality of writing was criticized by Koorders. Firmly believing that he knew Sundanese better than the Sundanese authors themselves, he made a large number of corrections to the writings of Moesa (and others) in his report to the Governor-General: he replaced words and sometimes totally rewrote passages.

Moesa, in short, was a bad author, according to Koorders, and his work should no longer be published. Koorders' criticisms and suggestions, however, were not taken seriously by the government, and one can only wonder why. Apparently, Moesa's authority and Holle's political power had already been established too firmly.

The Sundanese did not necessarily share the government's appreciation for Moesa's publications. A writer, in the *Volksalmanak Soenda* of 1919, for instance, affirmed that every literate Sundanese knew that Moesa was an author who wrote books for the Sundanese people but added that the books Moesa had composed in *dangding* were of questionable quality, and too long at that (Anonymous 1919: 318–9). On the other hand, one of the most respected and famous Sundanese intellectuals of the early twentieth century, Memed Sastrahadiprawira, a contemporary of Snouck Hurgronje, praised the literary talent of Moehamad Moesa, embedded as it was in the wealth of Sundanese literature. Sastrahadiprawira felt that Moesa's writings were admirable and wonderful, but at the same time his poetry was not as good as his contemporary poet Aria Bratawidjaja, who was well-known as *bujangga* (the best poet). Sastrahadiprawira carried out a counter-critique of an article written by an anonymous author who had underestimated Sundanese literature:[30]

> By acknowledging R. Haji Moehamad Moesa's talent as an author, the critic unconsciously contests his own opinion. Indeed, the recognition also implies the recognition of the existence of prizeworthy literature. That the *hoofdpanghulu*, who is now still known everywhere, indeed had a great literary talent might be evident from his many kinds of writings, which are still loved much, both in prose and in poetry, for example, *Panji Wulung, Dongeng Pieunteungeun, Ali Muhtar, Wulang Krama, Abdurahman jeung Abdurahim* and so forth. Haji Moehamad Moesa is rightly called a good writer while his contemporary R. Aria Bratadiwijaya has surely deserved the title of *Bujangga*, because it is generally said of him that he is superior in elegance of style, in the right choice of words and in depth of feeling to the famous *Panghulu*.

> Door het schrijverstalent van R. Hadji Moehamad Moesa te erkennen, bestrijdt de beoordeelaar onbewust zijn eigen meening. Immers, deze erkenning sluit tevens in zich de erkenning van het bestaan van prijzenswaardige literatuur. Dat de ook thans nog alom bekende hoofd-Pangoeloe inderdaad een groot literair talent bezat, moge blijken uit zijn veelsoortige, nog steeds uiterst geliefde werken, zoowel in proza als in poëzie, b.v. Pandji Woeloeng, Dongèng Pieunteungeun, Ali Mochtar, Woelang Krama, Abdoerahman en Abdoerahim, e.a. Gold Raden Hadji Moehamad Moesa terecht voor een goed schrijver, zijn tijdgenoot R. Aria Bratadiwidjaja, heeft stellig den titel van *Boedjangga* verdiend, want algemeen wordt van hem gezegd, dat hij in sierlijkheid van stijl, in juistheid van woordkeus en in diepte van gevoel de meerdere is van den vermaarden Pangoeloe (Sastrahadiprawira 1929b: 18).

This was a time of expansion for Dutch school education, and as a result, print literacy in the Sundanese community was increasing: Moesa's books were used at schools and read by many people. Not only should Moesa's writings be read, wrote someone using the pseudonym Goeroe (Teacher) in *Poesaka-Soenda*, a Sundanese journal in 1926: Moesa should inspire us to read other older Sundanese stories as well (Goeroe 1926: 13–4). Moesa's reputation was to survive even the Revolution: in 1955, the well-known Sundanese author M.A. Salmoen could still write, albeit ironically:

> Even today, there are not a few old men born in the second half of the nineteenth century who think that the poetry of Moehamad Moesa was "by far the best", beyond comparison, without a single mistake. Many among the eldest generation are fanatical admirers of Moehamad Moesa.
>
> Bahkan kini, tidak sedikit kakek-kakek jang dilahirkan pada bagian kedua abad XIX jang beranggapan, bahwa puisi Muhammad Moesa itu adalah "non plus ultra" jang sudah tidak ada bandingnja lagi, sudah mustahil salah. Tidak sedikit diantara para Embah itu pemudja Muhammad Musa jang fanatik (Salmoen 1955: 437).

Salmoen himself did not think that Moesa was the greatest writer. His poetry was artificial, Salmoen felt, stretching the rules of verse form beyond every possible elegance. His prose was interesting, but his work had been almost the only reading material available to Salmoen's grandparents in their youth, exerting a deep influence on them, especially on those who were educated at government schools (Salmoen 1955: 435–7).

> Since they sat in *Kabupaten*-School (a kind of People's School in the second half of the nineteenth century), they had to swallow "Pieunteungeun". Then when they became a bit older, they studied works such as "Ali Muhtar" and "Panji Wulung". That was for the schoolchildren. Meanwhile, Muslim pupils were taught to read "Ki Santri Gagal" and "Hibat". Peasants were given "Elmu Nyawah". When they started a household, "Wulang Krama" (meaning more or less "A Guide for the Perfect Married Life") was prepared by their parents. When the time came to teach their children, they would go back to "Pieunteungeun", continuously moving from one to another of Moesa's works. So it is clear how far and deep the influence of Moehammad Moesa reached.

Sedjak mereka itu duduk di Sekolah-Kabupaten (sedjenis Sekolah Rakjat pada bagian ke II abad XIX), sudah mesti menelan "Pieunteungeun". Agak besar sedikit dikunjahnja misalnja "Alimuchtar" dan "Pandjiwulung". Itu untuk anak-anak sekolah. Sedang untuk santri-santri diusahakan agar dapat dibatjanja "Ki Santri Gagal" atau "Hibat". Kaum tani diberinja "Elmu Njawah". Bila hendak berumahtangga, disadjikanlah oleh orangtuanja "Wulangkrama" (Kira-kira maksudnja "Petundjuk Untuk Perkawinan Jang Sempurna"). Datang masanja mengadjar anaknja nanti, kembali lagi ke "Pieunteungeun" ... dan selandjutnja berputar-putar dari Muhammad Moesa ke Muhammad Moesa lagi. Djadi njata dan tegaslah, sampai dimana mendalamnja pengaruh Muhammad Moesa itu (Salmoen 1955: 437–8).

One of the most influential critics of Sundanese literature after independence, Ajip Rosidi, was willing to appreciate Moesa's *jasa* (contribution) to Sundanese literature. Moesa had introduced a new style of composition, but that did not make him one of the best authors or his work creations of an outstanding quality (Rosidi 1966: 13). Moreover, Ajip Rosidi had critical words for Moesa's writings, which praised colonial policies (Ajip Rosidi in Musa 1990: 5). The most recent research on Moesa's *Wawacan Panji Wulung*, by Elis Suryani Nani Sumarlina, gives a well-balanced evaluation:

> It can be said that R.H. Moehamad Moesa was a pioneer or innovator in the framework of Sundanese literature, because he was the first to compose literary works of a realistic character. In his writings, Moehamad Moesa left behind the supernatural world and did not believe the superstition and mystery that coloured the other literary writings of his time. [...] The views and ideas expressed by Moehamad Moesa in his writings were greatly influenced by K.F. Holle, his close friend. No less important than this influence was the fact that Moehamad Moesa left behind Javanese as the literary language.

> R.H. Moehamad Moesa dapat dikatakan sebagai pelopor atau inovator dalam khazanah susastra Sunda, karena dialah yang mula-mula mengarang karya sastra bercorak realistis. Dalam karangan-karangan, Moehamad Moesa telah meninggalkan alam supernatural dan tidak percaya terhadap takhyul dan hal yang gaib yang pada periode itu masih mewarnai karya-karya sastra sezamannya. [...] Pandangan dan gagasan yang ditampilkan Moehamad Moesa dalam karya-karyanya mendapat pengaruh besar dari K.F. Holle sebagai teman dekatnya.

Hal lain yang tak kalah pentingnya dari pengaruh tersebut ialah bahwa Moehamad Moesa telah melepaskan bahasa Jawa sebagai bahasa tulis (Sumarlina 1990: 41–2).

## Moesa's writings

In a manuscript culture of a largely oral-aural character, readers vocalize the handwritten text in front of them, reading aloud slowly, even when alone: there always seems to be a feeling of community in that the words have to be shared. Reading aloud has yet another, material motivation: in manuscripts, words are run together or the spaces between them minimal, so that reading is an activity that literally makes sense of the words in the process of pronouncing them: one interprets the text by voicing it.

Clear punctuation as we know it in printed books did not exist in the Sundanese manuscript tradition, and this absence gives the writing a certain flow, a certain fluidity which only reading could bring to a halt.[31] This is different from printed texts in which commas, periods, and paragraph breaks bring reading to a halt. The new way of organizing discourse had effects on ways of thinking (Ong 1982: 117). In printed texts, the words are more visible, and hence they are far easier to read than manuscripts, especially for modern readers. This greater legibility tends to facilitate rapid, silent reading — which in turn leads to other forms of conceptualization and to other worldviews in which the accumulation of information prevails over the sharing of information.

The introduction of printed books into the world of Sundanese writing did not change reading habits at once. Manuscripts kept a place next to the books and (later) periodicals that spread in the wake of education and commodification. Only gradually did a substantial group of people emerge who were used to reading books, and concurrently developed new ideas of the world — ideas of "modernity", as will be seen in Chapter 4.

The books had the appearance of their European counterparts. In Moesa's books, title pages come first. They tell their readers the title of the book, the author, the printer and publisher (usually the same), and the place and year of publication. For instance, we can read such information on the title page of *Ali Moehtar* (see Plate 5). The layout of the printed book was designed by the Landsdrukkerij, run by the Dutch. Thus, printed books were modelled on the European book concept.

# ALI MOEHTAR

DOOR

**RADEN HADJI MOEHAMAD MOESA,**

HOOFD-PANGHOELOE

VAN

**LIMBANGAN.**

Gedrukt te Batavia, ter Lands-Drukkerij — 1864.

---

I

ASMARANDANA.

1 Ije tjarita di goerit, lalakon djalma ajena, hadé ékér baris tjouto, hanté anggang noe di tiṅgal, boekti ajéna pisau, tjitjingna di dajeh Garoet, inahna toekaṅgén pasar.

2 Djeṅg boga pakoewon déi, ngaraña kéboer Badama, bilangan Distrik Panémbong, kebon legana di Ngamlang, pinoeh koe pépélakan, pirang-pirang réwoe waroe, sarta salijan tidinja.

3 Pirang-pirang dapoer awi, asal tégal léga pisau, ajéna, béjak koe kébon, noe matak pantés di karang, niṅgal tina réjana, somahau di dajeh Garoet, noe tohaga ugan saoerang.

4 Toerta lain asal boemi, ka Garoet sedja ngoembara, oerang Bantén asalna téh, ngaraña ki Ali Moehtar, réja anoe oeniṅga, jén éta djalma téh boetoeh, datangna té mawa banda.

---

Plate 5. *Ali Moehtar*, published in 1864

Differences between printed books and the Sundanese manuscript tradition are obvious. The manuscripts usually had no titles in the European sense. For convenience, people used the name of the main protagonist of the story to identify the manuscript, or called them by generic names. Meanwhile, printed books had titles for the writing. They also had an independent title page, and even two title pages, one in Dutch and one in Sundanese (see Plate 5). Presumably, the Dutch title page was for the convenience of the Dutch authorities and readers — but it was intended to have an effect on Sundanese readers too: local culture is put into the context of European culture, the culture of the power-holder in the colony.

Printed books in the nineteenth century offered the name and identity of the author on the title page. The name and occupation, or rank in the colonial administration of the author were printed on the very first page. The writer became an "author", with a personal "authority", thus pushing the manuscript tradition aside. The title and name set him free from the task of transmitting the knowledge of the ancestors: he transmitted his own knowledge, so to speak, and he sanctified that knowledge by giving his own name and status. The author made himself visible, offering his readers new ways of organizing knowledge.

In the history of Sundanese writing, Moesa was regarded as a pioneer in writing that followed the European example:

> Because of Holle's influence, Moehamad Moesa began to write following European standards. Before Moehamad Moesa began the new style, the Sundanese people were used to texts written in a continuous flow without breaks. The writing had no commas and no full stops. Moreover, beginning a new paragraph after a full stop was very strange.
>
> More than that, manuscripts written before the time of Moehamad Moesa did not have the title of the work and the author. We would know the name of the book or story after we read it. Usually the titles are given following the names of the main protagonist. For instance, *Rêngganis, Abdulmuluk, Surianingrat, Anglingdarma, Lutung Kasarung, Mundinglaja, Tjiung Wanara* and many others. These stories have titles only because they are called so by the people. The author or copyist did not mention the titles.
>
> Ku pangaruh Holle, Muhammad Musa mimiti ngarang nurutkeun patokan[2] Barat. Da tadina mah, samemeh Muhammad Musa, urang Sunda teh lamun ngarang sok "ngagêbleg", tulisan teh djadi hidji teu

puguh komana, teu puguh peunna. Sumawaonna marake djadjaran anjar sabada peun mah, pohara asingna.

Leuwih ti kitu, naskah[2] samemeh Muhammad Musa mah hênteu disêbut ngaran bukuna djeung ngaran nu ngarangna. Kanjahoan soteh ngaran buku atawa ngaran tjarita, êngke lamun geus dibatja. Biasana mere ngaran tjarita teh nurutkeun ngaran anu njêkêl paranan utama. Upamana bae: *Rêngganis, Abdulmuluk, Surianingrat, Anglingdarma, Lutung Kasarung, Mundinglaja, Tjiung Wanara*, djeung pirang[2] deui. Kitu soteh si Tjarita bogaeun soteh ngaran, dingaranan ku djalma rea, lain ditulis ku nu ngarang atawa ku nu njalinna (Salmoen 1958: 131).

The list of Moesa's publications shows that many of his creations are in verse form (*dangding*). In this, he followed Sundanese tradition, and by doing so, he and his friends Holle and van der Chijs tried to reach out to Sundanese students who were familiar with this traditional way of conveying information and knowledge. *Dangding* was customarily chanted or recited and much loved by the people. Hence, its traditional poetic form would be pleasing to those who attended modern school because of its oral orientation, and at the same time effective in conveying content because of its popularity among the Sundanese. *Elmu Nyawah* (A Guide for the Cultivation of Rice in Sawah) is a good example. Traditional verse form notwithstanding, Moesa's writings were inspired by a new aesthetic and ideology in which practical information and colonial deference competed with traditional knowledge. In this sense, they were between tradition and modernity. Broadly speaking, Moesa's books have a strongly didactic and rationalistic character. They were meant to enlighten the public. Moesa tried to teach by way of showing good and bad examples. The influence of European allegories and fables is obvious. Moreover, Moesa often gave a short summary of events in a tale. The best example is the summary he gave of *Wawacan Panji Wulung* at the end of the book:

| | |
|---|---|
| 1010. Geus tamat ieu carita, | The story ends, |
| supaya jadi pepeling, | hopefully it will become a lesson, |
| rea keur bade tuladan, | many are the good examples |
| picontoeun anu bukti, | and models which are testified |
| lampah barang mimiti, | from the beginning of events. |
| katembong bohongna dukun, | It is evident that the *dukun* was a liar. |

| | |
|---|---|
| dukun jaman ayeuna, | Among *dukuns* of today |
| aya nu kitu deui, | there are some like that, |
| bohong bae caturna kasarumahan. | they lie and their words are mystified. |※

1011. Sanajan jaman ayeuna, / Even these days,
rea nu dadaku sakti, / many insist they possess supernatural powers,

majar maneh awas tingal, / saying that they have clear insight,
nyaho di nu gaib-gaib, / and knowledge of the supernatural.
ku jalma hanteu mikir, / People who do not think carefully
digugu caturna lepus, / believe their false stories.
ajar gunawisesa, / The *ajar* Guna Wisesa
norahna ka Tunjungsari, / foretells the destiny of Tunjungsari,
nyebut nyaho asal tina di bejaan. / he knew it but in fact he was informed.

1012. Jeung deui jadi tuladan, / Another suitable model is
menak anu lantip budi, / the aristocrat who thinks deliberately,

nurut piwuruk sepuhna, / follows the teaching of his parents and

satindak polah jeung budi, / any admirable wise behaviour.
tungtungna manggih mukti, / In the end [he] meets happiness
lulus jumenengna ratu, / and succeeds in becoming a king.
nya kitu deui jalma, / The same holds for people,
nu estu ngabdi ka gusti, / who are really loyal to the king
bersih pikir cara Patih Sokadana. / and think sincerely, like the viceroy Sokadana.

1013. Tungtungna manggih kamulyan, / In the end he meets glory
beurat beunghar sugih mukti, / and prospers in wealth and happiness.

putrana jumeneng raja, / His child becomes a king.

| | |
|---|---|
| lain asal tina dengki, | but not based on envy. |
| jeung jadi conto deui, | And what becomes another model is |
| | |
| jalma babari kawujuk, | one who is easily persuaded, |
| cara Papatih Cempa, | as is the viceroy of Cempa. |
| tungtungna balangsak diri, | In the end he suffers. |
| hirup soteh ngan manggih raja darana. | He only breathes by the king's grace. |
| | |
| 1014. Sumawonna eta jalma, | Even the man |
| nu hiri dengki ka gusti, | who envies his Lord |
| gede omong jijieunan, | and speaks lies with a big mouth, |
| tungtungna manggih balai, | in the end he meets disaster |
| tina kagedean ati, | because of his conceit. |
| wani ngamusuh ka ratu, | He dares to rebel against the king. |
| ratu rea baladna, | The king has many soldiers. |
| cacandran ti nini aki, | In the proverbial words of the old, |
| paribasa pacikrak ngalawan merak. | The proverb says "like a tailor-bird opposing a peacock". |
| | |
| 1015. Jog-jog neureuy buah loa, | He has a foolish wish. |
| tegesna lain paranti, | Apparently they are not in the same category. |
| ngahuap lain layanna, | He wishes wrong things. |
| nya-eta upama kuring, | The same as, if common people, |
| anu wani ka gusti, | who dare to oppose the king, |
| ngahangu-hangu ka ratu, | who insult the king, |
| nya cara ki Andaka, | will become like Andaka, |
| tungtungna dihukum pati, | who in the end is executed |
| paeh nista hulu dipanjer di jalan. | and dies in humiliation, his head exhibited in the street. |

In these stanzas, various words and expressions can be found that are key concepts in Moesa's writings and appear repeatedly. The first group of words has a positive meaning: *bukti* (testified to be true), *pepeling* (teaching), *budi* (wise, right thinking), *bersih pikir* (thinking sincerely). The second group of words has a negative connotation: *bohong* (lying), *dukun* and *ajar* (someone possessing spiritual power), *sakti* (supernatural, having divine power), *lepus* (highly esoteric but having false knowledge), *dengki* (envy, hatred). The third group of words is functional, serving to introduce examples and models: *tuladan* and *picontoeun*. Summarizing the tale's central points is the most effective way of showing the readers what they should learn and to make sure that they learn it. This is the first characteristic of Moesa's writing. This form of ending was new to the tradition of Sundanese writing. Moesa's explanation of the new way of learning can be read in his preface to *Dongeng-dongeng Pieunteungeun* (Model Stories), published in 1867. The word *pieunteungeun* means "something for a person to mirror". Teaching through examples (*tuladan, conto, kaca*) is in fact a tried-and-tested approach. Moesa said in the book, "reading only as a pastime is useless. Of course, sometimes we need such stories as *Rama* and *Anglingdarma* for enjoyment.[32] But, we should read useful (*manpaat*) stories" (Moesa 1867: 4). Reading, in short, was expected to yield useful and practical knowledge. The agricultural texts illustrate this: *Lampah Sebar* (Seeding Guide) explains how to plant rice, and *Wawacan Seca Nala* (Wawacan of Seca Nala) gives a picture of village life by portraying the protagonist Seca Nala as a farmer. Practical knowledge was presented in the form of *dangding* so that the readers could easily relate to the stories, so Moesa (and Holle) thought.[33]

The second characteristic of Moesa's writing is rationality,[34] which Salmoen described as follows:

> What can be said to be the "special" feature of Moehammad Moesa is that he makes a serious and resolute attempt to eradicate superstition, heresy and faithlessness in most of his books. Almost all books contain a scene in which a *dukun* who is said to be a master of black magic and other "supernatural" knowledge is confronted with the protagonist of the story who is sober and rational.
>
> Jang boleh dikatakan "chusus" mendjadi tjiri Muhammad Moesa, ialah hampir dalam setiap bukunja, dengan tegas dan njata, ditjobanja memberantas tachajul, bidäh dan kuchannah. Hampir semua bukunja pasti memuat satu pragmen tentang konfrontasi antara dukun jang katanja pandai ilmu sihir dan ilmu-ilmu "gaib" lainnja, dengan pahlawan-tjerita jang nuchter dan rasional (Salmoen 1955: 437).

Moesa himself wrote about this in the preface of the above-mentioned *Dongeng-dongeng Pieunteungeun*. The point Moesa made relates to the education of children: untrue stories only agitate children's minds and then reading bears no fruit. In the preface he says:

| | |
|---|---|
| Sanget paneda kawoela, | I sincerely ask |
| ka Goesti raboel alamin, | the Lord of the world |
| ijeu teh djadi manpaät, | that this become useful |
| keur watjaeun moerangkalih, | as reading for children, |
| soepaja djadi lantip, | so that they will become clever |
| ahirna manggih rahajoe, | and in the end will meet peace. |
| anoe kagoengan poetra, | Those who have children, |
| oelah rek koerang pamerdih, | do not neglect to urge |
| ka poetrana sing matja ijeu tjarita. | children to read this story. |
| | |
| Malaoer djeung matja tjrita, | It is better than reading a story |
| anoe bohong taja hasil, | that is deceitful, leading nowhere, |
| matak bae kasamaran, | leading to confusion |
| manahna maroerangkalih, | in the minds of children. |
| maroekan enja boekti, | They believe it to be true. |
| noe diseboet sakti wedoek, | Those said to be powerful and invulnerable, |
| boga pikir noeroetan, | [children] want to imitate them |
| hajang wedoek reudjeung sakti, | wanting to be invulnerable and powerful. |
| anoe kitoe eta kasasar pikirna. | Those who do this will go astray in their thinking. |

(Moesa 1867:4)

Moesa denies superstition and irrationality, represented by words such as *sakti* (supernatural power) and *weduk* (invulnerable).

The third characteristic is that Moesa does not hide his loyalties: the colonial government is praised again and again. He clearly states that people should show gratitude to the colonial government and never violate its regulations. The second and third stanzas at the very end of

*Wawacan Panji Wulung* offer a good illustration:

| | |
|---|---|
| 1016. Paneda kula nu ngarang, | I, as the author, ask |
| ka gusti Rabul Alamin, | God, Lord of the world that |
| muga tetep kumawula, | we will be always loyal |
| ka nu agung nyakrawati, | to the great person who rules here, |
| nu estu jadi gusti, | who is the real Lord, |
| Jeng Gusti Tuwan Gupernur, | His Excellency the Governor, |
| nu ngareh pulo Jawa, | who rules over the island of Java |
| sarta salianna deui, | and other islands as well. |
| wawakilna sri Maha Prabu Nederland. | He is the representative of the King of the Netherlands. |
| | |
| 1017. Nu estu ngertakeun jaman, | He peacefully organises our time, |
| ngangeunahkeun abdi-abdi, | makes his people happy, |
| nu jadi panyalindungan, | he is the shelter, |
| nu kagungan hukum adil, | he upholds fair laws. |
| eta sadaya puji, | All praise him. |
| sarta ati nu sa-estu, | from their sincere heart. |
| mugi tetep harjana, | I wish that he will always be happy |
| Gupernemen mangkubumi, | and that the government |
| nyakrawati di bumi Indi Nederland. | rule all the lands of the Dutch East Indies. |

(Moesa 1901: 131)

These stanzas read like propaganda for the colonial government: the reader is asked to pray to Allah that the colonial order will last forever — and the Dutch authorities must have been very pleased with Moesa's words.

Judging from his writings, which include the above-mentioned characteristics, Moesa had a knowledge of the world which in many ways was different from that of his people, and he wanted to share this with his readers. There was an emerging group of "modern" intellectuals, just like him, who were to question the authority of "traditional values" and "ancestral knowledge".

# Chapter 4

# Reading Modernity in *Wawacan Panji Wulung*

## 1. The Reception of *Wawacan Panji Wulung*

When I was in Bandung in October 1994, an old man born in the early 1920s told me that he had read *Wawacan Panji Wulung* when he attended *volksschool* (primary school) as a young boy in the early 1930s.[1] "All students read the book, and we all loved it". That was a long time ago. Recently, he had bought a new edition of the *wawacan* written in Roman script at a small bookstore near the bus terminal in downtown Bandung and discovered that he still loved it, for reasons he could not explain well. They were probably different from the reasons why he had loved the poem of *Wawacan Panji Wulung* 60 years earlier. Memories had gotten hold of him and, like everywhere else, memories of days of old are often very sweet. Did nostalgia give the past a strange glow to him?

Memories notwithstanding, the old man's tale is revealing: copies of *Wawacan Panji Wulung* were circulated and known in West Java in the 1920s and 1930s, more than 50 years after it was first published in 1871. In addition, people who went to school in the Dutch colonial period had read this particular *wawacan*, and they apparently liked it so much that they still remembered it after 60 years.

The new edition of the *wawacan* that the old man referred to must have been the 1990 version that was edited by Ajip Rosidi, the prominent Sundanese literary critic. Ajip had added a preface in which he complained that the younger generation did not even know the title of the *Wawacan Panji Wulung* any longer, let alone the text.[2] His intention may have been to introduce a revered masterpiece to his fellow Sundanese, but as it turned out the older people were probably the only ones willing to read his new edition, for remembrance sake.

*Wawacan Panji Wulung* was written by Moehamad Moesa, the *hoofdpanghulu* of Limbangan, in 1862 and was first published by

Landsdrukkerij in 1871. These apparent facts may conceal a fiction, as there are persistent rumours that a *kalipa* (substitute for *panghulu* and head of mosque personnel) in Limbangan wrote the text and that Moesa had just put his name on the manuscript, to ensure that it was printed under his name.[3] Such vague authorship was not uncommon in those days, since the idea of authorship itself was a new concept. Rumours are not necessarily true, however; judging from the style and content of the *wawacan*, Moesa may have indeed co-authored at least parts of the poem. Nonetheless, there is usually a grain of truth in rumours too: they suggest some kind of dislike or distrust of Moehamad Moesa, the collaborator and opportunist who knew all too well how to protect his family's interests.

Two manuscripts of the *Wawacan Panji Wulung* have been preserved, both containing only fragments of the tale. They were part of the collection of K.F. Holle, and must therefore be autographs or archetypes close to the autograph (see Plate 6). The manuscripts are now in the *Perpustakaan Nasional* (National Library) in Jakarta.[4] They offer readings that are slightly different from the 1871 printed edition, but have so much in common that they could be called mere variants (Sumarlina 1990).

*Wawacan Panji Wulung* was published nine times between 1871 and 1922: four in Javanese script and five in Roman script (see Appendix 1).[5] There is even a Javanese translation — which is very unusual, although Javanese texts were often translated into Sundanese — published in 1879.[6] On the title page, the name Pangeran Adipati Ario Mangkoe Negoro IV (1809–81) is given as the author.[7] In 1973 the Ministry of Education in Jakarta published the revised version once again, with the addition of a short introduction. Altogether there have been 11 printed editions of *Wawacan Panji Wulung* in Sundanese.[8]

## Reception

The colonial government supervised the publication of schoolbooks from the beginning of the school system in the mid-nineteenth century. Most Sundanese books were printed under the supervision of Dutch administrators, at government expense. Even in the motherland, these activities were occasionally followed with a certain critical interest. Education was an important issue, and the Indies' experts in The Hague wanted to be heard not only on the desirability of economic expansion. The colonial government gave full credit to K.F. Holle and considered

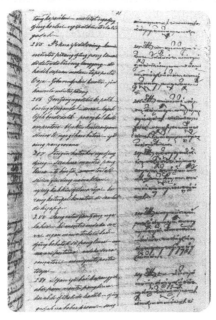

**Plate 6.** Manuscripts of *Wawacan Panji Wulung*
SD No. 127 (above) and SD No. 70 (below)
*Source: K.F. Holle collection, National Library of the Republic of Indonesia.*

his selection of schoolbooks good and appropriate. The government printing house Landsdrukkerij received and printed the manuscripts sent by Holle, but it is not clear whether the books he saw to print were effectively evaluated. The reports that Koorders wrote for the government, as described in the previous chapter, were exceptional, and it is unfortunate that he died before he could make his — no doubt scathing — comments on the published version of *Wawacan Panji Wulung*.

Ten years after the publication of *Wawacan Panji Wulung*, G.J. Grashuis mentioned it, together with two other works by Moehamad Moesa, in his anthology of Sundanese literature, which was a survey of available materials that were used in teaching Sundanese to aspirant civil servants. He characterizes them as "lengthy works", written "in an impure language" (Grashuis 1881: xiv). On the other hand, S. Coolsma, the missionary with a knowledge of things Sundanese that surpassed all others, expressed a deep admiration for Moesa's creation (see also Chapter 1, Dutch view of *Dangding*). At that time, Coolsma was compiling his Sundanese-Dutch dictionary. In the preface of the dictionary published in 1884, a number of titles of manuscripts can be seen in the list of consulted works, including *Wawacan Panji Wulung* and many other poetic works (Coolsma [1884]). Coolsma's appreciation of Sundanese poetry was rare among nineteenth-century Dutch scholars, officials, and missionaries.

*Wawacan Panji Wulung* was the most frequently printed Sundanese work. The colonial government wished to provide the new literates among the local population, which was slowly growing in number, with "good" and "proper" books that would help them think in politically and culturally correct ways. *Wawacan Panji Wulung* was seen as a proper book. It was made mandatory reading in government-subsidized schools — and apparently it was very popular among the students (AVVIO 1880–90: 8).

At the turn of the century, the new generation of students also appreciated it: reports of the *Bureau voor de Volkslectuur* placed *Wawacan Panji Wulung* in the top group of books borrowed at the Bureau's libraries in the 1920s and early 1930s, together with other publications of Moesa.[9] However, not everyone agreed with this appreciation. Mr. Goeroe, for example, was clearly annoyed about the appreciation of *Panji Wulung*. Students, he wrote, should read other tales as well:

> Thus, students at V.I.O. schools (Secondary Indigenous Education) have to know the ancient stories. Not only always "Abdurahman

jeung Abdurahim" (another work of Mr. Moehamad Moesa) and "Panji Wulung" (a work of Mr. Moehamad Moesa), while "Sulanjana" (printed in 1907) and "Lutung Kasarung" (printed in 1910) or other stories do not receive any attention.

Kitoe deui moerid-moerid di sakola-sakola V.I.O. (Voortgezet Inlandsch Onderwijs) koedoe pisan sina njaho kana eta tjarita-tajrita koena. Oelah deui-deui "Abdoerahman djeung Abdoerahim" karangan djoeragan Moehamad Moesa), deui-deui "Pandji Woeloeng" (karangan djoeragan Moehamad Moesa keneh) noe di batja teh, ari "Soelandjana" (tjitakan taoen 1907) djeung "Loetoeng Kasaroeng" (tjitakan taoen 1910) atawa tjarita-tjarita sedjen, taja noe ngagomeng-gomeng (Goeroe 1926: 13-4).[10]

It is hard to find concrete reasons why the *Wawacan Panji Wulung* was loved by the people. The *Volksalmanak* of 1919 seems to point to the main reason: its length (Anonymous 1919: 319). A long narrative was considered as a comprehensive series of fragments, giving a complete view of the language, allowing one to read only fragments but resulting in the reader's satisfaction (cf. Maier 1999: 355-6) — considered a positive element in this *wawacan*. Since its publication, *Wawacan Panji Wulung* has been mentioned in discussions about Sundanese writing, but it is impossible to even try to give a complete survey of these discussions. The appreciation may be organized around the two following themes.

Firstly, *Wawacan Panji Wulung* was felt to be a *wawacan* belonging to the period of change in the configuration of writing. "There is a very dominant tendency in *Panji Wulung* to attack irrational beliefs by way of (European) education. *Panji Wulung* is a fictional narrative in transition, between narratives full of fantasy and those written on the basis of reality" (Sumarga 1983: 9; Sumarlina 1990: 49). The central point is the transitional character: *Wawacan Panji Wulung* moved its readers, so to speak, from fantasy to realism. This particular *wawacan* is a rationalized (*rasionalisasi*) and humanized (*memanusiakan*) one, according to Ekadjati (Ekadjati 1994: 94).

Secondly, sometimes the appreciation focused on the *dangding* form in which *Wawacan Panji Wulung* was written. Some people in colonial times were of the opinion that the *dangding* of *Wawacan Panji Wulung* was unnatural, lacking elegance (Anonymous 1919: 319). Others expressed a deep admiration for its composition, a judgment which was most recently repeated by Sumarlina: "The composition forms a mature totality; the text is full of beautiful Sundanese phrases, of wonderful constructions and expressions" (Sumarlina 1990: 4).

## An alternative reception

Two titles[11] on Sundanese literature published in the 1950s and 1960s quote a number of stanzas of *Wawacan Panji Wulung* as examples of "good poetry". Fragments and excerpts of the poem were used to teach *dangding* at schools (Sumarga 1983: 8). Copies of *Wawacan Panji Wulung*, however, were hard to find, and that situation did not change even when Soeharto's New Order began to propagate and impose its idea of "preserving the local heritage" (*melestarikan warisan daerah*). In New Order jargon, heritage must be preserved for posterity as a rich treasury of a vanished culture. Sumarga, a Sundanese literary critic, made an appeal to his readers to preserve this *wawacan*:

> Who knows whether the original book (*Wawacan Panji Wulung*) still exists? If someone has preserved it, it could be submitted to the "Project for Publishing Readers and Indonesian and Local Literature", Department of Education and Culture in Jakarta. Although the "Project" prints a limited number (not for the public), it will never cease to show the evidence of our ancestors' heritage. At least it will be available at libraries as reading material for someone who wants to read it.
>
> Duka tah, naha aya keneh buku aslina? Upami aya nu leukeun nyimpen, tiasa diajukeun ka "Proyek Penerbitan Buku Bacaan dan Sastra Indonesia dan Daerah". Dep. Pendidikan dan Kebudayaan Jakarta. Sanajan eta "Proyek" nyitakna terbatas (lain keur umum), moal leungit keur pisarateun bae mah, titinggal karuhun teh, sakurang-kurangna bakal aya di Perpustakaan-Perpustakaan, bacaeun nu panasaran (Sumarga 1983: 9).

Apparently it was considered as "our ancestors' heritage": the Ministry of Education and Culture decided to publish the work in order to preserve it as a treasure of a vanished or vanishing culture in a local language.

Why is *Wawacan Panji Wulung* no longer read by the people? There may be at least four reasons. The first is a matter of language: Sundanese language and writing has been marginalized by the national language, Indonesian, and by publications in that national language. Again, Sundanese writing is viewed as a "minor literature" in a "local language" (cf. the opinions of Crawfurd in the early nineteenth century), and has now been seized on to evoke and preserve the heritage in support of the policy to build and preserve national unity. *Wawacan Panji Wulung* became a good example of this heritage-forming movement:

> [...] wawacan is a part of the wealth of Sundanese literature, not necessarily vanished from the spiritual life of the Sundanese people. In fact, if someone composes *wawacan* nowadays, he might be regarded as a person being left behind by the train; however, if *wawacan* is ever written in Sundanese, it will be required reading so that the Sundanese people know their forefathers' spiritual heritage.
>
> [...] wawacan minangka bagian tina kakayaan sastra Sunda, sawadina ulah nepi ka leungit tina kahirupan batin urang Sunda. Memang, lamun kiwari aya nu ngganggit wawacan, baris dianggap tinggaleun karetaapi, tapi ari wawacan anu kungsi ditulis dina basa Sunda mah perelu dibaraca sangkan urang Sunda wanoh kana warisan rohani karuhunna (Ajip Rosidi in Moesa 1990: 12).

The second reason is a commercial one: publications in Sundanese have hardly ever been subsidized by the government in independent Indonesia, especially during Soeharto's New Order, and only a few publishing houses in West Java have had the courage to publish books in the local language, as Indonesian has been the more self-evident language of publications in an era of nationalist fervour.

The third reason is the change that took place in Sundanese reading practice. People used to enjoy reading *wawacan* because of their form. The *Wawacan Panji Wulung* is in verse, so it could be recited and listened to. After independence, silent reading gradually took the place of intoning: people no longer read aloud in the way they did in the nineteenth century, and in silent reading the form of *wawacan* became more bothersome than entertaining because it was complicated and difficult for modern Sundanese literates. The following quotation suggests the change in reading practice:

> [...] *Panji Wulung*, a work of Haji Muhammad Musa, shall not be in vain if it is printed again, even though readers these days will no longer like the form of verse composition *dangding*. It does not need to be chanted in *tembang* melody, but may be read as all other poems (verse *dangding*), which contain lyrical elements (rhyme in the last words and so forth); one will never be bored reading it, especially if the contents are interesting.

> [...] Pandjiwulung karya Haji Muhammad Musa sanajan wangunan dangding bisa jadi teu dipikaresep ku nu maca jaman kiwari — moal mubadir, mun dicitak deui teh, teu kudu ditembongkeun,[12] dibaca biasa ge da kangaranan puisi mah (puisi-tembang) bogaeun unsur liris tea (purwakanti jeung kecap-kecap pinilih jspp) tara matak bosen maca komo mun eusina narik hate keneh mah (Sumarga 1983: 9).

The fourth reason for the demise of *Wawacan Panji Wulung* may be the fact that it was produced by the colonials, and anything that reflected colonialism was treated with scepticism and disgust. The work of Moehamad Moesa and his contemporaries was supposed to contain colonial elements, and to be based on a colonial ideology. In the very last part of the text, Moesa asks "I, as the author, ask Allah" (*Paneda kula nu ngarang, ka gusti Rabul Alamin*) to make the political order under the Dutch government last forever, expressing the hope that the Dutch governor would continue to be the sole king on the island of Java. Such phrases were an affront to nationalist readers, and it is telling, but not surprising, that these stanzas were omitted from the 1973 edition published by the General Director of Culture of the Republic of Indonesia. The editor and translator of this edition, R.S. Subalidinata, wrote:

> The two penultimate stanzas I have not included and translated, because the contents are only private hope and admiration for the colonial masters at that time and do not have any relation to the contents of the story or to the colophon that consists of the author's notes about the finishing of the writing.
>
> Dua bait tembang kedua dan ketiga dari akhir, tidak saya sertakan/ terjemahkan, sebab isinya hanya harapan dan pujian pribadi kepada Penguasa Jajahan waktu itu, samasekali tidak ada sangkut paut dengan isi cerita, maupun dengan penutup yang merupakan catatan pengarang mengenai selesainya karya-tulisnya (Subalidinata 1973: 238).

After Indonesia became an independent nation, Malay became the national language and named as Indonesian. Other languages of the Islands, such as Javanese, Sundanese, Balinese, Madurese, Minangkabau, and Batak, were now called *bahasa daerah* (local languages), their literatures became *sastra daerah* (local literatures), and they were supposed to make, in one way or another, a contribution to the construction of the national culture of Indonesia. To steer these contributions, the Department of Education and Culture designed a variety of projects, such as *Proyek Inventarisasi dan Dokumentasi Kebudayaan Nasional* (Project to keep Inventory and

Document the National Culture), under which *Wawacan Panji Wulung* was translated into Indonesian (Salmoen 1955: 438). Local literature was collected and appreciated through the national language. A Sundanese literary work was to be appreciated as being a part of the national literature of Indonesia, in Indonesian. In Soeharto's New Order, an increasing amount of money was made available to explore the meaning of these regional languages and literatures: according to the ideology of unity in diversity. This ideal of a proud Sundanese people living in harmony with the united Indonesian nation, and the significance of an anthology of Sundanese writing within that ideal picture becomes very clear in the following quotation from Ajip Rosidi:

> Hopefully this book shall not only inform Sundanese people of the richness of their own culture, but it can also make them proud of their own cultural heritage as well as of the cultural achievements of others [other ethnic groups], which as a whole form the basis of a lofty and dignified Indonesian national culture.
>
> Mudah-mudahan ieu buku teh lain bae baris ngawanohkeun urang Sunda kana kabeungharan banda budayana, tapi oge bisa nimbulkeun kareueus ku warisan karuhun katut ciptaan baturna saseler nu jadi tatapakan ngadegna budaya nasional Indonesia nu pengkuh tur tohaga (Rosidi 1995: 2).

Long ago in the Priangan Regencies, Malay and Sundanese narratives were read and discussed side by side in schools and beyond. Now *Wawacan Panji Wulung* was made an antique masterpiece and remains but a name, while Malay/Indonesian novels such as Abdul Muis' *Salah Asoehan* (1928) are still being read as national classics.

## 2. Reading Modernity in *Wawacan Panji Wulung*

Why was this *wawacan* so successfully introduced by the Dutch in the government-subsidized schools? How was it superior to other *wawacan*, and why did its reputation reach beyond the schools? In the following section it will be argued that *Wawacan Panji Wulung* was a perfect blend of traditional features of narrative in terms of form of writing and contents, and at the same time introduced innovations inspired by the experiences of modernity in the second half of the nineteenth century. *Wawacan Panji Wulung* was, as it were, old but also new.

## Modernity

> Modern! How fast that word had surged forward and propagated itself like bacteria throughout Europe. (At least, according to what people were saying.) So allow me also to follow them by using this word, even though I still cannot fully fathom its significance.
>
> *Modern!* Dengan cepatnya kata itu menggelumbang dan membiak diri seperti bakteria di Eropa sana. (Setidak-tidaknya menurut kata orang.) Maka ijinkanlah aku ikut pula menggunakan kata ini, sekalipun aku belum sepenuhnya dapat menyelami maknanya (Pramoedya 1980: 4).

This is the monologue of the main protagonist, Minke, in *Bumi Manusia*, one of the novels of the Indonesian author Pramoedya Ananta Toer about the rise of modernism and nationalism in Java. Minke was modelled on the Javanese journalist R.M. Tirto Adhi Soerjo (1880–1918), who established a printing business in Bandung in the early twentieth century. At that time, the people in Java were going through drastic changes, concurrent with the so-called Ethical Policy as well as the emergence of Muslim modernism, nationalism, and communism. About 20 years after Moesa died, Minke was asked by one of his enlightened friends, Miriam de la Croix, about the meaning of the word "modern". His answer was:

> That word isn't in the dictionary. But according to a knowledgeable teacher of mine it is the name for a spirit, an attitude, a view that emphasises the conditions of scholarship, aesthetics and efficiency. I don't know any other explanation...
>
> Tak ada kata itu dalam kamus. Hanya menurut guruku yang jagoan itu adalah nama untuk semangat, sikap, pandangan, yang mengutamakan syarat keilmuan, estetika dan effisiensi. Keterangan lain aku tak tahu... (Pramoedya 1980: 128).

Changes in forms of communication, the introduction of steamships, the building of railways and the development of electricity were manifestations of new times in which parts of the world were becoming more closely tied together than ever before. These innovations made people think of efficiency, and new and strange things also seemed to evoke a new aesthetics in public buildings, houses, clothes, the performing arts and writing.

The islands of the Dutch Indies were being divided into discrete administrative units with clear borders. Networks of roads, railways, telegraph wires and postal systems connected the urban centres with their hinterlands, or such divided units. The hypocentre of modernity was always in the towns. These innovations induced insecurity and unpredictability as a characteristic feeling of urban culture. Concurrently, human relationships and social structures changed. A new style of administration came into existence, characterized by clearly defined, formal and impersonal institutions, bureaucratic functionaries, anonymous laws, routinization and huge piles of paper. The state, in short, started to prevail over personal loyalties, client-patron relations, and differential connections between court and periphery (Trocki 1992: 79). Peasants were hindered in their relative mobility, their dwelling compounds fenced, their houses built into more or less orderly patterns, and their rights to surrounding fields and forests became ever more precisely demarcated. A period of delineation and alienation set in. This was the new order of modernity.

In the second half of the nineteenth century, when the burgeoning of such changes in all aspects of life became visible and was experienced in the Dutch East Indies, the author of *Wawacan Panji Wulung*, Moehamad Moesa, lived in a small town called Limbangan in West Java, but he and his circle of relatives and friends breathed the air of novelties. Correspondence among members of Moesa's family between 1882 and 1885 reveals some concrete manifestations of modernity and reminds us of Minke's ambiguous feeling and excitement. A letter from the chief prosecutor of Garut addressed to the Regent of Lebak, Moesa's eldest son R.A.A. Soeria Nata Ningrat, tells us of the benefit of the railway (*sepoerweh*, from the Dutch *spoorweg*) — one of the most evident symbols of modernity and economic development.

| | |
|---|---|
| Soemawon ajeuna gampil, | Moreover it is easy now |
| lampah anggang djadi senang, | travelling far becomes pleasant, |
| rehna geus aja sepoerweh, | because there is a railway. |
| lalakon anoe djamdjaman, | A journey of hours |
| ajeuna miminoetan, | is now one of minutes. |
| gampang lamoen hojong tepoeng, | It is easy if we want to meet |
| reudjeung kadang kaoela-warga. | with our family now and then. |

(Danoeredja, 1929: 11)

Travelling to distant places had been troublesome, but now it was "pleasant" (*senang*). The concept and experience of time changed, and so did notions of space; witness, for instance, the way Moesa's wife described in slight amazement her train journey from Batavia in a letter to her daughter-in-law (Danoeredja 1929: 20–33).[13] She and her husband and two family members were brought to Kota station in Batavia by *panghulu* Hadji Anwar and Antaredja at 8:30 in the morning of Saturday 19 November. They took a second-class coach, and reached Bogor at about 10 o'clock the same morning, after passing the stations of Noordwijk (*tasiun Norbek*), Gambir, Pagangsan, Meester Cornelis, Tandjoeng, Pondoktjina and Depok. In Bogor, they were welcomed by their friends Kuneman and van der Chijs, who showed them around the *kadaton Goepernoer Djendral* (palace of the Governor-General). Kuneman told her in Malay (use of that language being another consequence of modernity):

| | |
|---|---|
| Ini nama kamar madjlis, | This is called the conference room, |
| tempat Kangdjeng Toean Besar, | the place where H.E. Governor-General |
| menerima radja laen, | receives other kings |
| atawa oetoesan radja, ... | or royal envoys, ... |

(Danoeredja, 1929: 23–24)

Moesa's wife describes the guided tour of the residence in loving astonishment. Everything impressed her. It was the very first time in her life that she had seen modern European things with her own eyes. The bathroom was something unbelievable for her:

| | |
|---|---|
| Ladjeng kana kamar mandi, | Then we entered the bathroom, |
| pasiraman Toean besar, | where the great master takes his baths. |
| bo! Enden geus moetoeh bae, | Oh! my daughter, it is unbelievable. |
| aja noe kitoe anehna, | It is so bizarre. |
| tina loteng bidjilna, | From the ceiling emerges, |
| ana dipoeterkeun iskroep, | when the tap is turned, |
| njoeroeloek tjara tjihoedjan. | water spouts as if it rains. |
| Koe bawaning herang tjai, | How transparent the water is |
| kawas moetiara ragrag, | as if pearls are falling |

| | |
|---|---|
| atawa djeg inten bae, | or like diamonds. |
| dadasarna pasiraman, | The floor of the bathroom is |
| marmer nomer satoena, | first quality marble. |
| kawas angkik herang-hoeroeng, | It is like pure agate, |
| moenggoeh pikiran kang raka. | so my husband thought. |
| | |
| Asa moal manggih deui, | I guess I will never find again |
| pasiraman tjara eta, | such a bathroom |
| sanadjan dina tjarios, | not even in stories. |
| pasiraman Dewi Sinta, | The bathroom of Goddess Sinta |
| di taman Argasoka, | in the Argasoka garden |
| mangga taroeh moal kitoe, | is not like this, I dare say. |
| satengahna oge moal. | It is not even half as beautiful. |

(Danoeredja 1929: 24)

Neither Moesa nor his wife could help being excited by the things they saw, even though Moesa's good friend may have prepared him. Though he lived in a small town far away from Batavia, the motor of modernization, new things, and perspectives penetrated Moesa's world of tradition, in turn changing the world of those who were most directly exposed to it.

Another example of the representation of modernity can be found in the travel accounts written by a Sundanese lady, Raden Ajoe Abdoerachman, who started her journey to Europe on 25 February 1928 from the port of Batavia, Tandjoeng Prioek. When her ship arrived in Singapore after a two-day voyage, the lady was astonished to see things like *betja* (rickshaw) and *lift* (elevator):

> I discovered something else we do not have. In a huge shop was something called a "lift", whose shape looked like a cage for a canary. It is one and a half times the height of a man and the space inside is about one square meter. That is what is called a lift, whose purpose is to lift, lifting people from the shops downstairs to the shops upstairs, so that people do not have to climb many stairs.

> Aja deui pependakan anoe tjan aja di oerang, ajana di lebet toko, namoeng toko noe galede. "Lift" disebatna, bangoenna sapertos koeroeng paranti manoek kanari, loehoerna satangtoeng satengah

djalma, legana kinten sameter pasagi. Eta noe disebat lift teh gawena paranti oenggah, ngoenggahkeun djelema, ti toko handap ka toko loehoer, soepaya oelah sesah ngambah tangga anoe roa (Abdoerachman 1930: 6).

In the same period Moesa and his wife were surprised to see the bathroom, another archipelago, some, 8,000 kilometres to the northeast of the island of Java, was being exposed to modernity. The bacteria of modernity, in Minke's words, was reaching Japan at the same time, that is, during the Meiji Restoration of 1868.[14] The traditional worldview had been centred on the transcendental, in the terms of one Japanese critic (Karatani 1993: 21): it was not concerned with the relationship between the individual and a "thing": one did not look at an object but envisioned the metaphysical "model". A good example of this transcendental vision can be seen in Japanese painting that predates European influence: "[...], *place* is conceived of in transcendental terms. For a brush painter (of *sansuiga*, paintings of natural scenes done in traditional styles) to depict a pine grove meant to depict the concept (that which is signified by) 'pine grove', not an existing pine grove. This transcendental vision of space had to be overturned before painters could see existing pine groves as their subjects. This is when modern perspective appears" (Karatani 1993: 27). In the case of the modernization of Japanese literature, the modern worldview took hold when Japanese writers discovered their internal landscape. A similar change took place in Sundanese literature.

Moesa could also be compared to Abdullah bin Abdulkadir Munsyi (1797–1854), a writer living in the Malay Peninsula and one of the first Malay intellectuals who tried to define a "modern self" struggling to see and describe the "real" world rather than experiencing the transcendental one. Just like Abdullah, the narrator of *Wawacan Panji Wulung* was struggling to represent the world in a new way, trying to be conscious of a "modern self", the expression of an individual being.[15] Rapid modern developments confused him as they did Abdullah, but it seemed difficult for him to write consciously distinguishing the outer world from the inner world as its counter-concept. He lived in-between the traditional and the modern, and the mixture disturbed his consciousness. His "realistic" description calls the reader to see the outer world, but he remained the captive of a transcendental world. Realism is a new way to describe the world one can see and in which one can find oneself — in other words, to objectivize the world in a modern way: "to be modern is to find ourselves in an environment that promises adventure, power, joy, growth, transformation of ourselves and the world — and, at the same time, that threatens to destroy everything we have, everything we know, everything we are" (Berman 1982: 23).

## *Wawacan*

The story of *Wawacan Panji Wulung* reads roughly as follows:

The kingdom of Sokadana is flourishing. The king falls in love with one of his concubines. She is almost executed by the king because of the evil-hearted queen's conspiracy, but then saved from execution by the faithful viceroy. Soon she gives birth to a beautiful son in a hermitage. The baby is named Panji Wulung and brought up by the viceroy until he comes of age. Panji Wulung departs on an adventurous journey which brings him to several places where he has successful encounters with the rulers. Eventually, he arrives in Cempa and one day saves a beautiful princess from an elephant trainer in a forest. Panji Wulung falls in love with her and the king of Cempa allows them to marry. After the demise of the king, Panji Wulung succeeds to the throne according to the monarch's dying wish. The faithful viceroy of Sokadana visits Panji Wulung in Cempa, and in return Panji Wulung visits his real father in Sokadana who now knows the secret of Panji Wulung's birth. The son of the viceroy is made king of Sokadana as a reward for his father's loyalty. Panji Wulung returns to Cempa after overcoming a rebellion led by the unfaithful viceroy of Cempa. The kingdoms of Cempa and Sokadana continue to prosper (see an extended summary in Appendix 2 [2]).

The title *Wawacan Panji Wulung* gives several hints about the form and content of the work. The word *wawacan* designates that this writing is a verbal composition in poetry and constitutes a narrative; it belongs to a traditional genre and its form dictates a certain kind of content.

The combination of *panji* and *wulung* in the title must have appealed to the contemporary reader as well. In local literary traditions, the word *panji*[16] was the name of a hero who set out on a journey of adventures and was closely linked to the two kingdoms, Kuripan and Daha. Panji, the prince of Kuripan, was betrothed to the princess of Daha, but for various reasons the wedding was postponed. Only when the problems had been resolved by the prince in disguise could he reveal himself and claim the princess so that the world order would be restored.[17] The word *wulung* was rarely found in Sundanese texts. It referred to the colour blue-black (Coolsma 1913: 723) and was associated with the hawk (Gericke and Roorda 1901: vol. 2, 60). The hawk's fierce alertness, its large, dark eyes, and its lofty bearing marked this species as a "bird of nobility". Thus, *Wawacan Panji Wulung* means the narrative of Panji Hawk. In the *wawacan*, the hero goes on a quest, but the narrative does not follow the above-mentioned *panji* storyline, because the kingdoms of Kuripan and Daha are not mentioned at all. Although the story is set in the kingdom of Sokadana, *Wawacan Panji Wulung* may be read as a *panji* story in which the hero travels through several kingdoms, overcomes all kinds of problems and in the end marries his princess, after which they return home and live happily ever after. Therefore, it seems that *Panji Wulung* was chosen as a kind of generic title for the known stories of *Panji*.

*Wawacan Panji Wulung* begins with the word *dangdanggula*, which is the name of a certain verse form (*pupuh*), one of the 17 verse forms introduced by Javanese tradition. Each verse form has its own metrical structure which governs the number of lines per stanza, the number of syllables of a verse line, and the last vowel of a particular verse line (Satjadibrata 1953, Arps 1992: 4–7). *Dangdanggula* has ten lines. The first line consists of ten syllables with the final vowel "i"; the second has ten syllables with the final vowel "a"; the third has eight syllables with a final "é" or "o", and so on.

Below is the first stanza of *Wawacan Panji Wulung* (see also Plate 6):

| | |
|---|---|
| 1. Dangdanggula nu awit di gurit, | *Dangdanggula* is the start to compose metrically. |
| nu di anggit carita baheula, | What is embellished is an old story. |
| nurun tina kitab kahot, | It came from an ancient book and |
| di turun kana lagu, | it is transmitted in song. |
| nu di pambrih rea nu sudi, | Hopefully many are willing [to read] and |
| malar rea nu suka, | even many will like it. |
| ari nu di catur, | What is told is that |
| aya sahiji nagara, | [once upon a time] there was a kingdom. |
| Sokadana nagara gede teh teuing, | Sokadana was an enormously large country |
| murah keur kahirupan. | and life was comfortable. |

Plate 7. *Wawacan Panji Wulung,* published in 1871
(The title page of the Javanese script is missing.)

The rules of the verse form are not always strictly applied, but as long as the reader can sing the text in a certain melody, it is acceptable (Satjadibrata 1931: 17). Extra syllables can be added and a vowel may be changed, particularly in the last syllable of the line. In this *wawacan*, however, the traditional rules of metrical structure are faithfully applied, which drew some criticism that the poem is rather artificial (Salmoen 1955: 435–7).[18]

Each verse form is associated with a certain mood or feeling. *Dangdanggula*, for instance, is a verse form that evokes joy and grandeur, while *asmarandana* accords with the themes of love and affection[19] — but these are just tendencies. For example, the scene in which the viceroy of Sokadana and Panji's mother Tunjungsari are delighted to receive a letter from Panji Wulung is depicted in *asmarandana*. However, the episode of the departure of Panji Wulung and his parting with the viceroy and his own mother should have been depicted in the *kinanti* or *maskumambang*, which evokes sorrow, but the verse form *sinom*, which accords with happiness and joy, is used instead for this scene. Ten kinds of verse metres are used in *Wawacan Panji Wulung*, and it consists of 28 cantos (see Appendix 2).

The change of scene often coincides with a change of verse form, which may also draw renewed attention to the story among the listeners as well as the chanter of the poem. This change is clear from the following quotation of stanzas 566 and 567, in which the narrator mentions the next verse form (*magatru*), and the narrative changes from disclosing the content of a reply to a letter to Panji Wulung from the loyal viceroy of Sokadana to Panji's faithful assistant Bramani and his preparations for a journey:

| | |
|---|---|
| 566. Eta budak di pundut ku gusti, | "My child is required by the king |
| rama anjeun raja Sokadana, | who is your father, king of Sokadana. |
| di kukut aya di jero, | [He] is brought inside the palace |
| di piasih ku ratu, | cherished by the queen. |
| tapi mungguh bapa pribadi, | But concerning me, myself, |
| hanteu pisan katalang, | I am neither relieved |
| atawa kalipur, | nor consoled, |
| ka anjeun taya mendana, | because I am constantly thinking of you |

| | |
|---|---|
| gegel owel beurang peuting hanteu lali, | yearning for you day and night without forgetting." |
| magatru ganti tembang. | *magatru* changes the verse form. |

567.

| | |
|---|---|
| Raden patih geus nyerat tuluy di tutup, | The Viceroy finished writing and closed his letter. |
| di tampi ku Bramani, | It was received by Bramani. |
| sarta geus di leler sangu, | And he was given provisions. |
| geus dangdan tuluy arindit, | After dressing himself, he departed. |
| pada nyusutan cipanon. | The people wiped their tears away. |

Another storytelling device consists of the use of certain phrases such as *sigegkeun* (leaving out the topic), *kocapkeun* (let us say), and *teu kacatur* (nothing is told). These words represent a shortcut to speed up the story or change the topic. For instance, Panji Wulung sends an envoy to the viceroy of Sokadana and the envoy returns with a letter from Sokadana as follows:

| | |
|---|---|
| 644. Gancangna anu ngagurit, | The one who composes is speeding up. |
| utusan enggeus bral mulang, | The envoy has already come back |
| ngabantun serat pangwalon, | bringing an answer to the letter. |
| hanteu kacatur di jalan, | Nothing is told about the journey. |
| kocapkeun enggeus dongkap, | Let us say, he has already arrived. |
| torojag ka jro kadatun, | Immediately he enters the palace, |
| nuju kangjeng raja lenggah. | His Majesty the king is seated. |

Let us return to the first stanza of the text (see p. 158), a "performative opening", a formal inauguration of the tale (cf. Barthes 1970: 147). According to Coolsma's dictionary, the word *gurit* is exclusively used with reference to "metrical composition" (Coolsma 1913: 208)[20] and never with reference to prose or other poetic genres, such as *pantun*. The reader is thus told: this is a *dangding* composition. Then the narrator declares "*nu di anggit carita baheula*" in the second line, where the word *anggit* refers to embellishing (often in poetry) a tale that is already known; the poet is going to polish an old tale in poetry, and the old tale, we are told, is from *kitab kahot* (an ancient book). A connection is evoked with tradition, with memory, with the past. The following line "*di turun kana lagu*" (it is transmitted in song) suggests that the narrator expects the story to be intoned and recited in song.[21] This type of declaration is common in traditional texts; the connection with tradition and the genre of writing are shown in the very beginning. *Wawacan Rengganis* illustrates such an opening:

3. Ka sadaja nu dipudji,
kaula nêda hampura,
mugi dipadangkeun hate,

gampang sakur nu disêdja,

sarêng kaula nêda,
dunga bêrkahna karuhun,
nu geus sami tilar dunja.

To all I praise,
I ask apologies,
Hopefully [this] will enlighten your heart,
to be easily [understood] is all that I wish
and I ask,
for the blessing of our ancestors
all of whom have left this world.

4. Djeung sakabeh kulawargi,
nu masih aja di dunja,
ka kolot nu kahot-kahot,

djeung ka anu widjaksana,
kaula nêda dunga,
sarehing dek mangun tjatur,
nurutan lampah budjangga.

And all relatives
who are still in this world,
to the old who lived in ancient time
and to those who are wise,
I ask blessing
because I will compose a story
following the ways of the poets.

5. Ditulis bisina leungit,
disêrat bok paburisat,

djadi tjonto tamba poho,

nurutan djalma budiman,
nu geus meunang pudjian,
djeung pilangbara kajungjun,
ngan sugan kanggo lumajan.

Written down so it will not be lost,
written down so it will not be blown away,
becoming a remedy against forgetting,
following virtuous people,
those who are praised,
and it will not be too favoured,
perhaps even of little value.

| | |
|---|---|
| 6. Kumaki diadjar nganggit, | Supposedly learned to embellish stories, |
| beak-beak hênteu lajak, | but never appropriate, |
| ngan sêdja nadah pamojok, | only wishing to prevent mockery |
| wantu basa teu diajak, | because the language is not purified, |
| garihal matak djuhal, | and unrefined leading to confusion. |
| dibasakeun Sunda dusun, | Written in rural Sundanese |
| wantuning djalma padesan. | because [I] am from the country. |

(Abdoessalam 1957: 3)

With this performative opening, the reader is introduced to the familiar world of Sundanese writing. The tale was expected to be read in the context of tradition. This meant reading the handwritten text aloud. But then *Wawacan Panji Wulung* had a printed text, and the narrator tried to place this visually new form of text in the tradition, hoping that "many people would be willing to read it" (*malar rea nu suka*). In short, the opening lines were meant to make the text familiar and to invite the reader, and this is where ambivalence is seen, as the tale of old is presented in print.

This new form of the old story starts off in the kingdom of Sukadana, a name that has several associations and opens up a number of interpretations. Firstly, the word "Sukadana" refers to the homonymous kingdom on the west coast of the island of Borneo, which was prosperous in the seventeenth century.[22] Secondly, the name Sukadana refers to a kingdom in Javanese literature; it is found in *Serat Kandhaning Ringgit Purwa* (The Book of Wayang Purwa Story) together with Gilingwesi, the name of another kingdom that is referred to in this *wawacan* (Pigeaud 1970: vol. 3, 356). Thirdly, there was (and is) a place named Sukadana in West Java, south of Garut, the place where the author lived at the time he wrote the tale. In one of his letters, he calls himself *amil Sokadana* (Islamic chief of the village Sokadana) (Danoeredja 1929: 51). Lastly, the word *sukadana* is a made up of *suka* (desire) and *dana* (wealth). Thus, this is the kingdom of the "desire for wealth". There are four possible interpretations because the text leads us into four directions at once.

The epilogue is as important as the performative opening; the conclusion of the poem provides reliability. It gives information about the text, such as the date of completion, or copying, and the name of the composer — in short, it provides an identification for the text. The last stanza of *Wawacan Panji Wulung* reads as follows:

| | |
|---|---|
| 1018. Tamatna kaula ngarang, | I finished composing |
| pukul tujuh malem kemis, | at seven o'clock Wednesday evening |
| di tanggal tujuh welasna, | on the seventeenth |
| kaleresan bulan April, | concurring in April, |
| tahun kangjeng Masihi, | the year of Lord Jesus |
| sarewu dalapan ratus, | one thousand eight hundred |
| jeung genep puluh dua, | and sixty two, |
| marengan hijrahna Nabi, | the year of the Prophet's migration, |
| sarewu dua ratus tujuh puluh dalapan. | one thousand two hundred seventy eight. |

The tale was finished on 17 April 1862. The narrator does not use the word "copy" (*salin*), but "compose" (*ngarang*). He claims, "I composed this story" (*kaula ngarang*). In the opening, however, he says that the text was passed down from ancient texts and their traditions. They constitute contradictory statements in the opening and the ending. In Malay and Javanese manuscript tradition, texts were copied and the narrator would often state in the prologue and epilogue that he copied a text (Koster 1993: 55–69), but this type of epilogue is not always added in Sundanese *wawacan*. The performative opening and informative ending, as found in *Wawacan Panji Wulung*, are not commonly found in tradition.[23]

## The driving force of the story

After the opening and description of the kingdom of Sokadana, the story is set in motion by the episode of the secret of Panji Wulung's birth, which is one of the most important episodes in this text. It is inserted repeatedly in the narrative, and retold in dialogue or in a letter. As a result of these repetitive fragments, the text is like a patchwork. This episode is told by the narrator at the beginning of the text in the following way:

22. Nyaur patih hanteu lila sumping,

ka karaton bari semu reuwas,

reh disaur tereh-tereh,

lajeng sang ratu nyaur,
he ki patih,
sing gasik-gasik,
ieu si Tunjung sekar,
nu cidra ka ratu,
ayeuna geuwat paehan,

ulah nitah kudu ku maneh pribadi,

mangke bawa ceulina.

The *patih* is summoned, he soon arrives

at the palace with a surprised look,

because he was called to come immediately.

Then the king says,
"Sir Patih,
you must do this quickly.
This is Madam Tunjungsekar
who insulted the king.
Now (she) must be killled immediately.

You may not order [others] but do it yourself.

Later you must bring [me] her ears."

23. Patih naros nun hampura gusti,

abdi dalem buta tuli pisan,

ku naon perkawisna teh,
nu matak gusti bendu,

rehna eta pun Tunjungsari,
kalangkung diasihna,
ti nu rea punjul,
Dewakeswari ngandika,
enya pisan ku kami dipikaasih,
leuwih ti anu rea.

The viceroy asks, "Forgive me, your Highness,

your servant is completely blind and deaf.

What is the matter
that made your Highness get angry.

Madam Tunjungsari
is loved very much,
more than many others."
Dewakeswari speaks,
"Indeed she was loved by me
more than many others.

24. Anu matak kami liwat ijid,
ka si Tunjung sabab salah tampa,

What made me extremely angry
at Madam Tunjung is that she misunderstood.

| | |
|---|---|
| dipisono nyolowedor, | She was not faithful though she was beloved." |
| ki patih nyembah matur, | The viceroy bows and says, |
| abdi dalem nu kirang harti, | "Your subject who has little understanding |
| seja nyundul unjukan, | would like to interrupt to express my opinion. |
| sumuhun bebendu, | Yes [I understand] your wrath. |
| manawi gamparan lepat, | But perhaps you are wrong. |
| kirang priksa bendu kagancangan | You may be ill-informed, your wrath is |
| teuing | precipitated, |
| tacan kamanah enya. | You are not really convinced in your heart yet." |

The viceroy's persuasive speech continues, and then in stanza 28, the following is told:

| | |
|---|---|
| 28. Tuluy patih mawa Tunjungsari, | Then the viceroy brings Tunjungsari |
| sarta reujeung ki Panolih tea, | together with Sir Panolih. |
| duanana dikantet, | The two are bound. |
| nyi Tunjung celuk-celuk, | Madam Tunjung is weeping, |
| sambat-sambat ka kangjeng gusti, | calling for the king. |
| kuring teu gaduh dosa, | "I have not sinned. |
| gusti naha kitu, | Why does your Highness act like this? |
| ratu kurang titi priksa, | Your Highness did not make a careful investigation. |
| puguh maru saakal-akal nu dengki, | Surely jealousy drove the concubines to conspiracy. |
| kasmaran teuing raja. | our Highness is infatuated with love." |

This episode is retold by different voices as well: Panji Wulung's companions, Janggala and Janggali; his foster father, the viceroy of Sokadana; and his confidant Jayapati. The reader knows the secret of the birth of Panji Wulung from the start of the tale, while the protagonist himself ignores the secret until he kills the *ajar*, making the tale a kind of detective story. This becomes the initial cause for all the incidents, and the motor driving the story forward.

Another driving force is the antagonist, the villain Andakasura. He propels the story forward by playing a role opposite the loyal viceroy. The evil-minded Andakasura makes several mistakes. Firstly, he tells a lie to the king of Cempa. The princess had been seduced by the Bengalese elephant trainer during the absence of the king. Andakasura finds the corpses of the Bengalese man and the elephant in the forest and he lies to the king in order to obtain the reward. When his lie is revealed, he is arrested. The king of Cempa, Panji Wulung's father-in-law, intends to execute him, but Panji Wulung asks the king's favour to set him free. Andakasura runs away to the kingdom of Gilingwesi. Secondly, Andakasura persuades the king of Gilingwesi to propose marriage to the princess of Cempa. The king feels humiliated because his proposal of marriage to the beautiful princess Andayaningrat is rejected. In the meantime she has become Panji Wulung's wife. The king of Gilingwesi sends his troops to attack Cempa but they are defeated. Thirdly, Andakasura persuades the viceroy of Cempa to plot a rebellion against the new king of Cempa, Panji Wulung, during his absence. Again the conspiracy fails, and the rebels are defeated by the forces of Cempa. In the end, punishment is meted out to the villain Andakasura by the king, Panji Wulung. The story ends with the execution of Andakasura. It reads:

| | |
|---|---|
| 1005. Lajeng ki Andakasura, | Then Andakasura, |
| dikudungan lawon putih, | has his face covered in a white cloth, |
| dibawa ka panggantungan, | is brought to the gallows, |
| diriung ku tumbak bedil, | surrounded by spears and rifles. |
| raden Patih ngalahir, | Lord Patih says, |
| Andaka tampa panaur, | "Andaka accept your retribution. |
| ieu adiling raja, | This is the king's justice, |
| pamales lampah nu julig, | the reward for your evil acts." |
| pek digantung ki Andaka geus paragat. | Andaka is hanged and dies. |

| | |
|---|---|
| 1006. Tuluy diteukteuk beuheungna, | Then his head is cut off |
| dipanjer dina paranti, | and exhibited as usual |
| tengah jalan parapatan, | in the middle of the crossing. |
| adat paranti sasari, | It is the usual manner, |
| supaya jadi bukti, | so that it becomes proof of |
| jalma ngamusuh ka ratu, | someone who opposes the king. |
| beja enggeus gurnita, | The news spreads and |
| kasohor ka mana mendi, | everywhere it becomes known |
| yen Andaka enggeus dipanjer sirahna. | that Andaka's head is exhibited. |

## Reading modernity

Loan words from the Dutch represent modernity: for instance, *sopi* (Dutch gin)[24] and *pestol* (pistol) are found in this text. The viceroy of Sokadana gives six admonitions — do not drink, use opium, steal, fight, associate with women or kill anyone — to the little boy Panji Wulung before he sets off on his journey.[25] The viceroy warns the boy not to drink alcohol in the following stanza:

| | |
|---|---|
| 65. Watekna nu nginum sopi, | As for the effect of drinking gin, |
| ana kaliwatan rea, | if [you] drink excessively, |
| tangtu jadi matak mabok, | certainly [you] will get intoxicated. |
| ari laku mabok teya, | The effect of the intoxication is |
| sok ngaleungitkeun akal, | losing [your] rational thinking, |
| leungit era tinggal napsu, | losing your sense of shame, leaving only lust. |
| tungtungna matak cilaka. | In the end it causes disaster. |

In warning against excessive drinking, the narrator tells his Sundanese young readers of the possible danger. Similar moralistic messages may be detected in the writings of other contemporary authors working closely with European patrons, such as Abdullah bin Abdulkadir Munsyi, Raja Ali Haji, and Haji Ibrahim (see Putten 2001: 239–44).

Another example of representation of modernity besides the loan words is the foreign ideas in the story, as is apparent in the scene in which the princess of Cempa tells Panji Wulung about the king's favourite elephant:

| | |
|---|---|
| 246. Nu gaduh urang Banggali, | The owner [of the elephant] was a Bengalese. |
| harga lima ratus real, | The price was five hundred *real*. |
| tina ama langkung hoyong, | Because my father loved to have it, |
| gajah sakitu hide(u)ngna, | the elephant was so black, |
| lajeng digaleuh kontan, | he bought it with cash. |
| tina taya anu ngingu, | Because there was no one who could look after it, |
| nu gaduh digajih bulan. | the owner was paid a monthly salary. |

Both payment by cash (*kontan*, derived from the Dutch word *contant*) and the salary system (*digajih bulan*) allude to the institutional change in the monetary system. Moreover, the currency is a foreign one (*real*, a Mexican dollar).[26] These loan words are clearly a representation of newness. Unconsciously, such novelties fill the narrator's everyday life in conceptual terms; he cannot free himself from the modernizing current in his surroundings.

Here and there the depiction becomes realistic, offering a vivid picture and a feeling of excitement to the reader. The villain Andakasura's execution quoted above is one such scene. Such realistic depiction can also be detected in the names of places: the narrator does not use fictitious names but real names of places, such as Cempa, Malayu, Keling, Patani, and Malaka. The scene described below is unusually realistic, which is rare in traditional writings, and filled with newness and foreignness to stimulate the reader's curiosity. The episode tells how the princess of Cempa is rescued from the Bengalese elephant tamer. The narrator describes the scene vividly as if he had seen with his own eyes the big elephant with an ugly man and a beautiful lady. The frequent use of the word *tingal* (look) deserves attention:

| | |
|---|---|
| 235. Panonpoe wanci lingsir, | As the sun is going down, |
| rahaden tuluy ningalan, | the Lord sees something |
| laur-laur tebeh kulon, | dimly toward the west. |
| beuki deukeut katingalna, | Coming closer, it is visible |
| teges nu tumpak gajah, | the figure riding the elephant becomes clear, |
| gajah alus gede jangkung, | the elephant is beautiful, big and tall. |
| ngadua jeung putri endah. | The pillion rider is a beautiful lady. |

236. Kaget manah raden Panji,
sarta bingung ngamanahan,
ieu teh jelema naon,
ngadua jeung putri endah,

di tegal ngentak-ngentak,
atawa paningal palsu,
lajeng raden ngusap soca.

Lord Panji is surprised
and feel difficult to understand it.
What kind of man is he?
with a beautiful lady as his pillion rider,
in the wide open field?
Or is it an illusion?
The Lord wipes his eyes.

237. Raden ngawaskeun nigali,
jalma turun tina gajah,
putri geulis teh dikaleng,
dikalemoh diciuman,
dipondong dititimang,

dirangkul sarta dipangku,
putri ceurik dedengekan.

The Lord carefully watches
the man dismounting the elephant.
The beautiful girl is in his arms.
He kisses her forcibly,
holding her firmly in his arms and cuddling,
hugging and embracing,
the girl is whining incessantly.

238. Rahaden welas ningali,
aya putri disangsara,
ku lalaki hideung goreng,
biwir jeding huntu bodas,
sarta ceulina rubak,
buuk rintit kumis nanggung,

mata beureum ngembang wera.

The Lord looks compassionately.
The girl is suffering
because of an ugly black man
with lips jutting out and white teeth
and large ears,
frizzled hair and a broad moustache.
His red eyes betray lust.

239. Tina watirna ki Panji,
lajeng mentang gondewana,
disipat dihade-hade,
belesat jamparing mesat,
mener kana matana,
sot nyi putri tuluy muru,
ka nu keur nyandak gondewa.

Because Panji feels sorry,
he draws his bow
and aims accurately.
The arrow swishes through the air,
and hits him precisely in his eye.
Immediately the girl runs away
toward the one who holds a bow.

240. Rahaden awas ningali,

nyingcet bari matek ladrang,

ditewek eukeur nolonjong,
walikatna terus pisan,
rubuh utah-utahan,
segar-segor gerang-gerung,
teu lila tuluy paragat.

241. Gajahna rek bela pati,
neuleu juragan geus modar,
meta ngagero ngadengek,
bubat-babit tulalena,
rek newak raden putra,
tangginasna Panji Wulung,
tulale disabet rampal.

242. Tina bedasna ki Panji,
pinter tangginas binekas,
cungcat-cingcet hanteu kagok,
Daeng Bramani nulungan,
newekan kekemplongna,
gajah teh rubuh dihurup,

gedebug tuluy sakarat.

243. Tuluy digorok sakali,
genggerongna sapat pisan,
lajeng sang putri dikaleng,
dicalikkeun dipariksa,

he nyai nu ti mana,
kumaha asal kapungkur,
nu matak kieu petana.

The Lord watches [the man] carefully

and jumps aside while whipping out a dagger.
He jumps forward stabbing
right through his shoulder blade.
[The man] falls down vomiting,
rattling and growling,
and soon dies.

The elephant tries to take revenge,
seeing his master is already dead.
It roars in rage
swinging his trunk
to catch the Lord.
Panji Wulung moves quickly
to beat off the trunk.

Because of Panji's strength,
he is prompt in action,
he jumps right and left smoothly.
Daeng Bramani helps him
to pierce the pit of the stomach.
The elephant falls down after they attack,
sinks down on the ground and dies.

Then in a single stab,
the neck is cut off.
Then the girl is held in his arms,
and helped to sit, and asked questions,
"Where do you come from?
How did you come
to be in this situation?"

To indicate how realistic this depiction is, a corresponding passage from a traditional text *Wawacan Jayalalana* is quoted as a contrast.[27] Lalana, the main protagonist, is almost caught by soldiers when he is saved by a crocodile. As may become clear from the following quotation, the scene is described in traditional terms, full of fantastic elements:

| | |
|---|---|
| 210. Pek diheumeheu Den Lalana ku buaya, | The Lord Lalana was caught by the crocodile in the mouth. |
| Raden nyaur bari nangis, | He said while crying, |
| he jurig sagara, | "Hey, sea monster, |
| kami tong dilila-lila, | do not take too long, |
| geura teureuy sing lastari, | swallow me so it will be over soon." |
| jawab buaya, | Answers the crocodile, |
| abdi teu seja mateni. | "I do not wish to kill, |
| | |
| 211. Jisim abdi ka Agan bade nulungan, | I will help you, Lord". |
| jawab Raden bagja diri, | Answers the Lord, "I am glad, |
| atuh ulah lila eungap, | please do not choke me so long |
| enggal dibawa ka darat, | bring me to the shore swiftly." |
| buaya nyurungkuy tarik, | The crocodile swam without a sound, |
| nepi ka peuntas, | to the other side of the river. |
| ngarandegna sisi cai. | He got up at the edge of the water. |
| | |
| 212. Diejagkeun Den Lalana ku buaya, | Lord Lalana was released by the crocodile, |
| geus ngadeg di sisi cai, | already got up at the edge of the water |
| bari ngandika, | and said, |
| nuhun pitulung bapak, | "Thank you for your help, |
| abdi teh bisa walagri, | I am all right. |
| teu ditulungan, | Had I not been helped, |
| tanwanda abdi balai. | no doubt I would be struck by misfortune." |

(Masduki *et al.* 1996: 48)

Another interesting example is the representation of the "modern self": the narrator tells the reader that the main protagonist wrote down his own adventures (*lalakon diri*) — that is, Panji Wulung himself wrote down the poem that is being read. It may be a well-known literary device in Western literature, but seems to have been an innovation in the manuscript traditions of Indonesia.

| | |
|---|---|
| 200. Isuk-isuk manggul pacul, | In the early morning [he] brings a hoe |
| burit-burit milu ngarit, | at dusk [he] joins the grass-cutting. |
| ti beurang anyam-anyaman, | In the afternoon [he] makes plaited materials, |
| nyieun boboko salipi, | making a rice basket and others. |
| ti peuting nyerat di lontar, | In the evening [he] writes on palm leaves |
| elingan lalakon diri. | memories of the things he experienced. |
| | |
| 201. Taya laku nu kalarung, | No action is passed over |
| di tulis ti bareng indit, | written from the time of his departure |
| ti nagara Sokadana, | from the kingdom of Sokadana, |
| jadi babad salirana, | it becomes his life story. |
| picontoeun enggeus sumping. | This serves a model. |

The description of the activity of writing about oneself every night was unknown in traditional texts.[28] In addition, writing a kind of autobiography (*babad salirana*) was unusual for the reader. This can be regarded as an activity of the modern individual: a sign of recognizing one's ego and a projection of the inner self, or the modern self.[29] Seeing the outer world with one's own eyes and looking into the inner self fuse into unity. However, the unity is "a paradoxical unity, a unity of disunity: it pours us all into a maelstrom of perpetual disintegration and renewal, of struggle and contradiction, of ambiguity and anguish". To be modern is to be part of a universe in which, as Marx said, "all that is solid melts into air" (Berman 1982: 15). Nothing seems to hold firm, and there is a feeling of insecurity.

In this text, the viceroy of the kingdom of Sokadana plays a prominent role; his words constitute the leitmotif of the story. The viceroy saves the lives of Panji Wulung and his mother, and he sees to it that Panji Wulung receives a good education, based on expressions of rational thinking, *karasa*. The root word of *karasa* is *rasa*, which means "feeling", "taste", "opinion" (Coolsma 1913: 507). In old Javanese, it means "the essential of something, content, substance, meaning, purport" or "how something is, (real) disposition or condition" (Zoetmulder 1982: vol. 2, 1515). In the context of *Wawacan Panji Wulung*, the word seems to be used in the sense of rational thinking, opposed to words like *jampe* (magic words), *weduk* (invulnerability) and *sakti* (supernatural power). His instruction in rational thinking serves Panji Wulung as a compass on his subsequent quest. The viceroy begins his instruction or advice with "My boy Panji Wulung, attend my lesson" (*he agus ki Panjiwulung, regepkeun pangwuruk bapa*) and continues:

46. Agus ulah wani-wani,
nyorang pibayaeun awak,
kudu pikir masing hade,
saupama cai caah,
ulah rek di peuntasan,
atawa ratu keur napsu,
ulah rek wani haturan.

"My boy, do not dare to
bring [your] body in danger.
You must think deliberately.
Like a flood
[you] do not want to cross it.
When the king is in a rage,
do not dare to address him.

47. Sajaba ti dinya deui,
naon-naon kalakuan,
nu katingal bakal awon,
nu pibayaeun ka awak,
eta kudu singkahan,
eta tegesna nya kitu,
nu ngaran kapaliyasan.

Other than this,
it is every kind of behaviour
which seems wrong and
which puts your body in danger
that you should avoid.
In short, everything is like this.
This is called *kapaliyasan*.

48. Kajayaan kitu deui,
kudu wanter pikiran,
ulah reuwasan jeung kaget,
sarta ulah sok borangan,

*Kajayaan* is so, too.
You must think courageously.
Do not be startled and surprised
and do not frighten easily.

| | |
|---|---|
| watekna nu borangan, | [One who has] a frightened nature, |
| rajeun lumpat tigedebug, | sometimes jumps away in a hurry |
| sieun ku polah sorangan. | [because of] fears of his own acts. |

49. Tapi kajayaan pasti,  
sarat kudu bener lampah,

But true *kajayaan* is the condition of having to behave correctly,

karana mungguh nu goreng,

because, for instance, one who has an evil mind

risi ku polah sorangan,  
ku kalangkang ge lumpat,

gets worried by his own behaviour  
Looking at his own shadow, he will jump,

marukan jalma nu nyusul,  
mana horeng kalangkangna.

believing that someone chases him.  
In fact, it was his own shadow.

50. Kajayaan anu bukti,

As to *kajayaan* which can be proved,

kudu bener laku lampah,  
tamba borangan jeung kaget,

[one] has to behave correctly.  
[It is] the remedy for fear and surprise.

nya eta taya masalah,  
nu kasieun manehna,

So there is no problem,  
because the only one who is feared is oneself.

jeung deui anu di sebut,  
elmu kabedasan tea.

And what is also mentioned is  
the knowledge of *kabedasan*.

51. Taya jampe anu matih,

There are no magic words which are effective

kajaba ti kudu tuman,  
nu ku bapa geus kailo,  
kapikir rea tuladan,  
saperti tatanggungan,  
ponggawa nu agung-agung,  
bedasna eleh ku cacah.

other than routine exercise.  
This is what I have seen.  
[I] think there are many models  
like carrying heavy loads.  
Respectable vassals *ponggawa* are inferior to the commoner in physical strength.

| | |
|---|---|
| 52. Tina tuman kuring-kuring, | The routine of the commoner's |
| gawena nanggung jeung mundak, | work like carrying and bearing on their shoulders |
| eta patut jieun conto, | is good to be made a model. |
| najan boga jampe tumbal, | Even though one has magical words, |
| ari kurang tumana, | if the routine exercise is not enough, |
| tangtu moal bedas nanggung, | it is certain that he is not strong enough to carry. |
| jampe teh taya gawena. | Magic words do not work." |
| | |
| 53. Ngawalonan raden Panji, | Lord Panji answers, |
| sumuhun pangwuruk bapa, | "Right are your teachings, |
| tapi kula ewed keneh, | but I am still confused. |
| karana enggeus gurnita, | Because it is common knowledge, |
| lumbrah omongan jalma, | a common rumour among the people. |
| mun hayang bedas jeung weduk, | If one wants to be strong and invulnerable, |
| kudu guguru ka ajar. | one has to learn with an *ajar*." |
| | |
| 54. Ki paith ngandika deui, | The viceroy says again, |
| enya pisan geus gurnita, | "It is very true that it is common knowledge, |
| tapi ngan omongan bae, | but it is only a rumour. |
| teu aya pisan buktina, | There is no proof of it. |
| nu matak bapa cuwa, | What makes me disgusted is |
| ngagugu ajar jeung dukun, | listening to teachings of *ajar* and *dukun*, |
| sabab taya karasana. | because there is no rational thinking." |

The viceroy is teaching three things to Panji Wulung: *kapaliyasan* (avoiding danger), *kajayaan* (mental strength), and *kabedasan* (physical strength). In a concrete manner, the viceroy explains how to acquire *kabedasan*: magic words (*jampe*) cannot help him, but physical exercise "has to be made routine" (*kudu tuman*). Panji Wulung is ordered to train his body through gymnastics and body-building: he has to lift copper and iron weights and carry them on his shoulders every morning from dawn to noon. Thus, he will obtain physical strength which will overpower magic words: rational thinking is underscored.

Another important teaching of the viceroy is finding *bukti* (proof): "but they are only words, there is no proof at all" (*tapi ngan omongan bae, teu aya pisan buktina*). The viceroy denies supernatural and spiritual powers, symbolized by the word *weduk* (invulnerable). This word is associated with *sakti* (supernatural and spiritual power) and *dukun* or *ajar* (fortune-teller, magic-holder, herbalist) which the viceroy hates. Words like *weduk* and *sakti* constitute important elements in the traditional texts, such as *Wawacan Jayalalana*.

In contrast to traditional *wawacan*, the negation of *sakti* and the affirmation of *bukti* permeates the entire story of *Wawacan Panji Wulung*: denying irrationality and superstition. This theme is resonant with the above-mentioned rational thinking. One of the most important examples of the *bukti* versus *sakti* theme is the episode of the killing of *ajar* Guna Wisesa. The evil character Guna Wisesa (literally meaning "almighty purpose") is the cause of the misfortune of the protagonist and his mother, Tunjungsari. Because of Guna Wisesa's lies to the king of Sokadana, Panji Wulung's mother is thrown out of the palace and he is born in a remote village. Panji Wulung by himself cuts the cause of his misfortune from its root and testifies to the teachings of his foster-father, the viceroy of Sokadana, who saved his mother from execution. He does not know the secret of his birth before he kills Guna Wisesa. The scene is as follows: Panji Wulung wants to pursue *elmu* (wisdom, knowledge) and becomes an apprentice to the famous *ajar* Guna Wisesa. Every day he studies *jampe bedas weduk sakti* (magic words which have supernatural and invulnerable power) because he believes that he can obtain *elmu* by memorizing *jampe*. He asks proof from the *ajar* because he cannot see the effects. This attitude is in accordance with the advice of his foster-father: do not believe the words but look for the proof. The dialogue between Panji Wulung and Guna Wisesa illustrates this:

| | |
|---|---|
| 147. Tapi taya anu nyoba, | But no one has ever tested them. |
| ngan jampena di aji beurang peuting, | The magic words are only intoned day and night. |
| raden haturan ka guru, | The Lord asks his teacher, |
| jampe mah geus apal, | "Magic words I have memorized |

| | |
|---|---|
| tapi jasad kula ayeuna nunuhun, | but I want to ask you now |
| dibuktikeun masing nyata, | to prove that their power is obvious, |
| kabedasan reujeung sakti. | physical strength and supernatural power." |

| | |
|---|---|
| 148. Ki ajar bengis tembalna, | The *ajar* gets angry and answers, |
| naha maneh mana campelak teuing, | "How come you are so rude, |
| kumawani ngomong kitu, | and dare to speak like this, |
| kawas nu teu percaya, | as if you do not believe them, |
| kudu-kudu ngabuktikeun sakti weduk, | so I have to prove *sakti* and *weduk*, |
| jampe teu beunang di unghak, | magic words may not be insulted, |
| jeung ulah dipake ulin. | and may not be used for play. |

| | |
|---|---|
| 149. Hanteu meunang lalawora, | You must not be careless. |
| kudu ngandel yen jampe eta matih, | You must believe magical words are powerful, |
| mangke ari manggih musuh, | in the future if you meet an enemy, |
| didinya kabuktina, | then the words will be proven", |
| raden Panji haturan barina imut, | Panji says with a smile, |
| nyasat masih keneh hamham, | "I still have doubts, |
| mun tacan kapanggih bukti. | if I have not found proof yet". |

In this short dialogue, the word *bukti* appears four times. Panji asks the *ajar* to show him proof (*bukti*) of the physical strength (*kabedasan*) and supernatural power (*sakti*) with unusual persistence. He needs to see them with his own eyes. Following the teaching of the viceroy, he believes that something visible and evident is more important than magic words (*jampe*): things must be proved (*ngabuktikeun*, stanza 54). There appears to be a confrontation between indigenous knowledge and Western empirical knowledge of the real world, which is associated with modernity. The visible proof is also underscored in another episode: the king asks for his beloved concubine's ear (*ceulina*) as proof of her execution (stanza 22). To see a concrete object with one's own eyes is different from the traditional way of understanding the world, to envisage the transcendental, in the Karatani's term (1993: 27).

After the above dialogue between the apprentice and his teacher, Guna Wisesa throws a stone at Panji Wulung in rage. Panji Wulung falls, briefly stunned, then whips out his *keris* and kills Guna Wisesa. His violence is justified because he suffers humiliation: the stone is thrown at his head. This incident is, of course, unusual because a disciple kills his teacher, but this development can be understood as the triumphant march of *bukti* and rational thinking (*karasa*): Guna Wisesa is the symbol of irrationality, superstition, supernatural power, and falsehood. Killing Guna Wisesa symbolizes the eradication of *sakti* and *weduk* (invulnerability). In fact, in this text there are few irrational or fantastic elements such as an invulnerable hero, talking animals or ogres, which are very common in traditional tales.

*Pikir* is another key word: it means "to think, see, understand". Not only the main protagonist but also other characters "think" in this text. First, *pikir* can be found in the viceroy's advice: "*kudu pikir masing hade*" ("you must think deliberately", stanza 46), "*kudu wanter pikiran*" ("must think courageously", stanza 48), "*kapikir rea tuladan*" ("[I] think there are many models', stanza 51). The lesson is not to believe the words of others, but to see with one's own eyes and think for oneself. Is this the "modern self who thinks" which tries to put reality into inner experience and give it order? Examples of other thinking characters are the peasant and the princess of the kingdom of Cempa:

| | |
|---|---|
| 293. Pirempugna juru tani, | The advice of the peasant is: |
| sae gancang ka nagara, | "Better go to the town fast |
| ngadeuheusan ka kadaton, | and visit the palace |
| nyanggakeun sang putri tea, | to bring the princess. |
| geus tangtu ditarima, | It is certain you will be accepted |
| jeung lajeng dianggo mantu, | and recognised as the son-in-law. |
| kitu pikir pun aki mah. | So I think". |
| | |
| 294. Putri nyaur bari nangis, | The princess says while weeping, |
| pikir aki bener pisan, | "His opinion is very true. |
| nya kitu pikir kula ge, | I think the same. |
| langkung sae enggal-enggal, | It will be better quickly |
| marek ka kangjeng raja, | to go to see the king [bringing me], |
| tada teuing rama ibu, | surely my father and mother |
| sukana ningali kula. | will be very pleased to see me". |

Both of them think (*pikir*) and have their own opinions. The princess addresses herself using the first pronoun *kula*. The expression "I think" (*pikir kula*) is rare in traditional texts: here we find the "emergence" of the individual who thinks.

Their opinions, however, are opposed to the thinking of the protagonist. Panji Wulung thinks in a different manner and refuses their proposal:

| | |
|---|---|
| 297. Meureun bae ayeuna mah, | It is probable that now |
| kitu manah nyai putri, | such is your mind, princess. |
| saperkara masih anyar, | The incident happened a little while ago. |
| ditulung dina balai, | You have been saved from disaster. |
| enggeus lawas mah lali, | But you will forget it as time goes by |
| mo eling satungtung rambut, | and will not remember even a hair of |
| kadua perkarana, | the two incidents. |
| mangke lamun enggeus mukti, | It will be proved later, |
| lali bae urut ayeuna masakat. | you will forget the trace of misery you have now. |
| | |
| 298. Kitu wateking manusa, | It is human nature, |
| pikirna sok gancang lali, | thoughts are easily forgotten. |
| pitulung anu katukang, | The help which one received in the past |
| babari leungit kalindih, | will easily be forgotten. |
| paribasa ti aki, | A proverb of the elders says, |
| cara halodo satahun, | the dry season continues one year, |
| lantis sakali hujan, | once it rains, all becomes wet. |
| kahadean kitu deui, | The good is the same. |
| leungit musna ari manggih kagorengan. | [It] disappears completely when it meets evil. |

Panji's refusal causes strong tensions. The princess Andayaningrat "challenges" him to vow that she will not forget her words; if she does, she will die (stanza 300). This is a new type of woman with a strong will, whereas the traditional type of female characters never clearly express their opinion. As an example of the latter type of character, Panji's mother, Tunjungsari, may be mentioned as a caring mother who cherishes her son, weeps often, and hardly speaks. A novelty expressed in this *wawacan* is that some female characters emerge as individuals who have their own opinions and discuss them with others. Another emerging "modern" woman can be seen in the episode in which the queen of Cempa accuses the unfaithful vassals of Cempa at the resthouse after the battle (stanzas 930–3). In this case, the woman plays a prominent role in the text.

Independent-thinking females are not the only novelty in this text; critically thinking young men who question the advice of the older generation also form a departure from traditional typecasting. Conflict between the young and the old is presented, something rare in traditional texts in which the young always respect the old and usually follow their advice. Such conflicts can be detected in the dialogue between Panji Wulung and the king of Cempa: the king intends to execute the deceitful Andakasura, but Panji Wulung asks the king to set him free (stanzas 331–4). Tension occurs between them and is solved differently from that in traditional texts: the older man is persuaded by the young protagonist to follow his opinion, because it is right in terms of rational thinking. In other words, the old and traditional is put aside by the young and modern. This can also be seen in the above episode, in the conflict between the old peasant and Panji Wulung. The conflicts in this text cause tensions: every character has his/her own opinion, and individuals are recognized.

In the end, Panji's followers, Janggali and Janggala, succeed in easing the tension between Panji and the princess with their jokes. The princess smiles. Then the solution is offered by Panji Wulung's faithful right-hand man, Daeng Bramani, who suggests writing a letter to the king to let him know that the princess is safe. The tension disappears.

A kind of sceptical feeling remains even though the tension has dissolved. Panji thinks of human nature: "it is human nature, [I] think she will forget soon; the help she received in the past will be quickly forgotten". He does not believe in human nature and thinks people forget the favours received from other people. It is as if a fragile feeling catches up with him: everything is passing away, fleeting and one can hold nothing firm. Is it a feeling of the modern? Is it, as Berman has it, that we are all poured "into a maelstrom of perpetual disintegration and renewal, of struggle and contradiction, of ambiguity and anguish" (Berman

1982: 15)? The narrator of *Wawacan Panji Wulung* lived in a changing world. Novelty and modern representation induce insecurity. Nothing is familiar or stable, and such feelings are likely to be evoked. A new political order arises based on impersonal bureaucratic systems operated by salaried government officials sent from Batavia to the small towns and rural areas throughout the island of Java. Borders, boundaries, and fences bring a feeling of alienation and isolation, especially in the towns. Thus, one is caught by feelings of insecurity and unpredictability. Trust is difficult to obtain in such a society. Instead, lies or honeyed words and feelings of danger surround the people: the anonymity of the administrative apparatus versus the visibility of those in power.

*Wawacan Panji Wulung* is permeated by such a feeling of anxiety, anguish, ambiguity, and uncertainty.[30] The expression *urang tambah susah* (we are increasingly in anguish) symbolizes the feeling of the narrator.[31] Of course, such expressions can also be found in other *wawacan* and are familiar to the reader. This particular text evokes tensions throughout, as we can witness in the tense dialogue between Panji Wulung and the princess of Cempa. To Panji's rejection of the princess's proposal to return immediately to Cempa, she reacts angrily: "you tell nonsense. I did make a vow, didn't I? I offered my life and body, is it still not enough? I am in deep anguish" (*ari kakang misaur nu moal-moal. Apan enggeus kuring sumpah, naruhkeun nyawa jeung diri, kutan masih keneh kurang, susah temen diri kuring*).

In Marshall Berman's terms, words like *susah* represent the body of experience of "modernity". The atmosphere surrounding the people in the Dutch East Indies was similar to his vision of modernity; it seems to be "an environment that promises us adventure, power, joy, growth, transformation of ourselves and the world — and, at the same time, that threatens to destroy everything we have, everything we know, everything we are" (Berman 1982: 15). In such a society, one can "not believe" (*teu percaya*) each other, and much *bohong* (lying) and *napsu* (lust, passion) are around, causing *susah* (anguish) and *kaduhung* (regret) for the people. Their state of mind was becoming insecure. The existing values and norms of the communities were being questioned and new ones were beginning to infiltrate Sundanese society, both materially and spiritually. *Wawacan Panji Wulung* reflects the struggle of its narrator with certain modern developments and his attempts to introduce novel ideas and concepts to his readers. It may therefore be interpreted as an expression of the burgeoning of modernity in Sundanese writing.

One reason why *Wawacan Panji Wulung* is superior to other printed *wawacan* is the good blend of traditional narrative and modern elements. This *wawacan* was printed and published by the colonial government among other *wawacan* which provided practical knowledge or moralistic education. These new types of *wawacan* in print were a mismatch, as shown in Chapter 2. *Wawacan Katrangan Miara Lauk Cai* (Explaining the Cultivation of Freshwater Fish) or *Wawacan Wulang Guru* (*Wawacan* of Lessons for Teachers) are good examples of those providing practical knowledge. *Wawacan Dongeng-dongeng Tuladan* (*Wawacan* of Model Stories) is a compilation of moralistic stories. *Wawacan Ali Muhtar* (*Wawacan* of the Story of Ali Muhtar) is a narrative that teaches moral through the protagonist Ali Muhtar. *Wawacan Panji Wulung,* however, mainly provides amusement although moralistic teachings are interwoven in the long narrative. New elements of modernity do not interfere with reading but rather add fascination and excitement. *Wawacan Panji Wulung* is old but at the same time new.

Another reason for its superiority is its comprehensiveness. *Wawacan Panji Wulang* is the longest narrative among the other printed *wawacan*. All other printed *wawacan* are much shorter and less comprehensive as a story. A suitable length is necessary for *wawacan* to tell an exciting story in the tradition of Sundanese writing. When *Wawacan Panji Wulung* was published and widely read by the people in the second half of the nineteenth century, traditional *wawacan* were still being produced in manuscript form and read. Thus, *Wawacan Panji Wulung* was not exclusively read. Print technology provided the people with more reading books than ever before. This was the time when modernity was burgeoning in the community — a period of transition. This *wawacan* fitted in with the time and was the complete product of modern innovations: printing technology and the Western school system.

# Chapter 5

# The Change in the Configuration

## 1. The Changing Configuration of Sundanese Writing

Sundanese writing in print came into public circulation after 1850. These printed materials could not but have an effect on the configuration of Sundanese writing as a whole. Selected writings began to appear in print, designed according to European ideas of what a book should look like, and presenting the public with new elements and features. One of the changes in the configuration was the remarkable advance of prose. Printing technology and prose became a good match as will be detailed below. On the other hand, poetry, especially *wawacan*, or narrative poetry, seemed to fail in print because of the mismatch of the traditional form of writing and new content, which was moralistic and practical, whereas traditional *wawacan* was primarily for entertainment. This was not foreseen by the colonial administrators, scholars, and educators. They thought that poetry would be a good medium to educate and enlighten the Sundanese. It was not wrong, but it was not compatible with printing. The one exception was *Wawacan Panji Wulung*, which was to remain well-known for a long time. Its reputation seemed to confirm the Dutch belief that the Sundanese favoured poetry.

Printed materials as well as the European type of schools had a great impact on the indigenous communities. It is possible that these innovations stimulated reading activities in the communities. Schools certainly produced more literate people and the printed materials indirectly affected the notion of reading. More people became interested in reading activities, it seemed. Witness the number of manuscripts that were produced during this period, as Ekadjati's inventory tells us. Many *wawacan* in manuscript form were created and old ones were copied in the late nineteenth century.[1] It seems that *wawacan* was constantly a popular genre among the Sundanese although printed *wawacan* was not.

However, some *wawacan* that were circulating in manuscript form began to be printed in the first decade of the twentieth century, such as *Wawacan Angling Darma* (The Story of Angling Darma). A traditional work, it was published under the author's name, Martanegara, in 1906 by a private firm in Bandung, Toko Tjitak Afandi. Forty years earlier, Moesa had written that it was a story purely for entertainment purposes and that it was not suitable for children because it did not contain any useful knowledge (Moesa 1867: 5). This example suggests that *wawacan* for entertainment were widely favoured. The popularity of *wawacan* and its poetic form *dangding* lasted for a long time among the Sundanese.

## *Kalimah, Omongan, Basa Dilajur:* prose

Printing, however, was more suited to prose than to traditional poetry. One of the most knowledgeable missionaries on Sundanese writing, Coolsma, believed that prose should be developed among the Sundanese because it would embody the novelties of modernity (Coolsma 1881: 145). The most productive Sundanese writer, Moehamad Moesa, explains why prose should be preferred to poetry (*dangding*) in the preface to one of his books, *Dongeng-dongeng Pieunteungeun* (Model Stories), published in 1867.

| | |
|---|---|
| Eta dongeng anoe reja, | Most of the stories are |
| teu dianggit make dangding, | not composed in *dangding*, |
| ngan make pada kalimah, | but in *kalimah*. |
| lain soesah njijeun dangding, | Not that it is difficult to make *dangding*, |
| ngan eta leuwih hasil, | but [*kalimah*] will be more effective. |
| tara kasedek koe lagoe, | [They will] never be disturbed by songs. |
| tjarita bisa kebat, | Stories can progress fast, |
| tara katarik koe dangding, | unperturbed by *dangding*, |
| didangoena ngeunah gampang kahartina. | pleasant to listen to and easy to understand. |

(Moesa 1867: 5)

*Kalimah* is the key word here, and it can best be translated as "prose".[2] Moesa explains why prose should be preferred to poetry (*dangding*): stories in *kalimah* can progress faster than in poetry, as the course of a story in poetry is often slowed down by ornamentations. Moreover, prose is more transparent and clear. Thus, in the wake of new printing techniques, Sundanese writing was to follow a new path in which legibility and easy understanding were to become more important than artfulness. Of course, it is ironical that Moesa felt compelled to defend the expedience of prose by way of a poem before starting his prose tales — it reads like a symbolic moment of transition. In due course, the voice, so self-evident for Moesa, was to be silenced and poetry came to lose its superior position in the configuration of Sundanese writing.

A similar symbolic moment can be found in the work of Kartawinata, a son of Moehamad Moesa, who not only recognized the preference of prose to *dangding* but also tried to make prose an artistic form equivalent to poetry. In the preface to *Carita Kapitan Bonteku*, published in 1874, he explained why he did not compose in *dangding* to attract the reader's attention, and he too used *dangding* to explain the superiority of prose:

| | |
|---|---|
| Tapi teu didjieun dangding, | But [this is] not composed in *dangding*, |
| lain sabab soesah ngarang, | not because it is difficult to compose. |
| nja eta dihadja bae, | But it is done intentionally. |
| ngan diatoer kalimahna, | Prose is arranged |
| make pada omongan, | by means of *omongan*. |
| diwatjana koedoe njemoe, | When reading it one should follow |
| ninggang kana wirahmana. | the right rhythm. |
| | |
| Moen kitoe ngeunah teh teuing, | If you do so, it will be very pleasant. |
| tetela ti batan tembang, | [It will be] clearer than sung poetry. |
| matjana oelah digorol, | The reading may not be rattled off. |
| | |
| hanteu poegoeh ngarandegna, | It will be incoherent and faltering |
| da ieu basa Soenda, | because this is Sundanese. |
| koedoe njemoe tjara pantoen, | You have to follow the way of *pantun*, |
| ngan montong make aleuan. | as long as you do not stretch your voice. |

(Kartawinata 1874: 3)

Here the key word is no longer *kalimah* but *omongan*, something that is spoken (Coolsma 1913: 424). To make sure that his prosaic tale would not lead to too much confusion among his readers, Kartawinata still saw to it that it could be read aloud as if it were a *pantun*, the verse form used by Sundanese storytellers. *Omongan*, he seems to claim, is a new artful form of writing, closely related to the artful forms of performing tales. *Carita Kapitan Bonteku* was clearer and more pleasant to read (or even to recite) than *dangding* could ever be.

*Carita Kapitan Bonteku* was not the only book written in *omongan* in the late nineteenth century. Kartawinata himself had translated *Cariyos Tuwan Kapitan Marion* into prose two years earlier, and in the following years his sisters translated other European stories into a form of prose. These writings could be seen as the beginnings of *omongan*, the artful prose that by the 1920s was given the name *basa dilajur* (literally, "free words") by a new generation of literates (Goeroe 1926: 14).[3]

Kartawinata's younger sister, Lenggang Kantjana, also made some intriguing remarks on prose and reading:

| | |
|---|---|
| Ijeu koe koela disalin, | This is translated by me. |
| dipindahkeun kana soenda, | It is changed into Sundanese |
| tapi diomongkeun bae, | but uttered just in prose, |
| hanteu dikarang koe tembang, | not composed in *tembang*, |
| saperkara soesahna, | Firstly, it is difficult |
| neangan omongan roentoet, | to search for *omongan* in harmony |
| parele bener dangdingna. | with the coherence of *dangding*. |
| | |
| Sanadjan teu salah dangding, | Though *dangding* is not wrong, |
| ari teu beres omongan, | if *omongan* is in disorder, |
| tangtoe henteu djadi sae, | certainly it will not become good. |
| kaoela remen manggihan, | I often come across |
| noe ngarang basa soenda, | people composing Sundanese, |
| ngan ngoeroes bae dangdingdoeng, | but only taking care of formal aspects of *dangding*, |
| basana pabeulit pisan. | so the wording is very confusing. |
| | |
| Kadoea anoe dipambrih, | Secondly, what is meant here, |
| noe matak henteu koe tembang, | the reason writing is not composed in *tembang* |

| | |
|---|---|
| baris aoseun diilo, | is that it is to be read silently |
| njalira di pagoelingan, | when you are alone in your bed |
| djeung dina korsi gojang, | or in a rocking chair. |
| eta kitoe noe dimaksoed, | That is what I mean by |
| noeroetan oerang Eropa. | following Europeans. |

(Lenggang Kantjana 1887: 1–2)

In the preface to her compilation of translated stories, Lenggang Kantjana used the word *omongan* to mean artful, *pantun*-like prose, much like her brother did. She gave it an additional nuance: *omongan* stood for "harmonious phrasing". Indeed, the echoes of *dangding* were still being heard.

At the time Kartawinata was writing about *omongan*, reading aloud was still common; it was even advocated by Kartawinata. Reading was usually voiced, done by intoning or reciting the way a *pantun* was performed. Lenggang Kantjana may have been the first to express in writing that reading could be done by oneself, for oneself, perhaps even in silence. Tales were *baris aoseun diilo* "something to be read silently", she suggests — *diilo* referring to reading alone or with a soft voice, and skimming over (Coolsma 1913: 240).[4] Reading a book could be a personal, silent activity that Sundanese readers could do lying on a bed or sitting in a rocking chair, just as the Europeans did. *Kalimah, omongan, diilo*: these are terms that indicate the emergence of a new way of reading, a new way of writing that was to lead to the introduction of the novel, a genre that changed the configuration of Sundanese writing as a whole.

Lenggang Kantjana tells her readers that she reads Dutch stories to dispel boredom (*kesel*), yet another phenomenon that may have been a major tool in the creation of modernity (Maier 1993a: 147–50).

| | |
|---|---|
| Tina rasa kesel pikir, | Because of feeling bored, |
| waktoe taja pagawejan, | when there is no work, |
| tamba hees sore-sore, | as a remedy for sleeping in the late afternoon. |
| heug matja boekoe walanda, | [I] read Dutch books. |
| tjarita warna-warna, | There are various stories, |
| reja noe matak kajoengjoen, | most of which made me interested. |
| kaoela datang pikiran. | So I had an idea. |

| | |
|---|---|
| Bowa hade moen disalin, | How nice it would be if they were translated. |
| soegan aja manpaätna, | Probably they would be useful |
| baris ngabeberah hate, | and would be entertaining. |
| malaur ngomong ngatjomang, | It is better than talking and chatting |
| anoe taja pedahna, | which has no use |
| atawa tjitjing ngadjentoel, | or sitting and pondering |
| mikiran noe lalamoenan. | and daydreaming. |

(Lenggang Kantjana 1887: 4)

A new type of reader was being born, one who read silently and to alleviate boredom. Feelings of modernity were infiltrating people's minds in the East Indies.

After 1870, an increasing number of translated stories were published in Sundanese. They could be called transitional writings in terms of form as well as content, in that they prepared the way for the novel. The most important person engaged in the production of translations was the above-mentioned Kartawinata (1846–1906). Kartawinata realized that the island of Java was facing many new phenomena through his carrier. Figures like him may have been rare in West Java, yet they became the motor behind the change in Sundanese writing.

## Carita Kapitan Bonteku

Kartawinata, together with his brothers and sisters and other Sundanese children, had learned Dutch in Garut[5] and he later became a student of K.F. Holle (Snouck Hurgronje 1927: 119). Kartawinata translated Dutch texts into Sundanese, Javanese, and Malay on a wide variety of subjects: Dutch stories such as *Kapitan Bonteku;* a handbook of agricultural knowledge in 14 volumes written by K.F. Holle, *Mitra nu tani*; and government publications such as *Aturan Ngurus Sakit-sakitan di India Nederland* (Regulations for the Application of Punishment in the Dutch East Indies).[6] He also compiled an arithmetic book, a Sundanese-Dutch conversation manual (*Pagoeneman Soenda jeng Walanda*), and a Dutch-Sundanese dictionary (*Hollandsch-Soendaasch Woordenboek*) with P. Blussé.

Kartawinata was appointed adjunct translator for Sundanese language in February 1874 and later raised to the rank of official translator.[7] The government in Batavia regarded him as a very reliable translator and awarded him a silver medal. Along with his work as a translator, he was appointed *patih* of Sumedang in 1883, and later served as a *zelfstandig patih*[8] of Sukabumi (1892–1904). He died in 1906. Kartawinata could write faultless Dutch and had many friends and acquaintances in the Dutch community.

His elder sister, Lasminingrat, had similar talents for languages and composition but stopped her writing activities when she became the wife (*raden ayu*) of the Regent of Garut, and focused her attention on the education of Sundanese girls, an activity reminiscent of those of her contemporary Kartini.[9] Like her brother, she had good Dutch friends, among whom was Levyssohn Norman, Secretary-General of the Dutch East Indies Government, who called her Saartje in his memoirs (Levyssohn Norman 1888b: 95). They had become acquainted when as a young girl she stayed at the house of his brother-in-law, the *controleur* of Sumedang.

In a letter to P.J. Veth, K.F. Holle expresses his admiration for Kartawinata and Lasminingrat:

> The son of the *panghulu*, who writes and speaks Dutch rather well, translated in prose the travels of Bontekoe, Robinson Crusoe, the travels of Marion to New Zealand, and a number of fragments of *The Javanese Farmer's Companion, Mitra nu tani*. The daughter of the *panghulu*, who was married to the Regent of Garut, faithfully adapted the fairy tales of Grimm, the stories from Wonderland (by Goeverneur) and others in Sundanese. The government has already given authorisation to print one of her compilations.
>
> De zoon v. d. pangh, die vrij goed Holl. schrijft en spreekt, vertaalde in proza de reis van Bontekoe, Robinson Crusoë, de reis van Marion naar Nieuw Zeeland, menig stukje van de Vriend v. d. Javaanschen landman: Mitra noe tani. De dochter v.d. pangh., welke den Regent v. Garoet huwde, vertelt de Märchen v. Grimm, de vertelsels uit het wonderland (v. Goeverneur) etc. zeer goed in 't Soend. na. De Regeering gaf reeds magtiging om een bundel v. haar te doen drukken.[10]

Kartawinata's first translation was *Carios Tuwan Kapitan Marion*, an abridged prose version in Sundanese of *The Story of Captain Marion*.[11] It was published in 1872 and printed in Javanese script by the government printing house Landsdrukkerij; his Javanese version of the same story was published in the same year.[12] It is the story of the journey of Captain Marion to New Zealand, where he and his crew established friendly relations with the local population until something went wrong and the captain was killed.

**Plate 8.** Kartawinata (above) and Lasminingrat (below)
*Source: Royal Netherlands Institute of Southeast Asian and Caribbean Studies (KITLV), Department of Archives & Images.*

**Table 11.** Sundanese Translations of European Stories in the Nineteenth Century

| | |
|---|---|
| 1872 | Kartawinata, *Cariyos Tuwan Kapitan Marion/Geschiedenis van den Kapitein Marion*, Javanese script, 5015 ex. |
| 1874 | Kartawinata, *Carita kapitan Bonteku*, Javanese script, 5015 ex.; translated from a version of *Journael ofte gedenckwaerdige beschrijvinghe van de Oost-Indische reyse van Willem Ysbrandtsz Bontekoe*. |
| 1883 | – 2nd edition, Javanese. |
| 1903 | – new edition, Javanese. |
| 1924 | – [4th edition], Roman. |
| 1875 | Lasminingrat, *Carita Erman*, Javanese, 6015 ex.; translated from: Christoph von Schmid, *Hendrik van Eichenfels*, Dutch version translated from German in 1833. |
| 1911 | – 2nd edition, Javanese. |
| 1922 | – 3rd edition, Roman. |
| 1876 | Lasminingrat, R.A., *Warnasari atawa rupa-rupa dongeng*, Javanese; translated from: Märchen von Grimm and J.J.A. Goeverneur, *Vertelsels uit het wonderland voor kinderen, klein en groot*, 1872, and some others. |
| 1903 | – new edition, Javanese. |
| 1907 | – [3rd edition], Javanese. |
| 1879 | Kartawinata, *Carita Robinson Crusoë*, Javanese script, 10015 ex.; translated from: Daniel Defoe, *De geschiedenis van Robinson Crusoë*; Dutch version translated by Gerard Keller, 1869. |
| 1887 | Lasminingrat, R.A., *Warnasari*, vol. 2, Roman; translated from: Märchen von Grimm and J.J.A. Goeverneur, *Vertelsels uit het wonderland voor kinderen, klein en groot*, 1872, et cetera. |
| 1909 | – [2nd edition], Roman. |
| 1887 | Lenggang Kantjana, R., *Warnasari*, vol. 3, Roman., 6015 ex. |
| 1909 | – [2nd edition], Roman. |
| 1912 | – [3rd edition], Roman. |

Perhaps an even greater accomplishment was the above-mentioned *Carita Kapitan Bonteku*. This was the translation or adaptation that Kartawinata made in 1874 of the *Journal of Willem Ysbrandtsz Bontekoe*, a well-known book about the adventures of Captain Bontekoe and his ship during his voyage from Hoorn in Holland to the Dutch East Indies between the years 1618 and 1625. Since its first publication in the seventeenth century it had appeared in some 80 editions, and almost every Dutch student must have been familiar with it at the time (Schendeveld-van der Dussen 1993: 289; Hoogewerff 1952: xlix).[13] Just like the original Dutch version, the Sundanese translation contained many lessons. Holle, who clearly supported this publication by his student, hoped that the story of Bontekoe would contribute to a positive attitude towards the Dutch among the local population:

> Especially books that do not contain dogma, but nevertheless sometimes convince indigenous people that we also have high moral standards, can be very effective in moderating their antipathy towards Europeans and weakening their feeling that we are infidels. Bontekoe's travels, which are published in Sundanese and Javanese, have already elicited exclamations from more than one indigenous person such as "he [Bontekoe] truly was a pious person", or "I did not realise that the Dutch fostered such deep God-fearing feelings."

> Vooral boeken waarin van geen dogma sprake is, doch waardoor de inlanders zijns ondanks soms tot de overtuiging komt dat wij ook zedelijk hoog staan kunnen veel doen, om den tegenzin tegen de Europeaan te temperen en het gevoelen dat wij kafirs zijn te verzwakken. De reis van Bontekoe in het Soendaasch en Javaansch uitgegeven, ontlokte reeds meer dan een inlander de uitroep dat was een waarlijk vroom man of ik dacht niet dat ook de Hollanders zulke diepe godvrezende gevoelens koesterden.[14]

Bontekoe's piety and trust in the Lord must have struck the young native readers. Facing disaster, only God (*Allah, Pangeran, Gusti, Gusti Allah*) can determine the fate of human beings, the book told them.[15] The Dutch believed in God, and this message was repeated throughout the text. For instance:

> Bonteku snarled: "Have patience and show resignation, within 3 days we will surely find land. Have faith in God, the Creator of mankind who decides between happiness and misfortune, between life and death. If we have patience and show resignation to fate as decided by God, are tenacious towards the Lord, and do not give up our efforts, certainly God will provide help to us. With God's will, believe in me and in 3 days we will find land."

> Bonteku nyentak: "Sing salabar tawekal bae, 3 poe deui ge urang tangtu manggih daratan, masing percaya ka Gusti Allah nu ngadamel

mahluk kabeh, sarta bagja cilaka paeh-hirupna, mun urang sabar tawekal pasrah kana takdirullah pageuh muntang ka Pangeran, jeung teu tinggal ihtiar, tangtu Gusti Allah maparin pitulung ka urang, insya Allah masing percaya ka kami 3 poe deui manggih daratan" (Kartawinata 1924: 18).

Apart from this belief in God, the tale of Bontekoe also portrays the supremacy of the civilized West over the wild "native" and, as a consequence, the hostile relationship between them. Passages from *Carita Kapitan Bonteku* depicting the natives of the island of Sumatra, where Bontekoe and his crew arrived after a fire on their ship, indicate European views of the natives, who were backward in their eyes.

*Cariyos Tuwan Kapitan Marion* and *Caritana Kapitan Bonteku* were in accordance with the colonial ideology. Unlike the English Robinson Crusoe,[16] they suggest strong differences between the Europeans and natives, and one will fail to find indications of successful, let alone pleasant, interracial contacts. The Dutch colonial ideology was based on the idea that the natives should be kept at a proper distance, but directly discriminatory depictions of the natives were to be avoided so as not to create local antipathy against the colonizers. However, the publication of Kartawinata's translations, in which this discrimination is expressed, should be seen as an exception to this policy. Perhaps the relative success of *Carita Kapitan Bonteku* — it became well-known among the Sundanese and was reprinted three times after its first impression of 5,015 copies — might be explained by the fact that the Sundanese literates, mostly elites, read this as merely a foreign story: the island of Sumatra was foreign land for them at that time.

The extensive depiction of European behaviour and ideas was not the only novelty in Kartawinata's translation. Equally intriguing and shocking for indigenous readers must have been the foreign objects and persons illustrated by etched drawings, in a very concrete and realistic manner (see Plate 9). In comparison with Balinese and Javanese manuscripts, the Sundanese ones contained few illuminations and drawings (Ekadjati 1996: 101–28). The combination of writing and drawing in a book must have been a radical novelty for Sundanese readers, who could now read a story and develop a vision of its events. Readers were forced to look and watch, so to speak, a new way of experiencing the world which, as described in the previous chapter, is an important key to modernization. Realistic illustrations could be found in other Sundanese books such as *Kitab Atoeran Bab Maradjian*

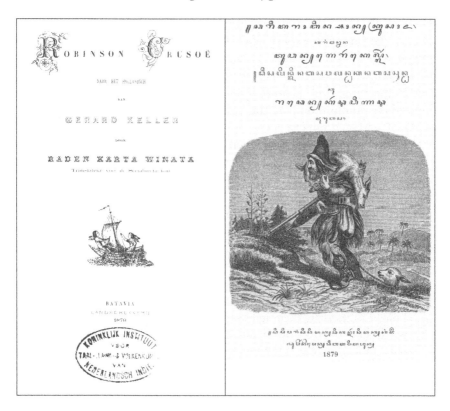

Plate 9. The title page of *Carita Robinson Crusoë*, published in 1879.

*Djelema Noe Ngedjoeroe* (The Handbook of Midwifery), written by Moehamad Saleh Mangkoepradja (a "Dokter Jawa" or indigenous doctor in Sumedang who had studied Western medicine) and published in 1901.[17] The book explains the Western method of assisting in childbirth, and it must have caused a sensation among Sundanese readers because of the novel and realistic drawings of female bodies in it — once again, the visual element was given a strong emphasis.

The third novelty in these translations was the narrative voice. In the original story of Bontekoe, Captain Bontekoe himself tells of his adventurous journey to the Dutch East Indies. In the Sundanese version, the narrator tells us the story of Captain Bontekoe in the third person. Kartawinata did not attempt to translate the story using the first person narration, as this style of storytelling was unknown to Sundanese readers.

He himself says in the preface that this story "is not composed by others, but by the one who experienced it himself" (*lain dianggit koe batoer, anggitan noe ngalakonan*). By this, he meant that the story was not fiction but written on the basis of real incidents. The statement was novel but at the same time it must have confused its readers because of the unfamiliar combination of the third person's narrative voice and the story of personal experiences.

Kartawinata's sister went even further than this. Lasminingrat used the word *kula*, denoting "I" in the preface of *Warnasari atawa roepa-roepa dongeng* (Colourful Essence or various tales), a compilation of her translations that was published in 1876.[18] This must have been one of the first cases in which the first person pronoun was used to address the reader directly in Sundanese writing, apart from the instances of reported speech in the traditional narrative:

> These are stories composed by authors in the old days in the Netherlands. When I read the books, the idea came to my mind that I ought to translate them into Sundanese so that the Sundanese, too, would like to read them because of their entertaining value. At the same time, I hope that the essence will be harvested and the lessons followed by many people.

> Ari eta mah karangan bujangga baheula bae, nu ngarang eta dongeng di nagara Walanda. Barang kula ilo eta buku datang inget tanda salin kana basa Sunda, supaya urang Sunda milu suka maca, tina karameanana. Malih mandar kapetik acina, kaalaranana, katurut wurukna (Lasminingrat 1876: [1–2]).

Most of the books that Moesa's children translated were children's books that were widely read in the motherland. They were used as reading materials in schools in West Java[19] at the recommendation of Holle, who introduced the didactic and moralistic elements.[20] Meanwhile, Lasminingrat tried to combine those elements with entertainment in her translations. In this, she differed from her father, who had argued that books should be read not for entertainment but for useful knowledge only (Moesa 1867: 4). It turned out that such a combination in a book was desirable and became favoured reading materials in the age of modernity, as seen in Tables 8 and 9 (Chapter 2). *Wawacan Panji Wulung* was no exception either, although it is unlikely that Moesa intended it.

## 2. The Rise of a Kind of New Writing

Not only did the predominant position of prose together with the emergence of new writings such as European translations, cause the changes in the configuration of Sundanese writing, but colonial institutions and local entrepreneurs were also significant instruments in disseminating the new forms of writings. The establishment of the *Commissie voor de Inlandsche School- en Volkslectuur* (Committee for Indigenous Schoolbooks and Popular Reading Books) in 1908 created a new context for Sundanese writing. Another context was the advent of commercial printing houses financed with local capital. These new contexts caused changes in Sundanese writing, but they were not considered drastic, but a kind of shift — a new literary stream emerged paralleling the existing tradition of manuscript and oral tradition.

Symbolically, this shift is best represented in the rise of the "novel" (*roman*) in Sundanese, which in terms of its form and the introduction of "realism" can be regarded as the successor of the *omongan* writings introduced through European prose translations. The Sundanese novel, fiction in prose, emerged in the 1910s, according to Solomon, a specialist in modern Sundanese literature (1993: 11-3). This was apparently stimulated by the Dutch *roman* or novel (Teeuw 1986: 53-4),[21] in part through intermediary Malay language prose. *Wawacan* and other traditional writings were gradually pushed aside by the novel and became forms of writing that lagged behind the times, especially those in printed form.

In 1914, the first Sundanese novel, *Baruang Ka Nu Ngarora* (Poison For The Youth), was published. D.K. Ardiwinata, chief editor of the Sundanese section in the above-mentioned Committee, may be identified as the author, although the title page of the first volume does not mention his name. The book was published in two volumes consisting of 63 and 48 pages each by a large private printing house, G. Kolff & Co. in Weltevreden, as number 90 in the series of the Committee for Indigenous Schoolbooks and Popular Reading Books.

The title pages of the two volumes had the words "*carita hiji jalma cilaka lantaran meunang kanyeri ti pamajikan*" (the tale of a man made unfortunate by the pain suffered from his wife) below the title. The word *carita* meant "tale" in conventional Sundanese writing (Coolsma 1913: 662). The translations and adaptations of the European stories in prose were also called *carita*, as in *Carita Kapitan Bonteku*. However, the title of this new writing, *Baruang Ka Nu Ngarora* (Poison For

The Youth), clearly suggests a moralistic story in contrast to the titles of traditional writings and translations, which sounded much more neutral in this respect. The "titles" of traditional writings normally contain a reference to the genre, and the name of the main protagonist only. Moreover, the subtitle of this writing introduces the contents of the story in a concrete manner, a feature never before found in Sundanese writing. Subtitling itself was rare. The form of writing is *omongan*, in Kartawinata's terms. The language is less ornamental and contains fewer idiomatic expressions and clichés than traditional writing. The difference with traditional writing becomes immediately apparent at the start of the novel. The first passage of *Baruang Ka Nu Ngarora* reads as follows:

> Sunday evening 14 Hapit 1291 (23 December 1874) at the house of Mr. Haji Abdul Raup in the village of Pasar, it was unusually busy. As if something strange had happened. The shutters were opened, all the lights were lit, the house was really bright and glittering; the floor in the centre of the house was covered by a carpet. In the kitchen people moved to and fro, apparently busy preparing food. Many passers-by stopped for a while, and asked themselves, "What is going on in the house of Mr. Haji? Why are there so many people?"

> Malem Senen tanggal 14 boelan Hapit 1291 di boemina toean Hadji Abdoel Raoep, di kampoeng Pasar, haneuteun pisan, teu cara sasari, kawas aja perkara noe aneh. Tingkeban diboeka, lampoe kabeh diseungeut, mani tjaang marakbak; tengah imah di kepoet koe alketip. Di dapoer djelema pasoeliwer, semoe keur oeroes[2] popolah. Djelema noe ngaliwat loba anoe ngarandeg, bari ngomong di djero atina: "Aja naon di boemi toean Hadji, bet haneuteun teuing?" (Ardiwinata 1914: 3).

The time is definite (the 14th day of the month of Hapit in 1291), the place is concrete (at the house of Mr. Haji Abdul Raup in the village of Pasar), and the protagonist has his own name. The setting of *carita* is quite individual, being different from a passage like "once upon a time, there was a kingdom", as in traditional writing. The monologue of passers-by is in everyday style. The description is realistic in terms of the setting and characters, and they are individualistic at the same time. This individualization can be considered the representation of the "modern self", as discussed in the preceding chapters. As Ian Watt suggests, "the novel is surely distinguished from other genres and from previous forms of fiction by the amount of attention it habitually accords both to the individualisation of its characters and to the detailed presentation of their environment" (Watt 1974: 17–8). This realism cannot be found in traditional Sundanese writings. There are examples where traditional writings tried to depart from conventions, but they still reflect the tendency to conform to traditional practices.

*Wawacan Panji Wulung* can be placed in between the traditional and modern. There is a burgeoning of individualization and realism, but the extent found in the *wawacan* is different from the novel. The translation and adaptation of European stories may be considered as occupying a transitional position that is closer to the novel: the same form of writing, *omongan*, was employed but the above-mentioned concepts of modern writing had not yet developed fully.

Changes in the context of indigenous writing were partly caused by the establishment of the Committee for Indigenous Schoolbooks and Popular Reading Books. The idea of institutionalizing the publication of indigenous writing dates back to the 1860s. Government publications in Sundanese had already started at that time. A high-ranking Dutch official for Javanese, A.B. Cohen Stuart (1825–76), suggested establishing a bureau for indigenous languages in his report to the Board of the Batavian Society for Arts and Science in 1866:

> This [lack] could to a certain extent be repaired by the proposed establishment of a bureau for indigenous languages, which as far as necessary may also be given the task of that evaluation [of textbooks], and for that purpose should be provided with every possible means.
>
> Hierin zou reeds eenigermate worden voorzien door de voorgestelde oprigting van een bureau voor de inlandsche talen, hetwelk mede, voor zooveel noodig, met die beoordeeling zou belast, en daartoe door alle beschikbare hulpmiddelen zooveel mogelijk in staat gesteld worden (Cohen Stuart 1866: 77).

His report claims further that the bureau was necessary in order to limit government expenses (Cohen Stuart 1866: 70–9),[22] a common strategy of Dutch officials to strengthen their arguments.

From the 1850s onwards, the publishing of indigenous books, especially schoolbooks, had been financed from the government budget, as seen in Chapter 2. Publishing was very costly indeed, as Cohen Stuart said. Choosing "good" drafts, printing and distributing them — everything was undertaken by the government printing house Landsdrukkerij, and Sundanese books were no exception. Cohen Stuart proposed to put a stop to this and turn over the task to private printing houses. In the mid-nineteenth century, some European and Eurasian printing houses had begun printing a few indigenous books alongside books in the European languages, mostly in Dutch, on a commercial basis. Cohen Stuart said that the government should take only a small role in the publication of books in the indigenous languages and may help the private printing houses to collect payments for their publications using the administrative network exclusively. The bureau in question would then proceed to publish after passing judgement on the proposed books. Nearly forty years passed before his suggestion was realized.

The Committee, headed by G.A.J. Hazeu, the Honorary Adviser for Native Affairs, was installed by government decree in September 1908 (Jedamski 1992: 25). The duty of the Committee was to *"memberi pertimbangan kepada Direkteur Onderwijs dalam hal memilih karangan-karangan jang baik untuk dipakai disekolah-sekolah dan untuk didjadikan batjaan rakja"* (advise the Director of Education in the selection of good writings to be used in schools and to designate reading materials for the people) (Balai Poestaka [1948]: 6). In 1913 D.A. Rinkes succeeded Hazeu as head of the Committee, and in 1917 the independent bureau, which became detached from the Office of the Adviser for Native Affairs, was established under the name Balai Poestaka.[23] In that same year, Rinkes became the first Director of the Bureau. Under his guidance, Balai Poestaka started to streamline its management to assist the colonial government in influencing the public discourse conducted in vernacular languages in the colony. Javanese, Sundanese, Malay, and Madurese editorial boards were set up, and D.K. Ardiwinata, the author of the first Sundanese novel, was appointed chief editor for the Sundanese section. Sundanese writings were examined and selected according to the judgement of the bureau. The indigenous language was checked and standardized following the guidelines of the Balai Poestaka: that "proper" language should be disseminated through the bureau's publications. Needless to say, so were the contents of the publications. A kind of censorship unknown before was applied to writing (Yamamoto 1995: 75–89). Before the establishment of the Committee, the choice of materials for publication had been made in a rather ad-hoc fashion by a particular group of people in line with their ideas and taste. Thus, starting in 1908, an institution was put in place to oversee publication in a more systematic, structured and business-like (*zakelijk*) manner. The publications were sold methodically and also supplied to newly-established public libraries that were attached to schools. In 1918 all phases of publication were undertaken by the institute, and in 1924 it moved to the old Landsdrukkerij (Balai Poestaka 1948). The publications of Balai Poestaka increased and became dominant, as Rinkes had expected.

Another factor that brought about change in the configuration of Sundanese writing was the increase of local printing houses. As mentioned in Chapter 2, a small number of private printing houses started to publish Sundanese books in the late nineteenth century. Most of them were European or Eurasian companies. Up to the early twentieth century, a market economy in the publishing business did not exist. Printing Sundanese books was not profitable because there was little readership for the books. Furthermore, most of the printed books were in Roman script and literacy in that script was severely limited. Printing presses were also rare and expensive.

The situation did seem to have changed by the 1920s. Local entrepreneurs began to participate in the publishing business, and the population growth in the Indies and the increase in literacy may have supported their businesses. Added to this was the increasing availability of printing presses and paper. The conditions for a publishing business gradually emerged, books became a commodity in the Indies, and publishers found opportunities to make a profit from printing Sundanese books.

There were two types of local printing houses. One type consisted of Dutch, Eurasian or Chinese printing houses[24] which received printing orders from Balai Poestaka. The other type was the indigenous printing house — small and "wild" (*liar*), and difficult to put under the control of the colonial government. The bureau of the Committee sometimes sent orders to the first type of printing houses. Their own printing house, Landsdrukkerij, started to limit its offerings of indigenous language books. Sundanese books were printed less often. Still, it is important to bear in mind the role that Landsdrukkerij played in printing schoolbooks and general books in the second half of the nineteenth century, thereby laying the groundwork for commercial printing houses. Through the private printing houses, Sundanese titles were published under the name *Volkslectuur*: *Serie uitgaven door bemiddeling der Commissie voor de Volkslectuur* (A Series of Publications by the Committee for Popular Reading Books), which was displayed on each title page. Most of these printing houses gradually withdrew from the business of printing Sundanese books, especially when the Balai Poestaka itself tried to monopolize the publishing market and stopped sending printing orders to them under the policy of director Rinkes.

Meanwhile, "wild" printing houses sprang up like bamboo shoots after rain (Moriyama 1990: 115–6). Sundanese books printed by such small printing houses increased remarkably from the second decade of the twentieth century. Most of them were in Bandung: they were Toko Boekoe M.I. Prawira-Winata, N.V. Sie Dhian Ho,[25] Insulinde, Sindang Djaja, H.M. Affandi, Dachlan-Bekti, Kaoem Moeda and Nanie. In terms of legibility and paper quality, their publications were usually inferior to those issued by the Balai Poestaka and the distribution was not as good, but the books were cheaper. Compared with those published by the Balai Poestaka, the contents were less moralistic, the language less artificial and the stories more exciting and nationalistic so that they were much loved by the people (Kartini *et al.* 1979: 8–10, 61–3). Some titles became well-known: for instance, books authored by Joehana, such as *Carios Agan Permas* (Tale of Madam Permas), published by Bandung-based Dachlan-Bekti in 1926 (Kartini 1979: 4–17). The authorities tried to control the local printing houses for the sake of order and peace in the colony, mainly through the Balai Poestaka, but this was not an easy task. The books were printed everywhere and circulated directly according to consumer demand. The context of Sundanese writing began to change, becoming freer, more secular, and more dynamic than ever before. The new genre of the "novel" could take advantage of this changed context to promote itself. Notwithstanding the emergence of the novel, traditional poems were still considered a prominent literary form by the Dutch authorities and some of the Sundanese intellectuals.

## *Disappearance of Wawacan*

In his book on early twentieth-century Sundanese writing, van den Berge, for example, has shown that one of the most authoritative magazines of Sundanese culture in the 1930s, *Parahiangan*,[26] featured a *dangding* on the third page of each issue (the most significant page after the front page), dealing with passion, fate, the monarch, nature, or culture (Berge 1993: 79–80). Another witness of the prominent position of poetry is Soewarsih Djojopoespito, a modern Sundanese author who highlights the soothing qualities of poems in a conversation between a young man, Sutrisna, and a young lady, Maryanah, in a novel she wrote in 1937:[27]

> "For me books are like good friends", said Sutrisna, while he let the ash of his cigarette fall into an ashtray. "When we are sad or looking

for the way in life, how great is the help of books! When we are happy, we can enjoy nothing more than reading *guguritan*; when we are in misery, we feel we are getting medicine for our sadness from reading something that shows there are still many things that bring more difficulties than ones we have. And also, when we are looking for the right way, books often guide us into the right direction."

Maryanah agreed and answered: "You mean the right way? [...]."

"Keur abdi mah sobat dalit buku teh", tjeuk Sutrisna, bari ngeprukkeun sekar rokok kana asbak. "Geuning ari urang keur sedih atanapi keur milari djalan hirup, sakitu agengna pitulung buku-buku teh. Dina keur bungah tiasa ngahening-ngahening, maos guguritan, dina keur larana asa kaubaran kasedihan teh, komo upami maos, perkawis nu mintonkeun jen seueur keneh anu langkung ti urang waluratna mah! Sareng deui, upami milari pangdjeudjeuh laku-lampah, buku teh sok nungtun urang kana pimendakeunnana."

Marjanah unggeuk, bari ngawalon:"Pangdjeudjeuh laku lampah urang? [...]" (Djojopoespito 1959: 74).

Djojopoespito seems to suggest that young people in the 1930s were still reading *guguritan*, a genre of traditional poetry different from *wawacan* but in the same form as *dangding*, in search of the meaning of life. The colonial authorities were of the same opinion, as evidenced by the remarks of Hidding, then Director of Balai Poestaka:

> Indeed, next to fairytales in prose and the above-mentioned *pantun* stories, most sagas, legends and traditional stories are composed in *tembang*, that is to say they are composed in a variety of *pupuh* in accordance with the contents of the story; such a compilation is called *wawacan*. This *wawacan* encompasses myths as well as historical narratives (*babad*), Muslim-saint legends and also fairytale-like narratives derived from *wayang*. This [genre] *wawacan* is the main representative of Sundanese literature, which indisputably at present still occupies the first place.

> Immers naast de in proza verhaalde sprookjes en de bovengenoemde pantoenverhalen zijn de meeste sagen, legenden, overleveringen en dgl. in tembang opgesteld, d.w.z. dat zij een naar den inhoud van het verhaalde afwisselende reeks poepoeh's vormen, die met elkaar *wawatjan* heeten. En deze wawatjan omvat zoowel mythen als ook geschiedenisverhalen (babad), Mohammedaansche heiligenlegenden en aan de wajang ontleende sprookjesachtige vertellingen. Deze wawatjan is de voornaamste representant van de Soendaneesche literatuur, die ook nu nog altijd onbetwist de eerste plaats inneemt (Hidding 1935: 128).

*Wawacan*, in short, were still loved by the people in the 1930s — and not only myths, historical narratives and *wayang* stories were composed in *wawacan*, but also experiences from daily life were told in traditional poetry, according to the Director of Balai Poestaka. Thirty years later, Ajip Rosidi has it that a "new" *wawacan* emerged:

> What was told in the form of *wawacan* was no longer only stories of kings, princesses and supernaturally powerful priests, but also the daily life of the writer's time.
>
> Jang ditjeritakan dalam bentuk wawatjan-wawatjan itu bukan lagi hanja hikajat-hikajat tentang radja-radja dan putri-putri serta pendeta-pendeta sakti, melainkan djuga tentang penghidupan sehari-hari pada djaman pengarangnya sendiri (Rosidi 1966: 29).

*Wawacan Enden Sari-banon; carios istri rayungan* (Wawacan of Lady Sari-banon; the story of a skittish lady) by Memed Sastrahadiprawira, published in 1923, *Wawacan noe Kaleungitan Caroge* (Wawacan of One Who Lost a Husband) in 1931, and *Wawacan Rampog di Cimahi tahun 1900* (Wawacan of the 1900 Riot in Cimahi) are good examples of the "new" *wawacan*. The genre was changing in nature: realism, if not journalism, infiltrated this so-called traditional form of writing, to the degree that Wendy Solomon concluded that "realistic *wawacan* could be regarded as novels", *roman anu didandingkeun* (Solomon 1993: 12). Even though it remains to be seen whether the Sundanese term *roman* is equivalent to the English term "novel", it is evident that the notions of *wawacan* were fundamentally changing and that a number of "new" *wawacan* had been published.

The flexibility of *wawacan*, however, was limited in the wake of the introduction of print in the nineteenth century. Printing brought about a change to reading; in addition to reading aloud and singing, other forms together with silent reading gradually spread in the early twentieth century. The people not only enjoyed sound but also obtained knowledge through reading books, especially schoolbooks. The beauty and art of writing became less important than the legibility and intelligibility provided by print technology. Therefore, ornamental and idiomatic expressions and clichés in traditional poetry became an unnecessary requirement in Sundanese writing. Moreover, the rules and metres in poetry were felt to interfere with the progress of the story. Stories written with realism and individuality did not need any rules, only "freedom" to develop. In other words, the new spirit was to fit prose which is more transparent and clear. Prose began to steadily and completely push *wawacan* and *dangding* to the margins of Sundanese writing.

In an article in the Sundanese magazine *Poesaka-Soenda* in 1926, a writer using the pseudonym Goeroe (Teacher) predicted the demise of *wawacan* or stories composed in *dangding* (*"tjarita-tjarita anoe digoerit"*) as follows:

> Now times have changed, as we are experiencing. Stories that are composed in *dangding* have become few in number; what has emerged is free composition. Ideas coming from the west on various things have had enormous influence on Sundanese literature. Many books have been published. Principally they are translations of Dutch or old stories adapted to recent times so that they suit recent developments.
>
> Ajeuna geus ganti djaman nja oerang anoe ngalaman. Tjarita-tjarita anoe digoerit beuki lila beuki koerang; anoe madjoe karangan-karangan noe make basa diladjoer. Pikiran-pikiran anoe datang ti bangsa koelon tina roepa-roepa perkara, gede pisan pangaroehna kana kasoesastran Soenda. Pirang-pirang boekoe anoe kaloear, babakoena salinan tina basa Walanda atawa tjarita-tjarita koena beunang masieup, soepaja soeroep kana kadjadian-kadjadian kaajeunakeun (Goeroe 1926: 4).[28]

The second and third decades of the twentieth century witnessed a short and final boom in the publication of narrative poetry, traditional *wawacan* and "new" *wawacan*; most of them were published by Balai Poestaka, and only a few by private publishers. Thirteen *wawacan* were published in the 1910s, 30 in the 1920s, and only 10 appeared in the 1930s, none in the 1940s, and one in the 1950s.[29] These numbers show the gradual disappearing of *wawacan* from the literary scene. Thus, the change in the configuration of Sundanese writing took place with the demise of traditional poetry and the rise of the novel.

# Appendix 1

# List of Sundanese Printed Books Before 1908

*Abbreviations:*

Jw: Javanese script
Ab: Arabic script
Rm: Roman script
Rm/Jw: Roman and Javanese script
LD: Landsdrukkerij (Government Printing House)
Wa: *wawacan*
ex: copies
litho: lithograph.

## (1) By Year of Publication

[1850]
Anonymous, *Kitab Pangajaran Basa Sunda* (Soendasch spel- en leesboekje). n.d., n.p., Jw., 1,490 ex.

1851
Holle, A.W.; Holle, K.F. [*Carita Kura-kura jeung Monyet*]. Batavia: Lange en Co., Jw.

1853
Anonymous, *Caritana Ibrahim*. 1st ed. Batavia: LD, Jw. 1888, rep. ed.

1854
Anonymous, *Indjil anoe Kasoeratkeun koe Mattheus*. Batavia: Lange & Co., translated by [I. Esser], Rm., Wa.

## 1858
[Ibnoe Hadjar al Haitami], *Ieu Pepetikan tina Kitab Tupah*. Batavia: Langeh jeung paseroan, translated by Soerjadilaga, Jw.

## 1859
Anonymous, *Wawacan Carita Ibrahim*. Batavia: Lange en Co., Jw., Wa.

## 1860
Anonymous, *Wawacan Carita Nurulkamar*. Batavia: LD, Jw., Wa.

## 1861
[Holle, K.F.], *Katrangan tina Prakawis Miara Lauk Cai*. Batavia: LD, translation, Jw.

[Holle, K.F.], *Kitab Conto-conto Surat pikeun Murangkalih anu Ngaskola (Soendasche modellen van verschillende brieven)*. Batavia: LD, Jw., 10,000 ex.

## 1862
Adi Widjaja, *Wulang Putra (Soendasch Gedicht Woelang Poetra)*. Batavia: LD, Jw., Wa.

Danoe Koesoemah, *Wawacan Raja Darma (Soendasch Gedicht Radjadarma)*. Batavia: LD, Jw., Wa.

Holle, K.F., *Kitab Tjatjarakan Soenda No.1 (Soendasch spel- en leesboekje met Latijnsche letter, vol. 1)*. 1st ed. Batavia: LD, Rm., 20,015 ex. 1876, 2nd ed.

Moehamad Moesa, *Wawacan Raja Sudibya (Soendasch gedicht Radja Soedibja)*. Batavia: LD, Jw., Wa.

Moehamad Moesa, *Wawacan Dongeng-dongeng (Soendasche gedichten en fabelen)*. Batavia: LD, Jw., Wa.

Moehamad Moesa, *Wulang-tani*. Batavia: LD, Jw., Wa.

Moehamad Moesa, *Wawacan Wulang Krama (Soendasch Zededicht Woelang-krama)*, 1st ed. Batavia: LD, Jw., Wa. (1923, reprinted in *Soendaneesch Volksalmanak*. Batavia: Balai Poestaka, Rm.)

Wira Tanoe Baija, *Wawacan Jaka Miskin* (*Soendasch Gedicht Djaka Miskin*). Batavia: LD, translation from Malay, Jw., Wa.

1863
Danoe Koesoemah, *Wawacan Cariyos Si Miskin*. Batavia: Lange en Co., Jw., Wa.

Moehamad Moesa, *Tjarita Abdoerahman djeng Abdoerahim* (*Geschiedenis van Abdoerahman en Abdoerahim*), 1st ed. Batavia: LD, translated from Arabic via Malay, Rm/Jw. 1884, 2nd ed. 1885, reprint. 1906, 3rd ed. 1908, reprint, 3rd ed. (1911, 4th ed.) (1922, 5th ed.) (1877, Javanese translation by Raden Angga Baja. Batavia: LD. 1925, Malay translation, Djakarta: Balai Poestaka.)

Moehamad Moesa, *Wawacan Seca Nala* (*Geschiedenis van Setja Nala, Bevattende lessen voor den boeren- en handelstand*). Batavia: LD Jw/ Rm., Wa., 3,050 ex.

Prawira Koesoema, *Wawatjan Dongeng-dongeng Toeladan*, 1st ed. Batavia: LD, Rm/Jw., Wa., 3,050 ex. 1888, 2nd ed. Rm/Jw. (1922, 4th ed.) (1911, 3rd ed. Batavia: LD, Rm.)

1864
Moehamad Moesa, *Ali Moehtar/Wawacan Carios Ali Muhtar*, 1st ed. Batavia: LD, Rm/Jw., Wa., 3,030 ex., f. 0.08. 1883, 2nd ed. Rm/Jw., Wa.

Moehamad Moesa, *Elmu Nyawah* (*Handleiding voor de kultuur van padi op natte velden*). Batavia: LD, Jw/Rm., Wa., 4,050 ex., f. 0.22.

['Abd as-Samad al-Palimbani], *Wawacan Petikan Bidayatussalik*. Batavia: LD, translated by R.D. Bratawidjaja under the supervision of Aria Koesoemah Diningrat, Jw/Rm., Wa., 3,050 ex., f. 0.15. (On the title page, in Javanese script, the year printed was 1863.)

1865
Moehamad Moesa, *Wawacan Wulang Murid*, 1st ed. Batavia: LD, Jw., Wa., 2,050 ex., f. 0.06. 1865, Rm. ed.

Moehamad Moesa, *Wawacan Wulang Murid* (*Lessen voor den leerling*). Batavia: LD, Rm., Wa. See 1865, 1st ed.

Moehamad Moesa, *Wawacan Wulang Guru*, 1st ed. Batavia: LD, Jw., Wa., 550 ex., f. 0.04. 1865, Rm. ed.

Moehamad Moesa, *Wawatjan Woelang Goeroe* (*Wenken voor den onderwijzer*). Batavia: LD, Rm., Wa. See 1865, 1st ed.

1866
Moehamad Moesa, *Dongeng-dongeng nu Araneh* (*Vertellingen*), 1st ed. Batavia: LD, translation from Malay, Jw., 3,050 ex., f. 0.16. 1884, new ed. Jw. 1890, 2nd ed., Jw.

Moehamad Oemar, *Wawatjan Katrangan Miara Laoek Tjai* (*Handleiding voor de teelt van zoetwatervisch*), [1st ed.]. Batavia: LD, Rm., Wa., 5,050 ex., f. 0.24. 1866, Jw. ed.

Moehamad Oemar, *Wawacan Katrangan Miara Lauk Cai* (*Handleiding voor de teelt van zoetwatervisch*). Batavia: LD, Jw., Wa. See 1866 [1st ed.]

Nederlandsche Zendingsvereeniging/[G.J. Grashuis], *Tjatjarakan Soenda* (*Soendaneesch spelboekje*), 1st ed. Rotterdam: E.H. Tassemeijer, Rm.; [1883], revised 2nd ed.

Nederlandsche Zendingsvereeniging, *Kitab Elmoe Itoengan no.1, pikeun maroerangkalih anoe kur iskola*. Rotterdam: D. De Koning, Rm.

Nederlandsche Zendingsvereeniging, *Kitab Indjil Dikarang koe Loekas*. Rotterdam: E.H. Tassemeijer, translated by G.J. Grashuis, Rm.

Nederlandsche Zendingsvereeniging, *Kitab Elmoe Itoengan* (*Rekenboekje voor de scholen*), vol. 1. Rotterdam: D. De Koning, Rm. 1866, vol. 2. 1867, vol. 3. 1868, vol. 4.

Nederlandsche Zendingsvereeniging, *Kitab Elmoe Itoengan* (*Rekenboekje voor de scholen*), vol. 2. Rotterdam: D. De Koning, Rm. See 1866, vol. 1.

[1866]
Nederlandsche Zendingsvereeniging/[Albers, C.], *Kitab Itoengan, pangmimitina pisan keur baroedak iskola*, 1st ed. Schoonhoven: S.E. van Nooten & Zoon, Rm. 1902 [3rd ed.]. Rotterdam: D.van Sijn & Zoon, Rm.

## 1867

Moehamad Moesa, *Dongeng-dongeng Piêntêngên* (*Spiegel der jeugd*), 1st ed. Batavia: LD, Rm., 3,050 ex., f. 0.28. 1867, Jw. ed. 1888, new ed. 1901, [3rd] ed. 1904, [4th] ed. 1907, [5th] ed. (1912, [6th] ed.)

Moehamad Moesa, *Dongeng-dongeng Pieunteungeun* (*Spiegel der jeugd*). Batavia: LD, Jw., 6,050 ex., f. 0.48. See 1867, 1st ed.

[Holle, K.F.], *Kitab Nuduhkeun Ngelmu Itungan* (*Rekenboekje over de benoemde getallen*). Batavia: LD, Jw.

Nederlandsche Zendingsvereeniging, *Kitab Elmoe Itoengan* (*Rekenboekje voor de scholen*), vol. 3. Rotterdam: D. De Koning, Rm. See 1866, vol. 1.

## 1868

Perdjandjian Anjar. *Iju kitab bunang njoetat tina Kitab Soetje*, vols. 1 & 2. n.p., Rm.

Nederlandsche Zendingsvereeniging, *Kitab Elmoe Itoengan* (*Rekenboekje voor de scholen*), vol. 4. Rotterdam: D. De Koning, Rm. See 1866, vol. 1.

## 1871

Moehamad Moesa, *Panji Wulung*, 1st ed. Batavia: LD, Jw., Wa. 1876, Rm. ed. 1891, 2nd ed. Jw. 1901, new ed. Jw. 1904, new ed. Rm. 1908, 3rd ed. Jw. (1909, 3rd ed. Rm.) (1913, revised ed. Rm.) (1922, 4th ed. Rm.) (1879, Javanese translation by Soerjodidjojo in the name of Pangeran Adipati Ario Mangkoe Negoro IV, Jw.) (1928, Madurese translation by R. Sosro Danoe Koesoemo, 2 vol., Jw.)

Anonymous, *Iju Tjariosna Para Nabi*. Mèstèr: Rèhobot, Rm.

Anonymous, *Iju Doewa Kitab Indjil anoe Soetji* (*De Evangelien van Loekas en Johannes*). Meester-Cornelis: Rehoboth-Zending Press, translated by S. Coolsma, Rm.

## 1872

Moehamad Moesa, *Wawatjan Lampah Sebar*. Batavia: LD, Rm/Jw., Wa. 1872, Lampah Sebar. Rm/Jw. 1874, Katrangan Lampah Sebar, Jw.

Moehamad Moesa, *Lampah Sebar*. Batavia: LD, Rm/Jw. See 1872, [1st ed.]

Kartawinata, *Cariyos Tuwan Kapitan Marion* (*Geschiedenis van den Kapitein Marion*). Batavia: LD, Jw., 5,015 ex. (1872, Javanese translation by Kartawinata)

Albers, C., *Elmoe Boemi Tanah Hindia Nederlan*. Batavia: Ogilvie & Co., Rm.

1873
*Kitab Cacarakan Sunda* (*Soendaasch Spelboek*), vol. 1. Batavia: LD, Jw.

Anonymous, *Poepoedjian pikun Njanji, sareng pikun moedji ka pangeran*, 2nd ed. Meester-Cornelis: Rehoboth-Zending Press, Rm. (1st ed. unknown)

1874
Moehamad Moesa, *Katrangan Lampah Sebar*. Batavia: LD, Jw., Wa. See 1872, *Wawacan Lampah Sebar*.

Kartawinata, *Carita Kapitan Bonteku* (*Reis van den kapitein Willem Ysbrandtsz Bontekoe*), 1st ed. Batavia: LD, Jw., 5,015 ex. 1883, 2nd ed., Jw. 1903, new ed., Jw. (1924, Rm. ed.)

Holle, K.F. ed., *Mitra nu Tani*, vol. 1, translated by Kartawinata from Dutch. Batavia: LD, Jw. 1877, vol. 2, Jw. 1877, vol. 3, Jw. 1878, vol. 4, Jw. 1878, vol. 5, Jw. 1879, vol. 6, Jw. 1879, vol. 7, Jw. 1892, vol. 8, Rm. 1893, vol. 9 & 10, Rm. 1894, vol. 11, Rm. 1895, vol. 12, Rm. (1897, vol. 13, Rm. ed. by H. de Bie.) (1899, vol. 14, Rm. ed. by H. de Bie.)

1875
Lasminingrat, *Carita Erman*, 1st ed., translated from Dutch. Batavia: LD, Jw., 6,015 ex. (1911, 2nd ed. Jw.) (1922, Rm. ed.) (1919, Hikajat Erman, Malay translation by M.S.Tjakrabangsa, n.y.; 2nd ed., 1930, 3rd ed.)

*Besluit Betreffende de Regeling der Heerendiensten in het Soendaneesch*. Batavia: LD, Rm.

1875/76
Staatsblad voor Ned. Indie. *Soendasche vertaling van verschillende nummers*. Batavia: LD, Rm.

## 1876

Kartawinata, *Kitab Conto-conto Surat Anyar (Nieuw Brievenboek voor de Soendasche Scholen)*. Batavia: [LD], under the supervision of K.F. Holle, Jw., 10,000 ex.

Kartawinata, *300 Masalah, Elmu Itungan (300 Rekenkundige voorstellen voor eerst beginnenden)*. Batavia: LD, Jw.

Lasminingrat, *Warnasari atawa Rupa-rupa Dongeng*, vol. 1. Translation from Dutch. Batavia: LD, Jw. 1887, vol. 2, Rm. 1887, vol. 3 (translated by Lenggang Kantjana), Rm. 1903, vol. 1, new ed., Jw. 1907, vol. 1, Jw. (1909, vol. 2, Rm.) (1909, vol. 3, Rm.) (1912, vol. 3, Rm.)

[Coolsma, S.], *Ijeu Wawatjan eukeur Moerangkali anoe di Iskola*. Rotterdam: D. De Koning, Rm.

Holle, K.F., *Kitab Tjatjarakan Soenda Make Aksara Walanda (Soendaasch spel- en leerboekje met Latijnsche letter)*, vol. 1. 2nd ed. Batavia: LD, Rm. 20,015 ex. See 1862, 1st ed.

Moehamad Moesa, *Pandji Woeloeng*. Rm. ed. Batavia: LD, Wa. See 1871, 1st ed.

## 1877

Nederlandsch Bijbelgenootschap, *Ieu Kitab Injil Sutji anu Dikarang ku Lukas (Het Evangelie van Lucas)*, translated by S. Coolsma. Leiden: A.W. Sijthoff, Ab.

Nederlandsch Bijbelgenootschap, *Perdjandjian Anjar, hartosna sadajana kitab noe kasebat indjil goesti oerang Jesoes Kristoes*, translated by S. Coolsma. Amsterdam, Rm.

Holle, K.F. ed., *Mitra nu Tani*, vol. 2. Batavia: LD, Jw. See 1874, vol. 1.

Holle, K.F. ed., *Mitra nu Tani*, vol. 3. Batavia: LD, Jw. See 1874, vol. 1.

## 1878

Holle, K.F. ed., *Mitra nu Tani*, vol. 4. Batavia: LD, Jw. See 1874, vol. 1.

Holle, K.F. ed., *Mitra nu Tani*, vol. 5. Batavia: LD, Jw. See 1874, vol. 1.

**1879**
Defoe, Daniel, *Carita Robinson Crusoë*, translated by Kartawinata. Batavia: LD, Jw., 10,015 ex. (orig. translated into Dutch by Gerard Keller.)

Holle, K.F. ed., *Mitra nu Tani*, vol. 6. Batavia: LD, Jw. See 1874, vol. 1.

Holle, K.F. ed., *Mitra nu Tani*, vol. 7. Batavia: LD, Jw. See 1874, vol. 1.

**1880**
Chijs, J.A. van der, *Babad Tanah Pasundan*, translated by Kartawinata. Batavia: LD, Jw.

Gelder, W. van, *Carita Pulo Jawa (Java en zijn bewoners)*, vol. 1, translated by Kartawinata. Batavia: LD, Jw. 1880, vol. 2. Jw. 1881, vol. 3. Jw. 1881, vol. 4, Jw.

Gelder, W. van, *Carita Pulo Jawa (Java en zijn bewoners)*, vol. 2. Batavia: LD, Jw. See 1880, vol. 1.

**[1880]**
*Parentah jeung Piwuruk baris Nuduhan Petana Amtenar-amtenar Eropa jeung Pribumi Rawuh Pangkat-pangkat Ngalamphkeunana Timbalan kana Ngajaga Paragan Sato*, translated by Kartawinata. Batavia: LD, Jw.

**1881**
Gelder, W. van, *Buku Bacaan Salawe Tuladan, pikeun murid-murid pangkat panghandapna di sakola Sunda*, [1st ed.]. Batavia: LD, Jw. 1889, rep. ed., Jw. 1898, 3rd ed., Jw. 1902, [4th] ed., Jw.

Gelder, W. van, *Buku Itungan nu Ka I, pikeun murid-murid pangkat panghandapna di iskola pribumi*, vol. 1. Batavia: LD, Jw. 1881, vol. 2., Jw. 1881, vol. 3., Jw. 1882, vol. 4., Jw. 1883, vol. 5., Jw.

Gelder, W. van, *Buku Itungan nu Ka I, pikeun murid-murid pangkat panghandapna di iskola pribumi*, vol. 2. Batavia: LD. See 1881, vol. 1.

Gelder, W. van, *Buku Itungan nu Ka I, pikeun murid-murid pangkat panghandapna di iskola pribumi*, vol. 3. Batavia: LD. See 1881, vol. 1.

Gelder, W. van, *Carita Pulo Jawa (Java en zijn bewoners)*, vol. 3. Batavia: LD, Jw. See 1880, vol. 1.

Gelder, W. van, *Carita Pulo Jawa (Java en zijn bewoners)*, vol. 4. Batavia: LD, Jw. See 1880, vol. 1.

1882
*Aturan Ngurus Sakitan-sakitan di Indiya Nederlan. Staatsblad 1871 nomer 78. (Soendasche vertaling van het reglement van orde en tucht onder de gevangenen in Nederlandsch-Indë. Staatsblad 1871. No. 78)*, translated by Kartawinata. Batavia: LD, Jw.

Gelder, W. van, *Buku Itungan nu Ka I, pikeun murid-murid pangkat panghandapna di iskola pribumi*, vol. 4. Batavia: LD. See 1881, vol. 1.

1883
Kartawinata, *Pagoeneman Soenda djeng Walanda (Soendasche Hollandsche samenspraken)*, [1st ed.], under the supervision of K.F. Holle. Batavia: LD, Rm. 1891, rep. ed., Rm. 1908, Rm. (1915, Rm.)

Nooij, H.A., *Buku Bacaan, pikeun murid-murid dina pangkat panghandapna di iskola Sunda*, [1st ed.]. Batavia: LD, Jw. 1894, new ed., Jw. 1896, 2nd ed., Jw.

Moehamad Moesa, *Ali Moehtar*, 2nd ed. Batavia: LD, Rm. See 1864, 1st ed.

Moehamad Moesa, *Carita Abdurahman jeung Abdurahim (Geschiedenis van Abdoerahman en Abdoerahim)*, 2nd ed. Batavia: LD, Jw. See 1863, 1st ed.

Kartawinata, *Carita Kapitan Bonteku (Reis van den kapitein Willem Ysbrandtsz Bontekoe)*, 2nd ed. Batavia: LD, Jw. See 1874, 1st ed.

Gelder, W. van, *Buku Itungan nu Ka I, pikeun murid-murid pangkat panghandapna di iskola pribumi*, vol. 5. Batavia: LD, Jw. See 1881, vol. 1.

[1883]
Nederlandsche Zendingsvereeniging/[G.J. Grashuis], *Tjatjarakan Soenda*

(*Soendaneesch spelboekje*). Revised 2nd ed. Rotterdam: D. De Koning, Rm. See 1866, 1st ed.

1884

Moehamad Moesa, *Carita Abdurahman jeung Abdurahim* (*Geschiedenis van Abdoerahman en Abdoerahim*), 2nd ed. Batavia: LD, Jw. See 1863, 1st ed.

Moehamad Moesa, *Dongeng-dongeng nu Araneh*. New ed. Batavia: LD, Jw. See 1866, 1st ed.

1885

Anonymous, *Mangle Lemboet keur Baroedak Leutik*. Bogor: Zending-Pers, Rm.

Nederlandsche Zendingsvereeniging, *Tjarijos Goesti Jesoes sareng Rasoel-Rasoelna*, [1st ed.]. Rotterdam: D. De Koning, Rm. 1901, 2nd ed. Rotterdam: D. van Sijn & Zoon, Rm.

Moehamad Moesa, *Tjarita Abdoerrahman djeung Abdoerrahim*, rep. ed. Batavia: LD, Rm. See 1863, 1st ed.

1886

Nederlandsche Zendingsvereeniging/[Albers, C.], *Elmoe Agama Oerang Kristen*. Rotterdam: D. De Koning, Rm.

[1886]

Anonymous, *Istruksi Kapala Desa*, translated by Rangga Adilaga. Batavia: LD, Jw.

1887

Lasminingrat, *Warnasari atawa Roepa-roepa Dongeng*, vol. 2. Batavia: LD, Rm. See 1876, vol. 1.

Lenggang Kantjana, *Warnasari atawa Roepa-roepa Dongeng*, vol. 3. Batavia: LD, Rm., 6,015 ex. See 1876, vol. 1.

1888

Anonymous, *Caritana Ibrahim* (*Geschiedenis van Ibrahim*), [Rep. ed.]. Batavia: LD, Jw. See 1853, 1st ed.

Prawira Koesoema, *Wawatjan Dongeng-dongeng Toeladan*, 2nd ed. Batavia: LD, Rm/Jw., Wa. See 1863, 1st ed.

Moehamad Moesa, *Dongeng-dongeng Pieunteungeun*. New ed. Batavia: LD, Rm. See 1867, 1st ed.

1889
Kartawinata, *Boekoe Wet Hal Pangadilan Hoekoeman baris Oerang Priboemi di Indië-Nederland*. Batavia: LD, Rm.

Kartawinata, *Boekoe Wet Hal Pangadilan Hoekoeman djeung Atoeran noe Djadi Babakoe Hoekoeman Politie baris Oerang priboemi di Indië-Nederland*. Batavia: LD, Rm.

Anonymous, *Pangatoeran Tjengtjelengan Limbangan*, in Sundanese and Dutch. Bandung: De Vries & Fabricius, Rm.

Gelder, W. van, B*uku Bacaan Salawe Tuladan, pikeun murid-murid pangkat panghandapna di sakola Sunda*, rep. ed. Batavia: LD, Jw. See 1881 [1st ed.]

1890
Gelder, W. van, *Mangle, nja eta roepa-roepa Tjarita reudjeung tjonto*, [1st ed.]. Leiden: Kantor Tjitak Toewan P.W.M. Trap, Rm. 1898, 2nd ed. 1901, 3rd ed. 1902, 4th ed. 1906, 5th ed. (1909, 6th ed.) (1911, 7th ed.) (1913, [8th ed.]) (1922, 9th ed. Rm.)

Moehamad Moesa, *Dongeng-dongeng nu Araneh*, 2nd ed. Batavia: LD, Jw. See 1866, 1st ed.

1891
Nederlandsch Bijbelgenootschap, *Kitab Soetji, hartosna sadajana kitab anoe kasebat Perdjandjian lawas sareng Perdjangdjian anjar*, translated by S. Coolsma, Amsterdam, Rm.

Moehamad Moesa, *Panji Wulung*, 2nd ed. Batavia: LD, Jw., Wa. See 1871, 1st ed.

Kartawinata, *Pagoeneman Soenda djeng Walanda (Soendasche Hollandsche Samenspraken)*. Rep. ed. Batavia: LD, Rm. See 1883 [1st ed.]

1892
Nederlandsche Zendingsvereeniging, *Tjarijos Para Nabi Ditoekil tina Kitab Perdjangdjian Lawas*, [1st ed.]. Rotterdam: D. van Sijn & Zoon, Rm. 1902, 2nd ed., Rm.

*Serat Pananggalan Sunda (Soendaneesche almanak)*, 1st year. Cheribon: A.Bisschop, Jw. 1893, 2nd year, Jw. 1894, 3rd year, Jw. 1895, 4th year, Jw. 1896, 5th year, Jw. 1897, 6th year, Jw.

Holle, K.F., ed., *Mitra Noe Tani*, vol. 8. Batavia: LD, Rm. See 1874, vol. 1.

[1892?]
Albers, C./Nederlandsche Zendingsvereeniging, *Hikajat Garedja*. Rotterdam: D. van Sijn & Zoon, Rm.

[1892]
Anonymous, *Atoeran Metakeun Herendines di Tanah Prajangan*. Batavia: LD, Jw. (enacted by J.D. Harders, Resident of Priangan).

1893
Holle, K.F., ed., *Mitra noe Tani*, vol. 9 & 10. Batavia: LD, Rm. See 1874, vol. 1.

*Serat Pananggalan Sunda (Soendaneesche almanak)*, 2nd year. Cheribon: A. Bisschop, Jw. See 1892, 1st year.

[1893]
Nederlandsche Zendingsvereeniging, *Poepoedjian Oerang Kristen, njanjikeuneun di garedja djeung di imah*. Rotterdam: D. van Sijn & Zoon, Rm.

1894
Haastert, C.J. van, *Boekoe Edjahan djeung Batjaan, pikeun moerid-moerid dina pangkat panghandapna di sakola-Soenda*, vol. 1. Batavia: LD, Rm. 1896, vol. 2., Rm. 1898, vol. 2, [2nd ed.], Rm. 1899, vol. 1, [2nd ed.], Rm. 1907, vol. 2, [3rd ed.], Rm. 1908, vol. 1, [3rd ed.], Rm. (1910, vol. 1, [4th ed.]), Rm. (1910, vol. 2, [4th ed.]), Rm.

Haastert, C.J. van, *Boekoe Itoengan Petjahan-perpoeloehan, pikeun moerid-moerid pangkat kadoewa di sakola-Soenda*, [1st ed.]. Batavia: LD, Rm. 1900, 2nd ed., Rm. 1906, 3rd ed., Rm.

Haastert, C.J. van, *Boekoe Itoengan Petjahan Bener, pikeun moerid-moerid pangkat kadoewa di sakola-Soenda*, [1st ed.]. Batavia: LD, Rm. 1900, 2nd ed., Rm. 1904, 3rd ed., Rm.

Holle, K.F., ed., *Mitra noe Tani*, vol. 11. Batavia: LD, Rm. See 1874, vol. 1.

Nooij, H.A., *Buku Bacaan, pikeun murid-murid dina pangkat panghandapna di iskola Sunda*. New ed. Batavia: LD, Jw. See 1883, [1st ed.]

*Serat Pananggalan Sunda (Soendaneesche almanak)*, 3rd year. Cheribon: A.Bisschop, Jw. See 1892, 1st year.

[1894]
Nederlandsche Zendingsvereeniging, *Tjarijos Joesoep Beunang Nembangkeun*, [1st ed.], translated by N. Titus. Rotterdam: D. van Sijn & Zoon, Rm., Wa. [1902]; 2nd ed., Rm.

1895
Nederlandsch Bijbelgenootschap, *Kitab Injil Sutji anu Dikarang ku Johanes (Het Evangelie van Johannes)*, translated by S. Coolsma. Leiden: A.W. Sijthoff, Ab.

Holle, K.F., ed., *Mitra noe Tani*, vol. 12. Batavia: LD, Rm. See 1874, vol. 1.

*Serat Pananggalan Sunda (Soendaneesche almanak)*, 4th year. Cheribon: A.Bisschop, Jw. See 1892, 1st year.

1896
Anonymous, *Tjarita Djahidin*, [1st ed.], translated by Soerja Karta Legawa. Batavia: LD, Rm. 1903, rep. ed., Rm.

'Utman bin Abdallah ibu Aqil bin Jahja (Sayyid 'Uthmân), *Irsjad Al-anam Fi Tarjmat Arkan Al-Islam*, translated by the *mantri goeroe* in Soekaboemi. Batavia, Ab., litho.

Nederlandsch Bijbelgenootschap, *Kitab Lalampahan Para Rasul Saruci Beunang Ngarang Lukas*, translated by S. Coolsma. Leiden: A.W. Sijthoff, Ab.

Nooij, H.A., *Buku Bacaan, pikeun murid-murid dina pangkat panghandapna di iskola Sunda*, 2nd ed. Batavia: LD, Jw. See 1883 [1st ed.]

*Serat Pananggalan Sunda (Soendaneesche almanak)*, 5th year. Cheribon: A.Bisschop, Jw. See 1892, 1st year.

Haastert, C.J. van, *Boekoe Edjahan djeung Batjaan, pikeun moerid-moerid dina pangkat panghandapna di sakola-Soenda*, vol. 2. Batavia: LD, Rm. See 1894, vol. 1.

[1896]
Anonymous, *Wawacan Gendit Birajung*. Title written by Snouck Hurgronje? found in Banten region, Ab., Wa., litho.

1897
Ardiwinata, *Buku Cacarakan Anyar (Soendaasch spel- en leesboekje)*, vol. 1 & vol. 2, [1st ed.]. Batavia: LD, Jw. 1903, revised 2nd ed., Jw. 1907, revised 3rd ed., Jw. 1908, revised 4th ed., Jw.

Anonymous, *Wawacan Piwulang Panulak Panyakit Kolera*, translated by Raden Tumenggung Djajadiningrat. Batavia: LD, Ab.

Nederlandsche Zendingsvereeniging, *Njanjian baris Moedji di Iskola reudjeung di Imah*. Rotterdam: D. van Sijn & Zoon, Rm.

'Utman bin Abdallah bin Aqil ibu Jahja (Sayyid 'Uthmân), *Taftih Al-uyun Ala Fasadi Al-dhunun*, translated by Raden Haji Azhari. Batavia, Ab., litho.

'Utman bin Abdallah bin Aqil ibu Jahja (Sayyid 'Uthmân), *Islah Al-hal Bi Talb Al-halal*, translated by Raden Azhari. Batavia, Ab., litho.

'Utman bin Abdallah bin Aqil ibu Jahja (Sayyid 'Uthmân), *Kamus Kecil Arabiyah-Malaju-Sunda*, translated by Raden Hadji Azhari. Batavia, Ab., litho.

'Utman bin Abdallah bin Aqil ibu Jahja (Sayyid 'Uthmân), *Cempaka Mulia*, translated by Raden Hadji Azhari with Hadji Irsyad. Batavia, Ab., litho.

R. Demang Soerja Nata Legawa (Kartawinata), *Pangeling-ngeling ka Padoeka Toewan Karel Frederik Holle*. n.p., Rm.

*Serat Pananggalan Anggoeun dina Taun Walanda (Soendaneesche Almanak)*, 1st year. Samarang: G.C.T.van Dorp & Co., Jw. 1898, 2nd year, Jw. 1899, 3rd year, Jw. 1900, 4th year, Jw. 1901, 5th year, Jw. 1902, 6th year, Jw. 1903, 7th year, Jw.

Bie, H. de, ed., *Mitra noe Tani*, vol. 13. Batavia: LD, Rm. See 1874, vol. 1.

*Serat Pananggalan Sunda (Soendaneesche Almanak)*. 6th year. Cheribon: A. Bisschop, Jw. See 1892, 1st year.

1898
Gelder, W. van, *Buku Bacaan Salawe Tuladan, pikeun murid-murid pangkat panghandapna di sakola Sunda*, 3rd ed. Batavia: LD, Jw. See 1881 [1st ed.].

Gelder, W. van, *Mangle*, 2nd ed. Den Haag: Kantor tjitak De Swart en Zoon, Rm. See 1890 [1st ed.].

Haastert, C.J. van, *Boekoe Edjahan Djeung Batjaan, pikeun moerid-moerid dina pangkat panghandapna di sakola-Soenda*, vol. 2, [2nd ed.]. Batavia: LD, Rm. See 1894, vol. 1.

*Serat Pananggalan Anggoeun dina Taun Walanda (Soendaneesche Almanak)*, 2nd year. Samarang: G.C.T. van Dorp & Co., Jw. See 1897, 1st year.

1899
Bie, H. de, ed., *Mitra noe Tani*, vol. 14. Batavia: LD, Rm. See 1874, vol. 1.

Haastert, C.J. van, *Boekoe Edjahan djeung Batjaan, pikeun moerid-moerid dina pangkat panghandapna di sakola-Soenda*, vol. 1 [2nd ed.]. Batavia: LD, Rm. See 1894, vol. 1.

*Serat Pananggalan Anggoeun dina Taun Walanda (Soendaneesche almanak)*, 3rd year. Samarang: G.C.T. van Dorp & Co., Jw. See 1897, 1st year.

## 1900

Anonymous, *Serat Rama*, translated from Javanese by R. Toemenggoeng Arija Martanagara, supervised by Bratadiwidjaja. Samarang: D.C.T. van Dorp & Co., Jw., Wa.

*Serat Pananggalan Bahasa Sunda (Soendaneesche almanak)*, 1st year. Samarang: G.C.T. van Dorp & Co., Ab. 1901, 2nd year, Ab. 1902, 3rd year, Ab. 1903, 4th year, Ab.

Lenderink, *Roepa-roepa Pangadjaran Hal Mijara Boedak Lolong keur Waktoe Aja di Imah Kolotna*, translated by the colonial government. Batavia: LD, Rm.

Haastert, C.J. van, *Boekoe Itoengan Petjahan-perpoeloehan, pikeun moerid-moerid pangkat kadoewa di sakola-Soenda*, 2nd ed. Batavia: LD, Rm. See 1894 [1st ed.].

Haastert, C.J. van, *Boekoe Itoengan Petjahan Bener, pikeun moerid-moerid pangkat kadoewa di sakola-Soenda*, 2nd ed. Batavia: LD, Rm. See 1894 [1st ed.].

*Serat Pananggalan Anggoeun dina Taun Walanda (Soendaneesche Almanak)*, 4th year. Samarang: G.C.T. van Dorp & Co., Jw. See 1897, 1st year.

## 1901

Moehamad Saleh Mangkoepradja, *Kitab Atoeran Bab Maradjian Djelema noe Ngedjoeroe*. Batavia: Albrecht & Co., Rm.

'Utman bin Abdallah bin Aqil ibu Jahja (Sayyid 'Uthmân), *Nasihat Datang buat Ngalarang Nyieun Nyeri kana Binatang*, translated by Mohamad Bisri bin Hadji Abdullah. Batavia, Ab., litho.

Moehamad Moesa, *Dongeng-dongeng Pieunteungeun*, [3rd ed.]. Batavia: LD, Rm. See 1867, 1st ed.

Moehamad Moesa, *Panji Wulung*, new ed. Batavia: LD, Jw., Wa. See 1871 [1st ed.].

Nederlandsche Zendingsvereeniging, *Tjarijos Goesti Jesoes sareng Rasoelrasoelna*, 2nd ed. Rotterdam: D. van Sijn & Zoon, Rm. See 1885 [1st ed.].

Gelder, W. van, *Mangle*, 3rd ed. Den Haag: Kantor tjitak De Swart en Zoon, Rm. See 1890 [1st ed.].

*Serat Pananggalan Anggoeun dina Taun Walanda (Soendaneesche Almanak)*, 5th year. Samarang: G.C.T. van Dorp & Co., Jw. See 1897, 1st year.

*Serat Pananggalan Bahasa Sunda (Soendaneesche Almanak)*, 2nd year. Samarang: G.C.T. van Dorp & Co., Ab. See 1900, 1st year.

1902
Gelder, W. van, *Buku Bacaan Salawe Tuladan, pikeun murid-murid pangkat kadua di sêkola Sunda* [1st ed.]. Batavia: LD, Jw. 1907, rep. ed., Jw. (1913, rep. ed., Jw.)

Nederlandsche Zendingsvereeniging/[Albers, C.], *Kitab Itoengan, pangmimitina pisan keur baroedak iskola*, [3rd ed.]. Rotterdam: D. van Sijn & Zoon, Rm. See 1866 [1st ed.].

Gelder, W. van, *Buku Bacaan Salawe Tuladan, pikeun murid-murid pangkat panghandapna di sêkola Sunda*, [4th ed.]. Batavia: LD, Jw. See 1881 [1st ed.].

Gelder, W. van, *Mangle*, 4th ed. Den Haag: Kantor tjitak De Swart en Zoon, Rm. See 1890 [1st ed.].

Nederlandsche Zendingsvereeniging, *Tjarijos Para Nabi Ditoekil tina Kitab Perdjangdjian Lawas*, 2nd ed. Rotterdam: D. van Sijn & Zoon, Rm. See 1892 [1st ed.].

*Serat Pananggalan Anggoeun dina Taun Walanda (Soendaneesche almanak)*, 6th year. Samarang: G.C.T. van Dorp & Co., Jw. See 1897, 1st year.

*Serat Pananggalan Bahasa Sunda (Soendaneesche almanak)*, 3rd year. Samarang: G.C.T. van Dorp & Co., Ab. See 1900, 1st year.

[1902]
Nederlandsche Zendingsvereeniging, *Tjarijos Joesoep Beunang Nembangkeun*, 2nd ed. Rotterdam: D. van Sijn & Zoon, Rm. See [1894], [1st ed.]

1903
'Utman bin Abdallah bin Aqil ibu Jahja (Sayyid 'Uthmân), *Saun Ad-din 'An Nazgrat Al-mudallin*. Arabic, Malay, Javanese, and Sundanese poligrot text. Batavia, Ab/Rm., litho.

Kartawinata, *Carita Kapitan Bonteku (Reis van den kapitein Willem Ysbrandtsz Bontekoe)*, new ed. Batavia: LD, Jw. See 1874, 1st ed.

Lasminingrat, *Warnasari atawa Rupa-rupa Dongeng*, vol. 1. New ed. Batavia: LD, Jw. See 1876, vol. 1.

Anonymous, *Tjarita Djahidin, kalawan Piwoeroek Sêpoehna*. Rep. ed. Batavia: LD, Rm. See 1896 [1st ed.]

Ardiwinata, *Buku Cacarakan Anyar (Soendaasch spel- en leesboekje)*, vol. 1 & vol. 2. Revised 2nd ed. Batavia: LD, Jw. See 1897 [1st ed.]

*Serat Pananggalan Anggoeun dina Taun Walanda (Soendaneesche Almanak)*, 7th year. Samarang: G.C.T. van Dorp & Co., Jw. See 1897, 1st year.

*Serat Pananggalan Bahasa Sunda (Soendaneesche Almanak)*, 4th year. Samarang: G.C.T. van Dorp & Co., Ab. See 1900, 1st year.

1904
Nederlandsche Zendingsvereeniging, *Poepoedjian Garedja Pasoendan, njanjikeuneun di garedja djeung di imah*. Rotterdam: D. van Sijn & Zoon, Rm.

Moehamad Moesa, *Dongeng-dongeng Pieunteungeun*, [4th ed.]. Batavia: LD, Rm. See 1867, 1st ed.

Moehamad Moesa, *Pandji Woeloeng*. [New ed.]. Batavia: LD, Rm., Wa. See 1871, 1st ed.

Haastert, C.J. van, *Boekoe Itoengan Petjahan Bener, pikeun moerid-moerid pangkat kadoewa di sakola-Soenda*, 3rd ed. Batavia: LD, Rm. See 1894 [1st ed.].

1905
Anonymous, *Rupa-rupa Katerangan nu Netelakeun Bab Kasakit Kolera jeung Sarat-sarat pikeun Ngurus Awak Bisi Katerap Panyakit eta*. Batavia: LD, Ab.

1906
Martanagara, *Wawacan Angling Darma*. Bandung: Toko citak Afandi, Jw., Wa.

Ardiwinata, *Piwoelang ka noe Tani [I & II]*, [1st ed.], supervised by H.C.H. de Bie. Batavia: LD, Rm. 1907, 2nd ed., vol. 1. Semarang: H.A. Benjamins, Rm. 1908, 2nd ed., vol. 2. Semarang: H.A. Benjamins, Rm. (1914, 3rd ed. Semarang: H.A. Benjamins, Rm.)

Moehamad Moesa, *Carita Abdurahman jeung Abdurahim (Geschiedenis van Abdoerahman en Abdoerahim)*, 3rd ed. Batavia: LD, Jw. See 1863, 1st ed.

Gelder, W. van, *Mangle*, 5th ed. Den Haag: Kantor tjitak De Swart en Zoon, Rm. See 1890 [1st ed.].

Haastert, C.J. van, *Boekoe Itoengan Petjahan-perpoeloehan, pikeun moerid-moerid pangkat kadoewa di sakola-Soenda*, 3rd ed. Batavia: LD, Rm. See 1894 [1st ed.].

[1906]
Nederlandsche Zendingsvereeniging, *Tjarijos Radja Saoel djeung Radja Dawoed Beunang Nembangkeun*, translated by N. Titus. Rotterdam: D. van Sijn & Zoon, Rm., Wa.

1907
Nederlandsch Bijbelgenootschap, *Kitab Indjil Soetji anoe Dikarang koe Markoes*. Amsterdam: ?, Rm.

Anonymous, *Wawatjan Soelandjana nja eta Tjaria Tatanen Djaman Koena*, edited by C.M. Pleyte. Bandoeng: G. Kolff & Co., Rm.

Among Pradja, *Boekoe Batjaan Sesela, pikeun moerid-moerid pangkat kadoewa*, [1st ed.]. Batavia: LD, Rm. (1911, vol. 2, Rm.) (1913 [2nd ed.], Rm.)

Hekker, Ch., *Pangadjaran Basa Soenda, pikeun moreid-moerid pangkat panghandapna di sakola Soenda*, vol. 1, 2nd ed. Batavia: LD, Rm. (1st ed. unknown)

Moehamad Moesa, *Dongeng-dongeng Pieunteungeun*, [5th ed.]. Batavia: LD, Rm. See 1867, 1st ed.

Lasminingrat, *Warnasari atawa Rupa-rupa Dongeng*, vol. 1. Batavia: LD, Jw. See 1876, vol. 1.

Haastert, C.J. van, *Boekoe Edjahan djeung Batjaan, pikeun moerid-moerid dina pangkat panghandapna di sakola-Soenda*, vol. 2 [3rd ed.]. Batavia: LD, Rm. See 1894, vol. 1.

Ardiwinata, *Buku Cacarakan Anyar (Soendaasch spel- en leesboekje)*, vols. 1 & 2, revised 3rd ed. Batavia: LD, Jw. See 1897 [1st ed.].

Gelder, W. van, *Buku Bacaan Salawe Tuladan, pikeun murid-murid pangkat kadua di sêkola Sunda*, rep. ed. Batavia: LD, Jw. See 1902 [1st ed.]

Ardiwinata, *Piwoelang ka noe Tani, I.*, 2nd ed., supervised by H.C.H. de Bie. Semarang: H.A. Benjamins, Rm. See 1906 [1st ed.].

1908
Mangoen Di Karia, *Tembang Piwoelang, pikeun moerid-moerid di iskola Soenda*. Batavia: LD, Rm.

Hekker, Ch., *Pangadjaran Basa Soenda, pikeun moerid-moerid pangkat kadoewa di sakola Soenda*, vol. 2, 2nd ed. Batavia: LD, Rm. (1st ed. unknown).

D.K. Ardiwinata, *Tatakrama Oerang Soenda*, vol. 1. 1st ed. Bandung: Kaoem Moeda, Rm.

Moehamad Moesa, *Carita Abdurahman jeung Abdurahim* (*Geschiedenis van Abdoerahman en Abdoerahim*). Rep, 3rd ed. Batavia: LD, Jw/Rm. See 1863, 1st ed.

Moehamad Moesa, *Panji Wulung*, 3rd ed. Batavia: LD, Jw., Wa. See 1871, 1st ed.

Kartawinata, *Pagoeneman Soenda djeng Walanda* (*Soendasche Hollandsche Samenspraken*). Batavia: LD, Rm. See 1883 [1st ed.].

Haastert, C.J. van, *Boekoe Edjahan djeung Batjaan, pikeun moerid-moerid dina pangkat panghandapna di sakola-Soenda*, vol. 1, [3rd ed.]. Batavia: LD See 1894, vol. 1.

Ardiwinata, *Buku Cacarakan Anyar* (*Soendaasch spel- en leesboekje*), vol. 1 & vol. 2. Revised 4th ed. Batavia: LD, Jw. See 1897 [1st ed.].

Ardiwinata, *Piwoelang ka noe Tani. II*, 2nd ed., supervised by H.C.H. de Bie. Semarang: H.A. Benjamins, Rm. See 1906 [1st ed.].

n.d.
Anonymous, *Cacarakan Sunda, pikeun murangkalih anu mimiti diajar maca*. n.p., Jw. (published before 1865)

n.d.
Anonymous, *Tjarijos Djalma noe Sangsara*. n.p., Rm. (title page missing)

n.d.
Hadji Mohamad Nuh, *Kitab ieu Landong tina Kabaluwengan Urusan Gogoda Zaman Ayeuna*. Bogor: Ikhtiar, Ab.

## (2) By Author's Name

['Abd as-Samad al-Palimbani], *Wawacan Petikan Bidayatussalik*, 1864. Batavia: LD, translated by R.D. Bratawidjaja under the supervision of Aria Koesoemah Diningrat, Jw/Rm., Wa., 3,050 ex., f. 0.15. (On the title page, in Javanese script, the year printed was 1863.)

Adi Widjaja, *Wulang Putra* (*Soendasch Gedicht Woelang Poetra*), 1862. Batavia: LD, Jw., Wa.

Albers, C., *Elmoe Boemi Tanah Hindia Nederlan*, 1872. Batavia: Ogilvie & Co., Rm.

_____, Nederlandsche Zendingsvereeniging, *Hikajat Garedja*, [1892]. Rotterdam: D. van Sijn & Zoon, Rm.

Among Pradja, *Boekoe Batjaan Sesela, pikeun moerid-moerid pangkat kadoewa*. [1st ed.], 1907. Batavia: LD, Rm. (1911, vol. 2, Rm.) (1913 [2nd ed.], Rm.)

Anonymous, *Kitab Pangajaran Basa Sunda (Soendasch spel- en leesboekje)*. [1850], n.p., Jw., 1,490 ex.

Anonymous, *Caritana Ibrahim*, 1st ed., 1853. Batavia: LD, Jw.

Anonymous, *Caritana Ibrahim (Geschiedenis van Ibrahim)*, [rep. ed.], 1888. Batavia: LD, Jw.

Anonymous, *Indjil anoe Kasoeratkeun koe Mattheus*, 1854. Batavia: Lange & Co., translated by [I. Esser], Rm., Wa.

Anonymous, *Wawacan Carita Ibrahim*, 1859. Batavia: Lange en Co., Jw., Wa.

Anonymous, *Wawacan Carita Nurulkamar*, 1860. Batavia: LD, Jw., Wa.

Anonymous, *Cacarakan Sunda, pikeun murangkalih anu mimiti diajar maca*. n.d., n.p., Jw. (published before 1865).

Anonymous, *Perdjandjian Anjar. Iju kitab bunang njoetat tina Kitab Soetje*, vol. 1 & 2. 1868, n.p., Rm.

Anonymous, *Iju Doewa Kitab Indjil anoe Soetji (De Evangelien van Loekas en Johannes)*. 1871. Meester-Cornelis: Rehoboth-Zending Press, translated by S. Coolsma, Rm.

Anonymous, *Iju Tjariosna Para Nabi*. 1871, Mèstèr: Rèhobot, Rm.

Anonymous, *Poepoedjian pikun Njanji, sareng pikun moedji ka pangeran*. 2nd ed., 1873. Meester-Cornelis: Rehoboth-Zending Press, Rm. (1st ed. unknown)

Anonymous, *Kitab Cacarakan Sunda (Soendaasch Spelboek)*, vol. 1, 1873. Batavia: LD, Jw.

Anonymous, *Mangle Lemboet keur Baroedak Leutik*, 1885. Bogor: Zending-Pers, Rm.

Anonymous, *Pangatoeran Tjengtjelengan Limbangan*. In Sundanese & Dutch, 1889. Bandung: De Vries & Fabricius, Rm.

Anonymous, *Tjarita Djahidin*, [1st ed.], translated by Soerja Karta Legawa, 1896. Batavia: LD, Rm.

Anonymous, *Tjarita Djahidin, kalawan Piwoeroek Sêpoehna*, rep. ed., 1903. Batavia: LD, Rm.

Anonymous, *Wawacan Gendit Birajung*. Title written by Snouck Hurgronje? found in Banten region, [1896], Ab., Wa., litho.

Anonymous, *Serat Rama*, translated from Javanese by R. Toemenggoeng Arija Martanagara, supervised by Bratadiwidjaja, 1900. Samarang: D.C.T. van Dorp & Co., Jw., Wa.

Anonymous, *Wawatjan Soelandjana nja eta Tjaria Tatanen Djaman Koena*, edited by C.M. Pleyte, 1907. Bandoeng: G. Kolff & Co., Rm.

Anonymous, *Tjarijos Djalma noe Sangsara*. n.d., n.p., Rm. (title page missing)

Ardiwinata, *Buku Cacarakan Anyar (Soendaasch spel- en leesboekje)*, vol. 1 & vol. 2, [1st ed.], 1897. Batavia: LD, Jw.

―――――, *Buku Cacarakan Anyar (Soendaasch spel- en leesboekje)*, vol. 1 & vol. 2. Revised 2nd ed., 1903. Batavia: LD, Jw.

―――――, *Buku Cacarakan Anyar (Soendaasch spel- en leesboekje)*, vol. 1 & vol. 2. Revised 3rd ed., 1907. Batavia: LD, Jw.

―――――, *Piwoelang ka noe Tani. I*. 2nd ed., supervised by H.C.H. de Bie, 1907. Semarang: H.A. Benjamins, Rm.

―――――, *Buku Cacarakan Anyar (Soendaasch spel- en leesboekje)*, vols. 1 & 2. Revised 4th ed., 1908. Batavia: LD, Jw.

―――――, *Piwoelang ka noe Tani, II*. 2nd ed., supervised by H.C.H. de Bie, 1908. Semarang: H.A. Benjamins, Rm.

―――――, *Piwoelang ka noe Tani, [I & II]*. [1st ed.], supervised by H.C.H. de Bie, 1906. Batavia: LD, Rm. (1914, 3rd ed. Semarang: H.A. Benjamins, Rm.)

Ardiwinata, D.K., *Tatakrama Oerang Soenda*, vol. 1. 1st ed., 1908, Bandung: Kaoem Moeda, Rm.

Bie, H. de, ed., *Mitra noe Tani*, vol. 13, 1897. Batavia: LD, Rm. See 1874, vol. 1.

―――――, ed., *Mitra noe Tani*, vol. 14, 1899. Batavia: LD, Rm.

Chijs, J.A. van der, *Babad Tanah Pasundan*, translated by Kartawinata, 1880. Batavia: LD, Jw.

[Coolsma, S.], *Ijeu Wawatjan eukeur Moerangkali anoe di Iskola*, 1876. Rotterdam: D. De Koning, Rm.

Danoe Koesoemah, *Wawacan Raja Darma (Soendasch Gedicht Radjadarma)*, 1862. Batavia: LD, Jw., Wa.

―――――, *Wawacan Cariyos Si Miskin*, 1863. Batavia: Lange en Co., Jw., Wa.

Defoe, Dan., *Carita Robinson Crusoë*, translated by Kartawinata, 1879. Batavia: LD, Jw., 10,015 ex. (orig. translated into Dutch by Gerard Keller.)

Gelder, W. van, *Carita Pulo Jawa (Java en zijn bewoners)*, vol. 1, translated by Kartawinata, 1880. Batavia: LD, Jw.

## Appendix 1

_____, *Carita Pulo Jawa (Java en zijn bewoners)*, vol. 2, 1880. Batavia: LD, Jw.

_____, *Carita Pulo Jawa (Java en zijn bewoners)*, vol. 3, 1881. Batavia: LD, Jw.

_____, *Carita Pulo Jawa (Java en zijn bewoners)*, vol. 4, 1881. Batavia: LD, Jw.

_____, *Buku Itungan nu Ka I, pikeun murid-murid pangkat panghandapna di iskola pribumi*, vol. 1, 1881. Batavia: LD, Jw.

_____, *Buku Itungan nu Ka I, pikeun murid-murid pangkat panghandapna di iskola pribumi*, vol. 2, 1881. Batavia: LD

_____, *Buku Itungan nu Ka I, pikeun murid-murid pangkat panghandapna di iskola pribumi*, vol. 3, 1881. Batavia: LD

_____, *Buku Itungan nu Ka I, pikeun murid-murid pangkat panghandapna di iskola pribumi*, vol. 4, 1882. Batavia: LD

_____, *Buku Itungan nu Ka I, pikeun murid-murid pangkat panghandapna di iskola pribumi*, vol. 5, 1883. Batavia: LD, Jw.

_____, *Buku Bacaan Salawe Tuladan, pikeun murid-murid pangkat panghandapna di sakola Sunda*, [1st ed.], 1881. Batavia: LD, Jw.

_____, *Buku Bacaan Salawe Tuladan, pikeun murid-murid pangkat panghandapna di sakola Sunda*. Rep. ed., 1889. Batavia: LD, Jw.

_____, *Buku Bacaan Salawe Tuladan, pikeun murid-murid pangkat panghandapna di sakola Sunda*. 3rd ed., 1898. Batavia: LD, Jw.

_____, *Buku Bacaan Salawe Tuladan, pikeun murid-murid pangkat panghandapna di sêkola Sunda*, [4th ed.], 1902. Batavia: LD, Jw.

_____, *Buku Bacaan Salawe Tuladan, pikeun murid-murid pangkat kadua di sêkola Sunda*, [1st ed.], 1902. Batavia: LD, Jw.

_____, *Buku Bacaan Salawe Tuladan, pikeun murid-murid pangkat kadua di sêkola Sunda*. Rep. ed., 1907. Batavia: LD, Jw. (1913, rep. ed., Jw.)

_____, *Mangle, nja eta roepa-roepa Tjarita reudjeung tjonto*, [1st ed.], 1890. Leiden: Kantor Tjitak Toewan P.W.M. Trap, Rm.

_____, *Mangle*. 2nd ed., 1898. Den Haag: Kantor tjitak De Swart en Zoon, Rm.

_____, *Mangle*. 3rd ed., 1901. Den Haag: Kantor tjitak De Swart en Zoon, Rm.

_____, *Mangle*. 4th ed., 1902. Den Haag: Kantor tjitak De Swart en Zoon, Rm.

_____, *Mangle*, 5th ed., 1906. Den Haag: Kantor tjitak De Swart en Zoon, Rm. (1909, 6th ed.) (1911, 7th ed.) (1913 [8th ed.]) (1922, 9th ed. Rm.)

Haastert, C.J. van, *Boekoe Itoengan Petjahan-perpoeloehan, pikeun moerid-moerid pangkat kadoewa di sakola-Soenda*, [1st ed.], 1894. Batavia: LD, Rm.

——, *Boekoe Itoengan Petjahan-perpoeloehan, pikeun moerid-moerid pangkat kadoewa di sakola-Soenda*, 2nd ed., 1900. Batavia: LD, Rm.

——, *Boekoe Itoengan Petjahan-perpoeloehan, pikeun moerid-moerid pangkat kadoewa di sakola-Soenda*, 3rd ed., 1906. Batavia: LD, Rm.

——, *Boekoe Itoengan Petjahan Bener, pikeun moerid-moerid pangkat kadoewa di sakola-Soenda*, [1st ed.], 1894. Batavia: LD, Rm.

——, *Boekoe Itoengan Petjahan Bener, pikeun moerid-moerid pangkat kadoewa di sakola-Soenda*, 2nd ed., 1900. Batavia: LD, Rm.

——, *Boekoe Itoengan Petjahan Bener, pikeun moerid-moerid pangkat kadoewa di sakola-Soenda*, 3rd ed., 1904. Batavia: LD, Rm.

——, *Boekoe Edjahan djeung Batjaan, pikeun moerid-moerid dina pangkat panghandapna di sakola-Soenda*, vol. 1, 1894. Batavia: LD, Rm. 1896, vol. 2., Rm. (1910, vol. 1 [4th ed.]), Rm.

——, *Boekoe Edjahan djeung Batjaan, pikeun moerid-moerid dina pangkat panghandapna di sakola-Soenda*, vol. 2, 1896. Batavia: LD, Rm.

——, *Boekoe Edjahan Djeung Batjaan, pikeun moerid-moerid dina pangkat panghandapna di sakola-Soenda*, vol. 2, [2nd ed.], 1898. Batavia: LD, Rm.

——, *Boekoe Edjahan djeung Batjaan, pikeun moerid-moerid dina pangkat panghandapna di sakola-Soenda*, vol. 1, [2nd ed.], 1899. Batavia: LD, Rm.

——, *Boekoe Edjahan djeung Batjaan, pikeun moerid-moerid dina pangkat panghandapna di sakola-Soenda*, vol. 2, [3rd ed.], 1907. Batavia: LD, Rm.

——, *Boekoe Edjahan djeung Batjaan, pikeun moerid-moerid dina pangkat panghandapna di sakola-Soenda*, vol. 1, [3rd ed.], 1908. Batavia: LD. (1910, vol. 2 [4th ed.]), Rm.

Hekker, Ch., *Pangadjaran Basa Soenda, pikeun moreid-moerid pangkat panghandapna di sakola Soenda*, vol. 1, 2nd ed., 1907. Batavia: LD, Rm. (1st ed. unknown)

——, *Pangadjaran Basa Soenda, pikeun moerid-moerid pangkat*

*Appendix 1* 231

*kadoewa di sakola Soenda*, vol. 2, 2nd ed., 1908. Batavia: LD, Rm. (1st ed. unknown)

Holle, A.W.; Holle, K.F., [*Carita Kura-kura jeung Monyet*], 1851. Batavia: Lange en Co., Jw.

[Holle, K.F.], *Katrangan tina Prakawis Miara Lauk Cai*, 1861. Batavia: LD, translation, Jw.

_____, *Kitab Conto-conto Surat pikeun Murangkalih anu Ngaskola (Soendasche modellen van verschillende brieven)*, 1861. Batavia: LD, Jw., 10,000 ex.

_____, *Kitab Tjatjarakan Soenda No.1 (Soendasch spel- en leesboekje met Latijnsche letter)*, vol. 1, 1st ed., 1862. Batavia: LD, Rm. 20,015 ex.

_____, *Kitab Tjatjarakan Soenda Make Aksara Walanda (Soendaasch spel- en leerboekje met Latijnsche letter)*, vol. 1, 2nd ed., 1876. Batavia: LD, Rm., 20,015 ex.

_____, *Kitab Nuduhkeun Ngelmu Itungan (Rekenboekje over de benoemde getallen)*, 1867. Batavia: LD, Jw.

_____ ed., *Mitra nu Tani*, vol. 1., translated by Kartawinata from Dutch, 1874. Batavia: LD, Jw. (1897, vol. 13, Rm., ed. by H. de Bie.) (1899, vol. 14, Rm., ed. by H. de Bie.)

_____ed., *Mitra nu Tani*, vol. 2, 1877. Batavia: LD, Jw.

_____ed., *Mitra nu Tani*, vol. 3, 1877. Batavia: LD, Jw.

_____ed., *Mitra nu Tani*, vol. 4, 1878. Batavia: LD, Jw.

_____ed., *Mitra nu Tani*, vol. 5, 1878. Batavia: LD, Jw.

_____ed., *Mitra nu Tani*, vol. 6, 1879. Batavia: LD, Jw.

_____ed., *Mitra nu Tani*, vol. 7, 1879. Batavia: LD, Jw.

_____ed., *Mitra Noe Tani*, vol. 8, 1892. Batavia: LD, Rm.

_____ed., *Mitra noe Tani*, vol. 9 & 10, 1893. Batavia: LD, Rm.

_____ed., *Mitra noe Tani*, vol. 11, 1894. Batavia: LD, Rm.

_____ed., *Mitra noe Tani*, vol. 12, 1895. Batavia: LD, Rm.

[Ibnoe Hadjar al Haitami], *Ieu Pepetikan tina Kitab Tupah*, translated by Soerjadilaga, Jw, 1858. Batavia: Langeh jeung paseroan.

Kandjeng Goepernemen, *Besluit Betreffende de Regeling der Heerendiensten in het Soendaneesch*, 1875. Batavia: LD, Rm.

_____, *Staatsblad voor Ned. Indie. Soendasche vertaling van verschillende nummers*, 1875/76. Batavia: LD, Rm.

_____, *Parentah jeung Piwuruk baris Nuduhan Petana Amtenar-amtenar Eropa jeung Pribumi Rawuh Pangkat-pngkat Ngalamphkeunana Timbalan kana Ngajaga Paragan Sato*, translated by Kartawinata, [1880]. Batavia: LD, Jw.

_____, *Aturan Ngurus Sakitan-sakitan di Indiya Nederlan. Staatsblad 1871 nomer 78. (Soendasche vertaling van het reglement van orde en tucht onder de gevangenen in Nederlandsch-Indë. Staatsblad 1871, No. 78)*. translated by Kartawinata, 1882. Batavia: LD, Jw.

_____, *Istruksi Kapala Desa*, translated by Rangga Adilaga, [1886]. Batavia: LD, Jw.

_____, *Atoeran Metakeun Herendines di Tanah Prajangan*, [1892]. Batavia: LD, Jw. (enacted by J.D. Harders, Resident of Priangan).

_____, *Wawacan Piwulang Panulak Panyakit Kolera*, translated by Raden Tumenggung Djajadiningrat, 1897. Batavia: LD, Ab.

_____, *Rupa-rupa Katerangan nu Netelakeun Bab Kasakit Kolera jeung Sarat-sarat pikeun Ngurus Awak Bisi Katerap Panyakit eta*, 1905. Batavia: LD, Ab.

Kartawinata, *Cariyos Tuwan Kapitan Marion (Geschiedenis van den Kapitein Marion)*, 1872. Batavia: LD, Jw., 5,015 ex. (1872, Javanese translation by Kartawinata).

_____, *Carita Kapitan Bonteku (Reis van den kapitein Willem Ysbrandtsz Bontekoe)*, 1st ed., 1874. Batavia: LD, Jw., 5,015 ex.

_____, *Carita Kapitan Bonteku (Reis van den kapitein Willem Ysbrandtsz Bontekoe)*, 2nd ed., 1883. Batavia: LD, Jw.

_____, *Carita Kapitan Bonteku (Reis van den kapitein Willem Ysbrandtsz Bontekoe)*, new ed., 1903. Batavia: LD, Jw. (1924, ed., Rm.)

_____, *Kitab Conto-conto Surat Anyar (Nieuw Brievenboek voor de Soendasche Scholen)*, 1876. Batavia: [LD], under the supervision of K.F Holle, Jw., 10,000 ex.

_____, *300 Masalah, Elmu Itungan (300 Rekenkundige voorstellen voor eerst beginnenden)*, 1876. Batavia: LD, Jw.

_____, *Boekoe Wet Hal Pangadilan Hoekoeman baris Oerang Priboemi di Indië-Nederland*, 1889. Batavia: LD, Rm.

_____, *Boekoe Wet Hal Pangadilan Hoekoeman djeung Atoeran noe Djadi Babakoe Hoekoeman Politie baris Oerang priboemi di Indië-Nederland*, 1889. Batavia: LD, Rm.

_____, *Pagoeneman Soenda djeng Walanda (Soendasche Hollandsche samenspraken)*, [1st ed.], under the supervision of K.F. Holle, 1883. Batavia: LD, Rm.

_____, *Pagoeneman Soenda djeng Walanda (Soendasche Hollandsche Samenspraken)*, rep. ed., 1891. Batavia: LD, Rm.

_____, *Pagoeneman Soenda djeng Walanda (Soendasche Hollandsche Samenspraken)*, 1908. Batavia: LD, Rm. (1915, Rm.)

Lasminingrat, *Carita Erman*. 1st ed., translated from Dutch, 1875. Batavia: LD, Jw., 6,015 ex. (1911, 2nd ed., Jw.) (1922, Rm., ed.) (1919, *Hikajat Erman*, Malay translation by M.S. Tjakrabangsa, n.y. 2nd ed. 1930, 3rd ed.).

_____, *Warnasari atawa Rupa-rupa Dongeng*, vol. 1, translation from Dutch, 1876. Batavia: LD, Jw. 1887, vol. 3 (translated by Lenggang Kantjana), Rm.

_____, *Warnasari atawa Roepa-roepa Dongeng*, vol. 2, 1887. Batavia: LD, Rm.

_____, *Warnasari atawa Rupa-rupa Dongeng*, vol. 1, new ed., 1903. Batavia: LD, Jw.

_____, *Warnasari atawa Rupa-rupa Dongeng*, vol. 1, 1907. Batavia: LD, Jw. See 1876, vol. 1. (1909, vol. 2, Rm.) (1909, vol. 3, Rm.) (1912, vol. 3, Rm.)

Lenderink, *Roepa-roepa Pangadjaran Hal Mijara Boedak Lolong keur Waktoe Aja di Imah Kolotna*, translated by the colonial government, 1900. Batavia: LD, Rm.

Lenggang Kantjana, *Warnasari atawa Roepa-roepa Dongeng*, vol. 3, 1887. Batavia: LD, Rm., 6,015 ex.

Mangoen Di Karia, *Tembang Piwoelang, pikeun moerid-moerid di iskola Soenda*, 1908. Batavia: LD, Rm.

Martanagara, *Wawacan Angling Darma*, 1906. Bandung: Toko citak Afandi, Jw., Wa.

Moehamad Moesa, *Wawacan Wulang Krama (Soendasch Zededicht Woelang-krama)*, 1st ed., 1862. Batavia: LD, Jw., Wa (1923, reprinted in Soendaneesch Volksalmanak. Batavia: Balai Poestaka, Rm.)

_____, *Wawacan Dongeng-dongeng (Soendasche gedichten en fabelen)*, 1862. Batavia: LD, Jw., Wa.

_____, *Wawacan Raja Sudibya (Soendasch gedicht Radja Soedibja)*, 1862. Batavia: LD, Jw., Wa.

_____, *Wulang-tani*, 1862. Batavia: LD, Jw., Wa.

_____, *Wawacan Seca Nala (Geschiedenis van Setja Nala, Bevattende lessen voor den boeren- en handelstand)*, 1863. Batavia: LD, Jw/Rm., Wa., 3,050 ex.

_____, *Tjarita Abdoerahman djeng Abdoerahim (Geschiedenis van Abdoerahman en Abdoerahim)*, 1st ed., 1863. Batavia: LD, translated from Arabic via Malay, Rm/Jw.

_____, *Carita Abdurahman jeung Abdurahim (Geschiedenis van Abdoerahman en Abdoerahim)*, 2nd ed., 1883. Batavia: LD, Jw.

_____, *Carita Abdurahman jeung Abdurahim* (*Geschiedenis van Abdoerahman en Abdoerahim*), 2nd ed., 1884. Batavia: LD, Jw.
_____, *Tjarita Abdoerrahman djeung Abdoerrahim*, rep. ed., 1885. Batavia: LD, Rm.
_____, *Carita Abdurahman jeung Abdurahim* (*Geschiedenis van Abdoerahman en Abdoerahim*), 3rd ed., 1906. Batavia: LD, Jw.
_____, *Carita Abdurahman jeung Abdurahim* (*Geschiedenis van Abdoerahman en Abdoerahim*), rep. 3rd ed., 1908. Batavia: LD, Jw/Rm. (1911, 4th ed.) (1922, 5th ed.) (1877, Javanese translation by Raden Angga Baja. Batavia: LD. 1925, Malay translation. Djakarta: Balai Poestaka.)
_____, *Ali Moehtar/Wawacan Carios Ali Muhtar*, 1st ed., 1864. Batavia: LD, Rm/Jw., Wa., 3,030 ex., f. 0.08.
_____, *Ali Moehtar*, 2nd ed., 1883. Batavia: LD, Rm/Jw., Wa.
_____, *Elmu Nyawah* (*Handleiding voor de kultuur van padi op natte velden*), 1864. Batavia: LD, Jw/Rm., Wa., 4,050 ex., f. 0.22.
_____, *Wawacan Wulang Guru*, 1st ed., 1865. Batavia: LD, Jw., Wa., 550 ex., f. 0.04.
_____, *Wawatjan Woelang Goeroe* (*Wenken voor den onderwijzer*), 1865. Batavia: LD, Rm., Wa.
_____, *Wawacan Wulang Murid*, 1st ed., 1865. Batavia: LD, Jw., Wa. 2,050 ex., f. 0.06.
_____, *Wawatjan Woelang Moerid* (*Lessen voor den leerling*), 1865. Batavia: LD, Rm., Wa.
_____, *Dongeng-dongeng Piêntêngên* (*Spiegel der jeugd*), 1st ed., 1867. Batavia: LD, Rm., 3,050 ex., f. 0.28.
_____, *Dongeng-dongeng Pieunteungeun* (*Spiegel der jeugd*), 1867. Batavia: LD, Jw., 6,050 ex., f. 0.48.
_____, *Dongeng-dongeng Pieunteungeun*, new ed., 1888. Batavia: LD, Rm.
_____, *Dongeng-dongeng Pieunteungeun*, [3rd ed.], 1901. Batavia: LD, Rm.
_____, *Dongeng-dongeng Pieunteungeun*, [4th ed.], 1904. Batavia: LD, Rm.
_____, *Dongeng-dongeng Pieunteungeun*, [5th ed.], 1907. Batavia: LD, Rm. (1912, [6th] ed.)
_____, *Dongeng-dongeng nu Araneh* (*Vertellingen*), 1st ed., 1866. Batavia: LD, translation from Malay, Jw., 3,050 ex., f. 0.16.
_____, *Dongeng-dongeng nu Araneh*, new ed., 1884. Batavia: LD, Jw.

———, *Dongeng-dongeng nu Araneh*, 2nd ed., 1890. Batavia: LD, Jw.
———, *Panji Wulung*, 1st ed., 1871. Batavia: LD, Jw., Wa.
———, *Pandji Woeloeng*, Rm. ed., 1876. Batavia: LD, Wa.
———, *Panji Wulung*, 2nd ed., 1891. Batavia: LD, Jw., Wa.
———, *Panji Wulung*, new ed., 1901. Batavia: LD, Jw., Wa.
———, *Pandji Woeloeng*, [new ed.], 1904. Batavia: LD, Rm., Wa.
———, *Panji Wulung*, 3rd ed., 1908. Batavia: LD, Jw., Wa. (1909, 3rd ed., Rm.) (1913, revised ed., Rm.) (1922, 4th ed., Rm.) (1879, Javanese translation by Soerjodidjojo in the name of Pangeran Adipati Ario Mangkoe Negoro IV, Jw.) (1928, Madurese translation by R. Sosro Danoe Koesoemo, 2 vol., Jw.)
———, *Lampah Sebar*, 1872. Batavia: LD, Rm/Jw.
———, *Wawatjan Lampah Sebar*, 1872. Batavia: LD, Rm/Jw., Wa.
———, *Katrangan Lampah Sebar*, 1874. Batavia: LD, Jw., Wa.
Moehamad Oemar, *Wawacan Katrangan Miara Lauk Cai (Handleiding voor de teelt van zoetwatervisch)*, 1866. Batavia: LD, Jw., Wa.
———, *Wawatjan Katrangan Miara Laoek Tjai (Handleiding voor de teelt van zoetwatervisch)*, [1st ed.], 1866. Batavia: LD, Rm., Wa., 5,050 ex., f. 0.24.
Moehamad Saleh Mangkoepradja, *Kitab Atoeran Bab Maradjian Djelema noe Ngedjoeroe*, 1901. Batavia: Albrecht & Co., Rm.
Mohamad Nuh, Hadji, *Kitab ieu Landong tina Kabaluwengan Urusan Gogoda Zaman Ayeuna*, n.d. Bogor: Ikhtiar, Ab.
Nederlandsch Bijbelgenootschap, *Ieu Kitab Injil Sutji anu Dikarang ku Lukas (Het Evangelie van Lucas)*, translated by S. Coolsma, 1877. Leiden: A.W. Sijthoff, Ab.
———, *Perdjandjian Anjar, hartosna sadajana kitab noe kasebat indjil goesti oerang Jesoes Kristoes*, translated by S. Coolsma, 1877. Amsterdam, Rm.
———, *Kitab Soetji, hartosna sadajana kitab anoe kasebat Perdjandjian lawas sareng Perdjangdjian anjar*, translated by S. Coolsma, 1891. Amsterdam, Rm.
———, *Kitab Injil Sutji anu Dikarang ku Johanes (Het Evangelie van Johannes)*, translated by S. Coolsma, 1895. Leiden: A.W. Sijthoff, Ab.
———, *Kitab Lalampahan Para Rasul Saruci Beunang Ngarang Lukas*, translated by S. Coolsma, 1896. Leiden: A.W. Sijthoff, Ab.
———, *Kitab Indjil Soetji anoe Dikarang koe Markoes*, 1907. Amsterdam: ?, Rm.

Nederlandsche Zendingsvereeniging, *Kitab Elmoe Itoengan (Rekenboekje voor de scholen)*, vol. 1, 1866. Rotterdam: D. De Koning, Rm.

_____, *Kitab Elmoe Itoengan no.1, pikeun maroerangkalih anoe kur iskola*, 1866. Rotterdam: D. De Koning, Rm.

_____, *Kitab Elmoe Itoengan (Rekenboekje voor de scholen)*, vol. 2, 1866. Rotterdam: D. De Koning, Rm.

_____, *Kitab Elmoe Itoengan (Rekenboekje voor de scholen)*, vol. 3, 1867. Rotterdam: D. De Koning, Rm.

_____, *Kitab Elmoe Itoengan (Rekenboekje voor de scholen)*, vol. 4, 1868. Rotterdam: D. De Koning, Rm.

_____, [Albers, C.], *Kitab Itoengan, pangmimitina pisan keur baroedak iskola*, 1st ed., [1866]. Schoonhoven: S.E. van Nooten & Zoon, Rm.

_____, [Albers, C.], *Kitab Itoengan, pangmimitina pisan keur baroedak iskola*, [3rd ed.], 1902. Rotterdam: D. van Sijn & Zoon, Rm.

_____, *Kitab Indjil Dikarang koe Loekas*, translated by G.J. Grashuis, Rm, 1866. Rotterdam: E.H. Tassemeijer.

_____, [G.J. Grashuis], *Tjatjarakan Soenda (Soendaneesch spelboekje)*. 1st ed., 1866. Rotterdam: E.H.Tassemeijer, Rm.

_____, [G.J. Grashuis], *Tjatjarakan Soenda (Soendaneesch spelboekje)*. revised 2nd ed. [1883]. Rotterdam: D. De Koning, Rm.

_____, *Tjarijos Goesti Jesoes sareng Rasoel-Rasoelna*, [1st ed.], 1885. Rotterdam: D. De Koning, Rm.

_____, *Tjarijos Goesti Jesoes sareng Rasoel-rasoelna*, 2nd ed., 1901. Rotterdam: D. van Sijn & Zoon, Rm.

_____, *Tjarijos Para Nabi Ditoekil tina Kitab Perdjangdjian Lawas*, [1st ed.], 1892. Rotterdam: D. van Sijn & Zoon, Rm.

_____, *Tjarijos Para Nabi Ditoekil tina Kitab Perdjangdjian Lawas*, 2nd ed., 1902. Rotterdam: D. van Sijn & Zoon, Rm.

_____, *Tjarijos Joesoep Beunang Nembangkeun*, translated by N. Titus, [1st ed.], [1894]. Rotterdam: D. van Sijn & Zoon, Rm., Wa.

_____, *Tjarijos Joesoep Beunang Nembangkeun*, 2nd ed., [1902]. Rotterdam: D. van Sijn & Zoon, Rm.

_____, [Albers, C.], *Elmoe Agama Oerang Kristen*, 1886. Rotterdam: D. De Koning, Rm.

_____, *Poepoedjian Oerang Kristen, njanjikeuneun di garedja djeung di imah*. [1893]. Rotterdam: D. van Sijn & Zoon, Rm.

_____, *Njanjian baris Moedji di Iskola reudjeung di Imah*, 1897. Rotterdam: D. van Sijn & Zoon, Rm.

_____, *Poepoedjian Garedja Pasoendan, njanjikeuneun di garedja djeung di imah*, 1904. Rotterdam: D. van Sijn & Zoon, Rm.

---, *Tjarijos Radja Saoel djeung Radja Dawoed Beunang Nembangkeun*, translated by N. Titus, [1906]. Rotterdam: D. van Sijn & Zoon, Rm., Wa.

Nooij, H.A., *Buku Bacaan, pikeun murid-murid dina pangkat panghandapna di iskola Sunda*, [1st ed.], 1883. Batavia: LD, Jw.

---, *Buku Bacaan, pikeun murid-murid dina pangkat panghandapna di iskola Sunda*, new ed., 1894. Batavia: LD, Jw.

---, *Buku Bacaan, pikeun murid-murid dina pangkat panghandapna di iskola Sunda*, 2nd ed., 1896. Batavia: LD, Jw.

Prawira Koesoema, *Wawatjan Dongeng-dongeng Toeladan*, 1st ed., 1863. Batavia: LD, Rm/Jw., Wa., 3,050 ex.

---, *Wawatjan Dongeng-dongeng Toeladan*, 2nd ed., 1888. Batavia: LD, Rm/Jw., Wa. (1922, 4th ed.) (1911, 3rd ed. Batavia: LD, Rm.).

*Serat Pananggalan Anggoeun dina Taun Walanda (Soendaneesche Almanak)*, 1st year, 1897. Samarang: G.C.T.van Dorp & Co., Jw.

---. 2nd Year, 1898. Samarang: G.C.T. van Dorp & Co., Jw.

---. 3rd year, 1899. Samarang: G.C.T. van Dorp & Co., Jw.

---. 4th year, 1900. Samarang: G.C.T.van Dorp & Co., Jw.

---. 5th year, 1901. Samarang: G.C.T. van Dorp & Co., Jw.

---. 6th year, 1902. Samarang: G.C.T. van Dorp & Co., Jw.

---. 7th year, 1903. Samarang: G.C.T. van Dorp & Co., Jw.

*Serat Pananggalan Bahasa Sunda (Soendaneesche Almanak)*, 1st year, 1900. Samarang: G.C.T. van Dorp & Co., Ab.

---. 2nd year, 1901. Samarang: G.C.T. van Dorp & Co., Ab.

---. 3rd year, 1902. Samarang: G.C.T. van Dorp & Co., Ab.

---. 4th year, 1903. Samarang: G.C.T. van Dorp & Co., Ab.

*Serat Pananggalan Sunda (Soendaneesche Almanak)*, 1st year, 1892. Cheribon: A. Bisschop, Jw.

---. 2nd year, 1893. Cheribon: A. Bisschop, Jw.

---. 3rd year, 1894. Cheribon: A. Bisschop, Jw.

---. 4th year, 1895. Cheribon: A. Bisschop, Jw.

---. 5th year, 1896. Cheribon: A. Bisschop, Jw.

---. 6th year, 1897. Cheribon: A. Bisschop, Jw.

Soerja Nata Legawa, R. Demang (Kartawinata), *Pangeling-ngeling ka Padoeka Toewan Karel Frederik Holle*, 1897, n.p., Rm.

'Utman bin Abdallah bin Aqil ibu Jahja (Sayyid 'Uthmân), *Irsjad Al-anam Fi Tarjmat Arkan Al-Islam*, translated by the *mantri goeroe* in Soekaboemi, 1896. Batavia, Ab., litho.

---, *Cempaka Mulia*, translated by Raden Hadji Azhari with Hadji Irsyad, 1897. Batavia, Ab., litho.

———, *Islah Al-hal Bi Talb Al-halal*, translated by Raden Azhari, 1897. Batavia, Ab., litho.

———, *Kamus Kecil Arabiyah-Malaju-Sunda*, translated by Raden Hadji Azhari, 1897. Batavia, Ab., litho.

———, *Taftih Al-uyun Ala Fasadi Al-dhunun*, translated by Raden Haji Azhari, 1897. Batavia, Ab., litho.

———, *Nasihat Datang buat Ngalarang Nyieun Nyeri kana Binatang*, translated by Mohamad Bisri bin hadji Abdullah, 1901. Batavia, Ab., litho.

———, *Saun Ad-din 'An Nazgrat Al-mudallin*. Arabic, Malay, Javanese, and Sundanese poligrot text, 1903. Batavia, Ab/Rm., litho.

Wira Tanoe Baija, *Wawacan Jaka Miskin (Soendasch Gedicht Djaka Miskin)*, translation from Malay, Jw., Wa., 1862. Batavia: LD.

# Appendix 2

# *Wawacan Panji Wulung*

## (1) The Construction of Verse Form and Stanza in *Wawacan Panji Wulung*

1. *dangdanggula* (stanza no. 1 to no. 28)
2. *asmarandana* (29–78)
3. *sinom* (79–124)
4. *pangkur* (125–56)
5. *kinanti* (157–213)
6. *mijil* (214–29)
7. *asmarandana* (230–96)
8. *sinom* (297–322)
9. *dangdanggula* (323–48)
10. *durma* (349–70)
11. *kinanti* (371–435)
12. *asmarandana* (436–84)
13. *sinom* (485–522)
14. *dangdanggula* (523–66)
15. *magatru* (567–600)
16. *kinanti* (601–25)
17. *asmarandana* (626–72)
18. *dangdanggula* (673–700)
19. *pucung* (701–16)
20. *asmarandana* (717–64)
21. *sinom* (765–81)
22. *maskumambang* (782–805)
23. *kinanti* (806–51)
24. *pangkur* (852–91)
25. *durma* (892–927)
26. *dangdanggula* (928–67)
27. *maskumambang* (968–87)
28. *sinom* (988–1,018)

## (2) Summary of *Wawacan Panji Wulung*

The kingdom of Sokadana is prospering. The king, Dewakeswari, is in love with a concubine, Tunjungsari, with whom he conceives a child. Jealous and angry, the queen together with the *ajar*, Guna Wisesa, conspires to drive Tunjungsari out. The *ajar* tells the king that one of the concubines committed adultery with a certain Panolih, and is rewarded by the queen. The king believes the *ajar's* words and immediately orders the viceroy to kill the concubine and the vassal. However, the viceroy, Lembu Jayeng Pati, does not carry out the execution but hides the concubine in a remote village, and sends the vassal out of the country. The king believes that Tunjungsari has been executed because the viceroy brings him a pair of ears that he has taken from a dead body in prison and presents them as hers (Stanzas 1–38).

Tunjungsari gives birth to a beautiful baby who looks exactly like his father. The baby is named Panji Wulung. The king of Sokadana does not know about the birth of his son. The viceroy loves him very much and becomes his mentor. Panji Wulung follows the foster father's advice and trains his body by lifting weights every day. The viceroy teaches Panji Wulung to be brave and polite, and tells him not to believe the *ajar's* supernatural powers or anything that cannot be verified by sight or other rational proof. The fourteen-year-old boy Panji Wulung is ordered to go on a quest to gain more experience, and he sets out on a journey accompanied by two vassals, Janggala and Janggali (stanzas 38–105).

On his journey, Panji Wulung demonstrates his physical strength against animals and robbers. He wants to pursue wisdom and so serves an ascetic apprenticeship under the *ajar* Guna Wisesa. He learns sacred words but cannot see their effect. He asks the *ajar* to show him proof, but the *ajar* rejects the request and takes offence. When the *ajar* becomes angry he throws a stone at Panji Wulung, who stabs the *ajar* with a dagger because he feels insulted and recognizes that the *ajar* is a liar. Panji Wulung and his followers then go to the sea to look for a boat. While they wait for the boat, Janggala and Janggali reveal to Panji Wulung the secret of his birth. They find a boat from Patani and depart for Keling. Panji meets a noble Buginese man, Daheng Bramani, on the boat and the two young men find each other to be congenial spirits (stanzas 106–95). After staying at Patani for a year, Panji Wulung, Bramani, Janggala and Janggali sail to Cempa and settle in a remote village, devoting themselves to farming. The village flourishes (stanzas 195–228).

A year passes. Panji Wulung and the three men go hunting in a forest. They encounter an ugly man on an elephant and a beautiful woman who is his captive. Panji Wulung fights to save the woman and kills both the man and his elephant. Crying, she explains what happened to her. She is a princess of Cempa. The dead man was a Bengali who had been appointed as the trainer of an elephant that her father, the King of Cempa, loved very much. She was seduced by the Bengali man while the king was away on a hunting expedition. Panji Wulung and the princess Andayaningrat immediately fall in love and promise to marry (stanzas 229–66). They go back to the peasant in the village. The surprised peasant tells them of the King's proclamation that he who finds the lost princess will be appointed prince and rewarded half the Cempa kingdom. Panji Wulung hesitates, but the peasant advises him to bring the princess to the palace immediately (stanzas 267–75).

Meanwhile, the king and queen of Cempa are full of sorrow. The king is waiting for news of the lost princess. In order to get the reward, a man named Andakasura tells a lie to the king that he has killed the Bengali man and the elephant, although in fact he only came across their bodies in the forest. However, the princess has not been found yet (stanzas 275–91). In the village, Panji hesitates to bring back the princess for fear of being accused of unfaithfulness. Accepting Bramani's advice, he writes a letter to the king of Cempa. Bramani takes the letter to the palace (stanzas 292–308). The king of Cempa is overjoyed to know that the princess has been saved. Immediately, the king orders the viceroy to send a welcome party for Panji Wulung and the princess in the village. The liar Andakasura is imprisoned (stanzas 309–15). The procession reaches the village, and the viceroy conveys a royal letter to Panji Wulung. The procession starts its return to the palace. The princess is reunited with her parents. After the feast, the king welcomes Panji Wulung and appoints him prince, giving him the name Pangeran Dewa Kusumah. Bramani is given a new name, Urawan, befitting his high position. The king intends to execute the lying Andakasura, but Panji Wulung asks the king to set him free (stanzas 316–35).

After running away from Cempa and reaching the kingdom of Gilingwesi, the villain Andakasura persuades the king to attack Cempa. The king agrees because he wants to marry the beautiful princess Andayaningrat. Before the departure of Gilingwesi's fleet, the king kills the viceroy who had admonished him for his lust and passions. The troops of Gilingwesi capture the harbour of Cempa (stanzas 335–46). The king of Cempa orders Panji Wulung to defend the kingdom against

Gilingwesi's attack. The princess is worried about Panji Wulung's safety and parts from him in tears. Panji Wulung and his troops depart to the harbour (stanzas 347–59). An intense battle between Cempa and Gilingwesi takes place on the shore. Panji Wulung notices that a Gilingwesi soldier, Sudarma, has taken revenge for his executed uncle, the viceroy of Gilingwesi. Sudarma and other vassals explain to Panji Wulung the reason for killing their king when Panji Wulung accuses them of disloyalty. The war is over and the remnants of the defeated Gilingwesi army are brought to the palace of Cempa by Panji Wulung (stanzas 360–98).

The king's procession with Andayaningrat sets out to meet Panji Wulung after receiving news of the victory. At the royal rest-house, Panji Wulung reports the outcome of the battle to the king and proposes that Sudarma be made king of Gilingwesi. The king of Cempa advises Panji Wulung to nominate Sudarma as viceroy. Everyone returns to the palace in a royal procession. The beauty of the princess is beyond description. A celebration feast is held in the palace. After the party, Panji and the princess take a walk in the garden before entering their bedroom at the crown prince's palace (stanzas 399–442). Sudarma is appointed viceroy of Gilingwesi and renamed Suraludira by Panji Wulung. After studying state affairs for a half month, Suraludira bids farewell. Panji Wulung advises him on statecraft and asks him to restrain his passions (stanzas 442–501).

The country of Cempa prospers as never before. Panji Wulung invites the peasant and his wife to visit him. Panji Wulung often feels sad when he remembers his foster-father, the viceroy of Sokadana and his wife. He orders Bramani and Janggala to take a letter to the viceroy. He informs them that he has become crown prince of Cempa and invites them to come (stanzas 502–26).

In Sokadana, the viceroy and his wife are always thinking of Panji Wulung, who had left a long time ago. They had a son named Panji Pamekas, who was asked by the king of Sokadana to become the crown prince because the king had no children. The wife of the viceroy hears that Panji Wulung has become crown prince of Cempa. Bramani and Janggala reach Sokadana, bringing Panji Wulung's letter and royal presents. The viceroy, his wife, and Panji Wulung's mother Tunjungsari are moved to tears by the letter. Every night, Bramani and Janggala tell stories of Panji Wulung's success. In return, the viceroy writes a letter to Panji Wulung giving advice: do not be proud of success, love your wife, do not have too many concubines, restrain your passions. He writes about his own son Pamekas, who has won the king's affection, and tells the secret of Panji Wulung's birth. After a two-month stay, Bramani and Janggala leave Sokadana for Cempa with the viceroy's letter (stanzas 526–68).

Reading the letter from his foster father, Panji Wulung cannot hold back his tears. He hopes that the viceroy's son Pamekas will become the crown prince of Sokadana in order to repay the viceroy's kindness and faithfulness (stanzas 569–84). The great king of Cempa loves his son-in-law and often advises the princess that she should obey her husband and not be too proud of her royal birth. The king becomes seriously ill. He calls his vassals to his sickbed and expresses his dying wish that Panji Wulung should ascend the throne. He also wants his men to make a vow of loyalty to Panji Wulung. Panji Wulung and the princess, both in tears, each promise the king that they will not remarry after the other's death. The king gives a royal ring to Panji Wulung as the symbol of the throne and breathes his last. The whole country enters a mourning period of forty days (stanzas 585–619).

In the solemn coronation ceremony, Panji Wulung ascends the throne of Cempa. The viceroy explains that the throne was given to the princess and the princess then gave it to her husband, Panji Wulung. A great feast is held. The kingdom of Cempa keeps prospering. Panji Wulung sends a letter to the viceroy of Sokadana telling of the death of the great king of Cempa and of his own coronation (stanzas 620–41). The viceroy of Sokadana and Tunjungsari receive the letter and are delighted with the news. The viceroy plans to visit Panji Wulung with his wife. Rejoicing at the news, Panji Wulung discusses preparations for their visit with the queen (stanzas 642–50).

In Sokadana, the old king goes hunting. He talks heart-to-heart with the viceroy. The king tells the viceroy that he wants to give the throne to the viceroy's son Pamekas. He confesses that he can never forget the executed Tunjungsari and tells the viceroy that the day before he had seen a woman who looked exactly like her. In tears, the viceroy discloses the truth about the false execution many years ago. The king is embarrassed and his face turns pale. He is astonished but pleased to hear this revelation. The two old men talk until dusk. The king decides to execute the disloyal queen, but the viceroy reproves him for his rashness. The king starts on his way home (stanzas 650–76). The queen, who notices the king's anger, applies black magic to obtain his affection but does not succeed. The viceroy prepares a ceremony for the new queen, and Tunjungsari makes preparations to ascend the throne (stanzas 673–82).

The procession of Tunjungsari to the palace is completed, and the king nominates Tunjungsari as the new queen, renaming her Sekarkancana during the royal coronation. The people welcome the new queen, while the old queen lives in grief. The king and queen live in happiness, but often think of their own son Panji Wulung. The king orders the viceroy to go to Cempa to invite the king of Cempa, Panji Wulung, and his queen to Sokadana. The viceroy and his wife embark on the trip to Cempa, and are cordially received by the harbour master there. After one night, they proceed to the palace. They are heartily welcomed by Panji Wulung at the royal rest-house along the way. The royal procession then proceeds to the palace (stanzas 683–94). The queen of Cempa warmly receives them in a grand ceremony, and a luxurious feast follows. The viceroy invites Panji Wulung and his wife to come to Sokadana in the name of the king. Panji Wulung accepts the invitation. He thinks that Panji Pamekas should become the crown prince as a token of kindness to his foster father. Panji Wulung orders the vassals to prepare for a journey to Sokadana after his foster parents stay of ten days (stanzas 694–711).

The procession of the king and queen leaves for the harbour. They embark on a ship in a grand ceremony and ten boats sail towards Sokadana. They reach the harbour of Sokadana and are cordially welcomed (stanzas 712–28). The king of Sokadana receives a letter and learns that the boats of Panji Wulung are on the way. He orders Panji Pamekas to welcome them outside the palace. Pamekas' procession comes to the royal rest-house and he makes all the preparations in advance. Panji Wulung and his vassals are received in a grand ceremony by Pamekas at the royal rest-house. The meeting of the two Panji is warm and full of respect for each other. The magnificent procession departs for the palace (stanzas 729–45).

Panji Wulung meets with his real father, the king of Sokadana and his real mother, the queen. They shed tears of joy. The king thanks the viceroy for his faithfulness and loyalty. Panji Wulung proposes that Pamekas deserves to become the crown prince, following the king's wish. The proposal is approved by everyone. Meanwhile, the vassals of Cempa feel relieved to know that Panji Wulung will not stay in Sokadana and will always be the king of Cempa. The grand feast begins. After fifteen days have passed, Panji Wulung proposes to the king that the royal coronation for Pamekas be held. Planning to retire, the king agrees and nominates Pamekas to the throne. He also wants to divide his inheritance. He orders the viceroy to prepare for the coronation and asks him to retire too. Tunjungsari's nephew Pamitra is to take the position of viceroy (stanzas 746–69).

Panji Pamekas ascends the throne and Pamitra becomes the new viceroy. Pamekas is renamed Dewabrata. The feast begins. Panji Wulung gives his advice on state affairs to the new king Dewabrata, teaching him faithfulness and loyalty just as the old viceroy of Sokadana had taught him in the distant past. The king should be fair and love the common people, and should undertake a journey to accumulate knowledge. The new king studies dutifully every day, and Panji Wulung teaches Pamitra as well. The kingdom of Sokadana prospers as never before. Panji Wulung then bids farewell to his father and mother. The old king divides his property between the old viceroy of Sokadana, Panji Wulung, Panji Pamekas, and himself. He is very proud of his two Panji. Panji Wulung's mother Sekarkancana feels deep sorrow to part with her son. After the three kings have a farewell dinner, the old king orders Dewabrata to make preparations for the departure of Panji Wulung, which is a sorrowful event. The new king Dewabrata sees Panji Wulung off, and Panji Wulung and his vassals embark on their journey (stanzas 829–44).

Meanwhile, the villain Andakasura has persuaded the viceroy of Cempa to plot a rebellion against the foreign king Panji Wulung during his absence, but his efforts fail. He does, however, persuade the viceroy's wife, who is blinded by avarice, to rebel against Panji Wulung. She tries to persuade her husband to rebel, and at last the viceroy agrees to the conspiracy of Andakasura. The misled viceroy and Andakasura gather the vassals of Cempa. Only one faithful retainer, Martadiguna, does not agree with the rebellion, and is put in prison with his son Katibaya. The rebellious vassals advance to the harbour to repulse Panji Wulung after dividing the treasure of the kingdom (stanzas 844–93). The harbour master surrenders, and the viceroy becomes king of Cempa, and renamed Dewasaksi. The new viceroy is Sudirapati, and Andakasura becomes chief commander. A letter arrives telling of the king's return to Cempa (stanzas 893–99).

The fleet of Panji Wulung is greeted with cannon fire from the shore. Panji Wulung is surprised. A loyal retainer, Jayaperbangsa, flees the rebel force and tells Panji Wulung what has happened during his absence. Hearing of the rebellion, Panji's fleet prepares for battle, and the king of Gilingwesi rushes to help him. An intense battle takes place between the loyal troops of Cempa assisted by the troops of Gilingwesi and the viceroy's rebellious troops on the sea and seashore. At last, Panji Wulung and Gilingwesi's forces defeat the rebels. The viceroy and Andakasura escape (stanzas 900–24). Both troops are completely exhausted. All the soldiers gather at a rest-house on the shore. Panji Wulung goes back to the royal ship to fetch the queen (stanzas 925–30).

Panji Wulung consoles the queen, who bursts into tears because of the disloyal viceroy and the vassals of Cempa. After he tells about the battle, they sail to the shore. The queen accuses the unfaithful vassals at the rest-house (stanzas 930–33). The king of Gilingwesi and Urawan are enraged and want to punish them, but Panji Wulung offers them amnesty. After one night, the procession goes back to the royal palace. Panji Wulung rides a horse, the king of Gilingwesi rides an elephant, and the disloyal vassals are tied up (stanzas 934–40). The town is desolate and the people are in grief. Only the most valuable royal treasures are saved, but the palace is in ruins. Panji Wulung asks the king of Gilingwesi to stay for a while. Panji Wulung decides to appoint Urawan as the new viceroy instead of the treasonous viceroy. Urawan becomes the new viceroy, renamed Surengjurit, in a coronation conducted by the king of Gilingwesi. Panji Wulung gives advice to the new viceroy about state affairs. The feast begins (stanzas 940–56).

The king of Gilingwesi teaches the new viceroy about his duties. Gilingwesi's vassals stay for one month. Their lessons include a denial of the *ajar*'s powers and supernatural phenomena, and advice on how to restrain passion and emotion. The king of Gilingwesi bids farewell to the king of Cempa. Panji Wulung and the queen prepare a magnificent feast and give him gifts of loyalty, such as a sword and a doll, symbolizing eternal brotherhood. On the following morning, the king of Cempa orders the new viceroy to see the king of Gilingwesi off. The king leaves (stanzas 957–69).

The rebellious viceroy and Andakasura wander in the forest as beggars. The viceroy regrets his disloyalty and has a grudge against his wife and Andakasura. One day they are found and caught by villagers. They are tied and brought to the palace in a procession. The new viceroy prepares for the king to pass judgement on them (stanzas 970–89). The rebellious viceroy and Andakasura are brought before the king and queen in court. The king pardons the viceroy, who repents of his sins, but sentences Andakasura to death. The faithful retainer Martadinata and the village chief who caught them are rewarded. Andakasura is wrapped in a white cloth and hanged, and his head is cut off. The country of Cempa becomes more prosperous (stanzas 990–1009). The lessons abstracted from the story are told by the narrator (stanzas 1010–15). A colophon concludes the narrative (stanzas 1016–18).

# Notes

## Introduction

[1] Sundanese is generally used in the province of West Java and Banten, but Javanese is spoken in the northern part of the Banten region and in the north coast of West Java, that is, the northern area of the Karawang and Indramayu districts. In more recent times, Indonesian has been spoken in the vicinity of Jakarta within the province of West Java, for example, in Bekasi and Tangerang. The total population of the province of West Java and Banten is 43.8 million according to the 2000 census conducted by the *Biro Pusat Statistik* (Central Bureau of Statistics). The former province of West Java was divided into two provinces (West Java and Banten) in the year 2001. According to estimates by Ekadjati, 75 per cent of the population of the former province of West Java were Sundanese (Ekadjati 1995a: 29–50).

[2] *Dangding* can be used for two genres of writing according to the contents — *wawacan* and *guguritan* — and the terms have often led to confusion. *Wawacan* is morphologically derived from a root word *waca* (read). The duplication of the first syllable "wa" and a suffix "an" makes it a noun, "something to be read". *Guguritan* is derived from the root word *gurit* (to compose in *dangding*); the duplication of the first syllable "gu" and an added suffix "an" makes it a noun, "something made in *dangding*". *Wawacan* is different from *guguritan* in terms of its function. *Wawacan* is entertaining, while *guguritan* is more didactic, mystic, philosophical, and sometimes practical. Stories of adventure and romance were written in *wawacan*, while Islamic teaching and philosophical discourse were conveyed in *guguritan*. With regard to the types of *pupuh*, Ajip Rosidi made a distinction between *wawacan* and *guguritan*: "the difference between *wawacan* and *guguritan* has to be looked for in their length. The form of poetry *dangding*, which consists of several stanzas, and in general has a single kind of *pupuh* (though there are some exceptions, but apparently the *pupuh* used are very limited), is called *guguritan*. Meanwhile, one which consists of hundreds of stanzas in total is called *wawacan*" (Rosidi 1983: 184). This explanation is regarded as only a tendency.

[3] For the importance of the Priangan Regencies to the Dutch, see Fasseur (1978), Knaap (1996).

4   The first part of Chapter 1 was published in the special issue, "In Memory of the Late Professor Kenji Tsuchiya", in Moriyama (1996) and a part of Chapter 3 was published in Moriyama (2000).

## Chapter 1

1   This citation was originally published in an article in the Sundanese magazine, *Poesaka Soenda*, in 1929. The article was written by Memed Sastrahadiprawira as a reaction to a book written by the Dutch scholar G. Schamelhout, titled *De Volkeren van Europa en de strijd der nationaliteiten* (European ethnicities and the struggle of nationality). Sastrahadiprawira translated several passages from the first of three volumes of the book, especially the second chapter, "*De taal als kenmerk der volken*" (Language as the identification of ethnicities). The above citation from the same chapter was originally a translation of a passage from the French linguist A. Meillet (Schamelhout 1932: 57–8). I owe this information to Benjamin G. Zimmer through personal communication.
2   The Dutch were very much influenced in the nineteenth century by the language studies of the German scholars Wilhelm von Humboldt and Herder. Humboldt described old Javanese language in his book, *Über die Kawi-Sprache auf der Insel Java* (On Kawi language on the island of Java); the first volume of which was published in 1836.
3   The kingdom was known as Pajajaran, by taking the name of the central place of the kingdom, Pakuan Pajajaran. However, local historical sources say that the name of the kingdom was Sunda (Ekadjati 1995a: 6–8).
4   Modern-day Sundanese are familiar with this tale, and it is one reason why Sundanese parents usually prefer not to marry their daughters off to Javanese men.
5   Tsuchiya discussed, in particular, this literary florescence and called it the "literary renaissance" (1990: 93–6).
6   Taco Roorda was the most prestigious scholar of the languages of the East Indies in the middle of the nineteenth century, but never went there.
7   A refined variant Sundanese used in the upland plains might differ from place to place, as was a plain variant spoken in the highland areas. This dialectal aspect adds confusion to the language map in West Java.
8   This is approximately half of the population of Cirebon and Banten; the remainder spoke Javanese (Roorda in Wilde 1841: v).
9   He revised the first edition because its contents were incomplete, adding considerable information about the Priangan Regencies in the revised edition (Wilde 1830).
10  De Wilde had ever been arrested as a sailor by the British authorities during the Napoleonic Wars. Afterwards he became a coffee planter in Sukabumi (Haan 1910: vol. 1, 284–309). His formal education was incomplete.

[11] For the usual layout in which *dangding* was published in the nineteenth century, see Plate 5, p. 135. For the reader's convenience, each stanza is formatted according to the verse form and its translation is given in the second column.

[12] Nowadays the language used in Cirebon, sometimes called Cirebonese, is linguistically a mixture of Javanese and Sundanese elements (Ayatrohaedi 1985).

[13] On the development of the study of Sundanese, see Uhlenbeck's survey (1964), and van den Berge's detailed discussion (1993).

[14] Art. 28. "Onderwijs voor Inlanders, Reglement op het lager onderwijs voor Inlanders. Ordonnantie van 25 Mei 1872" [Education for Indigenous People, Regulation on Lower Education for Indigenous People, Ordonnance of 25 May 1872], in *Gouvernements Inlandsche scholen of Staatsblad 1872*, no. 99 (Nationaal Archief Tweede Afdeeling).

[15] This catalogue includes a number of manuscripts in Javanese using Javanese script.

[16] Manuscripts were purchased mainly by foreigners in those days, and this might have stimulated people to produce manuscripts, especially using the Javanese script, to make money.

[17] Both had intensive contact with the locals and were seeking to discover Sundanese culture as it had been before Javanese influence affected it. In the process of their activities, though at different times, they amassed large collections of manuscripts.

[18] First published in Dutch by Kolff-Buning, and then in Malay by Balai Poestaka. See Watson (1993) for an article on Ahmad Djajadiningrat and his autobiography.

[19] In spite of Holle's insistence, Arabic script was used at the same time for Malay language education even at the secondary level for some time in the second half of the nineteenth century.

[20] E.M. Uhlenbeck erroneously sets the date of this publication as 1873 (1964: 10), whereas it is clear that the article was published in 1871.

[21] Koorders' successor, H.J. Oosting, published a large dictionary in 1879 and a grammar in 1884. He used the Javanese script rather than the Roman script, but his proposal was not taken seriously by the government, nor was his dictionary.

[22] This institution became the printing house of the Committee for Indigenous Schoolbooks and Popular Reading Books in the first decade of the twentieth century.

[23] The Sundanese text runs: "Ti semet sawatara taoen ka toekang geus karasa koe saréréja, jén perloe katjida aja katangtoean anoe pasti pikeun noeliskeun basa-basa oerang priboemi koe aksara Walanda, babakoena pikeun pangadjaran di sakola-sakola" ([Commissie voor de Volkslectuur] [1918]: 1).

24 Only Coolsma presented a part of the Bible in Arabic script, knowing that the Sundanese preferred it to the other two scripts.

25 Roorda's notions of the Sundanese were formed on the basis of the materials collected by de Wilde; it is noteworthy that the latter did not find any Sundanese writing during his long stay among the people of West Java.

26 Van den Berge's research on K.F. Holle was presented in a biography (Berge 1998). See also Berge (1993) for an account of Holle's career, especially pp. 11–30.

27 Engelmann wished to learn Sundanese from the manuscripts in order to compile a Sundanese dictionary, and intended to publish the texts since he considered them valuable from a scholarly point of view. At least he had already mastered *Carita Sama'un, Carita Raja Habib, Carita Raja Hindik, Carita Raja Jungjuman* and five other stories (Veth 1869: 259–61).

28 One of the reasons was to "hunt" manuscpripts for the collection. It is known that the search for Malay and Javanese manuscripts was going on during this period (Putten 1995a: 44–55). Snouck Hurgronje was one of the main Dutch collectors of Sundanese manuscripts as well as Malay and Javanese ones. His collection comprises no less than 400 in the Leiden Library collection.

29 Palaces (*kraton*) often played an important role in nurturing local culture in the archipelago. Language studies in the nineteenth century in the Dutch East Indies were carried out with and around such cultural centres (Putten 1995: 53).

30 Grashuis had an excellent command of the language, and it is a great pity that he could not find any artistic merit in Sundanese writing. How painful and odd it must have been to read so many writings without emotion or excitement and only respond to their linguistic features! This was an attitude many Dutch scholars were to keep, especially in colonial times.

31 They were *Soendaneesch leesboek* [Sundanese reader], published in 1874; *Soendanesche bloemlezing. Fabelen, brieven en verhalen* [Sundanese anthology. Fables, letters and stories], in 1881; and *Soendanesche bloemlezing. Legenden en Moslimsche leerboekjes* [Sundanese anthology. Legends and Islamic readers], in 1891. All were published by A.W. Sijthoff in Leiden. Grashuis included a few of Moesa's and Kartawinata's prose writings in the anthologies.

32 In many ways, Sastrahadiprawira can be compared with Poerbatjaraka, who did the same in his criticisms of Ranggawarsita (Tsuchiya 1990: 107–8).

33 The words *sastra* and *kasusastran* have been used to denote literature, or things pertaining to literature, in Sundanese until present times.

34 *Jangjawokan, pantun, sisindiran, kakawihan, sawer,* and *pupujian* belong to this *kawih* category. These can be categorized on the basis of content and function. *Jangjawokan, kakawihan, sawer,* and *pupujian* are poetry

used mainly for spiritual purposes, while *pantun*, although also used in ritual contexts, is used more for entertainment (Zanten 1993: 144–5). Regarded as the oldest genre of Sundanese verbal art, Sundanese *pantun* is generally a long narrative. It is markedly different from Malay *pantun*, which is composed of verses that rhyme every four lines. The repertoire consists of *Lutung Kasarung, Mundinglaya di Kusumah,* and others. *Sisindiran* is a generic term for verse in which "an allusion (*sindir*) is given by a combination of words". See van Zanten (1989: 68–70).

[35] Different from such traditional *kawih*, Mang Koko created a musical genre called *kawih* in the middle of the twentieth centry. This new genre consisted of a popular song in Sundanese accompanied by a new type of zither made by him too.

[36] This recitation of *pantun* is rather similar to the Malay *syair* reading, while *wawacan* parallels *hikayat* which, however, is in prose.

[37] Very bluntly (and importantly), in the same article van der Chijs claims that "the indigenous people do not know silent reading" (Chijs 1867b: 7).

[38] The writing entitled *Panata Istri* (Etiquette for Women), composed by the *panghulu* of Garut, that is, Moehamad Moesa, cannot be found anywhere.

[39] K.F. Holle to P.J. Veth, 16 November 1874, in BPL, no. 1756, Leiden University Library.

[40] Coolsma used the *Abdul Muluk* and *Rangganis* in manuscript form for compiling his Sundanese dictionary, together with the published *Wawacan Panji Wulung*. See *Opgave van Soendaneesche Geschriften* [List of Sundanese Writings] in Coolsma (1884: n.p.). *Abdul Muluk* was a story originating from the Malay-speaking communities, which has been reprinted several times in the Arabic script since the middle of the nineteenth century (Dumas 2000: 67). *Rangganis* was a famous story that originated in the Javanese literary tradition. Both stories were translated into Sundanese in verse form. The manuscripts are available at the National Library in Jakarta and Leiden University Library (Ekadjati 1988: 105, 349, 365). The Sundanese version of *Abdul Muluk* was never printed, while the Sundanese version of *Rangganis* was published in 1957 by Balai Poestaka.

[41] A Sundanese convert to Christianity, N. Titus of the Netherlands Missionary Union, was an unusual exception. He had a talent for language and could compose *dangding* himself. He translated two missionary books into *dangding*: *Carios Jusup beunang nembangkeun* [Tale of Yusuf composed in tembang], published in 1894, and a gospel translation *Carios Raja Saul jeung Raja Dawud beunang Nembangkeun* [Tale of King Saul and King David, composed in tembang], published in 1906. These translations were willingly read by the Sundanese for a long time, according to the late B.F.H. Arps, who spent his childhood in the Sundanese-speaking community in the 1930s to the 1940s (Private interview held on 11 November 1993 in Leiden).

42  According to Uhlenbeck, this translation of part of the New Testament was published by I. Esser, "apparently basing himself on a Malay version" (Uhlenbeck 1964: 12).
43  The word *omongan* in this quotation means "utterance", but in the late nineteenth century it meant "prose", as coined by Moesa's son, Kartawinata. This will be discussed in Chapter 5.
44  Such "colonial" discourse on literature is found in Malay literature, as pointed out by Amin Sweeney (1987: 291).
45  *Njawer* and *kakawihan* are included in the *kawih* genre. *Njawer* is for praying and petitioning while *kakawihan barudak* is a play for children to sing and dance.
46  Among the titles of manuscripts given by the people were: *kitab, suluk, wawacan, kawih, carios, carita, babad, parimbon* or *paririmbon, dongeng, lalakon, pantun, serat* or *surat, sajarah* or *sejarah, silsilah, jampe, sawer, doa, mantera, catatan, ilmu, mistik, risalah* or *risalat, buku, kidung, hikayat, layang, kanda* and *tarekat*. They did not have titles in the European sense. Many terms originated from Javanese, such as *suluk, babad, parimbon/paririmbon, lalakon, kidung, layang,* and *kanda,* while *kitab, carios/carita (cerita), dongeng, serat/surat, sajarah/sejarah, silsilah, catatan, ilmu, mistik, risalah/risalat, buku, hikayat,* and *tarekat* are terms that remind us of Malay writing.
47  Research was done on *beluk* performance and their manuscripts in different places and times: a village in kecamatan Cikalong Kulon, Cianjur, in February–May 1984; a village in Tambak Mekar, kecamatan Jalan Cagak, Subang, in August 1990; a village in Pagerageung, kecamatan Ciawi, Tasikmalaya in August 1990; a village in Cipinang, kecamatan Banjaran, Bandung in August 1990; a village in Ciapus, kecamatan Banjaran, Bandung in September 1990.
48  Van Zanten mentions *cigawiran* besides *tembang macapat* and *beluk* as solo singing genres without accompanying instruments. *Wawacan* is sung in all three genres (Zanten 1989: 31).

## Chapter 2

1  The remaining amount of Dfl. 2,300 was for the transportation expenses of the school teachers.
2  This school was different from the one partly financed by the Regent of Cianjur in 1820s.
3  According to AVSS (1859), there were 23 students at Cianjur, 36 at Bandung, 38 at Sumedang, 22 at Manonjaya, and 40 at Garut.
4  The island of Madura is usually taken together with the island of Java in the statistics. The categories frequently used in the nineteenth century were

"Java and Madura" or sometimes simply "Java" and "Buitenbezittingen" (Outer Possessions).
5   In comparison with the whole of the East Indies area, the number of schools per million inhabitants was higher than or nearly equal to that in the Priangan Regencies. This can be explained by the fact that in some of the Outer Possessions more schools had been established because of the prevalence of Christianity since the seventeenth century. The people were already familiar with the Dutch education system there. In addition, the population of the area in the second half of the nineteenth century was only a quarter of that in Java and Madura.
6   In the first established schools, the subjects taught were only reading Sundanese, writing Sundanese, reading Malay, writing Malay, and arithmetic in Malay.
7   Before the establishment of the Teachers' Training School of Surakarta, some training for teachers was done at the school in Cianjur, which had been the administrative centre (*hoofdplaats*) of West Java.
8   Soeria di Koesoemah was the son of a *wedana* (district chief) and received training at the school in Cianjur for ten months. The other teacher, Tjakra Wiria, had finished his studies at the school in Bandung.
9   A Javanese reading book (in *ngoko* and in *kromo*) adapted by C.F. Winter, a Malay spelling book with a reader, and a Javanese spelling book with a reader were sent to Batavia. The books numbered 3,990 copies collectively (AVSS 1853: 320–1).
10  According to Uhlenbeck, this 22-page book was published in Batavia in 1851. Uhlenbeck says, "A Dutch adaptation of this fable by K.F. Holle was published in 1885; in the same year a Malay translation made by A.F. von Dewall appeared" (1964: 28). This Sundanese book was deposited in the library of Leiden University but, according to the late J. Noorduyn, it disappeared soon after.
11  Holle to Governor-General, 25 May 1864, in Verbaal 1-2-1866, no. 27, Nationaal Archief.
12  Koorders criticized Holle in Parliament in Den Haag in 1868. Considering the population size in the Sundanese-speaking area, too many copies of his book were being printed, he argued. That was a waste of the government budget (Berge 1993: 23–7).
13  It is worth noting that every Sundanese book was distributed to Batavia. Moreover, the number of copies sent there was the second largest after the Priangan Regencies. It can be assumed therefore that a sizeable number of the Sundanese population lived in Batavia.
14  Holle to Governor-General, 25 May 1864, in *Verbaal*, 1 February 1866, no. 27, Nationaal Archief.
15  W. van Gelder, H.A. Nooij, C.J. van Haastert, and Ch. Hekker were among those teaching at the Teachers' Training School in Bandung.

16 There were few books printed in Arabic in the Sundanese-speaking area. More details are provided later in this chapter.

17 Gonggrijp (1827–1909) was sent to the Indies by the Dutch Missionary Society (NZG) of Rotterdam in 1849 and appointed lecturer of Christianity in Depok and Tugu until his departure in 1864. In 1872 he took up a professorship at the School for Colonial Officers in Delft. There he started the first course in the study of Sundanese in the Netherlands. See also van der Putten (2000: 116–21).

18 Derived from the Dutch word *boek* (book).

19 The term *kitab* was, however, also used in a few titles of books that did not have religious themes. *Kitab atoeran bab maradjian djelema noe ngedjoeroe* (Handbook for midwifery), published in 1901, is a good example of the use of this word.

20 There are a number of Sundanese *kitab kuning* in the special collection of the KITLV library, which was collected and inventoried by van Bruinessen. The total number of items in the collection is some nine hundred (Bruinessen 1990).

21 Cf. Braginsky (1993: 55–73), in which he explains that *faedah* (benefit) was important in Malay literary tradition.

22 The title was *Tijt-boek* (Time book), printed in 1659 (Chijs 1875: 1). Careful research has been done by Katharine Smith Diehl on the history of printing in the Dutch East Indies, especially in Batavia, until 1850 (Diehl 1990).

23 Two bibliographical works on Sundanese books, namely, those by Uhlenbeck (1964) and Ekadjati (1988), have been consulted. Other useful sources include the library catalogue at the KITLV, Royal Netherlands Institute of Southeast Asian and Caribbean Studies library (combining the collections of the Koninklijk Instituut voor de Taal-, Land- en Volkenkunde van Nederland Indie and the Indisch Genootschap in The Hague), and those of Perpustakaan Nasional in Jakarta and Perpustakaan Museum Konferensi Asia Afrika in Bandung. All the printed books were checked and a comprehensive list compiled (see Appendix 1). Technically, every book is counted once, whether it is a reprinted or revised edition. It is important to know the total number of printed books, and this is one way to approach it. For instance, the number of pages of each book and the number of copies printed can show other aspects, as Proudfoot did on early Malay books using the term "bulk" — the number of pages multiplied by the number of copies produced (Proudfoot 1986).

24 Exceptions are the books designed for language training for promising Dutch officials in Delft or Leiden (Studentencorps [1898]: 79–81). Good examples are *Tjarios Soepena of Geschiedenis van Soepena* (The story of Soepena's history), edited by H.J. Oosting in 1881, and books printed in Singapore which will be discussed later. There were at least three such exceptions.

25 An indigenous people-owned periodical, *Soenda Berita*, appeared in 1903, but it was published in Malay (Adam 1984: 109–10).
26 The list of printed books is not complete, but it seems that omissions are few because not many printing presses were available in the nineteenth century in the Dutch East Indies, especially in the Sundanese-speaking area. Few books were produced by the local printing houses before 1910, except Islamic ones by lithograph printing. Most printing houses and publishers operated by the Europeans/Eurasians, including missionaries, were registered by the government or documented elsewhere, and their publications were mostly collected in the library of the *Bataviaasch Genootschap van Kunsten en Wetenschappen* in Batavia. It should be noted that early printing houses were responsible not only for printing books but sometimes also for compiling and editing them. There was no clear distinction between printer and publisher.
27 See Kimman (1981: 73) and Departement van Gouvernementsbedrijven (1912: 7–14).
28 See also Klinkert (1868: 559–60), and cf. Putten (2000: 121).
29 On the lithograph machine in nineteenth-century Dutch East Indies, see also Putten (1997: 717–9).
30 He may have been a relative of Haji Muhammad Azhari in Palembang, whom Peeters mentions (1996: 182–4). Arab descendants often formed a wide network based on their family ties in the Archipelago. The community of Arab descent in Bandung, many of whom originated from Palembang, comprised 200–300 people in the late nineteenth century (Personal communication with Dr. J. Peeters on 16 August 1999 in Leiden).
31 Sayyid 'Uthmân was once introduced to K.F. Holle and Moehamad Moesa at Snouck Hurgronje's house (Snouck Hurgronje 1924: 78–85). Van Bruinessen pointed out that he was one of the pioneers in indigenous publishing and a prolific "Arab ally of the Dutch Indies government" (Bruinessen 1990: 231). For further information, see Steenbrink (1984: 134–7) and Kaptein (1997).
32 They were *Faslatin*, printed by lithograph in 1905; *Lataif al-Taharat*, printed by lithograph in 1906; and *Pupujian*, printed by the Methodist Publishing House in 1908 (Proudfoot 1993: 679).
33 The number of Islamic schools and their students in West Java were as follows: Bantam, 372 schools, 7,230 students; Karawang, 120 schools, 1,085 students; Cirebon, 817 schools, 8,975 students (*Algemeen Vijfjarig Verslag van het Inlandsch Onderwijs in Nederlandsch-Indie* 1878 t/m 1882: 260).
34 The Chinese were active in the Confucian revival movement, and had no intense contact with the Sundanese (Coppel 1986: 22–6).
35 *Regerings-Almanak* and *Handboek voor Cultuur- en Handersondernemingen in Nederlandsch-Indie* provide us with the data on printers and publishers

in the Dutch East Indies. See also the series of reports by van der Chijs (1875, 1880, 1903).
36   For an account of the activities of European/Eurasian capital printing houses, see Maier (1993a).
37   Javanese typography was developed in the 1820s and 1830s and used in printing in various languages in the Dutch East Indies (Molen 2000: 140–9).
38   For instance, *Wawacan Panji Wulung*, in Roman script, had only 122 pages, while the Javanese script version had 266 pages.
39   For example, a book reprinted in Javanese script by the Landsdrukkerij is Ayu Lasminingrat's *Warnasari atawa Roepa-roepa Dongeng* (Colourful Essence or Various Tales, 1901). A private publisher also reprinted in the Javanese script Martanagara's *Wawacan Angling Darma* (*wawacan* of Angling Darma), published by Toko Tjitak Afandi, Bandung, in 1906, but the quantity of the reprint was small.
40   This book was translated by Ahmad Djajadiningrat, who was the most credible indigenous high official.
41   Quotation from *Notulen Bataviaasch Genootschap* 1869, VIII, *Bijlagen Notulen* 05-01-1869, K.F. Holle aan Directie, 29-06-1868: III.
42   He changed his name to Raden Demang Soerja Nata Legawa when he was appointed to a higher position in Sukabumi in 1892.
43   In the Malay case, a professional author in Batavia, Muhammad Bakir, had 76 titles of manuscripts for rent in the late nineteenth century, while printed books were also being read (Chambert-Loir 1991). This provides a good example of the overlapping readership.
44   This was a poetic version of a tale in prose that had been published six years earlier.
45   Not all books indicate whether they are revised or reprinted editions.
46   The book is a kind of historical description of the region intended for higher level education. The Dutch edition was translated by the well-known official translator Kartawinata, a son of Moesa. The book was printed in Javanese script, and was very thick and costly. It was on the catalogue for more than 40 years without ever being reprinted.
47   Personal communication with some local Sundanese in August and September 1995, consisting of villagers, traditional music teachers at the high school, retired teachers at the elementary school, researchers of Sundanese literature, and Sundanese novelists.

## Chapter 3

1   When the contract between the ruler of Mataram and the East Indies Company at Kartasura was drawn up in October 1705, Limbangan was

not included in the "Western Area" that was given to the Company. It belonged to the Cirebonese Sultanate together with Sukapura and Galuh. Then in 1818, when the Preanger Regentschappen (Priangan Regencies) were formed, Limbangan was included in the same regency with Sumedang and Sukapura. It was not until 1859 that Limbangan became an independent regency, ruled by an assistant resident. In 1913, the Limbangan Regency changed its name to Garut (Encyclopaedie 1919: vol. 3, 506).

2 The salary system is one of the results of administrational reforms (*bestuurshervorming*) which Governor-General Sloet van de Beele (1861-6) instituted for the indigenous officials in 1866 (Doel 1994: 87).

3 In addition to the content of the correspondence, the letters are unique in two ways. One is that they were written in the traditional form of writing, *dangding*. Secondly, some letters were written in Javanese by Sundanese aristocrats, a community in which the Javanese language still held a prestigious status. This book was published in 1929 by Balai Poestaka in Batavia. The letters in this book tell us about the relationship between several members of his family, and provide indigenous views on their contacts within the Indies society of West Java and Batavia.

4 Holle's report in *Notulen der vergaderingen van het Bataviaasch Genootschap van Kunsten en Wetenschappen*, 5 Januari 1869, Bijlagen p. XVIII, footnote (2).

5 K.F. Holle to Veth, 16 November 1874, in BPL, no. 1756, Leiden University Library.

6 K.F. Holle to Governor-General, 20 August 1873, in Verbaal 3-6-1874, no. 31, Nationaal Archief.

7 According to Memed Sastrahadiprawira, Brata di Widjaja was one of the most talented authors in the Sundanese-speaking area (Sastrahadiprawira 1929b: 18).

8 According to A. Rachman Prawiranata, Moesa had 16 children, and 66 grandchildren. He claims himself to be a son of R. Ahmad Natalegawa, who was a son of the fifth wife of Moesa, and his wife, R. Koesaesin Sariakusumah. Moesa's six wives and children were as follows:

R.A. Perbata: 1. R.A.A. Soeria Nata Ningrat (regent of Lebak); 2. R.A.A. Soeria Nata Legawa or Kartawinata (*patih* of Sumedang); 3. R.S. Domas (F); 4. R.H. Zainal Asikin (*hoofdpanghulu* of Limbangan)

R.A. Banonagara: 1. R. Soeria Nata Madenda; 2. R. Radja Bodedar (F); 3. R. Niswan Radjanagara (F)

R.A. Rija: 1. R.A. Lasminingrat (F: wife of the regent of Limbangan); 2. R.A. Ratna Ningroem (F); 3. R.A. Lenggang Kancana (F: author of *Warna Sari*)

R.H. Djoehro: 1. R. Moerminah (F); 2. R. Siti Rahmah (F); 3. R.A.A. Prawirakoesoemah (regent of Serang)

R.A. Lendra Karaton: 1. R. Ahmad Natalegawa (*wedana* of Singaparna); 2. R. Moehamad Prawiradilaga (*wedana* of Cibeber) R. Tedjamantri: 1. R. Andu Surja Adi Widjaja (*hoofdjaksa* of Bandung) (Source: Personal communication from A. Rachman Prawiranata, on 27 October 1994, in Bandung).

9  Besides Suminto's book (1985), Steenbrink (1985: 16–7) and Kartodirdjo (1966: 161–2) give more detailed information.

10  Holle came to the Dutch East Indies with his family in 1844, at the age of 14. After working as a civil servant for ten years, he moved to a tea plantation at Cikajang in the Limbangan Regency. It was there, in 1857, that Holle came to know Moesa. Holle opened his own tea plantation, called Waspada, in 1862. Gradually, he earned the trust of the government and was appointed as the Honorary Advisor on Native Affairs in 1871, becoming one of the most influential persons in nineteenth-century Dutch East Indies. For more details, see van den Berge's biography of Holle (1998).

11  Moesa's younger sister.

12  Moesa to H. Holle, 20 November 1879 (Collectie 274, "Thee en familiearchief van der Hucht", no. 25, Nationaal Archief Tweede Afdeling).

13  A card reached Herman H. Holle in the Hague on the 24 September via Marseilles (Collectie 274, "Thee en familiearchief van der Hucht" no. 27, Nationaal Archief Tweede Afdeling).

14  This reading is uncertain.

15  This letter is dated 8 November 1886 (Collectie 274, "Thee en familiearchief van der Hucht", no. 28, Nationaal Archief Tweede Afdeling).

16  This article was immediately translated into Malay, although the translation was not made literally. A Chinese publisher released it in the same year, under the title *Hal Setijanja Kepala Bangsa Anak Negri di Tanah Hindia-Wolanda* (Loyalty of Indigenous People in the Dutch East Indies).

17  Here the poem switches from Sundanese to Malay, as if direct quotations were taken from their conversation, which apparently was conducted in Malay.

18  This letter with the motto "Ook verlichte Islamieten willen van het Christendom niets weten" (Even enlightened Muslims want to know nothing about Christianity) was sent by the missionary C. Albers to the head office of the Netherlands Missionary Union from Cianjur on 18 March 1879 (End 1991: 176).

19  K.F. Holle to Veth, 16 November 1874, in BPL no. 1756, Leiden University Library.

20  Besides being criticized by Koorders, Holle was ridiculed by the anonymous writer of "*Herinneringen uit het leven van een ambtenaar*" (Memories from the life of an official) published in *Javabode*, Wednesday 27 March 1872.

21  Levyssohn Norman to J. Louden, 4 January 1873, in Verbaal 2-10-10,

*Directeur Binnenlands Bestuur aan Gouverneur-Generaal*, Mr 1873, no. 98, Nationaal Archief.

22 Moesa became a member of the Society from September 1862 to December 1885. Other indigenous members in the list for the year 1885 were Raden Mas Ismangoen Danoe Winata, Raden Adipati Aria Koesoema Daningrat, and Raden Mas Toemenggoeng Aria Soegonda (Bataviasch Genootschap van Kunsten en Wetenschappen 1886: 57–62).

23 R.A.A. Musa Suriakartalegawa became the leader of Partai Rakyat Pasundan (People's Party of Pasundan) and proclaimed the establishment of Negara Pasundan (Republic of Pasundan) on 4 of May 1947 as its president. During the struggle for independence, he was fully backed by the Dutch government (Ekadjati 1995b: 14–6). From interviews in Garut it was apparent that he was not respected much by the people because of his attitude.

24 Personal interview with Soemarna W.S. (1909–95) in Balubur Limbangan on 25 and 26 October 1994, and H. Bahrum Sobandi (b. 1922) in Garut on 27 October 1994. They knew about these rumours and Moesa's family.

25 The special issue of *Handelingen van het Eerste Congres voor de Taal, Land- en Volkenkunde van Java* reported the lectures and the programme of the congress.

26 Personal interview with Soemarna W.S., in Balubur Limbangan, on 25 and 26 October 1994.

27 Only a few handwritten drafts of Moesa's work intended for print can be found, mostly in the Holle collection at the National Library (Perpustakaan Nasional) in Jakarta; SD. 127 and SD. 70 in the Holle collection.

28 This short story in prose was apparently written before 1869, because Holle gave a summary of the story in his letter to the board of the Batavian Society of Arts and Sciences (Holle 1869: xxvi–xxxi).

29 Snouck Hurgronje criticized Kohlbrugge in this article because the latter had underestimated the Sundanese schoolbooks.

30 In the same article, Memed Sastrahadiprawira ranked Moehamad Moesa above the renowned Javanese authors Jasadipoera I, II, III, and Ranggawarsita.

31 The poetic metre and rules found in *dangding* or *pantun* help readers understand units of content by using special signs or letters.

32 Both stories belong to the old corpus of writings that originated from Javanese literature. Moesa saw them as stories for entertainment purposes only (Moesa 1867: 5).

33 As seen in Chapter 1, Koorders did not approve of this form of writing. He argued in a report submitted to the Governor-General in Batavia (Rapport no. V, Bandoeng, 31 January 1864 [Koorders in Meinsma 1869]) that practical knowledge such as information about agriculture should be in prose, not in *dangding*,

34 This point was welcomed not only by Holle but also by Koorders. For instance, in a report submitted to the Governor-General in Batavia (Rapport no. IV, Bandoeng, 15 Januari 1864 [Koorders in Meinsma 1869]). Koorders praised this characteristic of Moesa's *Raja Sudibya*.

## Chapter 4

1. His name is Bahrum Sobandi. He had attended a three-year *volksschool* (primary school) in 1929 and continued his studies at a *vervolgschool* (secondary school) for two years. He did not learn Dutch in those schools, but he did learn Sundanese and Malay. The interview was held on 27 October 1994.
2. Some people might know the name of *Panji Wulung* from another book. In 1969 a series of *silat* (adapted form of Chinese martial arts) stories was published in Indonesian. This *silat* collection, comprising 22 volumes, was titled *Panji Wulung*, taking the main protagonist's name (OPA [1969]).
3. According to an interview with retired Lieutenant Colonel Soemarna at his house in Balubur Limbangan on 27 October 1994. See also Ajip Rosidi (1966: 13).
4. Elis Suryani Nani Sumarlina did a philological study of this *wawacan* in the published versions, in both Javanese and Roman scripts, and found that they are the same even though some misprints can be found (Sumarlina 1990).
5. The uniqueness of *Wawacan Panji Wulung* is that it never circulated in manuscript form and that people know the tale only through printed editions. In the nineteenth century, many *wawacan* were read in manuscript form, copied by hand, and hence constantly changing in form. The text of *Wawacan Panji Wulung* has hardly changed because the poem was not copied by hand (with all the changes that come with it) but printed and reprinted.
6. Sumarga and Ajip Rosidi said it was translated not only into Javanese, but also into Madurese. However, this Madurese version cannot be located. For more information, see Sumarga (1983: 9), and Ajip Rosidi in Musa (1990: 5).
7. Pangeran Adipati Ario Mangkoe Negoro IV was the prince royal of the royal house of Mangkunegara in Surakarta. He was famous because of his patronage for literature.
8. The total number of stanzas is the same in all the editions since 1871: 1018 stanzas in 28 cantos. There is some variety in the numbering of these stanzas: the first edition erroneously includes stanza 567 twice, and most editions (except the 1990 edition) have stanzas 946 to 948 out of order. The 1891 and 1908 editions are identical by accident, and could be seen

Notes to pp. 146–60

as the most correct ones in terms of the numbering of the stanzas. In the following discussions on *Wawacan Panji Wulung*, this 1990 edition will be used for practical reasons (Moesa 1990).

9 *Het Bureau voor de Volkslectuur*, or Balai Poestaka published their annual reports from 1922 to 1930. *Wawacan Panji Wulung* can always be found at the top of the list of borrowed books (Bureau voor de Volkslectuur 1924). For instance, it was borrowed 4.735 times in 1930 (Kantoor voor de Volkslectuur 1931: 51).

10 The latter two stories were part of the oral repertoire; they were written down and published for people to appreciate the stories of "old".

11 R.I. Adiwidjaja's *Kasusastran Sunda* I (Adiwidjaja 1952) and II (Adiwidjaja [1954]), and M.A. Salmoen's *Kandaga, Kasusastran Sunda* (Salmoen 1958).

12 The word *ditembongkeun* should be *ditembangkeun* (to be recited in *tembang* melody).

13 The letter is not dated, but must have been written after 1880, when her eldest son Suria Natadiningrat became the Regent of Lebak (Kartodirdjo 1966: 161). Her correspondence was edited and published later as a book.

14 VOC ships, which were only allowed to trade with Tokugawa Japan through Deshima, had brought in this "bacteria of modernity". The era of splendid isolation, effective in Japan for nearly 250 years, prevented the bacteria from growing. The isolation policy ended officially with the Meiji Restoration of 1868. The change of policy greatly affected the world of the Japanese.

15 Interestingly, Elis Suryani Nani Sumarlina makes a comparison between Moehamad Moesa and Abdullah bin Abdulkadir Munsyi on the basis of realism in their writings (Sumarlina 1990: 49).

16 Apart from this meaning, the word *panji*, or the duplicate form *panji-panji*, means a kind of flag or the name of a type of trousers which are usually worn by a king or prince.

17 The *panji* story was known in the Sundanese-speaking communities because of the long-standing Javanese influence on their literature (Sumarlina 1990: 42). The Sundanese seldom composed original *panji* stories (Ekadjati 1988), but the *panji* story can be found in Sundanese *pantun* repertoires (Sumarlina 1990: 45). Only *Wawacan Raden Panji Kerneng Pati* (*Wawacan* of Raden Kerneng Pati) was published, at least four times, by Balai Poestaka in the early twentieth century. This *wawacan* was set in Solo, not in Daha or Kuripan. It may be included in the "new *wawacan*" category, which will be discussed in Chapter 5. For *panji* stories in the Javanese and Malay tradition, see Rassers (1959), Robson (1971: 166), Koster (1993: 161–98).

18 For instance, the name of the kingdom Sokadana was changed to Sukadana, the name of the beloved concubine Tunjungsari, which was also changed to Tunjungsekar to end with the vowels "e" and "a" instead of the vowels "a" and "i".

19  The other examples are *sinom*, expressing happiness, and joy; *pangkur*, in passages dealing with departure, desire, and preparations for war; *kinanti*, expressing sorrow, anticipation, and hope; *mijil*, expressing trouble, difficulty, sadness and disaster (Salmoen 1958: 41–2).

20  Coolsma's first Sundanese-Dutch dictionary was probably compiled around 1884. The work was extensively revised and published in 1913, and reprinted in 1930. For my understanding of this text, I mainly made use of Coolsma's second edition (1913) and Satjadibrata's (1954).

21  The words meaning "to sing" or "to chant" a verse form, are *(nga)hariring* (hum, sing gently), *(nga)gending* (sing *dangding* text with gamelan instruments or sitar), *nembang* (chant or sing *dangding* text). The author Hasan Mustapa uses such words in his poem *guguritan* entitled, "Hariring nu hudang gering" (Hasan Mustapa in Rosidi 1989: 122). For instance, *sorangan nulis ngagending* (write *dangding* alone) (ibid: 157), and *nembang eukeur erang-erang* (chanting *dangding* at dusk) (ibid: 122). He often uses *ngagending* to mean writing *dangding,* and *nulis* to mean writing in general. Added to this, the word *(nga)haleuang* (sing aloud, sing louder [than *ngahariring*]) is used not only for singing *dangding* but also for other genres.

22  A manuscript entitled *Silsilah Raja-Raja Sambas* (History of the Kings of Sambas) gives information about the kingdom of Sukadana (Schulze 1991: 141–62). Another source says that "Sokadana was at this time (the end of the eighteenth century) enjoying great prosperity under Sultan Ahmad al-Din" (Raja Ali Haji 1982: 327, 376).

23  This kind of epilogue is not found in *wawacan*, such as *Wawacan Jayalalana, Wawacan Sajarah Galuh, Wawacan Ogin Amarsakti,* or in *wawacan* regarded as "traditional", such as *Wawacan Damar* (Sumarlina 1990: 48). However, a few *wawacan,* such as *Wawacan Rengganis,* do contain a performative opening and an informative epilogue (Abdoessalam 1957: 355).

24  The word *sopi* derives from the Dutch word *zoopje,* which means a glass of alcohol, such as *jenever* (Dutch gin).

25  Almost the same admonitions can be seen in the Javanese manuscript, *Serat Madat, Madon, Minum, Main, Maling,* kept at the Surakarta Court library (Wieringa 1994: 106; Florida 1993: 212–3).

26  The word comes from the old Spanish *real,* a Mexican dollar that was in use in international trade. The different form *rial* is more commonly used in Malay texts (Wilkinson 1932: vol. 2, 337). In the East Indies, *duit* is more commonly used, instead of *rial* (ibid.).

27  *Wawacan Jayalalana* is thought to be written in the eighteenth century (Masduki *et al.* 1996: 9). The text, judging from the wording and the way it is written, is in an old style and apparently not rewritten in the last 200 years, according to Undang Ahmad Darsa, a Sundanese specialist of

traditional writing. In general, existing *wawacan* were mostly adapted to contemporary writing when they were copied, so that the text does not preserve its old language usage even though the storyline remains the same. (Personal communication with Undang Ahmad Darsa, 8 September 2000, in Leiden). See also Darsa (1998).

[28] In this quotation, the narrator uses the words *nyerat* and *ditulis* to mean "write" the things Panji Wulung has experienced "without skipping any actions" (*taya laku nu kalarung*) "from the beginning of his journey" (*ti bareng indit*), instead of words such as *ngagurit* and *ngarang* to mean "compose and embellish" a narrative (Coolsma 1913: 691, 208, 264).

[29] The same can be seen in the writing of Abdullah Abdul Kadir: "He [an Englishman] suggested to me that I should write my autobiography in Malay. But in truth my heart felt sad and my limbs heavy as I thought of my dear friend's wish. For all the important events of my life now belonged to the past" (Abdullah 1970: 29).

[30] A similar feeling in the face of the advent of modernity in Malay writings is discussed by van der Putten (2001: 213–5).

[31] Words such as *sieun*, *watir*, *risi*, *borang* (all four words mean "afraid" or "worried"), *bohong* (lying), *teu percaya* (do not believe), *kaduhung* (regret), *napsu* (desire, greed) may be grouped together with words such as *susah* (anguish), which repeatedly appear in this text.

## Chapter 5

[1] Next to an expanding readership for printed materials, a readership of manuscripts remained until long after Independence. Even in the 1980s and 1990s, there were villagers who read manuscripts at certain rituals.

[2] The word *kalimah* is a loanword from the Arabic word *kalima* (*kalimat* for plural) to mean "word", "speech", "address", "utterance", "remark", "saying" (Cowan 1976: 838).

[3] In the 1920s, R.I. Adiwidjaja, a teacher at the Teachers' Training School, used the word *omongan* in a different and broader sense, that of "utterance". He said: *Atanapi gedicht teh kenging disebat kedalna rasa, anoe digambarkeun koe omongan, boh koe omongan biasa bae, boh koe dangding* (the verbal art can be called a representation of feeling, which is depicted by utterance, both in common utterance and in *dangding*) (Adiwidjaja 1926: 8). This interpretation was also short-lived.

[4] The word *diilo* is still used to mean "read by heart" (*maca ku hate*) (Satjadibrata 1954: 156). F.S. Eringa repeats Coolsma's interpretation, "to read by oneself" (*voor zichzelf lezen*) (Eringa 1984: 309).

[5] K.F. Holle to Veth, 16 November 1874, in BPL, no. 1756, Leiden University Library.

[6] This translation was part of the regulations issued in the Indies: *Het reglement van orde en tucht onder de gevangenen in Nederlandsch-Indië* (Regulations concerning order and discipline for prisoners in the Dutch East Indies). Kartawinata's translations numbered at least 20 books.

[7] *Koloniaal Verslag van 1876, Nederlandsch (Oost-) Indie*, pp. 69, 109, and 103, notes.

[8] The *zelfstandig patih* was the highest position for indigenous people in regencies that did not have a regent.

[9] Kartini (1879–1905) was the daughter of a progressive regent of Japara and devoted herself to women's right to education and freedom from polygamy and child marriage. She is famous for her letters in Dutch, published posthumously in the Netherlands.

[10] K.F. Holle to P.J. Veth, 16 November 1874, in BPL, no. 1756, Leiden University Library.

[11] I have been unable to find the original version for the translation. Alexandre Dumas' "*Le Capitaine Marion*", in the anthology *Les drames de la Mer* (Shipwrecks at Sea), published in 1860 in Paris, is probably not the immediate source of Kartawinata's version.

[12] Apart from the story of Marion, Kartawinata translated two other tales into Javanese: *Cariyosipun Wiliyam Ukele Tuwin Tiyang Kumed Kasam* (The Story of Wiliam Ukele and Kumed Kasam), published in 1872, and *Cariyosipun Kapitan Bonteku* (The Story of Captain Bontekoe), published in 1883.

[13] De Linschoten-Vereeniging travel series and Beekman's anthology of Dutch colonial literature give elaborate comments and notes about the corpus of Bontekoe's story (Hoogewerff 1952; Beekman 1988: 3–54; Bostoen 1996).

[14] K.F. Holle to Governor-General, 20 August 1873, in Verbaal 3-6-1874, no. 31, Nationaal Archief.

[15] God was translated as "Allah", not "Tuhan". In the late nineteenth century, missionaries had a polemic about the translation of "God" that ended with the conclusion that the word "Tuhan" should be used to avoid Islamic connotations of the word "Allah". Kartawinata probably translated God as "Allah" so that the people could understand the message in the story more easily.

[16] The world-famous story of Robinson Crusoe was also translated by Kartawinata into Sundanese and published in 1879. The title page states, "Robinson Crusoë naar het Hollandsch van Gerard Keller door Raden Karta Winata translateur voor de Soendasche taal" (Robinson Crusoë of Gerard Keller in Dutch [translated] by Mr. Kartawinata, translator of the Sundanese language). This Sundanese version appeared four years after the Malay translation by A.F. von Dewal was first published.

[17] One year later, this book was translated into Malay and published by Albrecht & Co. (1902). It was given the title *Kitab Pengajaran Bagaimana*

*Patut Orang Menulung Sa-orang Perempuan Yang Beranak* (Handbook of Midwifery), and it clearly mentioned that the original version was in Sundanese.

18 This book was a Sundanese adaptation of Grimm's fairy tales. The first volume was reprinted three times in Javanese script, while the second volume was in Roman script (see Table 12). The third volume of *Warnasari* was translated by Lasminingrat's younger sister, Raden Lenggang Kantjana, in 1887.

19 Lasminingrat's *Carita Erman* (Story of Erman, 1875) was the translation of *Hendrik van Eichenfels* (Hendrik van Eichenfels) by von Schmid. The Landsdrukkerij printed 6, 015 copies of this translation in Javanese script in 1875 (Table 12). In 1920, another of C. von Schmid's books, *Genoveva*, was translated from a Dutch version into Sundanese, and later in 1929 into Malay (Bureau voor de Volkslectuur or Balai Poestaka 1924, 1930). In the late eighteenth and early nineteenth centuries, many of the popular Dutch children's books were based on German books for children, which were translated into Dutch in the Netherlands (Knuttel-Fabius 1906).

20 Holle to J.A. van der Chijs, 24 March 1874, in Box no. 5, no. 19, Holle papers, Arsip Nasional Republik Indonesia.

21 Teeuw suggests a certain relationship between Indonesian novels and Western novels, but does not elaborate on this relationship (Teeuw 1986: 53–4).

22 Interestingly, Cohen Stuart started his report by criticizing and disagreeing with K.F. Holle's proposal that the government should send indigenous students to Holland to be trained in writing schoolbooks.

23 See Anonymous (1918), Salmoen (1939): Satjadibrata (1939): Jedamski (1992); as well as Setiadi (1991) and Balai Poestaka [1948].

24 The printing houses that printed Sundanese books by order of the *Volkslectuur* were mostly Batavia-based companies. These included Ruygrok (established in 1910), Papyrus (est. 1910; formerly called H. M. van Dorp & Co., est. 1853), Indonesische Drukkerij (est. 1914), N. V. Elect. Drukk. Favoriet (est. 1915, Chinese-owned), Kantor Tjitak Javasche Boekhandel & Drukkerij Batawi (est. 1896), Mercurius (est. 1907), J.B. Wolters' Uitgevers Maatschappij, Verwachting (est. 1915), and Kwee Khe Soei (est. c. 1926). After the 1880s there were a number of Chinese printing houses in Batavia, such as Goan Ho(ng), Kho Tjeng Bie, Tjoe Toei Yang, and Tjiong Hok Long, and after the 1910s Lie Tek Long (1911), Han Po, and Tan Thian Soe (Kitano 1993: 23–4, 89). However, they usually did not print Sundanese books.

25 A bookseller, Sie Dhian Ho started a printing business in Solo in 1902. This was apparently a branch of the Bandung operation (Kitano 1993: 23).

26 The magazine *Parahiangan* was published for the first time in 1929 by Balai Poestaka.

27 S. Djojopoespito is famous for her Dutch novel *Buiten het gareel* (A life

free from trammels) published in 1940 (later translated into Indonesian by the author as *Manusia Bebas* [Free People] in 1975). She wrote her first novel *Marjanah* in Sundanese; it was probably written in 1937.

28   The writer consciously uses the word *basa diladjoer* (free and open utterance) (Coolsma 1913: 317), to denote prose. He said elsewhere that Sundanese literature consisted of three forms of writing: *wawacan, basa diladjoer,* and poetry (Goeroe 1926: 14). Later on, Ajip Rosidi was to call prose *basa lancaran* (smooth words) (Rosidi 1995: 3). The term *prosa* is most common nowadays.

29   *Wawacan* or books composed in *dangding* are occasionally published even today, but are used only by a small circle of people who love singing *tembang*.

# Bibliography

*Abbreviations:*

AVSS: *Algemeen Verslag van den Staat van het Schoolwezen in Nederlandsch-Indie*
AVVIO: *Algemeen Vijfjarig Verslag van het Inlandsch Onderwijs in Nederland-Indie*
AVIO: *Algemeen Verslag van het Inlandsch Onderwijs in Nederlandsch-Indie*
VIO: *Verslag van het Inlandsch Onderwijs in Nederlandsch-Indie*

Abdullah bin Abdul Kadir, 1970. *The Hikayat Abdullah*, an annotated translation by A.H. Hill. Kuala Lumpur: Oxford University Press.
Abdoerachman, R. Ajoe, 1930. *Lalampahan ka Eropa*. Batavia: Bale Poestaka.
Abdoessalam, R. H., 1957. *Wawatjan Rengganis*. Djakarta: Balai Pustaka.
Adam, Ahmat B., 1984. *The Vernacular Press and the Emergence of Modern Indonesian Consciousness (1855–1913)*. Ph.D. thesis, University of London.
Adiwidjaja, I., 1926. "Gedichten (Basa kaboedjangan, basa kawen)", *Poesaka-Soenda* 4(1): 6–11.
———, 1952. *Kasusastran Sunda I*. Djakarta, Groningen: J.B. Wolters.
———, [1954]. *Kasusastran Sunda II*. Djakarta, Groningen: J.B. Wolters.
*Almanak en naamregister van Nederlandsch-Indie, voor 1863*, 1862. Batavia: Ter Lands-drukkerij.
*Almanak en naamregister van Nederlandsch-Indie, voor 1864*, 1863. Batavia: Ter Lands-drukkerij.
Anonymous, 1780. "Proeven van Hoog, Gemeen en Berg Javaans", in *Verhandelingen vanhet Bataviaasch Genootschap der Kunsten en Wetenschappen* 2: 289–98.
Anonymous, 1918. "Schets van een Werkprogramma voor de Commissie voor de Volkslectuur", *Vrijzinnig Weekblad* 26: 425–8.
Anonymous, 1919. "Toewan Karel Frederik Holle djeung Raden Hadji Moehamad Moesa". *Volksalmanak Soenda* 1920: 317–20.
Antlöv, Hans, 1995. *Exemplary Centre, Administrative Periphery, Rural Leadership and the New Order in Java*. Richmond: Curzon Press.
Ardiwinata, D.K., 1914. *Baroeang Ka Noe Ngarora*. Batavia: G. Kolff & Co., Serie uitgaven door bemideling der Commissie voor de Volkslectuur No. 90.

Arps, Bernard, 1992. *Tembang in Two Tradition. Performance and Interpretation of Javanese Literature*. London: School of Oriental and African Studies, University of London.

———, 1997. "Koning Salomo en het dwerghertje, Taalpolitiek, taalonderwijs en de eerste grammatica's in het Javaans", in Kees Groeneboer (ed.), *Koloniale taalpolitiek in Oost en West, Nederlands-Indië, Suriname, Nederlandse Antillen, Aruba*. Amsterdam: Amsterdam University Press.

———, 2000. "The regulation of beauty: J. Kats and Javanese poetics", in David Smyth (ed.), *The Canon in Southeast Asian Literatures*. Richmond, Surrey: Curzon.

AVIO *lopende over de jaren 1888 t/m 1892*, 1894. Batavia: Landsdrukkerij.

AVSS *onder ultimo december 1852,,* 1853. Batavia: Landsdrukkerij.

AVSS *onder ultimo december 1853*, 1854. Batavia: Landsdrukkerij.

AVSS, *Afgesloten onder ultimo 1858. b. voor Inlanders.*, 1859. Batavia: Landsdrukkerij.

AVSS, *Afgesloten onder ultimo 1860. b. voor Inlanders*, 1861. Batavia: Landsdrukkerij.

AVVIO *lopende over de jaren 1873–1887*, 1880. Batavia: Landsdrukkerij.

Ayatrohaedi; Abdurachman, 1991. *Wawacan Ogin Amarsakti*. Jakarta: Departemen Pendidikan dan Kebudayaan.

Ayatrohaedi, 1985. *Bahasa Sunda di daerah Cirebon*. Jakarta: Balai Pustaka.

Bakhtin, Mikhail Mikhailovich, 1981. *The Dialogic Imagination*. Austin: University of Texas Press.

Balai Poestaka, [1948]. *Balai Pustaka Sewadjarnja 1908–1942*. Djakarta: Balai Poestaka.

Bataviaasch Genootschap van Kunsten en Wetenschappen, 1886. "Bijlage VIII. Lijst der leden van het Genootschap op ultimo December 1885", *Notulen van de Algemeene en Bestuurs-vergaderingen van het Bataviaasch Genootschap van Kunsten en Wetenschappen*. Deel XXIII: 57–62.

Barthes R., 1970. "Historical Discourse", in Michael Lane (ed.), *Introduction to Structuralism*. New York: Basic Books.

Beekman, E.M., 1988. *Fugitive Dreams, An Anthology of Dutch Colonial Literature*. Amherst: The University of Massachusetts Press.

Benjamin, Walter, 1970. *Illuminations*. London: Collins; Fontana.

Bennett, Tony, 1992. "Marxism and Popular Fiction", in Francis Mulhern (ed.), *Contemporary Marxist Literary Criticism*, pp. 188–210. London, New York: Longman.

Berge, Tom van den, 1993. *Van Kennis tot Kunst, Soendanese Poezie in de Koloniale Tijd*. Ph.D. thesis, State Universiteit of Leiden.

———, 1998, *Karel Frederik Holle, Theeplanter in Indie 1829–1896*. Amsterdam: Bert Bakker.

Berman, Marshall, 1982. *All That is Solid Melts Into Air. The Experiene of Modernity*. New York: Simon and Schuster.

Bezemer, T.J., 1924. "De mislukte theologische student-een Soendaneesche vertelling", *Nederlandsch-Indie Oude Nieuw* 425: 32–6.
Boomgaard, P.; and A.J. Gooszen, ed., 1991. *Changing Economy in Indonesia, A Selection of Statistical Source Material from the early 19th century up to 1940. Population Trends 1795–1942*, Vol. 11. Amsterdam: Royal Tropical Institute.
Bork, G.J. van; and N. Laan, ed., 1986. *Twee Eeuwen Literatuur-Geschiedenis.* Groningen: Wolters-Noordhoff bv.
Bostoen, Karel *et al.*, 1996. *Bontekoe, De schipper, het journaal, de scheepsjonges,* Amsterdam: Walburg Pers in cooperation with Stichting Nederlands Scheepvaartmuseum.
Bourdieu, Pierre, 1991. *Language and Symbolic Power.* Cambridge: Polity Press.
Braginsky, V.I., 1993. *The System of Classical Malay Literature.* Leiden: KITLV Press.
Brata di Widjaja, Raden Aria, 1897. "Karangan Panggagas", in H.de Bie (ed.), *Mitra noe tani*, pp. 20–8. Batavia: Landsdrukkerij.
Brugmans, I.J., 1938. *Geschiedenis van het Onderwijs in Nederlandsch-Indië.* Groningen, Batavia: J.B. Wolters.
Bruinessen, Martin van, 1990. "Kitab Kuning: Books in Arabic Script used in the Pesantren Milieu", *Bijdragen tot de Taal, Land- en Volkenkunde* 146 (2 and 3): 226–69.
———, n.d, *Lijst van Kitab Kuning. Religieuze literatuur in het Arabisch, Maleisch schrift, [her] uitgegeven in Indonesia, Malaysia, Singapore, verzameld in 1987 door Martin van Bruinessen*, mimeographed.
Bureau voor de Volkslectuur (Balai Poestaka), 1924. *Resultaten van de Volkslectuur in het jaar 1922.* Batavia: Volkslectuur.
Chambert-Loir, H., 1991. "Malay Literature in the 19th Century; The Fadli Connection", in J.J. Ras and S.O. Robson, ed., *Variation, Transformation and Meanig. Studies on Indonesian Literatures in Honour of A. Teeuw*, pp. 87–114. Leiden: KITLV Press.
Chijs, J.A. van der, 1864. "Bijdragen tot de Geschiedenis van het Inlandsch Onderwijs in Nederlandsch-Indie", *Tijdschrift voor Indische Taal, Land- en Volkenkunde* 14 (4–5): 212–323.
———, 1867a. "Bijdragen tot de Geschiedenis van het Inlandsch Onderwijs in Nederlandsch-Indie", *Tijdschrift voor Indische Taal, Land- en Volkenkunde* 16 (5–2): 1–80.
———, 1867b. "Fragment uit het Rapport van den Inspecteur van het Inlandsch Onderwijs in Nederlandsch-Indie, van 20 December 1865, no. 187, over den toestand van het Inlandsch Onderwijs op Java", *VIO over 1865*: 1–43.
———, 1875. "Proeve eener Ned. Indische Bibliographie (1659–1870)", *Verhandelingen van het Bataviaasch Fenootschap van Kunsten en Wetenschappen* 17: 1–325.

———, 1880. "Proeve eener Ned. Indische Bibliographie (1659–1870), supplement I", *Verhandelingen van het Bataviaasch Fenootschap van Kunsten en Wetenschappen* 19: xxxix, 1–93.

———, 1903. "Proeve eener Ned. Indische Bibliographie (1659–1870), supplement II", *Verhandelingen van het Bataviaasch Fenootschap van Kunsten en Wetenschappen* 55 (3): 1–64.

Cohen Stuart, A.B., 1866. "Nota van 16 Januarij 1866 aan de directie van het Bataviaasch Genootschap", *Notulen van de Algemeene en Bestuurs-Vergaderingen van het Bataviaasch Genootschap van Kunsten en Wetenschappen* 4: 32–80.

Commissie voor de Volkslectuur, ed., 1912. *Palanggeran Noeliskeun Basa Soenda koe Aksara Walanda.* Batavia.

[———], [1918]. *Spellingstelsels voor Inlandsche Talen.* [Batavia].

———, [1941]. *Gedenkboek H.I.K. Bandoeng 1866–1941.* Batavia.

Coolsma, S, 1873. *Handleiding bij de beoefening der Soendaneesche Taal.* Batavia: H.M. van Dorp & Co.

———, 1881. *West-Java. Het land, de bewoners en de Arbeid der Nederlandsche Zendingsvereeniging.* Rotterdam: J.H. Dunk.

———, [1884]. *Soendaneesch-Hollandsch Woordenboek.* Leiden: A.W. Sijthoff.

———, 1901. *De Zendingseeuw voor Nederlandsch Oost-Indie.* Utrecht: C.H.E. Breijer.

———, 1913. *Soendaneesch-Hollandsch woordenboek*, 2nd edition. Leiden: A.W. Sijthoff's Uitgevers-Maatschappij.

Coppel, Charles A., 1986. "From Christian Mission to Confucian Religion: The Nederlandsche Zendingsvereeniging and the Chinese of West Java 1870–1910", in David P. Chandler and Ricklefs, M.C. (ed.), *Nineteenth and Twentieth Century INDONESIA, Essays in honour of Professor J.D.Legge,* pp. 15–39. Clayton, Victoria: Center of Southeast Studies, Monash University.

Cowan, J. Milton, ed., 1976. *A Dictionary of Modern Written Arabic,* 3rd edition. Ithaca: Spoken Language Service, Inc.

Crawfurd, J.F.R.S., 1820. *History of the Indian Archipelago,* 3 vols. London: Hurst, Robinson, and Co.

Danasasmita, Saleh; Tien Wartini Ayatrohaedi; and Undang Ahmad Darsa, 1987. *Sewaka Darma, Sanghyang Siksakandang Karesian, Amanat Galunggung: Transkripsi dan Terjemahan.* Bandung: Bagian Proyek Penelitian dan Pengkajian Kebudayaan Sunda (Sundanologi), Direktorat Jenderal Kebudayaan, Departemen Pendidikan dan Kebudayaan.

Danoeredja, 1929. *Serat-sinerat Djaman Djoemenengna Raden Hadji Moehamad Moesa.* Weltevreden, Batavia: Bale Poestaka.

Darsa, Undang Ahmad, 1994. "Aksara yang pernah digunakan menulis Bahasa Sunda". Paper presented in the Seminar Nasional Pengkajian Naskah HA-NA-CA-RA-KA, dalam rangka Dasawarsa Lembaga Javanologi.

———, 1997. "Aksara Sunda, Salah Satu Lambang Identitas Daerah", unpublished paper.
———, 1998. "Khazanah Naskah Sunda: sebuah pemahaman aspek keislaman", unpublished paper.
Deenik, A.C. n.y. *Soendaasch proza en poezie*. 2 vols., n.p.
Departement van Gouvernementsbedrijven in Nederlandsch-Indië, 1912. *Landsdrukkerij Verslag over 1911*. Batavia: Landsdrukkerij.
Derks, Will, 1994. *The Feast of Storytelling. On Malay oral tradition*, Jakarta: Leiden: ILDEP. Serial Joint Publication Pusat Pembinaan dan Pengembangan Bahasa and Leiden University.
Diehl, Katharine Smith, 1990. *Printers and Printing in the East Indies to 1850*, vol. I. Batavia, New Rochelle, New York: Aristide D. Caratzas.
Djajadiningrat, P.A. Achmad, 1936. *Herinneringen van Pangeran Aria Achmad Djajadiningrat*. Amsterdam-Batavia: G.Kolff & Co.
Djojopoespito, S., 1959. *Marjanah*. Djakarta: Balai Pustaka.
Doel, H.W. van den, 1994. *De Stille Macht. Het Europese binnenlands bestuur op Java en Madoera, 1808–1942*. Amsterdam: Bert Bakker.
Doorn, Jacques van, 1983. *A Divided Society, Segmentation and Mediation in Late-Colonial Indonesia*. Rotterdam: Faculty of Social Science, Erasmus University Rotterdam.
Drewes, G.W.J., 1985. "The life-story of an old-time Priangan Regent as told by himself", *Bijdragen tot de Taal-, Land- en Volkenkunde* 141 (4): 399–422.
Dumas, Robert Martin, 2000. *"Teater Abdulmuluk" in Zuid-Sumatra op de Drempel van een Nieuw Tijdperk*. Leiden: Research School of Asian, African, and Amerindian Studies, University of Leiden.
Eisenstein, Elizabeth L., 1983. *The Printing Revolution, in Early Modern Europe*. Cambridge: Cambridge University Press.
Ekadjati, E.S. 1981. *Wawacan Sajarah Galuh*. Jakarta, Bandung: Lembaga Penelitian Perancis untuk Timur Jauh, Ecole Francaise D'extreme-Orient.
———, 1984. "Sejarah Sunda", in Edi S. Edadjati (ed.), *Masyarakat Sunda dan Kebudayaannya*, pp. 75–124. Jakarta: Girimukti Pasaka.
———; Hardjasaputra, A. Sobana, 1987. *Bibliografi Jawa Barat*. Bandung: mimeograph.
——— ed., 1988. *Naskah Sunda: Inventarisasi dan Pencatatan*. Bandung: Lembaga Penelitian Universitas Padjadjaran. Tokyo: The Toyota Foundation.
———; Hardjasaputra, A. Sobana; Ade Kosmaya Anggawisastra, and Aam Masduki, 1994. *Empat Sastrawan Sunda Lama; Riwayat Hidup, Riwayat Kepengarangan, dan Konsep Sentral Karangan Mereka*. Jakarta: Departemen Pendidikan dan Kebudayaan, Direktorat Sejarah dan Nilai Tradisional, Proyet Penelitian dan Pengakajian Kebudayaan Nusantara.
———, 1995a. *Kebudayaan Sunda (Suatu Pendekatan Sejarah)*. Jakarta: PT Dunia Pustaka Jaya.

———, 1995b. *Sunda, Nusantara dan Indonesia, suatu tinjauan sejarah*. Pidato pengukuhan Jabatan Guru Besar Dalam Ilmu Sejarah Fakultas Sastra Universitas Padjadjaran Pada hari Sabtu, 16 Desember 1995. Bandung: Departemen Pendidikan dan Kebudayaan, Universitas Padjadjaran.

———, 1996. "Cultural Plurality: The Sundanese in West Java", in Ann Kumar and John H. McGlynn, *Iluminations*. Jakarta: The Lontar Foundation, New York and Tokyo: Weatherhill.

———; Undang A. Darsa, 1999. *Jawa Barat: Koleksi Lima Lembaga. Katalog Induk Naskah-naskah Nusantara* Jilid 5A. Jakarta: Yayasan Obor Indonesia; Ecole Francaise D'Extreme-Orient.

*Encyclopaedie van Nederlandsch-Indië*. 1905. 4 vols. 's-Gravenhage: Nijhoff; Leiden: Brill.

*Encyclopaedie van Nederlandsch-Indië*. 1917–1939. 2nd ed., 4 vols and 4 supplements ['s-Gravenhage: Nijhoff; Leiden: Brill].

End, TH. van den, 1991. *De Nederlandsche Zendingsvereeniging in West-Java 1858–1963. Een bronnenpublicatie*. Leiden: Raad voor de Zending der Ned. Herv. Kerk, de zending der Gereformeerde Kerken in Nederland en de Gereformeerde Zendingsbond in de Ned. Herv. Kerk.

Engelmann, W.H. 1867. "Nog iets over de Soendaneesche Vertaling van het Evangelie van Lukas", *Java-Bode*, 2 February 1867.

Eringa, F.S., 1984. *Soendaas-Nederlands Woordenboek (mede met gebruikmaking van eerder door R.A.Kern bijeengebrachte gegevens)*. Dordrecht, Cinnaminson: Foris Publications Holland.

Fasseur, C., 1978. *Kultuurstelsel en koloniale baten. De Nederlandse exploitatie van Java 1840–1860*. Leiden: Universitaire Pers Leiden.

———, 1980. "De "geest" van het gouvernement", in C. Fasseur (ed.), *Geld en geweten. Een bundel opstellen over anderhalve eeuw Nederlands bestuur in de Indonesische archipel*, pp. 32–50. Den Haag: Martinus Nijhoff.

———, 1993. *De Indologen*. Amsterdam: Bert Bakker.

Febvre, Lucien, and Henri-Jean Martin, 1984. *The Coming of the Book, the Impact of Printing 1450–1800*. London: Verso Editions.

Ferguson, C., 1959. "Diglossia". *Word* 15: 325–340.

Florida, Nancy K., 1993. *Javanese Literature in Surakarta Manuscripts Vol. 1*. Ithaca: Cornell University.

Foucault, Michel, 1985. *Politics, philosophy, culture: interviews and other writings 1977–1984*, ed. with an introduction by Lawrence D. Kritzman; translated by Alan Sheridan and others. New York: Routledge.

Gaarder, Jostein, 1995. *Sophie's World*. London: Phoenix.

Geerdink, A., 1875. *Soendaneesch-Hollandsch Woordenboek*. Batavia: H.M. van Dorp & Co.

Gericke, J.F.C., and T. Roorda, 1901. *Javaansch-Nederlandsch Handwoordenboek*. Amsterdam: Johannes Muller, Leiden: E.J. Brill.

Giddens, Anthony, 1990. *The Consequences of Modernity*. California: Stanford University Press.

Goeroe, 1926. "Kasoesastran Soenda", *Poesaka-Soenda* 4 (1): 11–16.
Gonggrijp, J.R.P.F., 1866. *Kitab pengadjaran akan goena anakh-anakh jang bahroe mengarti membatja*. Batavia: Landsdrukkerij.
Grashuis, G.J., 1870. "Over de Spelling van het Sondaneesch met Latijnsch Letterschrift", *Tijdschrift voor Indische Taal, Land- en Volkenkunde* 19: 490–500.
———. 1874. *Soendaneesch Leesboek*. Leiden: A.W. Sijthoff.
———. 1881. *Soendanesche Bloemlezing*. Leiden: A.W. Sijthoff.
———. 1891. *Bijdrage tot de Kennis van het Soendaneesch*. Leiden: A. W. Sijthoff.
Groeneboer, Kees, 1993. *Weg tot het Westen. Het Nederlands voor Indie 1600–1950 een Taalpolitieke Geschiedenis*. Leiden: KITLV Uitgeverij.
Haan, F. de. 1910–12. *Priangan, De Preanger-Regentschappen onder het Nederlandsch bestuur tot 1811*. 4 vols. Batavia: Bataviaasch Genootschap van Kunsten en Wetenschappen.
Haastert, C.J. van, 1894. *Boekoe Edjahan djeung Batjaan, pikeun moerid-moerid dina pangkat pangahandapna di sakola-Soenda*. Batawi: Kantor Tjitak Kangdjeng Goepernemen.
Habermas, Jürgen, 1993. "Modernity — An Incomplete Project", in Thomas Docherty, ed. and intro., *Postmodernism. A Reader*, pp. 98–109. Cambridge: Harvester Wheatsheaf.
Harris, Roy, 2001. *Rethinking Writing*. London: Continuum.
Harvey, David, 1990. *The Condition of Postmodernity*. Oxford; Massachusetts: Blackwell.
Hidding, K.A.H., 1935. *Gebruiken en Godsdienst der Soendaneezen*. Batavia: G.Kolff & Co.
Hisyam, Muhamad, 2001. *Caught between three fires; the Javanese Pangulu under the Dutch colonial administration, 1882–1942*. Jakarta: Indonesian-Netherlands Cooperation in Islamic Studies (INIS).
Hobsbawm, Eric, 1983. "Inventing Traditions", in Eric Hobsbawm and Terence Ranger, eds., *The Invention of Tradition*, pp. 1–14. Cambridge: Cambridge University Press.
Holle, K.F., 1862, *Kitab Tjatjarakan Soenda No. 1*. Batavia: Lands-Drukkerij.
———, 1867. "Vlugtig Berigt omtrent eenige Lontar-Handschriften, Afkomstig uit de Soenda-Landen, door Raden Saleh aan het Bataviaasch Genootschap van K. en W. ten geschenke gegeven, met toepassing van de inscriptiën van Kwali", *Tijdschrift voor Indische Taal, Land- en Volkenkunde* 16: 450–70.
———, 1869. *Bijlagen. Notulen Bataviaasch Genootschap 1869 II*. Bataviaasch Genootschap.
———, 1871. "Het schrijven van Soendaasch met Latijnsch Letter", *Tijdschrift voor Indische Taal, Land- en Volkenkunde* 20: 91–107.
———, 1890. "Dat, en hoe men in 1848 in de Preanger als diensttaal nog Javaansch gebruikte", *Tijdschrift voor het Binnenlandsch Bestuur* 9: 128–30.

Hoogewerff, G.J., 1952. *Journalen van de gedenckw aerdige reijsen van Willem Ijsbrantsz. Bontekoe 1618–1625*. 's-Gravenhage: Martinus Nijhoff, De Linschoten-Vereeniging.
Hoëvell, W.R. van, 1842. "Onderzoek naar de Oorzaken van het Onderscheid in Voorkomen, Kleeding, Zeden en Gewoonten, Taal en Karakter tusschen de Soendanezen en de Eigenlijke Javanen", *Tijdschrift voor Nederlandsch-Indië* 4 (2): 132–69.
Iperen, J. van, 1780a. "Vervolg van eene Javaanſche Hiſtorie Sadjara Radja Jawa", *Verhandelingen van het Batviaasch Genootschap der Kunsten en Wetenschappen*, pp. 263–88, Tweede Deel.
[_____], 1780b. "Proeven van Hoog, Gemeen en Berg Javaans", *Verhandelingen van het Batviaasch Genootschap der Kunsten en Wetenschappen*, pp. 289–97, Tweede Deel.
Jedamski, Doris, 1992. "Balai Pustaka: A Colonial Wolf in Sheep's Clothing", *Archipel* 44: 23–46.
Jurriëns, Edwin, 2001. *Cultural Travel and Migrancy. The Artistic (Re)Presentation of Globalization in the Electronic Media of West Java*, Ph.D. thesis, State Universiteit of Leiden.
Kamei, Hideo, 1999. *"Syosetsu" Ron, "Syosetu Shinzui" to Kindai*. Tokyo: Iwanami Shoten.
Kantoor voor de Volkslectuur, 1931. *Eenige Resultaten van den Arbeid in het jaar 1930*. Batavia: Volkslectuur.
Kaptein, Nico, 1997. "Sayyid 'Uthmân on the Legal Validity of Documentary Evidence", *Bijdragen tot de Taal, Land- en Volkenkunde* 153(1): 85–102.
Karatani, Kojin, 1993. *Origins of Modern Japanese Literature*. Durham and London: Duke University Press.
Kartawinata, 1874. *Tjarita Kapitan Bontekoe*. Batavia: Landskrukkerij.
_____, 1924. *Tjarita Kapitan Bontekoe*. Batavia: Drukkerij Volkslectuur.
_____, 1891. *Pagoeneman Soenda djeung Walanda*. Batawi: Kantor-Tjitak Goepernemen.
Kartini, Tini; Yetty Kusmiyati, Hadish; Sutedja Sumardipura, and Iskandarwassid, 1979. *Yuhana — Sastrawan Sunda*. Jakarta: Pusat Pembinaan dan Pengembangan Bahasa, Departemen Pendidikan dan Kebudayaan.
Kartodirdjo, Sartono, 1966. *The Pesants' Revolt of Banten in 1888*. 's-Gravenhage: Martinus Nijhoff.
Kimman, Eduard, 1981. *Indonesian Publishing, Economic Organizations in a Langganan Society*. Hollandia Baarn.
Kitano, Masanori, 1993. *Oranda Higashi Indo jidai no Peranakan kajin Bungaku no tanjo to hatten 1880–1924*. M.A. thesis, Osaka University of Foreign Studies.
Klinkert, H.C., 1866. "Antwoord op de antikritiek van de Heeren G.R.P.E. Gonggrijp, J.G.F. Riedel en N. Graafland", *Bijdragen tot de Taal, Land- en Volkenkunde* 15: 555–82.

Knaap, Gerrit, 1996. *Shallow Waters, Rising Tide: Shipping and Trade in Java around 1775*. Leiden: KITLV Press.
Knuttel-Fabius, Eliza, 1906. *Oude Kinderboeken, Paedagogie en moraal in oude Nederlandsche kinderboeken*. 's-Gravenhage: Martinus Nijhoff.
Kobayashi, Yasuko, 1991. "Penghulu no Shokuminti Kanryoka", *Asia Kenkyuu* 37 (3): 29–60.
Koorders, D., 1863. *Boekbeschouwing, A dictionary of the Sunda language of Java*, reprint from *Java-Bode* 1863.
Koster, Gijsbert Louis, 1993. *Roaming through seductive gardens: reading in Malay narrative*. Ph.D. thesis, University of Leiden.
Kumar, Aan, 1985. *The Diary of a Javanese Muslim: Religion, Politics and the Pesantren 1883–1886*. Canberra: Australian National University.
Kunto, Haryoto, 1984. *Wajah Bandoeng Tempo Doeloe*. Bandung: P.T. Grancsia.
[Landsdrukkerij], 1891. *Daftar Goedang Kitab goebernemen di Batawi tahon 1892 Djilid I. Menjataken segala barang jang boleh dipinta bagi sekola anak negeri Goebernemen di tanah Hindia Nederland*. Batavia: Landsdrukkerij.
Lasminingrat, Ayu, 1876. *Warnasari atawa rupa-rupa dongeng*. Batavia: Kantor Tjitak Goepernemen.
Lenggang Kantjana, 1887. *Warnasari jilid III*. Batavia: Landsdrukkerij.
Levyssohn Norman, H.D., 1888a. *Hal Setijanja Kepala Bangsa Anak Negri di Tanah Hindia-Wolanda*. Batawi: Ijap Goan Ho.
———, 1888b. "Ter Herinnering", *Eigen Haard*, pp. 93–6.
Maeda, Ai, 1989. *Kindai Dokusya no Seiritsu (The Formation of Modern Reader)*. Tokyo: Chikuma Syobo.
Maier, H.M.J., 1988. *In the Center of Authority*. Ithaca: Cornell University.
———, 1993a. "Boredom in Batavia: A Catalogue of Books in 1898", in D.M. Roskies (ed.), *Text/Politics in Island Southeast Asia, Essays in Interpretation*, pp. 131–56. Athens, Ohio: Ohio University Center for International Studies.
———, 1993b. "From Heteroglossia to Polyglossia: The Creation of Malay and Dutch in the Indies", *Indonesia* 56 (October): 37–65.
———, 1999. "Tales of Hang Tuah, In Search of Wisdom and Good Behavior", *Bijdragen tot de Taal, Land- en Volkenkunde* 155 (3): 342–61.
Masduki, Aam; Nandang Rusnandar, and Lina Herlinawati, 1996. *Wawacan Jayalalana*. Jakarta: Proyek Pengakajian dan Pembinaan Nilai-nilai Budaya, Direktorat Sejarah dan Nilai Tradisional Direktorat Jenderal Kebudayaan, Departemen Pendidikan dan Kebudayaan.
Matheson Hooker, Virginia, 2000. *Writing A New Society: Social Change through the Novel in Malay*. Australia: Allen & Unwin; Leiden: KITLV Press.
Matsuo, Hiroshi, 1997. *Batavia no Toshikukan to Bungaku, Kindai Indonesia Bungaku no Kigen (Literature in the Social Context of Batavia)*. Osaka: Osaka University of Foreign Studies Press.

Meinsma, J.J., 1869. "Iets uit de Nalatenschap van Mr. D. Koorders", *Bijdragen tot de Taal- Land- en Volkenkunde van Nederlandsch Indië* 4 (3): 253–397.
Mijer, P., 1843. "Prijsvragen, uitgeschreven door het Bataviaasch Genootschap van Kunsten en Wetenschappen", *Verhandelingen van het Bataviaasch Genootschap van Kunsten en Weenschappen* 19: v–xviii.
Milner, Anthony, 1995. *The Invention of Politics in Colonial Malaya*. Cambridge University Press.
Moesa, Mochamad, 1867. *Dongeng-dongeng Piêntêngên*. Batavia: Landsdrukkerij.
———, 1883. *Ali Moehtar*. Batavia: Landsdrukkerij.
———, 1901. *Wawatjan Pandji Woeloeng*. Betawi: Kantor Tjitak Kangdjeng Goepernemen.
———, 1990. *Wawacan Panji Wulung, kalawan panganteur ti Ajip Rosidi*. Jakarta: Girimukti Pasaka.
Molen, W. van der, 1991. "Huruf Jawa Cetakan", in *Ilmu-ilmu Humaniora*, pp. 69–84. Jogjakarta: Fakultas Sastra UGM.
———, 2000. "Hoe heeft zulks kunnen geschieden? Het begin van de Javaanse typografie", in van der Molen Willem, Arps, Bernard (ed.), *Woord en Schrift in de Oost. De betekenis van zending en missie voor de studie van taal en literatuur in Zuidoost-Azie*, pp. 132–62. Leiden: Opleiding Talen en Culturen van Zuidoost-Azie en Oceanie, Universiteit Leiden, Semaian 19.
Moriyama, Mikihiro, 1985. *Tjarios Wiwitan Radja-radja di poelo Djawa, aru Sunda no "ouchoshi"*. M.A. thesis, Osaka University of Foreign Studies.
———, 1990. "The Sundanese Epic Wawacan in Print", *Southeast Asian Studies* 28 (1): 108–22.
———, 1995. "Language policy in the Dutch colony: On Sundanese in the Dutch East Indies", *Southeast Asian Studies* 32 (4): 446–54.
———, 1996. "Discovering the "language" and the "literature" of West Java: An introduction to the formation of Sundanese writing in 19th century West Java", *Southeast Asian Studies* 34 (1): 151–83.
———, 2000. "Moehamad Moesa, print literacy, and the new formation of knowledge in nineteenth-century West Java", *Indonesia and the Malay World* 28 (80): 5–21.
Multatuli, 1949. *Max Havelaar, naar het authentieke handschrift uitgegeven en ingeleid door Dr. G. Stuiveling*. Amsterdam: G.A. van Oorschot.
Nataprawira, P., [1955]. *Riwajat Opat Budjangga Sunda: Katut Tjutatan tina Karangan-karangan anu Marunel*. Bandung.
Noordegraaf, J., 1985. *Norm, geest en geschiedenis: Nederlandse taalkunde in de negentiende eeuw, Dordrecht-Holland*. Cinnaminson-U.S.S.: Foris Publications.
Noorduyn, J., 1962. "Over het eerste gedeelte van de Oud-Soendase Carita Parahyangan", *Bijdragen tot de Taal, Land- en Volkenkunde* 118: 374–83.

Ohashi, Atuko, 1994. "Jawato Priangantiho ni okeru coffee yuso to gentijinsyucho Regent (Coffee Transportation and Regents in Priangan, Java: From the Early 18th Century to the 1820s)", *Southeast Asian Studies* 32 (1): 66–119.
Ong, Walter J., 1982. *Orality and Literacy. The Technologizing of the Word.* London, New York: Routledge.
Oosting, H.J., 1879. *Soendasch-Nederduitsch Woordenboek, op last van het Gouvernement van Nederlandsch-Indie.* Batavia: Ogilvie & Co.
———, 1884. *Soendasche Grammatica.* 's-Gravenhage: Martinus Nijhoff.
OPA (Oh Peng An), [1969]. *Pandji Wulung.* Djakarta: U.P. Dwi Tunggal.
Oshikawa, Noriaki, 1994. "On the Malay Version of Robinson Crusoe: An Introduction to the Study of Translated Literature", *Southeast Asia: History and Culture (Tonan Ajia: Rekishi to Bunka)* 23: 3–21.
Peeters, Jeroen, 1996. "Palembang Revisited: Further Notes on the Printing Establishment of Kemas Haji Muhammad Azhari, 1848", in Paul van der Velde (ed.), *IIAS Yearbook 1995*, pp. 181–90. Leiden: International Institute for Asian Studies.
Pigeaud, Th., 1970. *Literature of Java*, vol. 3, *Illustrations and facsimiles of manuscripts, maps, addenda and a general index of names and subjects.* Leiden: In Bibliotheca Univeristatis Lugduni Batavorum.
Pleyte, C.M., 1913. "De Patapaan Adjar soeka resi anders gezegd de kluizenarij op den Goenoeng Padang", *Tijdschrift voor Indisch Taal, Land- en Volkenkunde* 55: 281–427.
Poerbatjaraka, and Tardjan Hadidjaja, 1952. *Kepoestakan Djawa.* Jakarta: Djambatan.
Poeradiredja, R., and M. Soerijadiradja, 1919. "Bijdrage tot de kennis der Soendasche taal", paper presented in Eerste Congres voor de Taal, Land- en Volkenkunde van Java at Solo, *Djawa* 4: 401–12.
Pramoedya, Ananta Toer, 1980. *Bumi Manusia.* Jakarta: P.T. Hasta Mitra.
Proudfoot, I., 1986. "A Formative Period in Malay Book Publishing", *Journal of the Malaysian Branch of the Royal Asiatic Society* 59 (2): 101–32.
———, 1993. *Early Malay Printed Books. A provisional account of materials published in the Singapore-Malaysia area up to 1920, noting holdings in major public collections*, University of Malaya: Academy of Malay Studies and the Library.
Putten, Jan van der, 1995a. "Taalvorsers en hun informanten in Indie in de 19e eeuw. Von de Wall als politiek agent in Riau?", *Bijdragen tot de Taal, Land- en Volkenkunde* 151 (1): 44–75.
——— and Al Azhar, 1995b. *Di Dalam Berkekalan Persahabatan. "In Everlasting Friendship". Letters from Raja Ali Haji.* Leiden: Vakgroep Talen en Culturen van Zuidoost-Azie en Oceanie.
———, 1997. "Printing in Riau. Two Steps Toward Modernity", *Bijdragen tot de Taal, Land- en Volkenkunde* 153 (4):717–36.
———, 2000. "Als een hond bij de Turken? H.C. Klinkert en suiver Maleis", in Willem van der Molen; and Benart Arps (ed.), *Woord en Schrift in de*

*Oost; de betekenis van zending en missie voor de studie van taal en literatuur in Zuidoost-Azië*, Semaian 19. Leiden: Opleiding Talen en Culturen van Zuidoost-Azië en Oceanië.

———, 2001. *His word is the Truth: Haji Ibrahim's letters and other writings*. Leiden: Research School of Asian, African, and Amerindian Studies, University of Leiden.

Raffles, T.S., 1817. *The History of Java*, 2 vols. London: Black, Parbury [etc.].

Raja Ali Haji, Ibn Ahmad, translated by Virginia Matherson and Barbara Watson Andaya, 1982. *The Precious Gift (Tuhfat al-Nafis)*. Kuala Lumpur: Oxford University Press.

Rassers, W.H., 1959. *Panji, The Culture Hero. A structural study of religion in Java*. The Hague: Martinus Nijhoff.

Reid, Anthony, 1988. *Southeast Asia in the age of commerce, 1450-1680. The lands below the winds*. New Haven, London: Yale University Press.

Rigg, J. 1862. *A Dictionary of the Sundanese Language of Java*. (Verhandelingen van het Bataviaasch Genootschap van Kunsten en Wetenschappen 29). Batavia: Lange.

Robson, S.O., ed., 1971. *Wangbang Wideya; A Javanese Panji Romance*. The Hague: Martinus Nijhoff.

Rosidi, Ajip, 1966. *Kesusastran Sunda Dewasa Ini*. Bandung: Tjupumanik.

———; Raksanagara, Ami, 1980. *Puisi Guguritan Sunda*. Jakarta: Pusat Pembinaan dan Pengembangan Bahasa, Departemen Pendidikan dan Kebudayaan. Proyek Penelitian Bahasa dan Sastra Jawa Barat 1979/1980.

———, 1983. *Dengkleung Dengdek, kumpulan esey jeung kritik ngeunaan basa Sunda jeung sastra Sunda*. Bandung: Angkasa.

———, 1989. *Haji hasan Mustapa Jeung Karya-karyana*. Bandung: Penerbit Poestaka.

———, 1995. *Puisi Sunda jilid 1*. Bandung: CV Geger Sunten.

Rusyana, Yus, and Ami Raksanagara, 1979. *Novel Sunda Sebelum Perang*. Jakarta: Pusat Pembinaan dan Pengembangan Bahasa, Departemen Pendidikan dan Kebudayaan.

———, 1980. *Puisi Guguritan Sunda*. Jakarta: Pusat Pembinaan dan Pengembangan Bahasa, Departemen Pendidikan dan Kebudayaan.

Salleh, Muhammad Haji, 1986. *Cermin diri. Esei-esei kesusasteraan*. Selangor: Fajar Bakti Sdn. Bhd.

Salmoen, M.A., 1939. "Pangemoet-ngemoet", *Parahiangan* 11 (1): 2–4, 12.

———, 1955. "Raden Hadji Muhammad Musa", *Buku Kita* 1 (10): 435–38.

———, 1958. *Kandaga, Kasusastran*. Bandung, Djakarta: Ganaco.

Sastradiredja, 1931. *Wawatjan Damarwoelan*, 3rd ed. Batavia: Balai Poestaka.

Sastrahadiprawira, Memed, 1929a. "Basa sareng Kasoesastran Soenda", *Poesaka-Soenda* (7 and 8): 97–101.

———, 1929b. "Over de waardeering der Soendaneesche literatuur", *Djawa* 9: 16–21.

———, [1930]. *Soendaaasch proza en poezie*, 2 vols., n.p.
Sastrawinangoen, 1925. "Oenak-anik Basa Soenda", *Poesaka-Soenda* 3 (18): 346–47.
Satjadibrata, 1939. "Marganing kamadjoean", *Parahiangan* 11 (1): 9–10.
———, 1953. *Rasiah Tembang Sunda*. Djakarta: Balai Poestaka.
———, 1954. *Kamus Basa Sunda*. Djakarta: Perpustakaan Perguruan Kementerian P.P. dan K.
Schamelhout, G., 1932. *De volkeren van Europa en de strijd der nationaliteiten*, vol. 1 of 3 vols. Nederlandse Bibliotheek.
Schendeveld-van der Dussen, M.A., 1993. *Nederlandse Literatuur, een geschiedenis*. Groningen: Martinus Nijhoff.
Schulze, Frits, 1991. *Die Chroniken von Sambas und Mempawah, Einheimische Quellen zur Geshichte West-kalimantans*. Heidelberg: Julius Groos Verlag. Sammlung Groos.
Setiadi, Hilmar Farid, 1991. "Kolonialisme dan Budaya: Balai Poestaka di Hindia Belanda", *Prisma* 10.
Snouck Hurgronje, C., 1894. "Sajjid Oethman's gids voor de priesterraden", *Indisch Tijdschrift van het Recht* 63: 722–44.
———, 1924. *Verspreide Geschriften van C. Snouck Hurgronje*, vol. 4 of 6 vols. Bonn, Leipzig: Kurt Schroeder.
———, 1927. *Verspreide Geschriften van C. Snouck Hurgronje*, vol. 6 of 6 vols. Leiden: E.J. Brill.
Soeria Nata Atmadja, A.A.A., [193?]. *Regenten-positie*. Bandoeng: A.C. Nix & Co.
[Soerja Nata Legawa, Raden Demang], [1897], *Pangeling ngeling ka Padoeka Toewan Karel Frederik Holle, Adviseur-Honorair voor Inlandsche Zaken, enz.* n.p.
Solomon, Wendy June, 1993. *The Early Sundanese Novel, 1914–1940*. Ph.D. thesis, Australian National University.
Steenbrink, Karel A., 1984. *Beberapa Aspek tentang Islam di Indonesia Abad ke-19*. Jakarta: P.T. Bulan Bintang.
———, 1985. *Mencari garis besar sejarah dari berkas-berkas arsip suatu pedoman dalam bentuk laporan perjalanan dan penelitian kepada K.F. Holle, penghulu kampung di Jawa di Banda Aceh dan riwayat hidup Habib As Sagaf*. Lembaga Penelitian, Pengembangan dan Pengabdian Masyarakat, IAIN "walisongo" Semarang.
Studentencorps, Het Indologisch, [1898]. *Almanak van het Indologisch Studentencorps voor 1898*. Delft: Van Mrkens Drukkerij-Vennootschap.
Subalidinata, R.S., ed., 1973. *Cerita Panji Wulung, karya R. Haji Muhammad Musa (terjemahan)*. [Jakarta]: Proyek Inventarisasi dan Dokumentasi Kebudayaan Nasional, Direktorat Jenderal Kebudayaan, Departemen Pendidikan dan Kebudayaan.
Sudibyoprono, R. Rio, 1991. *Ensiklopedi Wayang Purwa*. Jakarta: Balai Poestaka.

Sumarga, Rusman Sutia, 1983. "Tutungkusan (1) Muhammad Musa", *Mangle* 889: 8–9.
Sumarlina, Elis Suryani Nani, 1990. *Wawacan Panji Wulung. Sebuah Kajian Filologis*. M.A. thesis, Universitas Padjadjaran.
Suminto, H. Aqib, 1985. *Politik Islam Hindia Belanda*. Jakarta: LP3ES.
Sweeney, Amin, 1987. *A Full Hearing. Orality and literacy in the Malay world*. Berkeley, Los Angeles, London: University of California Press.
———, 1991. "Literacy and the Epic in the Malay World", in Joyce Burkhalter Fluechiger and Laurie J. Sears, ed., *Boundaries of the Text. Epic Performances in South and Southeast Asia*, pp. 17–29. Michigan: Center for South and Southeast Asian Studies, The University of Michigan. Michigan Papers on South and Southeast Asia No. 35.
Taylor, Jean Gelman, 1983. *The Social World of Batavia, European and Eurasian in Dutch Asia*. Wisconsin: The University of Wisconsin Press.
Teeuw, A., 1986. *Modern Indonesian Literature*, 2 vols. Dordrecht, Riverton: Foris Publication.
Tio Ie Soei, [1963]. *Lie Kimhok 1853–1912*. Bandung: L.D. Good Luck.
Trocki, Carl A., 1992. "Political Structures in the Nineteenth and Early Twentieth Centuries", in Nicholas Tarling, ed., *The Cambridge History of Southeast Asia*, vol. 2, pp. 79–130. Cambridge University Press.
Tsuchiya, Kenji, 1990. "Javanology and the Age of Ranggawarsita: An Introduction to Nineteenth-Century Javanese Culture", in *Reading Southeast Asia*, pp. 75–108. Ithaca: Cornell University.
Tuuk, H. Neubronner, van der, 1851. "Varia, De Soendsche letterkunde", *Tijdschrift voor Nederlandsch Indië* 13 (1): 340–42.
Uhlenbeck, E.M., 1964. *A Critical Survey of Studies of the Language of Java and Madura*. 's-Gravenhage: Martinus Nijhoff.
Veth, P.J., 1869. "Aanteekeningen over de Soendaneesche Taal- en Letterkunde, Fragmenten uit de Correspondentie van W.H. Engelmann met het Hoofdbestuur van het Ned. Bijbelgenootschap", *Tijdschrift voor Nederlandsch Indië* 3 (1): 255–78.
———, 1875. *Java, geographis, ethnologisch, historisch*, vol. 1. Haarlem: Erven F. Bohn.
*VIO over 1863*, 1865. Batavia: Landsdrukkerij.
*VIO over 1864*, 1866. Batavia: Landsdrukkerij.
*VIO over 1865*, 1867. Batavia: Landsdrukkerij.
*VIO over 1866*, 1868. Batavia: Landsdrukkerij.
*VIO over 1867*, 1870. Batavia: Landsdrukkerij.
*VIO over 1868*, 1871. Batavia: Landsdrukkerij.
Watson, C.W., 1993. "The Metamorphosis of a Javanese Aristocrat: The Memoirs of Pangeran Achmad Djajadiningrat", in D.M. Roskies, ed., *Text/Politics in Island Southeast Asia: Essays in Interpretation*, pp. 157–90. Athens, Ohio: Ohio University Center for International Studies.

Watt, Ian, 1993. *The rise of the novel*. London: The Hogarth Press.
Wieringa, E.P., 1994. *Babad Bangun Tapa; De Ballingsschap van Pakubuwana VI op Ambon 1830–1849*. Ph.D. thesis, University of Leiden.
Wilde, A. de, 1829. *Berigten Betreffende de Landschappen, genoemd de Preanger Regentschappen, op Java gelegen*. Amsterdam: M. Westerman.
———, 1830. *De Preanger Regentschappen op Java gelegen*. Amsterdam: M. Westerman.
———, 1841. *Nederduitsch-Maleisch en Soendasch Woordenboek*, edited by Taco Roorda. Amsterdam: Johannes Muller.
Wilkinson, R.J., 1932. *A Malay — English Dictionary*, part 1. Mytilene Greece: Salavopoulos and Kinderlis.
Woordenboek, 1993. *Woordenboek der Nederlandsche Taal*. Leiden: Stichting Instituur voor Nederlandse Lexicologie. 's-Gravenhage: Martinus Nijhoff. Leiden: A.W. Sijthoff (first published in 1924).
Yamamoto, Nobuto, 1995. "Colonial surveillance and 'public opinion': The rise and decline of Balai Poestaka's press monitoring", *Keio Journal of Politics*, 8: 71–100.
Zanten, Wim van, 1989. *Sundanese Music in the Cianjuran Style*. Leiden: KITLV Press.
———, 1993. "Sung epic narrative and lyrical song; carita pantun and tembang Sunda", in Bernard Arps, ed., *Performance in Java and Bali: Studies of narrative, theatre, music and dance*, pp. 144–61. London: School of Oriental and African Studies, University of London.
Zoetmulder, P.J., with the collaboration of S.O. Robson, 1982. *Old Javanese — English Dictionary*, 2 vols. 's-Gravenhage: Martinus Nijhoff; Leiden: KITLV.

# Index

Abdoerachman, R.A.   155
Abdullah b. A. Munsyi   156, 168
Aceh   119
Adang   116
Adiwidjaja, R.I.   48, 49
Adi Widjaja   93
Albers, C.   23, 118–9
Albrecht & Co.   89–90
Allah   21, 193
Ambon   57
Amongpradja, M.   28
Arabic script   see script
Ardiwinata, D.K.   28, 197, 200
aristocracy   2
author   6, 37, 76, 81, 84, 88, 93, 127, 136, 168, 202

Bakhtin, Michael   9–10
Balai Poestaka   82, 200–2, 205
Bali, Balinese   86
Banda Aceh   109
Bandung   22–3, 57, 58, 67, 93, 101, 202
Banonagara, Raden Ajoe   110, 114
Banten   26, 60, 76, 108, 109
*basa lancaran*   see prose
Batak   23
Batavia   2, 25, 60, 75, 76, 81, 85, 89, 110, 112, 115, 120, 124
*Bataviaasch Genootschap van Kunsten en Weterschappen*   see Batavian Society of Arts and Science
Batavian Society of Arts and Science   120, 199

*beluk*   53
Benjamin, Walter   77
Bennett, T.   55
Berge, T. van den   11, 202
*bergjavaans*   see "mountain" Javanese
Berman, M.   182
Bible   20, 29, 46, 92
Bisschop, A.   89, 90
Bogor   see Buitenzorg
Bratadiwidjaja, Aria (Brata di Widjaja)   37, 93, 104, 108, 110, 131
Broek, P. van den   75
Bugis   13
Buitenzorg (Bogor)   18, 26, 76, 110, 112, 116, 117, 154
*bupati*   see regent

*cacah*   39, 104
Capellen, van der   56
*carita*   79
Central Java   101
Chijs, J.A. van der   39, 41, 56, 65, 67, 68, 75, 98, 137
Chinese   88–9, 201
Chinese script   see script
chirographic   2, 4, 77, 124
Christian or Christianity   6, 29, 44
Ciamis   58
Cianjur   22, 56, 57, 58, 59, 60, 66, 109, 124
Cikajang   32, 110
Cikalong Kulon   124
Cirebon   26, 58, 60, 76
Cohen Stuart, A.B.   199–200

*Commissie voor de Inlandsche Scholen Volkslectuur* see Committee for Indigenous Schoolbooks and Popular Reading Books
Committee for Indigenous Schoolbooks and Popular Reading Books   1, 77, 79, 82–3, 197, 199–201
Coolsma, S.   3, 23, 28, 44, 45–6, 87, 92, 146, 185
Crawfurd, John   11, 12–3, 30–1

Daendels, H.W.   56, 85
*dangding*   1, 2, 4, 33, 38–42, 45, 46, 48, 49–51, 68, 73, 127, 131, 137, 147–8, 188, 202, 205
dictionaries   29, 30, 32, 46, 146
Djajadiningrat, Ahmad   25, 100
Djenal Asikin   109
Djoeariah (Djoea)   110, 112, 116, 117
Djojopoespito, S.   202–3
*dongeng*   79
Dutch   26
Dutch East Indies Company (VOC)   85
Dutch Missionary Society   87, 92

Eisenstein, Elisabeth   78
Ekadjati, Edi S.   25, 53, 99, 147, 184
Engelmann, W.H.   23, 27, 111
Ethical Policy   152
ethnicity (*kabangsaan*)   8, 10, 17, 30
Eurasian   88–9, 200–1

Fort de Kock   57

G.C.T. van Dorp & Co.   89–90
G. Kolff & Co.   89–90, 197
Gaarder, Jostein   16

Garut   58, 93, 100, 105, 114, 123
*gedicht* see poetry
Geerdink, A.   23
Gelder, W. van   77, 80
*geschriften*   34
*goena*   80
Gonggrijp, J.R.P.F.   23, 79–80
Gospel   29, 46, 92
Governor-General   56, 57
grammar books   29, 46
Grashuis, G.J.   23, 34–6, 42, 44, 46–7, 52, 87, 127, 146
Greek   86
*guguritan*   53, 203

Haastert, C.J. van   76–7, 84
Habib As-Sagaf   109
Haji Ibrahim   168
handwriting   4
Hazeu, G.A.J.   25, 200
Herder, J.G.   16, 17
Hidding, K.A.H.   46–7, 203
Hoëvell, W.R. van   17
Holle, A.W.   69–70, 92–3
Holle, Herman   112–3
Holle, K.F.   4, 12, 20, 25, 26, 27, 32–3, 39, 42, 43, 44, 47, 57, 69–70, 71, 74, 76, 77, 84, 92–3, 96, 100, 104, 110–3, 129, 137, 144, 189, 190, 193, 196
Honorary Adviser on Arab Affairs   88
Honorary Adviser on Native Affairs   200
*hoofdenschool* (Chiefs' school)   63
*hoofdpanghulu*   7, 59, 71, 93, 100, 101, 107
Hurgronje, Snouck   25, 56, 88, 129
*huruf pegon* see script

Ikhtiar   188
Indramayu   58

Iperen, Josua van 12
Islam, Islamic 25, 35, 61, 67, 83, 87–8, 109
Islamic schools 26, 61, 65–6, 77, 88

Jager, Herbert de 10
Jakarta National Library 25, 144
*jaksa* 101
Java Institute 37
*Javaans, Javaansch* see Javanese
*Java-Bode* 109
Javanese 1, 3, 9–13, 15–21, 23, 57, 81, 82
*Jaware* 14
Jepara 57

*kacapi* (zither) 38, 53
*kafir* 56, 112
*kalimah* 48, 186
*kalipa* 144
*kangdjeng* 81
Karatani, K. 178
Karawang 26, 56, 60, 76
Kartawinata 6, 85, 93, 108, 113, 186–8, 189–94
Kartini, R.A. 190
Kasteel-drukkerij 85
*kasusastran* 49
*kawih* 38–9, 124
Kitab Indjil see Bible
*kitab kuning* 80
Koesmaningrat, R.A. 22
Kohlburgge 129
Koning, D. de 87
Koorders, Daniel 18–9, 23, 25, 27, 33–4, 40, 41, 46, 85, 90, 119, 129–30
Koran 25, 41, 56
*kromo-ngoko* 17, 31
Kuneman, J.H.B. 116
Kuningan 58

*kuring* 31
*Kweekschool* see Teachers' Training School

*lagere scholen* 57
Lampungese 86
Landsdrukkerij 5, 7, 28, 33, 75, 81, 83, 84–7, 89, 90, 91, 95–6, 98, 124, 134, 143, 146, 190, 199, 201
Lange en Co. 69, 89–90
Lasminingrat, R.A. 100, 108, 190, 196
Lebak 108, 110, 153
Leiden University 25, 34
Lenggang Kantjana 187–8
*letterkunde* 34
Lie Kim Hok 88
Limbangan 20, 58, 71, 73, 93, 100, 101, 108, 109, 124
Linden, D. J. van 23, 88
*lingua franca* 12, 70
literacy 1–4, 55, 65–6, 77, 88, 90, 92, 93–4, 184, 201
literariness 38
lithography 87, 88, 92
*littérature* 34
*litteratuur* 34, 37–8
*lontar* see palm leaf
Louden, J. 107

Moehamad Saleh Mangkoepradja 195
*macapat* 2
Macassarese 13
*madrasa* 56
Madurese 3, 57
Majalengka 58
Majapahit 9
Makassar 57, 86
Melaka 23

# Index

Malay 5, 12, 13–6, 18, 20, 23, 61–2, 67, 68, 70, 71, 74, 75, 81, 82, 87, 88, 121, 127, 150, 154
*mamaos* 38
Mandheling 23, 86
Mangkoe Negoro IV, P.A.A. 144
manuscript 1–4, 25, 27, 55, 77, 78, 80, 93, 134–6, 164, 184, 194
Martanegara 185
Mataram 2, 3, 12, 24, 47, 50, 101
Medan 115
Meiji Restoration 156
*menak* 24, 31, 38, 104, 107–8, 115
Mijer, P. 17
missionaries 20, 22–3, 43, 44, 46, 61, 83, 87, 118–9, 146, 185
missionary school 59, 61, 65
Moehamad Moesa 4, 5–6, 7, 20–1, 33, 35, 47, 48, 52, 70, 71, 73, 76, 77, 81, 82, 93, 96, 100–42, 143–83, 185–6, 196
Moehamad Rais, M. 28
Moehamad Soeëb 37
"mountain" Javanese 10–2, 14, 22
Musa Suriakartalegawa, R.A.A. 123
Muslim 24, 31, 45, 61, 105, 119

National Library *see* Jakarta National Library
*Nederlands Bijbelgenootschap see* Netherlands Bible Society
*Nederlandsche Zendingsvereeniging see* Netherlands Missionary Union
Netherlands Bible Society 25, 27, 87, 92, 111
Netherlands Missionary Union 27, 34, 44, 118
Norman, Levyssohn 82, 114–5, 190
novel 1, 6, 7, 188–9, 197, 198–9, 202, 204

old Sundanese 10
*omongan* 1, 4, 6, 7, 187–8, 197, 198–9
Oosting, H.J. 23
oral tradition 2
orality 4, 5
orthography 24, 27, 28, 29, 30

palm leaf 2, 43
Padang 57
*panghulu* 32, 101, 105
*panji* 158
*pantun* 2, 36, 38, 40, 44, 161, 187–8, 203
*papati* 59
Parakan Muncang 101
Partadiredja, M. 28
*pasantren* 56, 101
Pasuruan 56, 89
Pati 57
*patih* 93, 100, 101, 104
*pepet*
 long 27, 28
 short 27
*Perang Sabil* 109
*Perpustakaan Nasional see* Jakarta National Library
Pleyte, C.M. 25, 28
Poeradiredja R. 124
poetry, poem 3, 35, 36, 38, 40, 42, 44, 46, 49, 51, 52, 67–8, 127–8, 146, 149, 161, 184–6, 202, 203, 205
Pramoedya Ananta Toer 152
Preanger System 120
*Preangerstelsel see* Preanger System
Priangan Regencies 2, 12, 15, 22, 58, 59, 60, 62–3, 65, 67, 73, 74, 76, 87, 101, 104, 151
print literacy 2–4, 6, 7, 77, 132, 134
*prosa see* prose

prose 35, 42–3, 44, 46, 48, 51, 52, 94–8, 127–8, 130,132, 184–6, 197, 204–5
Protestant mission 87
*pupuh* 38, 158, 203
Purwakarta 101
*pusaka* 32

Radjapamerat, R.A. 120
Raffles, T.S. 12–3, 22
Raja Ali Haji 168
readership 188–9, 194, 200
*rebab* (fiddle) 53
Rees, Otto van 109, 120
*regent* (also *bupati*) 56, 59, 61, 101
*regentschaps-school* 57
Rehoboth-Zending Press 87
Riau 23
Rigg, Jonathan 18–9, 30–1
Rinkes, D.A. 25, 200, 201
Robinson Crusoe 190, 194
Roman script *see* script
Romantic, Romanticism 16
Roorda, Taco 11, 15, 16, 22–3, 25, 31, 43
Rosidi, Ajip 47, 51, 53, 133, 143, 151, 204

s'Jacob, Frederick 117
*sajak* 53
*sajarah* 79
Salmoen, M.A. 132, 140
Sanskrit *see* script
*sastra* 38
Sastrahadiprawira, Memed 8, 37–8, 131, 204
Sayyid 'Uthmân 84, 87, 88, 92, 109
script
    Arabic (*pegon*) 7, 10, 11, 24–5, 26, 27, 28, 32, 46, 55, 67, 77, 86, 87–8, 90, 92
    Chinese 86
    Javanese 10, 24–6, 27, 28, 32, 46, 55, 67, 71, 76, 77, 84, 86, 90–1, 92, 127, 130, 144
    Roman (*walanda*) 7, 24–5, 27, 28, 46, 55, 62, 65, 67, 71, 76, 84, 87, 90–1, 92, 124, 144, 201
    Sanskrit 86
Semarang 89, 115
Serang 124
silent reading 1, 41, 188, 204
Singapore 88, 119, 155
Soeharto 148–51
Soekaboemische Sneldrukkerij 88
Soeria Nata Atmadja 122
Soeria Nata Ningrat 108, 109, 153
Soerijadiradja, M. 124
Soerjadikoesoemah, R.R. 67, 100
Sokadana 157–8
Solomon, W. 197, 204
Stads-drukkerij 85
Steinmetz, C.P.C. 58–9
Subalidinata, R.S. 150
Sukabumi 109
Sukadana 163
Sukapura 58, 93, 101
*suling* (flute) 53
Sultan Agung 101
Sumarga, Rusman Sutia 148
Sumarlina, E.S.N. 133, 147
Sumedang 58, 101, 108
Sundanese almanac 90
Surabaya 89, 115
Surakarta 11, 23, 57, 66, 67, 89

*taalkunde* 68
*tarekat Naqshabandiyya* 109
Teachers' Training School 19, 49, 57, 63, 75, 76, 84
*tembang* 38–40, 43, 44–5, 52, 53, 71, 203

Tirto Adhi Soerjo, R.M.   152
Tjakra Wiria   67
Tjondro Negoro   75
Toko Tjitak Afandi   88, 185
Tuuk, H.N. van der   31–2, 34
typography   78, 92

Veth, P.J.   43, 44, 119, 190
*volk*   12

*wadana* (or *wedana*)   101, 123
*wawacan*   1–4, 6, 7, 33, 36, 51, 53–4, 79, 94, 95–9, 127, 130, 143–9, 184, 197, 203–4, 205

*wayang*   44
Weltevreden   86–7
Wilde, A. de   11, 14–5, 17, 18, 31, 32
Wilkens, J.A.   66–7, 69–70, 73
Willem III Gymnasium   28
Winter, C.F.   75
Wiratanoedatar, A.A.   100

Yogyakarta   11, 57

Zending Press   87
*Zondase taal*   10